GW00363773

LANDS OF SACRED PLACES

LANDS OF
SACRED PLACES

Dr F. Fleischer

The Book Guild Ltd
Sussex, England

First published in Great Britain in 2003 by
The Book Guild Ltd
25 High Street
Lewes, East Sussex
BN7 2LU

Typesetting in Times by
SetSystems Ltd, Saffron Walden, Essex

Printed in Great Britain by
Bath Press Ltd, Bath

A catalogue record for this book is
available from the British Library.

ISBN 1 85776 702 0

CONTENTS

PRELUDE

Sometimes the name of a place or country can remain tucked in a corner of one's mind from early childhood, conjuring up mysterious pictures from time to time. This was the case with 'Tibet', which almost haunted me for many years, but all I could do was to read books and dream.

When I started travelling in earnest in 1975 Tibet had been invaded by China and was firmly closed to tourists. In 1978 a small travel brochure dropped on the mat advertising the district of Ladakh as 'Little Tibet'.

Our first encounter with Buddhism was Ladakh, the Himalayan kingdom annexed to India by Mrs Gandhi. Ladakh left a deep impression on me. Since then I have visited all but Japan of the existing Buddhist countries which I have tried to describe in this book. Each country has its own 'personality' but the connecting thread is Buddhism.

Many of the other important sites, such as the sacred place of Sarnath in India and others in India, Pakistan and China, I have also seen but none of these are any longer Buddhist countries and hence I have omitted them.

Searching for Buddha is not a simple task and I am not certain that I have succeeded in my quest but leave it to the reader to ponder and to decide.

London, March 1998

FOUR FACES OF BUDDHA

Nepal, Sikkim, Bhutan, Burma

October 1982

Nepal

Every journey has a beginning and ours started last night when we left home with our suitcases packed, hand luggage ready to spend the night with friends. It was a dry and sunny morning when our host drove us out to London Airport. Heavy traffic streamed out of London.

Everything proceeded extremely smoothly, we had barely time to do any shopping in the duty-free shop before we were called to board our plane for Amsterdam.

Briefly we cast a last look down at the English countryside before clouds blotted out our view. Forty minutes later we landed on Dutch soil, where we had two hours to while away before we were airborne once more. Our flight continued across Germany via Frankfurt and Munich, crossing the Austrian Alps in brilliant sunshine by midday. The flight path led over Zagreb, Sarajevo in Yugoslavia, across Salonika in northern Greece and on to Athens, where we landed but were not permitted to leave the plane. It had taken two and a half hours from Amsterdam. Central Greece looked barren and parched, lying forsaken whilst all along the coast the countryside was built up. Circling above the harbour with its many ships we saw a number of islands rising out of the blue waters.

After a short burst of orange above the sea, darkness descended and our view was blocked out but we were told that we were flying across Baghdad, Bahrain and along the Gulf to Karachi, where we

1

landed five hours later. Here we were able to disembark. By the time we had been frisked it was almost time to return to our seats but at least we had been able to stretch our legs and wander quickly through the arcades of shops selling carpets, jewellery, trinkets, clothes. The last lap of our journey passed speedily and soon we landed bumpily in Delhi.

On our flight we talked to a young, voluptuous Indian lady who told us that her husband was a cardiologist at present working in London, where she had spent four months with him, and she was now returning to Delhi. He would follow her soon to continue his double practice, working during the day at home in general practice and seeing private patients at Connaught Place in the evening. They had twin sons aged ten who were at boarding school in Simla. She was sorry that we would not be staying long enough in Delhi to visit her. It surprised us to learn that she held a pilot's licence and had already flown seventy hours solo. It always amazes me how quickly you acquire knowledge about fellow passengers when en route.

In Delhi we had a long wait to collect our baggage and to have our passports checked carefully against a 'transit list'. A suitcase was found damaged, which caused further delays since endless forms had to be filled out in triplicate. Eventually we were ushered into the departure lounge where we were offered coffee or tea made with sweetened tinned milk. Having had plenty of food and drink on our flight we politely declined this (to us unpalatable) drink. Although we were unable to change money we could and did buy a book about Asia.

Four hours later we boarded a Nepalese plane. The stewardesses – one of them with Tibetan features – were charming, and managed to serve breakfast to everyone during our short flight of one hour and ten minutes. Although the grand total of our flying time was only eleven hours the time spent waiting had almost doubled this. The flight was swift; alas clouds were low and we could only see some of the snow-capped peaks piercing the dense mist fleetingly. As we descended we looked down on the Valley of Kathmandu. It lay beneath us like a patchwork quilt. Small fields appeared everywhere; they lay deep in troughs between the high peaks, at the foot of mountains or extended up slopes as far as the high saddles.

In Kathmandu each piece of luggage was taken off singly. Eventually all our baggage had been collected, none had been opened, our visas and all forms were correct and we were able to proceed to the waiting bus. Even on this short way from the airport to the bus we were besieged by hordes of little boys with outstretched hands asking for money. Cows lumbered slowly among the traffic; gaily painted trickshaws (sidecars attached to bicycles) and somewhat shabby *tempos* (motorised trickshaws) mingled with cars, buses and lorries. Having reached our comfortable Hotel Annapura we were thankful to be able to have a bath and short rest before we changed and met our courier to hear about plans for our short stay in Nepal. The rest of the day was free, hence we decided to go by local bus to Patan, Kathmandu's neighbouring city and the second biggest in the country. Everybody laughed at us, we did not know why. It was perfectly simple to walk out of the hotel, resisting all offers made by taxi drivers, trickshaws and *tempo* boys – who all hovered around the entrance – and stroll steadfastly along the road to a park where we found the noisy crowded bus stop. Every bus was hooting, or so it seemed to us. Each of them was manned by one driver and two conductors whose job it was to collect the money and close the two doors, one in front, the other at the rear. They hit the tin roof with the flat of their hand to make the driver stop whenever a passenger wished to get on or off between official stops.

Kathmandu is a very lively town with big crowds milling round. Many Tibetan faces bore the Hindu mark of the *tikka* on their forehead. The Hindu and Buddhist religion not only exist side by side in Nepal but frequently both are embraced simultaneously by the same person.

Faced by a string of buses, we asked each driver in turn whether his bus went to Patan. Each pointed to the one in front until we finally reached the first in line, the most dilapidated of them all. It actually did go to Patan. Having paid our fare we sat down and looked at our guidebook, which was almost snatched from under our noses by eager hands. Little boys as well as young men took great interest in the book.

A flute seller arranged his flutes to resemble a sweeper's brush, Tibetan ladies squatted on the ground knitting in vividly coloured wools, carriers balanced their wares suspended in baskets from the ends of a pole which they carried across their shoulders. Large red and white radishes were offered for sale, betel-nut was chewed and spat out, marking the ground blood-red. Sweetshops and eating

3

places lined the road and amidst this medley and confusion sat mothers placidly feeding their babies at their breasts, whilst others searched for lice in each other's hair. Men dragged reluctant goats along by ropes. A man, his wrist manacled to a soldier's, walked past as if on a daily morning stroll; nobody paid the slightest attention. Many buildings were covered in graffiti. A parade ground which we passed was festooned with flags, and soldiers had gathered in brilliant red uniforms which glittered in the sun. Festival time had arrived in Nepal, the Army was getting ready to give a display.

As we rode along, spellbound at all the sights, we saw many brick buildings still not completed but nevertheless fully occupied. One board outside a school proclaimed proudly that 'a reliable builder is adding a new classroom block'. Signs on numerous squalid buildings indicated that these served as nurseries, schools and even public schools.

Soon after we had passed the mighty Bagmati River we arrived at the bus terminal outside the city gate. The next few hours were passed pleasantly walking through this ancient town said to have been originally founded in AD 299. Almost every single house contained a courtyard with a stupa (domed shrine) in its centre. Entering through narrow doorways, we found ourselves frequently in the midst of a small community. A fountain always stood next to the stupa, where old and young women did their laundry whilst others swept the ground with rush brushes. Groups of women separated grain by shaking the full ears in a flat rush basket over straw mats. Babies and toddlers played stark naked in the yard, covered in dirt. Many of the old women sat fast asleep on the ground, shielding their faces from the flies.

Workshops seemed to be everywhere, even the tiniest cubby-holes were put to use. Old men as well as boys – mere children – sat in these diligently working away. Children performed skilled tasks.

Streets were unpaved. Most of the houses, however dilapidated they were, bore intricate woodcarvings around windows which were covered by delicate wooden lattice screens. Lintels and door posts were equally decorated with fine woodcarvings, ornate wooden columns stood outside many dwellings. Maize, peppers, garlic and other vegetables had been strung up and hung suspended from the eaves, drying in the sun.

Apart from temples listed in our guidebook we found many

more; some of these were Hindu shrines with bells outside to announce your visit and with Nandi, the sacred bull, or one of the other vehicles of Hindu deities in evidence. Buddhist temples were marked by their stupas. In one temple the tank was entirely overgrown with delicate mauve water hyacinth.

Anxious not to miss any of the most important shrines we asked a young boy if he knew the Hiranya Mahavihar (Golden Temple). He did not know but led us to the Durbar Square. This is the main square in every town in Nepal. 'Durbar' applied to royal receptions in former days. Patan's Durbar Square presented an amazing sight with its many temples and tall columns. Most of the buildings dated back to the 17th century, having been built by the famous King Siddhinar Singh Malla. Bhimsen Temple, with a pillar in front bearing a lion on its lofty top, was the first temple we looked at. It was three storeys high with a golden façade on the first floor. The second temple, dedicated to Siva – guarded by two elephants – had Nandi the sacred bull placed to one side. It was decorated with heavily carved friezes and equally ornate wooden struts. The third temple was a Krishna temple where a large Garuda, the mystic bird – half eagle, half man, with four arms – sacred to Hindus, sat with folded hands on top of a pillar in front of it. This pagoda-style building had been carved entirely out of stone whilst all the other temples had been constructed of wood. The statue of King Yogan-aredra, who had ruled Patan in the early 18th century, dominated the square from its lofty height on top of a pillar. Next to the King stood a white temple reminiscent of the classic Indian temples. Adjacent to this rose Siva's temple with a heavy bell inside it. An octagonal temple dedicated to Krishna completed the temples around the square. The Royal Palace – used as a museum – had been erected on the remaining side opposite the tall Malla column and was heavily adorned with artistic woodcarvings, its windows made of bronze. Unfortunately it was closed and all we could do was to admire the Golden Gate. The tallest of all temples towered beside it, but this too was firmly locked. Here we could only see the two figures of the River Gods Ganges and Jumna guarding the entrance and had to be content to just look up to the graceful four-sided pagoda.

To see the King's circular sunken bath we had to go through a heavily carved door next to the Palace. The marble bath was adorned with stone carvings where the King used to meditate

5

resting on a marble slab on top of three steps which led down into the bath. Three figures, those of Narasinga, Ganesh the Elephant God and Hanuman the Monkey God, stood in front of this building. At this point another little lad joined us who was fourteen years old and spoke English well and actually knew where to find the temples. Leisurely we followed the two boys, who took us back from Durbar Square towards the city gate to the Vhiranya Mahavihar Temple, which stood well tucked away amongst old buildings. This 12th-century monastery took its name from the gold-plated roof. To enter it we walked through a misleadingly small entrance. Nearby we visited the Kumbeshwar Temple, a five-storey building dedicated to Siva, surrounded by many smaller ones, one of them dedicated to Kali, another to Ganesh. The water of the tank in the courtyard, which is said to come directly from the holy cave of Godsainkunda, was covered by green slime.

The boys took us back to Durbar Square where children played five stones and marbles and called out 'Hello' and 'Goodbye' all in one breath. The colourful market behind the Krishna temple was in full swing. Leaving this fascinating square behind us we followed our two guides to a tank which they called 'public baths' where water gushed forth from shimmering taps in the shape of animal heads. Women and girls were laundering their clothes, cleaning their pots and pans and finally washing themselves. Men sat close by polishing traditional drums with stones, using powdered coal as abrasive.

The boys took us south of Durbar Square to the well-hidden Mahaboudna Temple – Temple of a Thousand Buddhas – built in the 14th century, constructed of terracotta tiles which each bore the image of Buddha. The shrine lay surrounded by a sunken gangway which in turn was enclosed by a low wall. Small bowls stood on this wall waiting to be filled with oil and lit on festive occasions. The bowls on each corner were decorated with little brass monkeys. Tiny shops filled to the brim with the most amazing merchandise surrounded the courtyard.

Our last visit took us to the Rudra Varna Mahabinar Temple, which we entered through a low, heavily carved door. A gallery ran around the sunken courtyard where the shrine stood – not in the centre but to one side. The centre was occupied by the life-sized statue of one of the Malla kings which stood facing the shrine. A collection of fearsome-looking animals protected the temple.

The Nepalese seemed friendly and tolerant and we did not have to remove our shoes once we had explained that they were not made of leather. I strolled behind the temple complex and found myself in a courtyard with its own stupa and its own tank in the middle of a microcosm of village life. By that time we had grown foot-weary and, parting company with our young friends, we retraced our steps past numerous stalls and small shops and one Hindu cinema back to the city gate and the bus stop, from where another battered vehicle took us back to Kathmandu. An earnest young man sitting in front of us was deeply engrossed in an old *Geographical Magazine*. Slowly we walked back to our hotel, stopping to explore the arcade of little shops inside the hotel complex before we retired to our room to rest before dinner, which was quite a hilarious affair since one member of our party, a lady who lived in Bahrain, entertained us with stories of a disastrous trip to Tibet and Mount Everest Base Camp under the auspices of the Chinese Mountaineering Research Council.

Everybody retired to bed early and we slept soundly until the first morning light woke us. It had been an angry-looking sky the night before and it was followed by a dull day with an overcast sky. Although only few raindrops fell, the mountains were shrouded in mist. A big bus took us on a trip of the countryside through the fertile and well-cultivated Valley of Kathmandu, with its terraced fields. Rice, the staple diet of the country, had been harvested. The main crops grown in rotation were rice, buckwheat, wheat and millet. Two harvests per year were gathered in the valley whilst three were collected in the Tarai, the humid lowland in the south of Nepal. Bananas and citrus fruit also grew in Nepal. Clumps of bamboo appeared, used for scaffolding and serving the poor people for fuel. Splashes of brilliant yellow stood out amongst the various shades of green, and proved to be cheerful French marigolds. Maize had been gathered some time ago and left to dry in the air, placed on stilts and cleverly arranged resembling a perfect Christmas tree. The prosperity of each farmer was judged by the size of this 'corn on the cob tree' and the wealth of the harvest depended entirely on the monsoon; too much rain was just as bad as too little.

The houses which clung to the steep sides of the valley were usually three storey high, with the ground floor providing shelter for the animals, the middle one being used by the family for living space and the top, where the smoke escaped through a hole in the thatched roof, serving as the kitchen. The buildings were constructed of mud bricks, painted with clay in brown and orange horizontal stripes. The women going barefooted into the fields and carrying wooden hoes across their shoulders wore black saris edged with red. The older women emerged from their homes to stare at us. Many of them wore large hooped gold or silver earrings, rings through noses and strings of coloured beads round their necks. Young boys carried bales of hay home on their backs which were so enormous that they obscured the little carriers and it seemed as if the bundles of hay had grown legs to walk on their own. Men and boys were threshing in the fields by rotating a spiked drum by foot-driven treadle whilst beating the sheaves of corn on the moving drum.

The road we were travelling on led to China and carried very little traffic, in contrast to the roads leading into India; whilst an uneasy atmosphere hung over the Nepal–China frontier, brisk exchange of trade existed between Nepal and India. Public buses passed us which were full to the brim with heavily laden baskets poised on their roofs. Once we even saw a goat swaying precariously on top. Baskets, which were triangular in shape, were used to hold everything. When carrying them on their backs the Nepalese used leather straps across their foreheads to take some of the weight. Many of them contained freshly cut leaves which were tightly rolled; these were used as wrappings and also as plates. Big round or oval baskets carried livestock such as chickens, cockerels and other birds.

Leaving the valley we climbed up a good mountain road with many steep curves to reach Nagarcot, 7,130 feet high. Unfortunately fog had gathered and it swirled around us as we arrived at this lookout, blocking our entire view. In Nepal only snow-covered peaks are classed as 'mountains', all else, regardless of height, is designated as 'hill'.

There was nothing else to do than return down into the valley again, where we visited Nepal's third city: Baktapur. Entering through the city gate we drove carefully through narrow unpaved lanes thronged with people and creatures of all sizes from water buffaloes to puppy dogs, chicken and ducks. The sacred cow was much in evidence, frequently obstructing our way. Finally we reached Taumadhi Square, which boasts the finest temple in all Nepal, the five-storey Nyatapola Temple towering high up into the sky. The staircase leading up to the entrance is flanked by two griffins and finally by two goddesses. Each pair of guardians ascending the stairs was said to be ten times as powerful as the preceding ones and even the wrestlers at the bottom rung were believed to be ten times stronger than any mortal man. Next to the Nyatapola stood the Bhairabath Temple, a two-storey building with heavy ornamental carvings. Something interesting presented itself to our astonished eyes wherever we looked at any point on Taumadhi Square; whether this was a house, a temple, a figure, a column, every inch of every building seemed to be exquisitely carved either in wood or stone. Little shops and stalls were colourful with a plethora of merchandise. To reach Durbar Square we walked through a narrow passage where the Golden Gate led to Durga's temple, which we, however, as non-Hindus, were not allowed to enter. Looking across a broken wall we saw the remains of the royal bath with Naga's golden head raised up into the air. On one side of the Golden Gate stood the museum (which we had no time to visit) whilst on the other rose the Palace of the Fifty-Five Windows. Each of these windows was latticed and heavily carved. Next to the Palace stood a small stone temple with exquisitely carved statues of animals leading up to the entrance. A big bell used in the past to summon all men to arms in case of emergency had its rightful place here; now it was only rung on festive days, no longer did it toll for war. The Army in Nepal is entirely voluntary, but once committed the men have to serve five full years. The last monument we admired was the now familiar King's Column which faced the Golden Gate.

Leaving Baktapur we passed the golden roofs of Pashupatinath Temple, the most important Hindu temple in all Nepal, standing on the shores of the River Bagmati, which is as holy to the Nepalese as the Ganges is to the Indians and it too has a burning gat for cremation: Our goal was Bodnath Stupa, one of the largest stupas in the world, which stands hemmed in by houses but its golden spire rises high above the hemisphere which represents the earth. The hemisphere stands on a rectangular base surmounted by a square column known as *torana* with the 'all-seeing eyes of supreme Buddhahood' painted on all four sides. Buddha's blue eye watched us wherever we went. Prayer flags swayed gently in the breeze. I walked round the stupa, stepping gingerly past a group of Tibetans squatting on the ground and totally engrossed in gambling. I did

9

not know what dice game they played with such intense concentration. Tiny shops surrounded the stupa. Finally I found an entrance into a small courtyard from where well-worn steps led up to the mighty edifice. Somehow, in spite of all the people around me, standing at the foot of the great white hemisphere I felt alone and at peace with the world.

This visit concluded our sightseeing for the morning. In the afternoon we first drove west of the city up a hill to Swayambubath Stupa. Taking the gentle gradual climb from the southern approach, we passed vendors trying to sell wooden stringed instruments, medicine, Gurkha knives, various other knives etc. laid out on trestle tables. Our path led past maimed beggars with outstretched hands asking for alms. Little brown monkeys sat on small stupas swinging gaily from tree to tree, jumping over roofs whilst keeping a beady eye on all visitors. Once again (apart from the monkeys) Buddha's ever-seeing eye was upon us, pursuing us from the base of the lofty stupa which rose from the centre of a paved platform on top of the hill. Many small stupas encircled the main one. Monasteries closed off two of the sides. A puja (prayer session) was about to start, preceded by the blowing of the long horn; and there was finger drumming on native drums before the chanting begun. A charming pagoda-style temple stood next to the big stupa; a new temple was being built and its roof covered with copper sheeting, whilst the freshly carved wooden doors and latticed windows exhibited the same skilful work as in the past. It was fascinating to watch a young man placing metal screens across each niche around the stupa and securing each with an ancient lock. Locks like these were frequently offered to tourists for sale but we had never seen one actually being used before. From a terrace – set slightly below the main complex – we enjoyed a panoramic view over Kathmandu. Unfortunately, the day remained cloudy and overcast.

Our bus took us down to Kathmandu to visit the old quarter of the city. It began to rain and darkness suddenly descended, which shortened our visit. Innumerable temples cluster around Durbar Square and wherever we looked we saw pagoda roofs and buildings entirely covered by woodcarving. A low entrance guarded by two fierce-looking stone lions led into the courtyard of the Kumari Temple, the 'Temple of the Living Goddess', which presented a picture of feverish activity with everyone engaged in preparations for the big Festival of Dashain, which commemorates the times when demons roamed the earth. Legend has it that the demon Mahisasaur, the buffalo demon, and his followers wanted to gain immortality by pleasing Brahma. By doing penance they convinced Brahma of their 'good intentions' and he granted them their wish never to be slain by a male adversary. This made them invincible and they turned out the gods so that they could rule over heaven and earth. The gods prevailed upon Durga, the great Mother Goddess, symbolising the primeval female power, to free heaven and earth from the demons. Devi Durga destroyed them in a mighty battle, thus Dashain celebrates the victory of good over evil. Here in the small courtyard surrounded by balconies with 18th-century carvings, preparations for the feast were well advanced. A group of men and women were slicing cooked buffalo liver and kidney with a sharp knife which was attached to a wooden block at one end. Women sat on the floor of the lower gallery and were eating their meal when suddenly a little girl peered surly down from the top floor. She was the Kumari's attendant. Legend told of the Malla King about a century ago who raped a prepubescent girl. She died and to do penance he installed a small girl in the temple, where she had to remain until puberty. This custom still prevails and whilst the chosen girl is cosseted she is not allowed to leave the temple except on three days in September at the end of the monsoon to celebrate the Festival of God Indra, when she is taken by chariot around Kathmandu to be feted. Before being elected the Kumari has to face a terrible ordeal. A little girl from an ordinary silversmith family is always chosen. This unfortunate child has to spend a night locked into a dark room full of horrifying animal heads staring at her with gruesome eyes accompanied by terrifying background noises. If she survives the night without shouting out in terror or crying out in anguish, she is elected. Sometimes it has taken as long as ten years to find a Kumari. When her time as 'the Living Goddess' is completed she is returned to her family hoping to get married. This, however, can prove difficult since the ex-Kumari brings bad luck to any husband of hers and every man has died within six months of marriage.

Only Hindus were permitted to climb up the stairs to have an audience with the Kumari. Our local guide called up to her to show herself, and after a short while a little girl dressed in red with a bow in her hair, her eyes outlined with kohl, looked down on us from an open window. Taking photographs was strictly forbidden.

11

Feeling somewhat shattered by our experience we emerged from this medieval scene, hoping to visit the Royal Palace, which stands next to the Kumari Temple. Hanuman the Monkey God, shrouded entirely in red cloth, kept guard with elephants which were being whitewashed whilst the courtyard was being cleaned – all in preparation for the Dashain. Because of all this activity the Royal Palace was closed and we were unable to visit it. Instead we looked at the terrifying huge stone image of the Black Bhairab which used to serve to bring criminals to justice. Any guilty person brought face to face with this horrifying monument was bound to confess. The face of the White Bhairab opposite, standing behind a grill, was even more frightening.

The Jagnath Temple with its erotic carvings rose the other side of the Royal Palace. These were supposed to keep the Goddess of Lightning at bay since she was a virgin.

The rest of our party decided to return to our hotel whilst we remained and continued to stroll around the busy town in spite of steady rain. Temples were all around us; one of them, the Talesu, was being used as a market, with its merchandise spilling outside all over the ground so that we had to pick our way carefully over yellow limes piled high in small heaps on sacking, over pale green squash and other fruit and vegetables. The crowd which surrounded us consisted mainly of Nepalese with just a handful of Europeans amongst them. In fact there were far fewer westerners than we had anticipated and some of them we had met before, most of them sightseeing on bicycles which were easily available on hire. Twice we were approached and asked whether we wanted to buy hashish or change any dollars. We politely declined on both accounts, which was readily accepted and there was never any hassle; if you said 'no' you meant it. Many of the tiny shops in Freak Street tempted us to step inside and finally we bought two jerkins and two Nepalese calendars. By the time we turned into New Street to make our way back to our hotel it was completely dark, but in spite of this the street was still as lively and crowded as it had been during daylight. Walking through the city gate, we passed the cattle market, which was heralded by the pungent smell permeating the air. Skirting the parade ground, we found ourselves at the bus terminal, which we recognised from our excursion to Patan on the previous day, and from there it was easy enough to find our way back to our hotel.

Next morning we were scheduled to catch a plane at 9.30 a.m. but our departure was delayed and all we were able to do was sit around the poolside and patiently wait. Eventually we left at 11 a.m. and actually took off at midday, when it was warm and sunny as we flew across the flat Tarai, the fertile plain, with its many fields, until we suddenly ran into a storm which blocked out all view. An hour later we landed at Biratnagar to continue our journey by road. Torrential rains, which unfortunately continued all day, greeted us as we climbed on the dilapidated bus, which meant that we saw little of the countryside as we passed through West Bengal, catching only tantalising glimpses of little scenes such as a herd of buffaloes with small boys sitting astride their backs beneath black umbrellas. Three graves suddenly appeared at the roadside, which seemed strange to us since cremation was the customary way of disposing of the dead. Local markets carried on 'business as usual' under a sea of umbrellas. Houses stood on stilts and most of them were constructed of matting sheltering the animals below whilst the families squatted on mats above. Our way appeared to lead across a large number of bridges.

After two hours we reached Mechi, where the driver had to pay a toll, and half an hour later we arrived at the border town of Jalmagup, where we had to wait in pouring rain since two members of our party were asked to step off the bus to see the officer who sat in a tent. One was an American living in Israel, the other a German resident in the Channel Islands. It was an unpleasant interlude since the officer demanded visas from them both although the gentleman from Israel had been issued with one in Tel Aviv by the American Consul. The Indian officer, never having heard of Tel Aviv, expected it to be issued by the Ambassador himself. The unfortunate German had been told in the Channel Islands before he left that he did not require a visa for India. Eventually our courier signed that she would be entirely responsible for the German and she was also able to persuade the officious officer that the American's visa was valid. This transaction took a whole hour.

When we reached our hotel at Siliguri at 7.30 p.m. we found that almost all our belongings were soaking wet since they had been carried on the roof of the bus, which had no boot, and, piled high, the luggage had been ineffectively covered by a minute plastic sheet. This was not a very happy ending to a very wet day but the staff of the Siliguri Hotel were extremely helpful and kind, opening a room specially for us where they kept a fan going all night to dry our things. Next morning most of our belongings were dry.

Glorious sunshine greeted us next day when we learnt that plans had been changed, we never knew why! Instead of travelling first to Darjeeling we were to proceed to Sikkim in seven Ambassador cars (the usual taxis in India) accompanied by a guide. After some time the guide appeared and went off with our courier to change the dates on our group visa at the appropriate office. Six taxis arrived, number seven remained missing. Having patiently waited our guide went off in search of another car; no sooner had he disappeared than the missing taxi arrived and somebody was dispatched to chase after him. Eventually everything had been sorted out and all luggage safely stowed away in the seven boots of the seven cars and after a short briefing in the sunny little garden amongst flowers of all sorts we were actually off on our way soon after 10 a.m. Since the Siliguri Hotel stood well outside the town at an important junction of two highways, we had not seen anything of the town.

Our journey had barely begun when our cavalcade grounded to a sudden halt to wait for one of the cars, which had stopped to change a wheel as it had sustained a puncture. Nobody seemed unduly perturbed and we all got out to stretch our legs. People working in the fields were not particularly friendly and just stared at us, not returning our well-meant wave. Much of this region was densely wooded and managed by the Forestry Commission, whose small houses stood dotted about in groups. Here we saw our first tea plantation, which was set out in neat rows in the shade of tall trees. Soon we left the flat landscape and began to climb almost imperceptibly. The scenery changed and we found ourselves amidst lush vegetation consisting of subtropical undergrowth under lofty trees. When we stopped in a small village along our route, men, women and children came out to stare at us. Orchids grew in hollow bamboo branches which hung suspended from trees, fences and roofs, whilst big pear-shaped marrows dangling above our heads covered most of the roofs with their prolific growth. Up to this village we had followed the rail track, watching the spectacle of Indian trains, which are always full to overflowing with passengers hanging on for dear life on the steps to every carriage and sitting or lying on the roofs. When we had to stop to let a train go by we were told under no circumstances to take a photograph (no explanation was given) although neither the train nor the location appeared to be of any special significance.

Sikkim

As we neared Sikkim we followed the River Testa until we reached the border, where we had our picnic lunch sitting on felled trunks under the shade of big trees. I recognised rubber trees, acacias and rhododendrons growing side by side. Finally we had our first glimpse of a Sikkim village lying across the Testa before we crossed over the border to reach Rangpong, having been simply waved across the bridge at the frontier checkpoint. Rangpong was as noisy as any Indian town, with music blaring from loudspeakers, and crowds of people walking up and down the unpaved streets, which were lined by the usual stalls to either side. Men, women and children were worshipping at a shrine and receiving red *tikkas* on their foreheads, whilst sacred water was sprinkled over their heads to keep their eyes bright and clear. These shrines had been temporarily erected for the Festival of Durga's puja (service) and were known as pendals, and consisted of bamboo frames hung with matting housing the deity. Durga represents the fierce aspect of Siva's consort and features as a yellow woman riding a tiger or lion. A procession came along the street, headed by a leader entirely dressed in white and carrying a bamboo pole, followed by two small boys bearing a red cloth made into a sling which hung suspended from a frame between them. I thought that a chicken ready to be sacrificed was inside the red cloth. A small band consisting mainly of drums accompanied them. Little scenes like this one never fail to fascinate me. Wandering on, we looked down a slope and realised that some other ritual was taking place down below. A man was walking clockwise around, holding a lighted candle, whilst a group chanted away. Gingerly we climbed down some slippery steps and found ourselves in the market of Rangpong where big black pigs were scavenging amongst the pile of dirt and decay. At 3.30 we left Rangpong for our last lap, following a steep mountain road which climbed higher and higher, offering breathtaking views of thickly wooded slopes and rivers flowing through picturesque gorges at the feet of high mountains. Poinsettia trees were in full bloom, peach trees were covered in delicate pink flowers, banana palms stood with bunches of fruit suspended from their branches whilst bougainvillea and hibiscus trees added a bold splash of brilliant colours. Vegetation even at high altitude was unbelievably varied and lush. We also saw the white trumpet flower which dies when touched.

The very first impression of Gangtok (capital of Sikkim) when we reached its outskirts was by no means one of beauty as it straggled up and down the mountainside. Most of the houses were tall, some of them not as yet completed though shops were already beginning to start to trade; maybe they never will be finished. The older properties had been built of stone, the new ones of concrete. Many of them were covered by the very ugly corrugated iron sheeting and sadly little had remained of the ancient architecture of Sikkim. Gangtok reminded us strongly of Simla.

Stadium Road leading down to the Nor-Khill Hotel, where we were to stay, was steep and led past the attractive Tibetan Hotel. A gentle lady clad in Sikkim dress greeted us graciously, handing us the traditional prayer shawl as we had seen it done in Buddhist monasteries. A welcome cup of tea with Ritz biscuits was served in the comfortable lounge. The hotel occupied a superb position from where we could look down across the colourful garden to the valley and up to wooded hills. Given a clear day, it was possible to catch a glimpse of snow-capped giants beyond the wooded slopes, with Kanchenjunga, the third highest peak in the world, towering above them all.

Settling down in our room we found to our great delight that it had a bathroom with a full-sized bath and a geyser which actually worked. What a pleasant surprise, since we had been forewarned that accommodation in Sikkim would be very basic. This was certainly not the case; our room was extremely comfortable and well furnished, with light warm stepped overlays on our beds as well as a small electric fire. Having installed ourselves we ventured forth taking a small torch with us, since it had become dark. Climbing up some steps we reached the steep Stadium Road which led on to the main street. Our way led past houses, shops, hotels, past a hospital and an imposing building called Elephant Mansion, until we found the market, which had shops to either side, many of which were Sikkim liqueur shops. This struck us as rather strange until we were told that Sikkim was famous for its liqueurs produced locally. For the first time we found lovely soft Kashmir knitting wool, which we bought to take home. A man sat at an old treadle machine working away patiently making cosy overlays.

By the time we returned to our hotel the stadium below the hotel garden had come to life. A screen had been erected in front of a small light aircraft which had been deposited on this 'multipurpose space'. At night it served as cinema when a film was being shown to a spellbound audience. All people in the East seem to be ardent cinema fans and advertisements announcing films on hoardings usually present quite lurid pictures, which are always painted by hand, adding an extra dimension to the film industry.

A small shop filled with trinkets of all kinds as well as rugs and thangkas (the Buddhist religious silk wall hangings) occupied one corner of the lounge; the shopkeeper hailed from Kargill (Ladakh), where we had been, and it was pleasant to talk to him about his country, where he spent the winter months. The goods displayed were all handmade and of excellent craftsmanship.

The sound of a bugle woke us next morning when we found to our amazement that each morning the stadium served as a parade ground – not for the Army as we thought but for the police, who carried guns. In the afternoon it was taken over by the boys of the town and used as a football pitch. The role of the light plane remained a mystery.

Soon after breakfast we were on our way to visit Rumtek Monastery, which meant retracing our steps up the steep Stadium Road, driving through town and following the winding road on which we had come. Before leaving Gangtok we stopped to watch people receiving blessings at a wayside shrine. Many were present at this ceremony and it was a pleasure to watch their bright faces. Most features were Tibetan with high cheekbones, slightly slanting brown eyes, warm golden skin, rosy cheeks and straight black hair. The children looked at us with trusting eyes and waved happily. I saw one small boy with a goitre; otherwise the children looked very healthy – healthier and cleaner than in Nepal. When we reached the river we saw shacks huddled together standing on its bank. Having crossed the Testa we started to climb, enjoying the perfect view of terraced fields, gold with ripening rice, which looked as if sculptured by human hand and covered the slopes as far as our eyes could see until they reached the dark green mountains. Many gaily coloured butterflies and birds and shimmering dragonflies flitted through the fields. An enormous spider spun a gigantic net, crickets chirped away, tiny oranges grew wild, caraway bushes were pointed out to us, peace and serenity lay over the sun-baked scene.

Rumtek Monastery, which lay high nestling below the peaks, was new, having been built in 1965, but followed the old Tibetan traditions. An elaborate gate led into the courtyard, which was dominated by the square yellow temple with its double-tiered pagoda roof. The usual golden emblems adorned the top whilst windows, doors and eaves as well as the columns of the porch were painted in brilliant red, white and blue.

I know very little of Buddhism but have been told that basically there exist two sects: the red and the yellow. Rumtek is the seat of the red sect, which is further subdivided into four groups, and Rumtek belongs to the Karpama sect, who follow the Mahayana school of Buddhism (the Greater Vehicle) and worship Maitreya, 'the Buddha to Come'.

A puja, prayer session, was in progress but we were allowed to enter, having dutifully removed our shoes. The large prayer hall was filled with monks of all ages who sat cross-legged in neat rows on the floor chanting away. The chanting sounded like the litany in a Roman Catholic church or the cantor's intonation in a synagogue. Many of the monks present were mere children, bright-eyed with shorn heads, whispering to us beseechingly: 'Pens.' They loved biros. It was of course impossible for us to walk round to look at the murals which adorned the wall, all we were able to do was to cast a quick glance at one wall with niches containing the statues of a thousand Buddhas. One year had passed since the death of the last Head Lama; the present one was the fifth incarnation amongst 300 monks. When the service was finished we took our turn to be handed the traditional muslin scarf as a welcome from the Head Lama, who sat cross-legged on a throne. With arms outstretched, slightly bent, we received this greeting; the scarf was gently laid across. The Head Lama blessed each scarf, and placed it round our neck before removing it again.

Having silently filed out of the prayer hall we climbed up on the roof, from which we could feast our eyes on the panorama of the lovely valley below us. Looking down into the courtyard we saw that small cells led off it, providing the monks' living quarters. Everything was of utmost simplicity. One cell served as kitchen, another one as latrine and there was also one used as a printing

18

works. A feeble old monk barely able to stand and almost blind sat in the sun until a young monk helped him back into his cell. Pilgrims received the customary yak tea and a crust of bread. Looking up towards the mountains we saw prayer flags dancing in the wind. These always indicated a monastery or *chorten* (chorten is the Tibetan for stupa); above Rumtek Monastery lay the remains of the old monastery, which were barred to visitors since they served as a place for meditation for the Head Lama.

Leaving this peaceful place we walked down the steep approach past pretty little 'dolls' houses' built of wood and whitewashed. Wooden struts painted blue divided the brilliant white walls into squares. Unfortunately most of the houses were covered by corrugated roofs. The inhabitants either sat at the window – which had no panes, just wooden shutters to be used during the harsh winter months – stood outside or leant over wooden balconies. One man sat at the window on the ground floor blissfully turning his prayer wheel and chanting the well-known phrase *'O mani padme hum'* (O the jewel of the lotus) whilst an old lady up above was completely absorbed counting her beads.

Sikkim must be a paradise for bird-watchers, butterfly experts and botanists alike since butterflies, birds and plants of every kind prevail. Here saplings were protected by bamboo cages whilst in Nepal bricks had been used. In both cases this protection had also served as a clothes line. As far as we could ascertain, rice was still the main crop of Sikkim and fortunately it had not been replaced by a cash crop as has happened so frequently in other parts of Asia, e.g. south India. Terraces planted with rice covered every inch of the steep slopes. On our way back to Gangtok we passed a lady dressed in a sari with a leather jacket on top watching her flock of sheep from beneath a blue umbrella. As in Nepal, most people when carrying heavy loads hoist these on their backs and place a leather strap across their foreheads.

Our afternoon sightseeing commenced with a visit to the Sikkim Institute of Tibetology and Buddhist Studies, which stood at the bottom of the town in its own grounds. Building work was in progress nearby and a hoarding announced that this was to be a campus for Gangtok. On our way to the Institute we had halted when we heard music and watched Durga being worshipped at a temporary wayside shrine. (Durga is of course a Hindu goddess).

The Institute had been built in Tibetan style. The eight lucky emblems of Sikkim adorned the outer gate in the shape of vases, whilst painted on the walls of the veranda were the symbols of various gurus and their patrons. The majestic silver image of Manjushri Bodhisattva, who excels in wisdom, dominated the main entrance leading into the library containing 3,000 new Tibetan books and periodicals on Buddhism and on Central Asia. Various showcases around the room exhibited ritual objects such as the bell and thunderbolt as well as traditional art. Lovely *thangkas* were displayed on the walls. Most of them were new but exquisitely painted and mounted on blue silk surrounded by a broad band of dark red. The first floor housed the big Tibetan Library containing the most important collection of Buddhist literature, written on long strips of parchment or paper placed between two wooden covers, carefully wrapped in brocade and neatly stacked on shelves. This collection comprised 30,000 Tibetan texts in the form of xylograms, manuscripts and printed works from all four of the red sects of red Buddhism. The eight great Mahayana Masters were portrayed on the walls of the veranda, whilst inside the hall stood the imposing image of one of the gurus flanked by a Tantric deity on either side. Exquisite *thangkas* lined the walls of this lofty room, cushions lay on the floor for lamas and students to sit and research the various manuscripts.

Further up on the flat roof was the Ajanta Hall, with reproductions of some of the frescoes from the Ajanta caves on its walls. Looking out from here across the grounds, white *chorten* shimmered through the trees, but since it had begun to rain we were unable to explore and visit the outdoor orchid sanctuary. Orchids grew in wild profusion everywhere; they literally sprouted from every tree, but sadly none of them was in bloom.

The plan had been to continue and visit the Government Institute of Cottage Industry, but this was closed owing to the fact that it happened to be a public holiday; banks and post offices were also firmly shut. Fortunately we had been able to change money in the hotel, but we had run out of stamps. Our next visit was to the nearby Royal Chapel, the Tsuk-La-Khang, which was the principal place of worship in Sikkim and impressive viewed from the outside. On the way our guide pointed out the simple palace which stood close by where the late King's son still lived. Inside the chapel were imposing murals such as the Four Heavenly Gods depicted to either side of the entrance. Statues of Buddha, Bodhisattva and Tantric deities stood on the lavishly decorated altar. The wood carvings around the chapel were very fine indeed.

Rain had stopped when we left Tsuk-La-Khang, the sky had cleared and we caught a splendid view of the snow-capped Kanchenjunga. Whilst we stood lost in admiration an attractive young man with sleek, well-groomed dark hair, immaculately dressed in the grey robes of the lama with snow-white cuffs, passed us. He was accompanied by two American girls and a young American man; we could hear that he spoke perfect English, and the soldiers saluted him: he was the late King's son (his mother was American).

With time in hand we decided to call on the Governor's wife, to whom we had a somewhat vague introduction. Ruth had visited an Indian exhibition at Selfridges during the 'Year of India' celebrations in London before we embarked on this journey. There she had chatted to a young girl from Bombay who was trying to promote travel to India. When she heard of our forthcoming visit to Sikkim she had given Ruth her card and asked her to call on the Governor's wife, who was a personal friend of hers. Unfortunately, when the time came we had lost the card but decided to try in any case and set off in one of our cars. The driver, who came from Darjeeling, was a stranger to Sikkim and had to ask various times for directions. The road led through woods winding uphill until we arrived at what appeared to be an English country house set in a beautiful garden. Having told the soldier standing guard that we wished to call on the Governor's wife, we were taken into an office where the soldier behind the desk directed us to another one. We repeated our request for the third time and were politely asked to sit down. One officer stood behind a desk, attending to the almost continuous telephone calls on three telephones, saying 'Yes, sir, certainly sir, very well, sir'. Somehow between all these incoming calls he managed to deal with our request. People wandered in and out again, bells rang in the distance, the little room buzzed with activity. A man who frequently clutched his head sat opposite us and asked where we came from, suddenly demanded to know the percentage of trees in the whole of the United Kingdom. Sadly we were unable to oblige with a reply. Another officer came and asked us for our names before we were finally summoned. Yet another officer appeared. First he took us to a viewpoint in the garden where we could admire a magnificent panorama of snow-capped mountains; our guide named various peaks for us. Next he led us through a conservatory where a cage containing a nocturnal animal stood amongst exotic plants.

At last we reached the house, walking through a porch full of flowering orchids to reach a heavy mahogany door, which was flung open as we approached. We were led into a delightful drawing room which was completely panelled and exhibited graceful wood carvings (Sikkim is famous for its highly skilled wood carving); elegant chairs stood on magnificent carpets, and everything seemed in its right place. Even the flowers in vases arranged around the room appeared to stand to attention. A photograph of Mrs Gandhi hung prominently on the wall. Our guide asked us politely to take a seat but to leave two chairs to the right and left of the bay window free. Here we sat and waited, listening to the tinkling of tea cups issuing from the next room.

Once again doors were flung open and Mrs T. appeared. She wore a simple blouse over dark blue slacks and was middle-aged, with well-coiffured grey hair. Her features strangely resembled Mrs Gandhi. It was extremely easy to talk to her, having first explained how we came by the introduction. She and her husband had been in residence in Sikkim for the past eighteen months. The house had been built by an Englishman who had chosen the location for its superb view across the mountains. Mrs T. came from Bombay. She was involved with the social welfare of the people of Sikkim and had just met some of her fellow workers over a cup of tea. Sitting in one of the chairs to the side of the bay window, she rang a bell attached to the arm of the chair (hence these two chairs were reserved for her), a servant appeared and she obviously ordered tea, which appeared very quickly, served on a silver tray in fine bone china cups. Tea was poured from the silver pot, delicious pastries were served using silver tongs.

Mrs T. seemed genuinely concerned about the 'backwardness of people in Sikkim' as she phrased it; she certainly sounded very earnest and sincere. Of course we could not point out to the good lady that we had found the poverty and dirt in Bombay even more distressing than the simple life in Sikkim, but I have no doubt that she meant well. When we told her that we had been unable to obtain information about the country she replied that there was little in print but her husband had collected some facts and figures and had written a small booklet. One of the many houseboys was summoned by the bell, orders were given in Hindi. He reappeared bearing the pamphlet on a silver salver which was presented to us. Our hostess spoke perfect English and told us that she had often been to England.

The time had come for us to take our leave. She graciously saw us off, summoning an officer to collect our bags and windcheaters which we had left in the office, then he was detailed to show us to our car. Thanking her, we shook hands and were on our way after a very satisfying afternoon, reaching our hotel just in time to pack, bath and change for a traditional Sikkim meal served on tables specially adorned with flowers along arches fashioned from serviettes. The dishes resembled Chinese food, with small glasses of Sikkim's special liqueur completing the feast. Before we retired we bought an attractive small prayer wheel made of silver, horn and bone in the little shop from the man from Kargill, Ladakh.

Walking along the corridor which led to our bedroom, we cast a last look at the attractive pictures worked in appliqué which lined the walls. One of them had borne a butterfly in one corner when we first arrived which we had mistaken for part of the handiwork but it had disappeared and obviously had been real, taking· the embroidered flowers for true plants to rest on for a little while.

Our bedroom overlooked the forecourt where the cars were parked. Our drivers slept in their vehicles and, waking at daybreak, they felt fresh and wide awake ready to clean the cars cheerfully and noisily, disturbing our sleep. But we did not mind, since we had a fairly early start. Before eight o'clock we had already joined the heavy traffic, which consisted mainly of buses belonging to the Sikkim National Co-operation, taxis, tourist jeeps and carriers – piled dangerously high with a multitude of goods. There were barely any private cars. Our way led back on the same road on which we had come to Gangtok two days ago and we stopped again at Rangpong, where life had already begun to stir since the day starts early in these parts of the world. In fact even the post office was open and we were able to buy stamps. I wandered off through narrow lanes and saw a cow tethered to a shed being watched by a friendly mouse.

Continuing our journey, we reached a Bailey bridge which had replaced the original concrete one, which had been swept away by floods in 1982; again we were not permitted to take a photograph. This time we had to wait to have our papers checked once we had crossed the River Testa before commencing our climb to Darjeeling, which lies 6,000 to 7,000 feet above sea level. As we ascended, all the rice terraces disappeared, mountains were less high and no longer densely wooded to their top; small thatched cottages stood at the roadside. To stretch our legs we got off and walked ahead for a short while. On our stroll we watched the ritual of disembowelling a goat slaughtered to celebrate a festival. Everything was spotlessly clean, clear water was running freely, fresh palm leaves were used as cover, all blood was washed away, no drop was left. Returning to our cars, we continued along an incredibly steep road but had to stop after a short time since one of our cars had run into trouble: its radiator was running hot. In spite of the narrowness of the road and given the unwillingness of all drivers to let vehicles pass, it was surprising that we only saw one accident, which was an upturned lorry hanging halfway over a sheer drop.

At Lopshu we stopped to enjoy the magnificent panorama down the valley across the sweep of tea plantations. Here, like everywhere else, the main activity of the village centred on the river. A small clear stream gushed forth from the mountainside high above where men washed their bodies and hair, women laundered their clothes and children splashed about. Women trudged along the steep road carrying large wicker baskets on their backs, filled with enormously long white radishes which they offered for sale further along the road. Features once again were very Tibetan and also the women's apparel was reminiscent of Ladakh: 'overdresses' with crossover fronts flowing down to their ankles in sombre colours, made from wool. Over these they had tied the most attractive little aprons made from brightly coloured hand-woven strips. Our driver bought some *peda*, the well-advertised sweet made locally from sweet boiled milk, tasting not unlike marzipan.

High above the valley we stopped for our picnic lunch and soon afterwards we saw Darjeeling spreading up and down the mountain-side. It lies on three levels; it is not a pretty town but its position is superb. As we entered through the village of Ghoman we saw the track of the famous narrow-gauge 'toy train' for the first time (after which point the track crossed and recrossed the road various times). All along the way we were thrilled by the view across the sea of dark green tea gardens beyond the wooded mountains up to the snow-clad range of Kanchenjunga. Since the clouds moved continuously the majestic peaks kept on disappearing only to reappear again mysteriously. Below the Oberoi Mount Everest Hotel we drew to a halt. It was a big old building which had burnt down four years ago and still had not been rebuilt; the charred remains were there for all to see. Two old Tibetan women and one man dealt with our luggage, carrying the heavy cases on their backs in slings which went across their foreheads. The entrance hall was vast, with two large coal fires burning brightly in their grates. There we were greeted with tea and biscuits. Ruth and I were privileged since our accommodation consisted of a high-ceilinged sitting room with comfortable chairs, standard lamp, low tables and a coal fire ablaze in the grate; next to this height of absolute luxury we found the spacious bathroom and finally the bedroom, which was somewhat dark but comfortable, with an electric fire fully turned on.

Having settled in, we wandered out along the unpaved streets amongst the dense throng of people in search of a taxi to take us up to the Tibetan refugee village. The houses almost without fail were old and dilapidated, with many people occupying each room. Many of them called themselves 'hotel' and 'lodging house' but I shudder to think what they were like inside. As we passed an orphanage we saw the children, dressed in their Sunday best, playing in the yard. They seemed happy and well fed; next day they wore grey school uniform, but still played happily. Various signs pointed to 'homes' up and down town. Apart from many Tibetans now living in Darjeeling there were many Indian families on holiday and a few European tourists. Traffic fought its way through the crowd, with taxis and tourist jeeps full to the brim edging their way carefully through the teeming mass and hooting their penetrating horns continuously. Amidst all this confusion people remained cheerful and friendly, calling out 'Hello' to us as we passed. Eventually we found ourselves at the taxi rank, where we were able to 'clinch a deal', which is the customary way of hiring a car, or tourist jeep in our case, and arranged for the driver to take us to the 'Tibetan Refugee Self Help Village', wait there and bring us back again, having – most importantly – agreed on the price. You always hire the vehicle rather than paying per person.

First of all we drove to the lowest level of Darjeeling to collect a tyre. Punctures were extremely common and a frequent occurrence and we noticed that most tyres did not even have a trace of tread on them. Having completed this business, we drove out of town along a narrow road which clung to the mountainside to reach the village, which lay high above and was approached via a very steep incline.

The village had been built by Americans and when we visited 700 people lived there. Many of them had actually been born in the village. Unfortunately we were disappointed, having expected much activity and a lively place; it lay almost deserted and all we saw were women carding and spinning wool and also weaving carpets, and one carpenter planing wood whilst another sanded one of their famous ceremonial masks before it was ready to be painted. Both men and women alike were engaged in knitting with brightly coloured wools. One man consulted an ancient script before painting a *thangka*. In a small temple we found an old man singing happily to himself whilst he cleaned the place. A house proudly proclaimed 'Vocational Training for the Young' but it lay forsaken; nobody seemed to be anxious to receive instructions of any kind. A crèche was there and tucked away in a corner stood a 'House for the Infirm'. The whole village was served by a communal kitchen and when the food was ready a bell was rung to call all able people, who came clutching a bowl ready to be filled. Finally we visited the shop which sold articles produced in the village but we only bought postcards.

It is difficult to know how to react to a situation like the one we had observed. Whether living in the village in the hills helps these families to preserve their dignity and their identity, whether they are able to maintain their roots or not, I do not know. They appeared content.

Later we walked out again past the orphanage, to the Tibetan street market, where vendors sat on the ground with their colourful knitwear spread around them. Some of them were busily knitting or crocheting the bright 'mop caps' little toddlers always wore. Everybody, large or small, proudly showed off their enormous 'rice tikka' on their foreheads. Men walked amongst the crowd tempting us to buy fine Kashmir shawls. We succumbed and bought two plain ones, both extremely soft and light.

Continuing our walk past numerous shops brimful with merchandise of every kind within their narrow confine, we reached Chowrasta Square, where little mules trotted forwards and backwards amongst the milling crowd, giving excited children a short ride on their backs. Here we found the Oxford Bookshop, which we had been looking for since we had heard from friends that this was a true treasure trove, a book-lover's paradise with old and new books on every conceivable subject. Our main object was to find books about Bhutan. Deciding to postpone our purchase until the next day, we wandered out into the busy square again and back to our hotel, where we discovered two shops: one selling antiques, the other a boutique selling clothes, attractive and reasonably priced handbags, jewellery, books and postcards. For some time we chatted to the charming saleslady, who came from Pakistan, from the Punjab, but had lived in Darjeeling for the past twelve years. Finally we returned to the comfort of our own apartment, where a coal fire burnt brightly in the grate, the beds had been turned down and hot water bottles had been slipped between the sheets.

Next morning we were called early and rose at 4 a.m. Tea and biscuits were waiting for us in the big entrance hall with a little hand-written note by the side saying: 'Two biscuits each person, thank you'. Dressed in every available garment, clutching a blanket which we had taken off our bed (as we had been instructed to do), we climbed into the waiting jeeps. A stream of traffic laboured up Tiger Hill, consisting of cars as well as people on foot with some even jogging up the steep hill. The last part of the trail we all had to walk, which was tough going since it was not only steep but also very slippery as we threaded our way amongst cars, buses, jeeps and hordes of people. On top it was unbelievably crowded and we were almost unable to move. The majority of people present were Indians. Everybody waited patiently until a pink glow diffused the sky in the east and a golden ring fringed a grey cloud heralding the rising sun, which suddenly burst forth majestically, sending a glorious reflection over the range of Kanchenjunga which disappeared and reappeared behind clouds. For the first time we caught sight of Mount Everest – in the far distance. Well satisfied with our morning's venture we returned to our hotel, stopping on our way to let the 'toy train' pass.

At breakfast we were joined by an Anglo-Indian couple from our party. Ruth was a very well-groomed lady and Peter a very pleasant gentleman who liked to tell stories. He told us about the time when, whilst fishing in the wilds, he had accidentally stepped on a snake and later found fang marks on his ankle. Becoming very concerned, he phoned his doctor, who in turn put through a call to the snake doctor miles up country. The message which came back to Peter

27

instructed him to rid himself of all tobacco, drink black coffee throughout the night and take a cold bath in the morning, by which time 'all would be well'. The couple spent an anxious night drinking black coffee and reliving their happy married life by looking at their long-neglected photograph albums. Two days later the fang marks had completely disappeared. Some time after this incident the snake doctor suddenly announced one morning that he had used up all his power and was no longer able to help and would retire. On the selfsame day a young girl in another village told her parents that she was able to heal. In this very mysterious way the power of healing had been transferred by the gods from the old healer to the unknown young girl. No money or presents must ever pass or even be offered to the healer. Peter continued from his fund of stories and related one about a favourite bull which had been bitten by a snake and lay unconscious on the ground. It was placed on a stretcher and carried to the nearest point from where the snake doctor could be contacted. Shortly after contact had been established the bull came back to life, prancing back as fit as it had been before. Peter also told us about his houseboy, a well-known rogue, who had the power to locate any lost article. One of the engineers at Peter's place of work missed his camera one day and Ahmed was asked to find it. The boy declared that it was hanging on a hook in a house miles away. When they went as directed, true enough the missing camera hung on a hook inside the house which Ahmed had described. There was no doubt in our minds that Peter himself firmly believed in supernatural power, demonstrated by the earnest way he related his tales.

Feeling refreshed after our meal and wide awake enough to explore Darjeeling, we set off for the upper town, once more stopping on our way in one of the many small shops to buy a splendid Tibetan jacket, which Ruth wore later that night for dinner since the large dining room was freezing cold. One of the sweet-faced Tibetan waiters complimented her on her apparel, assuring her that she looked like a true Tibetan. Further along the road we purchased three more Kashmiri shawls and were amused to hear the vendor quote a higher prize to a potential customer who stood beside me. Next we called at a large stationery shop where we had admired beautiful photographs of the Himalayan range. Here we bought some postcards before moving on to the tea merchant, who ruled over a fascinating shop. The sad-faced man who owned the store explained that for the finest tea only the tender top shoots were used; the next grade consisted of the two top leaves as well as the top shoots, that the third used only the two top leaves. Broken tea or teabags – on mentioning these he visibly shuddered – were just 'rubbish', and saying this he took a pinch of tea tenderly into his cupped hands and gently blew on it to warm it and release its fragrance for us to smell. The subsequent purchase of a few packets proved quite a ritual.

Reaching Chowrasta Square, we returned to the bookshop to purchase some fine books, choosing *Bhutan, Land of the Peaceful Dragon*, which was not available outside India, one book about Ladakh and a second one with superb photographs of this Himalayan kingdom. I also found a 1949 edition of John Murray's *Handbook of India*, which we bought just for fun, and a book by D. Murphy which Ruth unearthed and purchased since she had been unable to obtain it in England. The book about Bhutan we took with us and had the rest sent home to arrive in a few months' time. Whilst browsing in the shop we talked to two American ladies who were on their way to trek in Buthan and were anxiously looking for Michael Peissel's book *Lords and Lamas*, which was out of print. I happened to locate a second-hand copy for them with which they were very pleased. Before we parted we also told them where to look for a travel bookshop in London on their next visit there.

Having crossed Chowrasta Square we followed a shady path climbing up to the Windermere Hotel, which looked like a smaller edition of the Oberoi, with clock golf on the front lawn and a terrace offering a splendid view. A Tibetan lady had laid out her trinkets on a cloth on the ground outside the hotel entrance, ready for trade. Continuing along the narrow path, we walked through pine woods, past beggars with outstretched hands to the top of Observatory Hill, where an old Hindu temple stood surrounded by prayer flags. It was dedicated to Siva and contained a lingam; Nandi, Siva's vehicle – the square bull – stood outside, where four Buddhist monks sat on the ground chanting away. This was the only temple where both Buddhists and Hindus worshipped. A throng of devotees presented their offerings, a ceremony which we found interesting to watch. One young couple arrived with a shopping bag from which they unloaded tins of food and other goods, finishing off with the customary offering of rice. A woman placed dough on top of the lingam in another shrine before putting the remains on the fire which burnt in a small hearth at the base of it. A *chorten* stood close by.

On our way back we stopped in our leisurely walk to buy some of the typical Tibetan aprons woven in coloured strips sewn together and backed on cotton. A mother with her baby girl in her arms stood in front of our hotel and even this little girl had her eyes outlined with kohl. Children seemed to wear the most extraordinary garments, since the Tibetans were very poor and anything which would serve to cover their bodies was used.

It happened to be a festival day again, with a Hindu festival coinciding with a Muslim holiday as well as being the Nepalese New Year. Therefore Indian Muslims, Indian Hindus, Buddhists from Tibet and Nepalese all celebrated.

In the afternoon we went down town to a part of Darjeeling which was rather grim but very colourful, with almost every street turned into a bazaar. A procession carrying Durga on a crude wooden platform passed by.

After dinner we invited a couple from our party to our cosy fireside where we sat sipping Sikkim brandy and talked until it was time to pack. This was fraught with difficulties since the electricity went off, then returned briefly only to plunge everything once more into darkness.

A tea tray arrived with our wake-up call next morning, which found us already up and dressed reading and writing. An English newspaper lay on the tray.

Soon after 9 a.m. we left, driving through narrow lanes where life had already commenced, where shops were open and trading was brisk. This led us to Ghom Monastery, which had been built in the 14th century and belonged to the yellow sect. A paved courtyard lay in front of the building, with prayer wheels standing alongside. An old monk blew his long copper horn for our benefit. This was normally used to announce the New Year, which falls at the end of February or beginning of March. He blew it badly but certainly loud enough for all to hear. The prayer hall was square, with ancient murals on its wall; prayer books written in two scripts lay wrapped in brocade, whilst 'Buddha to Come' sat on a chair, which was most unusual, since normally he stands or sits on a lotus blossom. His eyes were blue; usually they are dark. Both these features indicated that this particular image of Buddha came from the West. The Dorje – which is Tibetan for thunderbolt and is also the Tibetan name for Darjeeling – lay in front of the statue. On his left stood the God of Compassion with his eleven heads, thousand arms and thousand eyes on the palms of his thousand hands. To the right was a Tantric deity. In one corner loomed a very ancient prayer wheel made from leather. The cells for the monks lay behind the temple, whilst a small room off the courtyard housed an enormous brass prayer wheel which was very ancient.

Our journey continued downhill, parallel to the track of the narrow-gauge railway, which followed the contours of the mountainside. It ran through enchanting forests where pines, rhododendrons and an unfamiliar tree bearing pink blossoms grew. Fuchsias, cosmos, hydrangeas, marigolds and many other colourful flowers added to the profusion of the mountain flora. Many of the homes were crudely constructed from packing cases, yet people emerging from these hovels looked neat and spotlessly clean. Wherever there was running water men washed their hair and, stripped to the waist, their upper torso, whilst women laundered their clothes, rubbing in soap with their hands and stamping on them with their naked feet.

After Curso, which appeared an important shunting station where many people waited patiently, slogans appeared such as: 'Speed has five letters, so has Death'. But in spite of numerous warnings such as this, drivers took incredible risks when overtaking on the narrow steep roads.

Our bus stopped a number of times on the way down the mountainside, to let the 'toy train' cross the track which gave us time to look at the surrounding countryside, where we saw a Hindu shrine, a Buddhist *chorten* and three stone graves (either Muslim or Christian resting places), all set amongst lush tropical vegetation. Little thatched houses as well as shacks, standing on stilts, clung to the steep slopes and tea plantations were everywhere. One notice proclaimed: 'Soil Conservation Terraces under the Auspices of the Forestry Commission', whilst well-kept 'resting places' invited travellers to 'Use Me'. Actually we availed ourselves of one of these attractive spots for our picnic lunch before reaching Siliguri again. These resting places were very peaceful with roses and other flowers, shrubs and trees, a sweet-smelling frangipani amongst them.

Back once again at Siliguri we had to wait for new transport, this time provided by the Bhutanese Tourist Board with Bhutanese drivers and a charming Bhutanese guide. After a short time we took the same road as before, following the River Testa as far as the Sikkim–Darjeeling road junction, where we branched off to continue through a beautiful gorge which was wooded by tall teak trees. Once again we found ourselves back in India, people with broad Mongolian features had disappeared, women wore saris whilst men rested on charpoys. Villages with thatched houses appeared, some of which consisting of straw matting built on a base of local stone. The poorest dwellings utilised anything that could be found, from flattened rusty metal tins to corrugated iron or metal sheeting.

Stopping briefly along the roadside in a Muslim village, we watched a show of juggling, stick fighting and dancing, beneath a flag displaying the half-moon and a star. Men wore turbans, and the women's saris were of brighter colours than their Hindu counter-parts. Ladies turned their faces, covering them with veils as soon as they saw us with cameras slung around our necks. This proved without doubt that we were watching a Muslim community.

Tea plantations stretched to either side of the road as soon as we had left Siliguri behind. These were shaded by tall trees planted at strategic intervals to provide adequate protection for the root of the tea plant. Up in Darjeeling the tea had been planted on steep slopes where each plant provided shade for the roots of the plants below, making trees superfluous. The tea plant belongs to the same family as camellias and two species are grown: the one on the hills yields the most fragrant tea, the second, cultivated in the lowlands, provides a very strong brew with little bouquet. This plant has larger leaves and is marketed as Assam tea. Plantations stretched for miles, continuing from West Bengal into Assam.

After we had left the Muslim village the scenery changed; the countryside grew flat, with houses clustering together beneath palm trees, lending the whole scene almost an African atmosphere. A shepherd stood under a bleached black umbrella watching his flock, whilst rice paddies lay to either side of the road. Small streams meandered through wide river beds amongst smooth pebbles. Suddenly it was dusk, and the sun hung like a fireball low over the horizon spreading a blood red band to either side.

Our journey followed the broad National Highway NH 39 where military encampments were very much in evidence. The road led through a number of villages but it had become too dark to be able to see much.

Bhutan

Soon after 5 p.m. we stopped at the Indian passport control and twenty minutes later we entered Bhutan through an ornamental archway. Everybody had to climb down from the bus to complete individual forms, all passports had to be deposited since our group visa for Bhutan had not arrived from Delhi, but nobody seemed particularly disturbed by this fact and our journey continued through the well-lit town of Pusholding, which means 'The Gateway to Bhutan'. Finally we arrived at our hotel, which stood above and outside the city. Only men looked after us in hotels and restaurants, mostly wearing their national costume of a handsome robe belted at the waist with wide sleeves neatly turned back, knee-length woollen socks and leather boots. Knees had to be kept bare as long as the Head Abbot was in town but once he left (which coincided with the beginning of winter) they changed into long robes which fell down to their ankles. Some men wore traditional boots with rigid leather soles and red embroidered felt uppers or even more elegant footwear with slightly upturned toes with leather caps, the rest consisting of rich silk which was heavily embroidered. They utilised their pouch – made from the fullness of their crossover garment – to carry everything they needed. The Bhutanese were charming people, friendly and always ready with a smile. Their skins were smooth and golden, and sometimes they sprouted a small moustache or wispy goatee. Their hair was straight and black, worn in a pageboy style – except for monks, whose heads were shaven. Until recently long hair for males had been a punishable offence but this law had been abolished. At times it was difficult to distinguish male from female when meeting an old person. Women usually wore robes, woven from wool, which fell from their shoulders to their ankles, fixed below their shoulders by a silver brooch on either side connected by a chain. A colourful woven belt was tied around their waist, and they wore short jackets with wide sleeves over their robe, made from brocade, velvet or simple woven cloth.

The boys who looked after us were most delightful, always courteous and extremely thoughtful, seeming to anticipate our every wish and taking great care of us, which made us feel privileged and cosseted.

Our friends from Hong Kong who travel frequently in Bhutan had written to us suggesting we contacted Mr Dorji, the barman at our hotel, whose wife – an accomplished weaver from eastern Bhutan – produced fine work which he sold. Unfortunately there was little choice since she had fallen ill and he only had the remains of the previous year's stock. Regretfully we did not buy anything.

Brilliant sunshine greeted us next morning but our onward journey was delayed since our visa still had not arrived from Delhi and we were told that we would utilise the waiting time to visit some of the local sites.

I remember our first breakfast in Bhutan quite clearly, starting with local apple juice followed by eggs cooked in any way we liked. A plate most artistically arranged with sausages, tomatoes, fried potatoes arrived. Toast and marmalade were placed before us and tea or coffee served.

A splendid panoramic view opened out before us from the terrace of our hotel down to the town and further along the valley. Lush vegetation surrounded us, birds twittered and crickets chirped away, and weaver birds' baskets hung from the trees. Our first visit took us to a nearby modern temple which had been built by the Queen Mother in 1967. Eight stupas stood in front of the temple, representing the different styles found in Bhutan. The whole complex was surrounded by well-kept gardens. Adjacent to the temple stood the old monastery, which was only used by the Queen Mother when she was in residence. The temple contained three main figures: the Buddha to Come presided in the centre, with Ngawang Mamgyal (also known as Shabdung Rimpoch the Unifier of Bhutan) to his right. He wore a benign expression on his face, sprouted a goatee and wore a pointed hat. The third figure was of Guru Padmasambhava, the Indian sage who introduced Buddhism to Bhutan.

Down town we visited another modern temple built by the merchants of the city and completed in 1980. It was constructed on three levels, with the temple on the ground floor housing the Second Buddha in Bhutan, whilst the Buddha of Compassion – also known as Bodhisattva Avalokitesvara – stood in the middle temple.

34

He is always shown with eleven heads and a thousand hands bearing a thousand eyes on their palms. The legend goes that when Buddha looked down on the suffering of the world with his piercing eyes he was so overcome with compassion and with the desire to alleviate all misery that he could not contain his feelings within his head and burst into eleven heads to take up the volume of suffering and to understand it. A thousand arms sprung forth with a thousand hands to encompass all misery and a thousand eyes appeared to be able to see all ills. Otherwise Buddha is always represented with four main arms, two of which are joined in the attitude of prayer whilst the other two hold the beads and lotus flower respectively. The second from top of the eleven heads of the Buddha of compassion exhibited terrifying features of the Lord of Death which is the other aspect of the Bodhisattva.

The pièce de résistance rose up on the third floor: the Tree of Life created in papier mâché. The Maitreya – the Buddha to Come – sat inside the temple.

Since we had time to spare and this last temple stood in the central square of Pusholding, we strolled around and visited the local store, which consisted of 'shops within shops'. Here we looked vaguely for suitable presents to take back with us but found nothing to tempt us. The store was fully air-conditioned and therefore pleasantly cool in strong contrast to the searing heat and dust outside. Traders in the square sat on the ground, sheltering from the fierce sun under bleached umbrellas.

Our next visit was a short distance from the square to see some alligators safely ensconced behind wire netting. They were ugly beasts, and most of them appeared to be asleep with massive jaws wide open; one only was awake, partially immersed in a small pond.

Our bus took us back to our hotel, where we were greeted with fragrant tea and biscuits served in the cool entrance hall. This had also been our welcome drink when we arrived the night before. The lunch, which was served later in the dining room, was quite excellent and finally – our visa having arrived – we left Kharbandi Hotel shortly after 2 p.m.

The drive was beautiful, through lush green rain forest with curve after curve taking us higher and presenting wonderful views down into the wide valley with the torturous River Toorsa shimmering like a silver snake in the bright sunshine, whilst range after range of mountains rose in the far distance. Heat haze hovered over the plain. It was dusk when we reached the Bunaka Cafeteria, where we stopped for refreshment. Again we had an introduction from our friends in Hong Kong and asked to meet the proprietor, Mr Buatt from Bangalore, with whom we had a pleasant chat, since he knew Brian and Felicity well.

The rest of our journey led through darkness following the ever-winding road which hugged the mountainside, descending down valleys only to climb up into the unknown mountains again. Travelling in the night added to the excitement. Finally we reached a river which brought us to the junction of two valleys: the Paro and the Thimpu, where the respective roads and rivers met. The headlights of our vehicle lit up four stupas standing in a row, presenting us with a dramatic sight as they made these silent edifices appear almost luminous in their stark whiteness against the velvet darkness of the night.

Following the road to Paro, we were greeted by the twinkling lights of the town in just under one hour. Our way led up above Paro to the Olatang Hotel, where we arrived shortly before 8 p.m. This complex had been originally built as a royal hunting lodge and had been extended in 1972 to house the royal guests for the coronation. It consisted of many chalets built in traditional Bhutanese style, with the largest of them in the centre containing the reception area, lounge and dining room. Our quarters comprised one large room, part of which served as sitting room, with a half wall providing privacy for two beds. It was extremely tastefully furnished with gaily painted handmade furniture. One door led to a veranda, a second to a small dressing room which in turn led to the bathroom. Colourful motives were painted on the wooden walls. The bathroom boasted a bathtub, basin and loo but had no hot water. There was an abundance of electric plugs but no power cable had been installed. A large building was under construction, destined to become a luxury hotel, fully centrally heated, with bar and all modern facilities.

In the meantime we were told to inform the desk about the time we required hot water. A young man then appeared carrying a bucket with hot water drawn from an enormous cauldron near our chalet, beneath which a wood fire crackled all through the night. The pail of steaming water was placed carefully next to the wash basin and tenderly covered with one of the bath towels. The other luxury thoughtfully provided for us was a hot water bottle placed between the sheets. Unfortunately calamity occurred on our second night when the young man with the sad face and drooping moustache had failed to secure the top of the hot water bottle properly and therefore my bed was awash. Apart from this, we heard a mouse – or maybe it was a rat – one or even more creatures, busily scratching away in our dressing room throughout the night. Sleep escaped us.

The morning air was crisp and cool but soon the sun rose high in the sky and rapidly warmed the day. The countryside was unbelievably beautiful with rice fields looking like an artistically designed patchwork quilt. Rice when cut was carefully and orderly arranged in a specific pattern.

The architecture in Bhutan was most attractive, with wooden roofs (unfortunately some of these had been replaced by corrugated sheeting) anchored by great stones – seen from the far distance the houses were reminiscent of Swiss chalets or the lovely homesteads found in the western Himalayas. Most houses were three storey high, the base being larger than the rest and serving to house the livestock, whilst the family occupied the middle floor; grain and dry victuals were stored in the loft, which was either open at both ends or closed by beautifully patterned matting. Brilliant red splashes appeared which were chilli peppers put out to dry in the sun. Walls were built of local stone, with gaps filled in by mud, then plaster was applied to serve as a base for whitewash to cover all. Older houses were partly wood-clad; whether old or new, much care had been taken to adorn window frames, door frames and eaves with carving painted in vivid colours. The wooden shingles on the old roofs were securely held in place by wooded struts and stone; no iron – not even nails – had been used to construct any of the buildings in Bhutan. Attractive murals had been painted to either side of the entrance of some houses, usually depicting animals, one of which was inevitable the tiger. Windows had no panes but wooden shutters were used to keep out the cold during the harsh winter months. Modern buildings using cement were finished off with wood cladding to blend in with the traditional houses.

Black pigs with their piglets scavenged in the dirt, whilst chickens scratched for food and cattle munched contentedly in the high meadows. Foothills were thickly covered with woods where autumn tints were beginning to show. Birch trees looked golden since their slender leaves had already changed colour, and larch trees which

37

bore longer needles than those we know had also turned a different shade before shedding them.

Our first stop was at the ruins of Drugyel Dzong standing dramatically in the shadow of the second highest mountain in Bhutan, the Jomor Zharri, 25,000 feet high. It is also known as the Tower of Victory, commemorating the victory over Tibetan invaders in the 8th century when quarrels had broken out between the yellow and red sects and Padmasambhava had to flee. He came to Bhutan at the invitation of the Guru King, who was his father. Drugyel Dzong also celebrates the unification of Bhutan. It was built in 1647 by Shabdung Ngawag Nagel (1594–1651), who unified the country. It was burnt down in 1951 but kept deliberately as a ruin to preserve the construction of the building for everyone to see. These ruins were very impressive, with thick walls enclosing a large courtyard which was designed to give refuge to the whole population, who normally lived at the foot of the hill, during time of war. Dzongs were originally built as watchtowers for specific regions; later they served as divisional or provincial headquarters and housed administrative offices as well as monasteries.

Below Drugyel Dzong stood a prayer wheel which was kept in continuous motion by water coming from high mountains. The gurgling of the little stream, the creaking of the old wooden wheel, the buzzing of insects and twittering of birds all added to the peace and tranquillity which hung over the valley and we were almost loath to tear ourselves away to journey on to visit the old monastery of Paro, which had been built in the 7th century AD and contained the statue of the Buddha to Come – the Maitreya – surrounded by a thousand Buddhas sitting on shelves. A modern monastery had been erected by the Queen Mother in 1967 next to the old one but was only used when she herself was in residence, which was twice a year.

The afternoon found us driving up the steep mountainside to Ta Dzong, which was a pleasant round building commanding a splendid view down the valley. Ta Dzong housed a very comprehensive museum with a most amazing collection of stamps displayed in the top gallery. Stamps had reached Bhutan relatively late. There were sets of three-dimensional stamps, a set of compact discs, a set of famous painters, one of sculptures, yet another one of famous statesmen, one to commemorate the Munich Olympics, another the

38

first journey to the moon etc. On the top floor, above this gallery, stood the Tree of Life forming the centre piece of a shrine. On all the other floors *thangkas* were on show which were extremely beautiful and some of them were very old. Another gallery contained a collection of costumes with a special section for hats; there were jewellery, ritual vessels, exquisitely carved Buddhas in silver, copper, wood and carved out of an elephant's trunk. One gallery displayed wooden water vessels, copper containers and wooden teapots, whilst in another one we saw weights and measures, one of which – a square one – when filled to the brim was meant to feed a hundred people.

Walking down a gentle slope we passed a school. Boys and girls alike were sliding down the hill, lying full length on a board. A whole crowd of giggling schoolgirls clustered around as soon as they caught sight of us, asking us eagerly all kinds of questions. When we had stopped at the foot of Drugyel Dzong we had been greeted cheerfully by small children who were bright-eyed but in rags.

Our path led to the imposing Ring Pung Dzong, where many well-worn stone steps led to the entrance. A crowd of young monks came running down the steps whilst many more watched from numerous windows of the tall building. To reach the temple we had to cross the courtyard and were shown a special room containing fantastic masks for use for certain festivals. They were usually made from papier mâché, sometimes carved from wood, occasionally constructed from clay, and looked quite terrifying.

Leaving the Dzong, we picked up our transport again to drive down town and walk along Paro's 'High Street', marvelling at the shops consisting of shacks to either side of the road and containing a great variety of merchandise. These shacks, the goods within them, the people, numerous cats, all were incredibly dirty, but everybody smiled and welcomed the strangers in their midst with great friendliness and warmth.

Our transport took us back to the Olatang Hotel standing above town amidst fir trees. As in Darjeeling afternoon tea was a daily custom; tea and coffee were always served at lunch and dinner. The days were short, darkness fell soon after 5 p.m. And because electricity was poor, making it difficult to read and write, this meant 'early to bed and early to rise'. In fact next morning we received our wake-up call (by mistake) at 3 a.m. but did not mind, realising that the unfortunate young man who had been detailed to wake us at 5 a.m. did not possess a watch.

It was 6.30 a.m. when we rose and six of us set off after breakfast to drive to a nearby bridge. Walking across the swaying planks trustingly festooned with prayer flags, we reached the other bank, where ponies stood waiting for us. With shaking knees and faint heart we each climbed on the steed allotted to us, but found to our great relief that our fears had been groundless. The path we took although quite steep led over meadows and up wooded slopes where no abyss threatened us. The horses were members of the 'nibbling brigade', with mine favouring thorny branches, which meant that I had thorns in my hair, on my sleeves, in my thighs, thorns everywhere by the time our ride had finished. None of the horses would have been suitable in a race since they had two speeds: slow and stop. At times they stood stock still, at others they vied for position on the narrow path.

Ruth, one of our party, kitted out in fur hat and fur cape (she and her husband always changed for dinner: Ruth into a long skirt and smart blouse, he into a dinner jacket and bow tie), was immediately in front of me and like in a slow motion film I watched her gently slipping off her horse; the saddle had loosened along the stony, uneven ground and had slowly moved towards the belly of the horse. I had to suppress my laughter since it was such a funny sight. Another of the riders came off her horse; one leg almost doubled beneath her since her stirrup had been unevenly fastened, but fortunately neither rider was hurt and we all survived the ride. Standing high up on the mountain beside some prayer flags fluttering in the wind, we all considered the effort well worth while as we looked at the majestic view into the fertile valley across the wooded slopes to the snow-capped mountains.

After two hours we parted company from our respective ponies and continued on foot. It was quite easy going at first but finally we had to traverse a gorge with a sheer drop down into a deep narrow gully and cross a narrow little bridge which spanned over turbulent waters of a mountain waterfall. A tiny hermit's hut stood nestling against sheer rock high above us as we negotiated the last lap. Monks came here to stay on their own to meditate for three months. It was relatively easy to climb up the other side of the gorge to reach Tangsang Monastery (Tiger's Nest). Stone steps led to the elaborate entrance gate which gave access to the four temples poised high on a vertical cliff. The first of these was quite small, built partially into the rock and contained the figure of Dorje Trolo in his furious guise riding on the back of the flying pregnant tigress, holding the Dorje – the thunderbolt – which signifies the indestructibility of Buddha's teaching in one hand and the Purba – the ritual instrument shaped like a triple bladed dagger symbolising the dynamic quality of energy associated with the Void – in the other. Many skulls hung on his belt. Pregnancy stands for the latent wisdom in all of us. Legend has it that Dorje Trolo rode on the flying pregnant tigress in one single day from Tibet to Bhutan, slaying all evil along his path before reaching his goal. The prostrated figures beneath the tigress's paws represented the vanquished evil. Seven bowls of water stood on the altar: two to wash either hand, the others representing the five senses. They were offering bowls. The ritual water jug was beautifully chased in silver shaped like a peacock, with real peacock feathers decorating the tail, whilst the spout formed the head and neck of the bird. The thunderbolt beside the jug pointed the way for the dead, and the bell kept beside it was used to call the dead for their meals. A sealed screen decorated with faces devouring snakes stood behind the altar, hiding a cave which contained a thousand thunderbolts originating from natural rock. This cave was only opened once a year on a very special day when many pilgrims made their way to this sacred place.

Legend has it that Guru Padmasambhava, the great Indian sage – came to Tangsang Monastery in the 8th century to meditate. Padmasambhava sat in the second temple with his four guides. His image was known as 'the 'Spoken Statue'. Unfortunately I was unable to follow the guide's story as to how it had acquired this name. The seven offering bowls, the peacock jug, the thunderbolt and bell were all proudly displayed. In a prominent position stood the charming statue of Shabdung Rimpoch, the precious Teacher, reverently shrouded in the ritual shawl. On the wooden floor in front of the altar were two footprints outlined in semi-precious stones for the pilgrim to place their own feet when paying homage to the Guru. The floor in the first temple had consisted of natural rock.

The murals, as in all temples, told the life story of the main figure in the shrine. An enormous butter lamp stood in one corner which when completely full and lit would burn for a whole year. Whilst the guide explained one of the young caretakers of Tangsang Monastery had followed us carrying with obvious pride a tape recorder which played temple music.

The third temple was a large rectangular room, where we found Guru Padmasambhava in all his eight guises with his two wives, one Tibetan the other Indian.

The fourth temple on a yet higher level, was quite small, with an enormous figure of the furious Padmasambhava on his flying tigress punishing one guru and one lama for marrying girls of their generation. These miserable sinners lay prostrated beneath the tigress's paws. An unfinished figure of a mother goddess stood in a corner.

Perched high above, we spent some time merely sitting in the sun and feeling entirely at peace with the world, just soaking up the atmosphere of beauty and tranquillity and enjoying the magnificent view.

Our descent was easy, reaching a small restaurant within an hour where a welcomed cup of tea greeted us. There was also a loo consisting of a wooden seat built across a sheer drop down into a ravine. The luxury of 'running water' was also provided thanks to a small clear mountain stream which ran through the courtyard. These bodily comforts barely counted compared to the ever present view of the monastery perched above, the sweep of the valley below bathed in golden sunshine and the wooded slopes leading up to snow-capped mountains encircling the whole scene in a wide embrace. Still unable to take our eyes off the glorious panorama, we had an excellent meal. A young woman, baby at her breast, smiled sweetly at us whilst a girl tried to sell us some tickets – I never found out what they were for. One member of our party had given our guide an electronic pocket game popular in the West. He had no time to look, no time to eat or drink, he had no time for anything apart from playing with his new toy.

The sun stood high in the sky and time had come to continue our way down. The path led through woods of pine trees, silver birches, willow trees, rhododendrons and magnolias. Sweet scent hung heavily in the air. I saw the yellow mustard flower, cotoneaster with its red berries, short stemmed Michaelmas daisies, forget-me-nots, dwarf delphiniums, hollyhocks and stocks. At one time I could smell the pungent smell of the curry flower quite distinctly but could not see it. There were many butterflies, big and small; tiny little blue ones hovered near the water, elegant dragonflies flitted past. As we neared the valley, men and women, usually with a few ragamuffins by their side, tried to sell us trinkets which were mostly overpriced shabby offerings. Emerging from the woods, fields and homesteads lay before us but somehow we managed to lose our way and had to plod through marshland before we regained the path which took us back to the prayer wheel kept in continuous motion by the stream. Finally we arrived at the swaying bridge, which we crossed to climb on the waiting bus. As soon as our party was complete we returned to the hotel. Whilst we were sipping the customary cup of tea in the comfortable lounge a royal shooting party arrived, consisting of two old men with bushy moustaches carrying guns and looking as if they had stepped out of a Wild West film in their high boots and wearing wide-brimmed hats. With a broad American accent one addressed his partner in a booming voice: 'Here is your tea, Bert,' and both downed a glass of beer. Two women joined them, behaving in a brash manner without finesse which jarred in this tranquil place.

I needed the key to my chalet to collect my hand luggage but nobody appeared to man the desk in the hall, therefore I walked to the back to help myself, barely avoiding the sleeping receptionist who lay fully stretched out on the floor. When I later said goodbye to him he told me that he would be coming to England to do a business course which surprised me since very few people seemed to leave Bhutan apart from a small number who were sent to India to take up specific courses.

Our little group who had been up to the Tiger's Nest left Paro to join the rest of our party, who had preceded us to Thimpu. As we followed the River Poncho along the lovely Paro Valley where we had travelled in the dark only two days ago, we saw that work was being done in the fields, rice was being harvested and piled up into round stacks; only very occasionally was it placed on the road for traffic to do the threshing, as we had seen it so often in south India. Wooden ploughs, harnessed to sturdy oxen, were generally used; rarely did we see a tractor or any other machinery.

Our advance party had visited the Sunday market in Thimpu but unfortunately most trading had finished by the time they got there; only fruit and vegetable stalls were still functioning but even so Ruth had managed to buy some trinkets. They had watched some archery, which was the national sport. Maidens dressed in their

43

national costume had sung to encourage the participants, one of whom had stood out in his splendid apparel. He had spoken to each member of our party and told them that he knew America well, that he liked the cinema best of all things there and particularly enjoyed Wild West films. The cinema plays a very important part in the East and we had remarked on the construction of an enormous building in Gangtok when we were told that it was to be a cinema. Later we learned that the handsome archer was the King's cousin.

As we were leaving Paro we passed a very special building on the outskirts of the town. This served for the Thronbol (a very unique *Thangka* which was enormous) to be suspended in its entire length from it during the famous Paro Festival, covering the four storeys from top to bottom. It was worked in appliqué, showing Guru Padmasambhava in all his eight incarnations. The Paro airstrip lay close by, symbolising the old tradition side by side with modern technology.

Forty minutes later found us at the end of the Paro Valley where the River Poncho joined the river Monchu to become the Wangchu. This junction of rivers and valleys was known as Chuzon, where the four stupas, which had impressed us with their still whiteness in the dark night when we had arrived, stood at a height of 7,000 feet, with one of them being square whilst two were built in the traditional round style, the fourth bore four domes on an oblong base. Stupas formed quite a landmark, standing dotted about throughout Bhutan, sometimes near a homestead, at other times they rose in splendid isolation all on their own.

I saw a leper in one of the villages we passed through being carefully led by a young man. First he hid his face behind a cloth but let it drop, showing his disfigurement. I had noticed one woman up in the hills with a large mixed parotid tumour and outside Paro Monastery had sat a dwarf counting his beads contentedly. On the whole, however, people, both old and young, looked healthy.

A delightful pack of grey monkeys with a ruffle framing their faces and with bushy tails crossed our path before it became dark. Once before, whilst we were travelling at night, a nocturnal animal had glided silently into the dense undergrowth. The last part of our journey was blotted out by the dark until the twinkling lights of Thimpu greeted us. Again we entered the town through an arch and drove along the market street, where shops filled with a variety of merchandise were still open. Our path climbed higher up to our hotel, passing pleasant houses on the way. The hotel was an imposing building situated at the fringe of woods and standing in its own grounds. In fact it consisted of two quite sizeable houses built in Bhutanese style which were in the process of being connected to each other. This meant that we had to traverse a draughty, dusty building site to reach our bedroom. At night it became very cold and although our bedrooms had some kind of central heating as well as a small electric fire, neither worked very efficiently and they failed to warm the room. The fluorescent light in our bathroom was temperamental too. Some of the friendly and courteous manner we had become accustomed to in Bhutan was slightly missing in Thimpu, so to console ourselves and warm ourselves we joined a couple of our party in their room after our meal to drink the last of the Sikkim cherry brandy and taste Bhutanese cake bought in the Swiss bakery in town.

At half past eight next morning with the dew still heavy on the ground we watched some dancing being performed in our honour in front of the hotel. They danced seven dances, some wearing masks, others without. Masked dances were usually only performed by monks on special festive days. For the first dance the performers wore many layered yellow and red skirts over leopard skin pants. In one of the other dances each dancer carried a drum which had a handle and used a drumstick shaped like a sickle. All dancers used hands, arms and shoulders in rhythmic movement and were very light on their feet. One dance was a cremation dance in which white masks were used. This was followed by two folk dances in which girls joined and moved gracefully in pleasant rhythm. Next the stag dance was performed, danced behind masks with horns which symbolised the subjugation of the evil spirit of the wind by the flying stags. A Nepalese dance was shown, danced by gentle maidens with fair skins and different features dressed in saris and partnered by their fair-skinned beaux. The rat dance preceded the final folk dance. Two musicians had accompanied most of the dances, but the Nepalese group had their own band, three in number, with a sophisticated-looking instrument which sounded like a harmonica. We were not only watching the performers but looked with great interest at the audience which had gathered at the fringe. All workmen had downed their tools to come along with their wives and children and squatted spellbound on the ground.

45

The little ones were incredibly dirty, barefoot and in rags; many of the women were nursing their babies at their breasts. All workmen lived on the site with their families and everything was constructed in situ: trees were cut and sawn into planks which were planed, doors and window frames were constructed and carved in traditional patterns. Babies were either carried in slings on their mothers' backs or placed in a crude wicker basket with barely a cover over them; bottoms were always left exposed.

Our morning tour started with a drive down town back to the market street to visit the Government Emporium. Although this was open, unfortunately the electricity had failed and the whole place lay plunged in utter darkness and all we could do was just peer at the goods. Therefore we walked out into the brilliant sunshine and along the dusty street, looking at the various shops, some of which were open whilst others had their shutters firmly secured over doors and windows. According to my book, shops only opened twice a week. The local population were about, with women sitting calmly on the ground knitting or spinning whilst men squatted lazily in the sun. At the post office we stopped to buy stamps before continuing on our way and were amazed at all we saw, amused at the writing on wooden boards, such as one hotel proclaiming proudly that this was 'where you could get lodging and feeding too'.

In the Swiss bakery we joined some members of our party to partake of coffee and cake to the accompaniment of Alpine music issuing from a tape in the background. Strange as it seemed to us, the owner was actually a Swiss-born Bhutanese.

Our city tour led us to the Tshecho Chorten, which was the memorial to the late King built between 1972 and 1974. A small group of old men with wispy beards, clutching their beads, sat in a corner of the small garden which surrounded the edifice, listening intently to the lama, who told them that when they died they would be reincarnated according to the way they had conducted their lives: if they had been bad they might reappear as insects crawling on the ground to be squashed by a careless foot; if, however, they had led a good life they might even assume the part of a lama. Death held no fear for these old men, who sat in the meantime contentedly in the sun, each holding their prayer wheel and their prayer beads.

The *chorten* itself gleamed in its whiteness with its shimmering golden top which was visible from any point in town. It had been

46

constructed on three levels and appeared quite brash and gaudy at first glance until we had taken time and trouble to study details. Each register symbolised a specific aspect of Buddha's teaching of the law.

The afternoon found us back in town again to visit Tongsa Dzong; by definition a *dzong* is a fort or castle serving as a seat of religion as well as for the secular administration of a specific district.

Tongsa Dzong was a most imposing complex built in 1642 and last rebuilt in 1961. The seat of Parliament had been moved to Thimpu in 1965 and the King's summer palace was now within the confines of the dzong. An archway took us inside, where sweet-smelling roses planted in well-tended beds greeted us. Our guide had donned the ritual shawl which every Buddhist wears when entering a monastery as a sign of reverence. The entrance hall was beautifully adorned with murals. The main wall depicted the four Kings of the Compass: the King of the South was shown in blue, the King of the East in white, holding a mandolin. I cannot recall the specific colour of the other two Kings. On each of the side walls stood a furious guardian protecting the Kings. Another charming picture showed a pyramid of animals stretching up to a tree to pick its fruit. The elephant was at the bottom, the bird on top. The monkey sat on the elephant's back, the rabbit crouched on the monkey. An emaciated pilgrim – reminiscent of the wonderful descriptive Buddhist monument of the Ascetic in Ajanta's Penance at Mahabalipuram in South India, which we had seen and which left a permanent impression on my mind – stood watching the scene. Apart from these paintings the Eight Auspicious Signs were also depicted around the walls; these we saw on many of the official buildings everywhere in Bhutan, as well as along the roads and in other public places. They are called Tashi Tangye and interpreted as follows.

1. The Banner of Victory symbolises the victory of enlightenment.
2. The Parasol of Authority stands for Buddha's teaching.
3. The Conch Shell demonstrates the reverberating sound of the Dharma. Dharma means the Law as taught by Buddha.
4. The Golden Fishes symbolise resurrection indicating eternal life. They can also be interpreted as perception since fish can see through muddy water.

47

5. The Lucky Net or Braha Sala represents all theories and all philosophies about the entire universe. Another explanation maintains that 'one extracts pearls of wisdom or jewels of enlightenment from the ocean of existence'.
6. The Wheel of Dharma or Law indicates the propagation of Buddha's wisdom.
7. The Vase of Immortality or Amrita or Nectar stands for the Immortality of the soul.
8. The Lotus Flower represents the ultimate goal, namely Enlightenment.

These signs also refer to different parts of Buddha's body: the vase to his throat, the lotus to his tongue, the fish to his eyes, etc.

A flight of stairs brought us into the courtyard surrounded by buildings in traditional style. Three of these dated back to the 17th century. The buildings on the periphery housed the administrative offices; one contained the throne room but was closed to the public. A very tall old construction housed the temple but the wooden ladder leading up to its entrance looked so precarious that we did not venture inside and were content to watch the young monks scramble up and down like agile monkeys swinging from tree to tree. Our next visit was the Assembly Hall, known as Tshodgu, which was elaborately decorated with a mandala displayed in the centre of the ceiling. A mandala is the mystic pattern used for initiation and meditation and consists of complex geometrical patterns. Its philosophical concept is equally complex: essentially it is looked upon 'as means by which microcosmic man can be brought into harmony with the macrocosmic universe by visualisation of the divine pattern'. The mandala has therefore been defined as the 'psycho-cosmogram', and when placed on the ceiling it will shower its blessing on those standing below it. The mandala in Tshodgu showed Buddha in the centre with a Guardian in each of the four gateways. The sixteen Ahrats stood within a circle around him; an Ahrat is a saint who has overcome greed, hate and delusion.

The royal seat stood in a prominent position at the head of the seats for the ministers. Modern equipment such as microphones were present. One entire wall of this magnificent hall was occupied by an enormous head of Buddha behind glass but it was difficult to obtain a clear view of this edifice. Having admired the colourful splendour of Tshodgu Hall we stepped out into the courtyard again.

48

Standing on top of the stairs, we were met by a stampede. Most of the three thousand monks living here came rushing into the court-yard to assemble; excitement hung almost palpably in the air, dinnertime was approaching. Large wicker baskets filled to the brim with cooked rice were carried up the stairs and lined up outside the dining hall, whilst monks holding thonged leather whips kept a watchful eye on the proceedings. They did not hesitate to flick their whips through the air and to let them fall decisively and ominously on the stony ground. A gong sounded, followed by a sudden surge of many naked feet into the enormous dark hall. Permission was given for us to step inside and watch. Each monk took up his allotted place and sat cross-legged in a long orderly row on the floor. Next came the overseer, who handed a slip of paper to each boy. After each boy had received his voucher, the baskets of rice were carried in by two of the bigger boys whilst each of the little monks spread a dirty piece of cloth on his lap, and quick as lightning a large measure of rice was placed on it. The boys deftly tied their portion of rice into a neat bundle, some having first shaped it into a round ball. One boy got the whip and no rice for some misdemean-our, whilst other boys fought with each other as their masters' backs were turned; boys will be boys, who and wherever they are. It was quite a medieval scene to watch in the dark, sinister, cavernous hall. Once each boy had his ration, he rushed out into the sunshine. They were allowed to exchange their vouchers at the storeroom for additional food or for two rupees, before returning to their tutors to eat their meal. Three meals a day were distributed, each consist-ing of rice. All the boys looked surprisingly healthy and alert, with clear skin and bright eyes.

Following along the river, we drove to Simtok Dzong, which was the oldest, built in 1627 by Namwang Namgyal, and now served as a boys' school. The *dzong* stood high above the river and to reach it we had to climb up a short but steep path. There were no lights in any of the three temples. Buddha to Come stood in the middle temple with the War God to his left and the Buddha of Compassion to his right. The oldest part was a large shrine containing Buddha Sakyamuni with four enormous Buddhas standing to either side as well as his twenty-four disciples, twelve from India and twelve from Tibet. A side shrine housed the Buddha of Confession. The murals depicted Buddha's life.

As soon as we stepped outside we were surrounded by boys and lamas, both tempting us to buy some artefact or other. To inspect the Wheel of Life mounted outside the prayer hall we crossed the courtyard. This was a modern painting not unlike one of Picasso's abstract works. Every monastery which we had visited had contained a conventional painting of the Wheel of Life on some wall. In fact outside the dining hall in Tshodgu we had admired a beautiful replica with almost cartoon-like pictures showing what would befall the sinners, such as the beheading and subsequent disembowelment by vultures for avarice and greed. Our gentle guide explained to us that Buddhists believe the world to be flat and yet he himself knew that it had been proven without doubt that the world is round. He indicated that this had caused a conflict within himself but his faith was of such strength that he remained convinced that the world was flat.

When we returned to our hotel we found that once the sun had disappeared it grew cold and since their was little comfort anywhere, this meant early to bed once again. I woke early next morning. Going through the lounge, I found most of the staff stretched out on benches fast asleep, but the front door was unlocked. Silently I slipped out into the still morning. Frost covered the ground. Behind the hotel I discovered a small community living in little houses tucked beneath trees.

Soon after breakfast we left for our journey back, stopping briefly at the Government Emporium and at the post office. It was a glorious morning, warm and sunny for the best part of the time as we drove through Thimpu Valley for 25 to 30 miles, following the river as before. The mountains rose stark and bare; an enormous sculpture of a double-headed statue represented the god of both valleys. All along the road were the Eight Auspicious Signs. Once again we retraced our steps and reached the confluence of the River Monchu from the Thimpu Valley with the River Poncho from Paro Valley. The scenery soon changed, trees and well-tended fields appeared. At the highest point – 8,250 feet – we stopped to admire the view and to stretch our legs. Well-hidden behind trees stood the Royal Lodge, where gladioli grew along the path which led up to it. Our journey continued, when we suddenly came upon a group of saried women sitting outside a shack and soon afterwards encountered turbaned Sikhs, one of whom drove a jeep whilst the other was engaged in lighting a fire. These were road workers from India.

Soon we reached a colony called Chumukotti, which boasted a

50

'Hydel-Work' – a hydro-electric plant – and also a timber and firework colony. The latter stood under the auspices of the Forest Commission. In fact we had noticed various 'colonies' on our way up, such as the Plywood Colony, Mushroom Colony, Piggery Colony. Chumukotti was quite a large place, with its huts huddled close together and cows and chickens looking for sustenance in between. It possessed a cinema; cinemas appeared to be of utmost importance. A stream of people had met us as we approached Thimpu on the Sunday evening when we arrived. They had walked purposefully along the road and we realised only later that they all had come from the cinema which stood outside town. Later we had seen a crowd almost storming a cinema in town. Chumukotti also had an entrance arch adorned by fragrant branches of pine. A short time after Chumukotti we arrived at Chukka, another development. Looking down the valley, it seemed to be an elegant new town with tall houses, but glancing across it, poor tin huts housing the workers clung to the slopes. Having climbed up the other side after crossing the river we read at two places: 'A Bird's Eye View of Chukka Hydel-Project could be obtained'. Soon after Chukka we passed a military station. At times our road rose to such lofty heights that we felt as if we were travelling on top of the world.

Bunaka Cafeteria greeted us in time for lunch. I set off on my own after our meal to walk along the road in the lazy lull of the midday sun, where bees were buzzing and birds singing their sweet songs. A new sound suddenly joined this pastoral symphony. Unable to identify this, I looked around until I saw a little boy blowing a whistle. Looking down on fields, I noticed a bar in many of them where boys would happily swing, stamping the rice with their bare feet. Cattle found plenty to feed on in this part of the valley and were in good fettle. Some were brown, others pure black and some had black markings on their hide. Men had downed their tools and lay fast asleep on the pile of wood which they had cut. Traffic had increased; public buses were incredibly crowded, and many passengers perched on top of heavy loads on public carriers. Even a cupboard had been hoisted up to balance precariously amidst diverse goods, whilst a lorry carried an armchair which had quickly found a grateful occupant for the long journey. Courtesy on the road ruled wherever we drove, with drivers being considerate, and therefore overtaking did not present a hazard on the steep mountain road. Most of the cars on the road were Japanese, mainly

51

Toyotas, but we had seen one shining Mini and an equally well kept Dyane (Citroën) in Thimpu. Roads were generally excellent, with some under repair. The workforce was mainly imported from India, predominantly from Madras. Women and children hammered away, breaking and sorting stones and helping the menfolk. Two women handled one shovel between them, with one using the tool and the other assisting with the aid of a rope tied to the handle. These road workers lived in poor huts fashioned from matting.

Teatime found us at the rest house just off the road, 6,425 feet above sea level. The garden was ablaze with roses and nasturtiums, whilst a luxurious bush of bougainvillea grew over the front door; French marigolds blossomed and a poinsettia was in full bloom. Having enjoyed our tea, we continued our journey and came to yet another colony, called Gedu, where a board proudly proclaimed that this was a 'Plywood Project' run by the Forestry Commission. A second board in front of a fairly large building stated that 'Retail Sale of Plywood' was on offer here. I pondered who might venture into this wilderness to buy plywood.

The vegetation became more luxurious as we neared Pusholding where we passed a cardamom plantation. Purple orchids flowered in thick undergrowth and pampas grass raised its graceful plumes beside a special grass which I had never seen before with soft honey-coloured fronds hanging from the slender stem, looking like numerous bright golden flags between all the exuberant greens of the subtropical vegetation. A prunus with delicate blossoms cast a faint pink cloud amongst the scene. There were elderberries with their fruit ripened to dark purple and monesteria climbed up trees. Reaching a clearing, we could look down into the wide valley of the River Toorsa, and following numerous hairpins we descended through lush vegetation to the Hotel Kharbandi above Pusholding. Our reception was almost royal, courteous and smiling; again we were greeted with the inevitable cup of tea.

Before retiring for the night we walked along the road to watch the sun go down and the moon rise over the enchanted scene. Alas our rest was soon disturbed by a forward mouse who had smelt food. I had forgotten to fasten a grip but the poor mouse met with little success since the plastic bag defeated it entirely.

Burma

Reluctantly we left Bhutan next morning having fallen under its magic spell. Strange to relate we had not seen a single yak nor had we been offered butter tea nor seen a prayer wall whilst in this lovely Buddhist country.

As we had done on our arrival, we passed again through the ornate gateway of Pusholding where vendors sat on the ground offering exotic fruit and chickens (which were kept in baskets akin to our lobster pots) whilst colourful blankets swayed gently in the breeze above their heads.

The scenery changed quite abruptly once we had entered India. Gone were the terraces, here the fields were flat. Banana groves alternated with coconut palms and the 'African look' was back again. Three graves with crosses stood almost hidden amongst the plantations. Dilapidated trickshaws crossed our path, and the villages to either side were dusty and shabby. Big-leafed Assam tea grew beneath the shade of lofty acacia trees, many of them with golden blossoms. Women wearing saris were harvesting tea, working quickly, carrying bundles on their heads. Men had loincloths girded round their waists. Traffic was heavy, with road carriers laden to their full capacity. One of them had come to grief. Many of the riverbeds which we crossed were bone dry. Dainty white egrets stalked near water, delicate mauve water hyacinth covered stagnant pools. Kanchenjunga was still visible to our right rising in majestic glory above the other snow-capped peaks. Grapefruit and avocado grew along the roadside. In one small village called Binnaguri we spotted a board which proudly announced: 'Fancy Corner. Please step inside for your cosiest article at reasonable rate'. Our road followed the rail track for some time as it skirted the foothills on its way to Assam. The trains were full to overflowing, with passengers clinging to the steps and even fast asleep on the roof. A small graveyard which we passed consisted of graves made of clay festooned with many coloured flags. Our journey took us to yet another shanty town, called Mal, on whose outskirts a sign proudly proclaimed 'Mal Parks'! The town itself was dusty and dirty, people sat on the ground under faded umbrellas mending shoes, trying to sell bits and pieces. A board saying 'Diamond Cutter' leant next to a collection of papier-mâché figures which were drying in the sun. Clay pots too had been placed outside stalls to take advantage of the searing heat. Every village appeared to have bicycle shops. In one of the villages we saw a huge live elephant outside a temple.

Finally we left this flat fertile area and drove through a shady grove. After crossing a river we found ourselves back at the junction where the road leads north to Sikkim. Traffic increased, public buses joined carriers. Approaching Siliguri, we drove again through tea plantations which stood under the auspices of the Forestry Commission. Official-looking offices stood beside mean shacks in the woods. Trickshaws waited outside the gate of an army camp. Rice fields reappeared and factory chimneys suddenly rose up on the skyline since light industry had been established in these parts of the country. Cattle grazed peacefully whilst buffaloes waded into the water to keep cool. Turning back, we could still see the snow-capped mountains in the distance.

Once again we stopped in Siliguri at the Sinclair Hotel, where as a very special treat they had prepared fish and chips to sustain us before we proceeded to Bagdora Airport for our flight to Delhi which left soon after 4 p.m. and stopped briefly at Patna. Patna seen from the air appeared to be a large town. During most of our flight the mountain ranges seemed to float mysteriously out of the clouds, suspended in mid-air. At 7 p.m. we landed in Delhi, and it was already dark when we drove along the well-kept, remarkably clean streets with immaculate lawns in the centre of the wide thoroughfare graced by sparkling fountains. We spent the night in the new, opulent Ashoka Hotel but the opulence did not deter large beetles from sharing our bathroom. To our delight Francis King (we had met the family in Mexico) had received my letter and was waiting for us in the sumptuous lobby. All eyes looked at this handsome young man with his red beard who greeted us with a big hug. He took us to the British High Commission, which stood just across the road from the hotel to spend the evening with the family. The British High Commission consisted of a large complex of offices, flats, restaurants, bars and other facilities. The bar, lounge and restaurant were tatty, with an air of past elegance hovering over it all, but it was comfortable and pleasant to sit and talk – catching up. The cane furniture was the remains of the days of the Great British Empire when sahibs and memsahibs used these premises. A few lonely men had lingered on and sat in the dining room on their own, reading *The Times* propped up against the cruet, eating their solitary meal. The menu was limited and very plain, with some of the frugal dishes no longer available.

Once again we received our wake-up call too early and were rudely woken just after we had dropped off to sleep after 1 a.m., therefore we had made little use of all the luxury around us. Looking for the coffee shop, we almost lost our way in this vast building, wandering past boardrooms, conference hall, lobbies, shops and swish restaurants until we finally found it tucked away in the basement. After a meagre continental breakfast we were on our way to the airport. Delhi Airport – never one of the best – was in a state of utter chaos, with millions of people milling around in seemingly aimless confusion. To have our passports checked we had to queue for a long time, being pushed around by the seething crowd. A group of men from an isolated village appeared suddenly, looking completely lost and bewildered, clutching their passports and flight tickets tightly to their chests. They were unable to read or write and could not cope with the interminable forms. Three of these lost souls were left behind when at last we passed our first hurdle and received our boarding cards and were handed our passports back, duly stamped. Next came the personal luggage check, which did not take too long for me since I just had to wait until the officer concerned had finished his private conversation and was ready to deal with me. My poor friend fared badly, her little man opened both her grip and flight bag, took everything out and unpacked the tea we had bought, which had been carefully wrapped in many layers of silver paper. He even made Ruth demonstrate how the lemon squeezer we had bought worked. Eventually a senior officer standing close by took pity on my friend and told the officious little man to call it a day and let her proceed.

Our plane was late. It was the same flight as the one we had taken from Amsterdam. Finally we left at 7.15 a.m. when the sun stood already high in the sky; mist covered Delhi and the countryside until we reached Pakistan and the Bay of Bengal. The Himalayan mountains with Mount Everest remained clearly in view floating on high clouds. Looking down, we saw the mighty Ganges gaining width until it resembled an inland sea. Our flight path actually took us across Rangoon before we landed in Bangkok. It had taken just under three hours, during which we had been served a second breakfast. The captain had been most informative, giving

55

us details about our whereabouts in the air. Heat engulfed us as soon as we stepped out of the plane. Bangkok Airport was spacious and very clean. A smiling Thai official greeted us and told us that a man in a green shirt would be waiting to take care of us. For miles we walked looking for our elusive friend in the green shirt; our route march took us past immigration to transit and transit back to immigration again along endless corridors, up and down many stairs. Finally we were asked to fill in forms, the selfsame ones we had been told on the plane to ignore since they did not appertain to passengers in transit. On one form we had to state the exact money we were carrying in cash and traveller's cheques, whilst a second form required us to fill in all particulars relating to our personal circumstances. It always puzzles me what happens to all these forms once they have been completed.

At last we were allowed to proceed. This time we had to pass through immigration. The man in the green shirt had finally materialised and, aided by a helper, ushered us to the top floor in a fast-moving lift and steered us through crowded corridors into a very busy restaurant. An excellent meal was served but we had barely time to do justice to the delicious soup and the equally luscious chicken before it was time to retrace our steps and make our way to the departure lounge. Before long we had boarded for our short flight to Rangoon. It was incredibly hot waiting in the plane for take-off. No sooner were we airborne than we were served yet another appetising meal accompanied by wine. Each lady received a mauve orchid.

One hour later we touched down in Rangoon. Having been forewarned that entering Burma was a frustrating and tedious affair, we were prepared for the long wait. Rangoon Airport was not much of an airport to start with and it certainly was not improved by the fact that the fan had broken. The single hall was overcrowded, humid and stifling hot. Whilst our tour leader dealt with the formalities, aided by cigarettes (which had to be Benson and Hedges) and whisky (which had to be Teacher's to be acceptable) we waited patiently. Once again forms had to be filled in, and all the forms which we had completed during our flight, stating once again the amount of money each of us carried, as well as jewellery, watches, cameras etc., had to be transcribed in minute details on a master plan, and each of us had to fill in yet another form with all these details. It took two hours before we were finally allowed to leave. As soon as we emerged we were surrounded by little urchins clamouring for our mauve orchids, which no doubt they wanted to sell. Private enterprise in the young!

Unfortunately we had no choice as to the hotel and had to stay in the Inya Hotel, standing on the lake of the same name about 6 kilometres out of town, a huge Russian-built building surrounded by large grounds. The entrance hall was palatial, but the bedroom with bathroom en suite was a nondescript hotel bedroom. A large number of staff were about; girls in long skirts hugging their slender figures, with pale smooth skin and dark shiny hair, glided along with utter grace. That everybody in the hotel was languid, ineffective and inefficient was quite another story. Mealtime was sheer purgatory when we sat waiting to be served. Slowly plates were placed on the table, sometimes rolls and butter appeared, then halfway through these preliminaries the waiter went off to serve on another table. It was quite a mammoth feat to obtain a drink or a second cup of tea or be victorious in getting hold of salt and pepper. Quantities were strictly rationed: 'Four lobster claws per person,' we were sternly told. Paintings hung on the walls of the big dining hall, all for sale, but none of them appealed to us.

The hotel stood too far out of town for us to be able to stroll into Rangoon. In fact it lay in splendid isolation with no other house or community in sight. Therefore we had to be content to walk around the grounds and watch the sun set over the lake, which reminded us of Bali – only the patient fishermen beneath their coolie hats were missing. Dinner was a very uncomfortable affair since one man in our party got tired of waiting and stormed out of the dining room, followed by his two friends.

Our room, which was fully air-conditioned, was pleasantly cool but once we were out on the balcony the steamy heat sucked us into its hold. Scanning the horizon, we saw the lofty spire of a pagoda. This was not the famous Golden Pagoda but one close by. Bamboo scaffolding shrouded its noble shape since it was being repaired.

Soon after sitting through the agony of breakfast with two congealed eggs plonked on the table regardless of whether these were wanted or not, and being strictly rationed to two pieces of bread, we set off for town.

It is difficult to describe my first impression of Rangoon. Driving into the city we noticed little bamboo houses along our road, many

57

of which served as shops or eating places. Small communal cars with benches either side (reminiscent of 'bimbos' in Bali) were on the road, as well as local buses. All public transport was over-crowded, with passengers sitting close together, standing or hanging on wherever they could find a hold. Trickshaws consisting of bicycles with two seats back to back attached at the side and horse-drawn carts joined in this medley of transportation. Since we could not decipher the script we were unable to avail ourselves of any form of public transport during our stay.

Many monks, old and young, tall and short, each with his begging bowl, were out. Nuns shorn like the monks wore pink shawls draped over their rust-coloured habits and had both shoulders covered. Monks carried umbrellas and fans as well as their begging bowls.

When we caught our first sight of Shwedagon Pagoda – the famous Golden Pagoda – we stopped, rooted to the spot. To behold the golden stupa framed between green trees and backed by a blue sky was breathtakingly beautiful, and we stood gazing at this majestic picture in front of our amazed eyes, trying to imprint it on our minds. The structure of the pagoda follows a definite plan: the bell, which is decorated at its shoulder with sixteen flowers, is topped by an inverted bowl. A number of concentric rings directed our gaze above the bell to two bands of lotus petals, one turned down, the other pointing upwards. The ring of the upturned petals carried the banana bud. This was crowned by the Hti, or umbrella. The Hti of the Shwedagon Pagoda has seven tiers which taper progressively as they soar heavenwards. A shaft projects from the highest tier, carrying huge gold and silver bells and sundry items of jewellery. A vane sits on top of the shaft, turning its flag in the wind. It is silver and gold plated and studded with 1,000 diamonds which total 278 carat, not to mention the 1,383 other precious stones. The very top is crowned by the Orb, which is a hollow golden sphere embellished with 4,351 diamonds totalling 1,800 carat. The very top of the Orb is tipped with a single 75 carat diamond. The lotus petals and the banana bud are covered by 13,153 foot-square golden plates, whilst the remaining structure is bedecked with gold leaf. These are just facts and figures which do not convey the splendour of this edifice.

Our bus parked at the foot of the southern stairway. There are four stairways, corresponding to the four points of the compass. Walkways are covered by tiered roofs and shelter every kind of shop. The Shwedagon Pagoda rises up on a hill 190 feet above sea level.

Before entering a cage-like lift which took us up to a corridor, we had to deposit our shoes and socks, obeying the notice which read: 'Foot wearing and umbrella holding forbidden'. Another notice as we left the lift asked: 'Please donate for taking photographs five kyots'. Having donated five kyots, we climbed up a few steps to reach the main platform. Above this platform rose a 21 foot-high plinth supporting the splendid Shwedagon surrounded by smaller pagodas, graded according to their height and position. The tallest of them marked the four cardinal points, four medium-sized ones stood at the corners of the square platform, whilst sixty small ones encircled the perimeter of the Shwedagon. The Shwedagon itself rose first in three terraces then in octagonal terraces followed by five bands. All these elements taken together add another 112 feet to the pagoda's height. The construction of terraces and bands are the accepted solution of standard architecture associated with pagodas, solving the problem of changing the shape from a square base to the circular upper elements. It is by the introduction of the octagonal section that the transition from square to circular is achieved. Similarly the circular rings mark the change from the horizontal design of the lower factions to the smooth vertical shape of the banana bud. The end result is an extremely elegant structure soaring high into the sky.

The main platform was inlaid with marble slabs and by the time we reached it the stones beneath our bare feet were mighty hot, but the onslaught on our senses was so immense that we took no notice of our burning soles. The profusion and confusion of shrines, pagodas, pavilions, resting places, elaborate décor and traditional roofs of five, seven or nine tiers overawed us. Eight planetary posts – one for each day of the Buddhist week – with gilded alabaster figures standing guard close by were arranged around the Shwedagon. Offerings of flowers, small flags, dainty gold and silver pagodas and little umbrellas lay deposited at each post. Each day corresponded to a specific planet and was associated with an animal. Mercury was linked to the tusked elephant and his special day (as in French) was Wednesday, starting at midnight and ending at noon. All Buddha images were ritually washed each day.

Some of the figures – especially those representing the spirits, the Nas – were painted in vivid colours, whilst most of the many statues of Buddha were covered by gold leaf. Next to each temple stood bells waiting to be struck with a stout branch which lay near at hand.

In the far north western corner grew two bo trees adorned with flowers and flags. The smaller of these was a cutting of the bo tree in Bodhgaya, India, under which Gautama Buddha had gained enlightenment.

The whole of this amazing complex was alive with devotees who strolled around in festive relaxed mood. Many prostrated themselves in front of a particular idol and tendered their offerings of garlands of flowers, little silver and gold parasols and lucky golden owls; money was placed in special glass-fronted boxes. Small children prostrated themselves of their own accord, then got up to play hide-and-seek behind temples and shrines whilst men and women sat on the marble floor smoking their cheroots. Families rested in a cool pavilion or lay on the floor of the special resting places or found a shady corner to have their meal. Apart from humans, dogs abounded; many puppies lay contentedly curled up fast asleep in the sun. We never felt surprised by any scene we met.

Most of the woodcarvings were quite exquisite, whilst some of the other decorations, such as the three-dimensional stucco pictures, looked garish. Delicate tile work formed a striking contrast to the extraordinary statues of Guardians with cheroots stuck into their mouths which loomed up menacingly in front of the many temples.

Suddenly a procession appeared, making for the bo trees. Hastily we followed and watched six beautifully dressed little boys with glittering silver headdresses undergoing Shin-Pyu initiation. This takes place between a boy's ninth and twelfth birthday when he is initiated as a novice into the order of monks. The novice monk will carry his alms bowl for a short time, maybe for a few weeks or for several months, and will return after this period to normal life. Whilst under the care of the monks he will be studying Buddhist scripture and will be taught to follow strictly the code to become a dignified human being.

The boys stood facing the trees surrounded by family and friends, whilst a monk (maybe he was a lama or the abbot himself) addressed them. Finally he threw coins into the air, which were quickly scooped up by the youngsters in the party whilst the six boys stood still. Each boy was tenderly lifted up by his father and carried shoulder high to another corner to be photographed before his head was shaved and he was garbed in a saffron robe, handed the begging bowl, a fan and umbrella and thus emerged a fully fledged novice. Girls undergo a special ear-piercing ceremony at this age.

Next morning we returned to the Shwedagon Pagoda on our own to be able to wander at our leisure and marvel at all we saw, but let me return to our first visit. Having spent some time walking and looking, we went down the covered stairway flanked by many stalls selling the most varied collection of merchandise. Apart from flowers, flags and parasols destined as offerings, there were bells and weights, brass and ironwork of every description, rosaries made from plain wood to finely carved ivory. Necklaces and other jewellery were for sale, as well as bags and baskets and a hundred other items. Food stalls stood temptingly at the foot of the stairs. Sweetmeats made from rice were specialities, guavas already peeled sprinkled with chilli powder were presented on sticks, oranges, hot noodles and many other delicacies had been lovingly prepared. The well-worn stone steps terminated in the bazaar. Until we stepped out into the sunshine our feet had still been bare. Finally we passed an ancient pressing machine extracting sticky juice from sugar cane and walked past vendors selling bottles of soda water and fruit juice.

Having visited the most important sight in Rangoon, we drove through the centre of town to spend some time in the Bogyoke Augsen Market, which was an enormous market selling almost everything on its many stalls from meat, fish, fruit and vegetables to household goods and furniture. People were very cheerful, full of fun and smiled easily, which made us feel happy to be there. Some of the girls were extremely beautiful and most of them, men too, wore their national dress. Men were clad in *longyis* (sarongs), usually topped by white shirts and edge-to-edge jackets which were coloured and short, fastened with toggles. Women also wore long sarongs but in plain colours, whilst men's were often patterned. They wore plain blouses, frequently white, beneath short jackets with crossover fronts.

On our way to the Kyauk Htat Gyri Pagoda we passed a home for the aged, a small hospital and a co-op market. The pagoda was a pavilion housing the 210-foot long reclining statue of Buddha, a comparatively new sculpture smiling benignly from soft full lips in a feminine face. The soles of his feet were divided into compartments which showed pictures telling his life story. Buddha's Hall was attached to a monastery where 600 monks lived to study sacred Buddhist manuscripts and to meditate. It was the centre for the ancient Pali script, which took its origin from Sanskrit. As we approached we saw rust-coloured robes spread out to dry in the sun. Under the same roof where Buddha reclined sat two lifelike figures behind glass; both showed lovely faces, one represented the very first abbot of the monastery, the second was a statue of the present one.

On our way back we stopped to admire the reflection of the Golden Pagoda in the Royal Lake, on the surface of which floated the Karaweik Restaurant which was built as a replica of the former royal barge.

Having a free afternoon, we set off on our own, asking the receptionist for a taxi. This message was passed to the doorman, who summoned one of the drivers from a special rank within the hotel grounds. Deciding to book the car for two hours, we had to fill in a form which we handed to the reception clerk. On our return we paid 44 kyots as arranged and signed the form. Our driver received 30 kyots, the hotel kept the rest. The driver of this car was a very gentle man, a father of eight who told us that he owned the taxi but had to pay a yearly licence to carry passengers. Most cars were Japanese, some right-hand others left-hand drives.

Our drive took us down town past some Victorian buildings such as the railway station, which displayed a steam engine in its forecourt. The Sula Pagoda, which we had come to see, stood in the centre of town in the midst of heavy traffic, surrounded by the flow of daily life. It was said to be 2,000 years old. This golden edifice was unusual since the octagonal shape continued right up to the bell and inverted bowl. A strange scene unfolded itself in one of the side halls, where a lama reclined in a wicker chair whilst monks sat cross-legged on the floor, forming a semicircle. Women with flowers tucked into their hair, a shawl thrown over their right shoulder, approached the lama one by one on their knees, offering him presents such as shirts, towels etc. – all useful articles – to be blessed. Once this had been done each lady presented one of the monks with their gift, which (so we were told) represented contributions towards the upkeep and repair of the pagoda. All pagodas, temples and shrines were entirely supported by voluntary contributions and gifts. For sometime we stood and watched this ceremony before we continued along the famous Strand past the old-fashioned Strand Hotel to visit the Botataung Pagoda, which stood in a very poor district. The stupa was quite unusual since it was hollow and open to the public. Glass mosaic covered the whole interior, recesses were provided for meditation and numerous treasures were displayed behind glass. Devotees threw money into a deep shaft in the centre. Walking across the courtyard we admired the large bell. Stalls sold popcorn and green vegetables to feed the thousand turtles and the eels in the nearby tank. This task served to acquire merit for a future existence. In utter amazement we watched the turtles and eels being fed, when a young couple offered us a shallow basket of food. Dutifully we fed the green stuff to the turtles and threw the popcorn to the squirming eels.

When we drove along the River Rangoon we asked our driver to stop in the harbour so that we could watch the lively scene of ships being loaded and unloaded, whilst vendors plied their trade at the quay amidst the ever present crowd who enjoyed it all. Trickshaws stood waiting patiently for fares. It was Friday and we had intended to go to the synagogue listed in our guidebook but were told that since there was no longer a congregation no service was being held.

The red carpet had been put out at our hotel to receive many elegant Burmese who arrived with presents tucked beneath their arms. Some of the gifts had been wrapped in Christmas paper although the occasion was the wedding of the house manager's daughter. Discreetly we stood near the entrance to the hall, watching the proceedings, then a sweet-faced lady asked us to step in. When we hesitated, not wishing to intrude on a family occasion, she urged us to accept the invitation, saying smilingly: 'I am the bride's mother and can invite whoever I please.' She introduced us to her son and his graceful wife, who gave up their table and seats for us. Everybody sat at small round tables. The bride and groom took their places on a raised platform facing their guests. In front of them stood a low table beautifully decorated with flowers. On the bride's left knelt a young girl, on the groom's right knelt a young man. An elderly man entirely dressed in white gave an address to the couple whilst cheerful music played in the background. Finally he showered the happy pair with rice. Hot sausage rolls, and bread and butter which had stood ready prepared carefully covered with a wet serviette, were offered, followed by small pieces of cake, and tea was poured into fine china bowls. The bridal pair were served by two maidens kneeling in front of their table. Tea finished, they walked along a centre gangway to take up position at the door, where they received the good wishes of their departing guests. Women shook hands with the bride, men with the groom. The bride looked beautiful, her dark sleek hair exquisitely coiffured, swept up into a chignon to the right side of her head and adorned with flowers and glittering jewels. She wore a straight pink dress with a short jacket of white lace. The long narrow dress had a slit in front and a short train at the back. A longer train of white lace was superimposed. She wore many jewels and looked like a fairytale princess from bygone days. Her groom resembled a prince, dressed entirely in an elegant shade of grey. He wore a *longyi*, a jacket over his shirt and a close-fitting turban. He looked nervous, whilst his bride – in spite of the fact that she had some difficulty in managing her train – looked self-possessed and at ease. Wishing them great happiness for many years to come, we left. All presents were taken out into the foyer, where they were carefully wrapped in calico cloth and put into neat bundles.

Next day we watched quite a different wedding couple leaving the hall. The bride wore a white European-style dress, the groom a brightly coloured striped suit. The first wedding had been Burmese, the second Chinese. In Rangoon all ceremonies took place in public halls, either in the Inya or the Strand Hotel.

As we walked away from the wedding through the coffee shop, four lovely young Burmese ladies who sat at a table sipping tea laughed openly at us in a completely friendly childlike way. For a little while we stood and talked to them but had to decline their invitation to join them since we had to get ready for an evening of Burmese dancing at the floating restaurant on the Royal Lake. The restaurant was extremely ornate; we sat in a big hall on long tables to have a meal before the show (specially for tourists) begun. Three more parties joined us. The dancers performed in traditional dress of brilliant colours, making much use of exquisite movements of their slender hands. The girls' hair was styled like the bride's we had seen a few hours ago; so were their dresses. The accompanying music was melodious, incorporating much drumming, which was performed with the flat of the hand, and also soft sounds on a harp. The harp was shaped like a toy boat covered with buffalo hide with thirteen silk strings attached to its wooden prow. Most of the dances were based on old legends. Unfortunately I could not

follow the interpreter, whose voice was distorted by the micro-
phone. The only story I could clearly hear was of a prince who
rescued his princess, who had been carried off into the wilderness,
by slaying a snake. All the dancing was extremely graceful. The last
act was a young girl juggler with a young boy as her assistant. She
performed remarkable feats with a hollow ball made from plaited
bamboo.

Next morning saw us back in town, where we strolled once more
round the Golden Pagoda in utter contentment. Our driver on this
occasion was less pleasant then our gentle one had been on our
previous ride. This one coveted our butane gas lighter and asked
for cigarettes.

Leaving our main luggage behind in the hotel, we picked up our
hand luggage and made for Rangoon Airport in the early afternoon
for our flight to Meho in Upper Burma. Our path took us across
rice paddies. We saw isolated villages surrounded by dense woods,
and a lake glistened between rice paddies. When we reached a high
plateau the soil was red and fields straddled mountain tops. Brilliantly white stupas and temples pierced the dark woods. Barely an
hour later we landed bumpily at Meho, where a tourist bus stood
waiting for us to drive through pleasant scenery with bamboo
houses set amongst the fertile plains. Sometimes these stood on
stilts, whilst others rose from mud floors. Walls consisted of specially patterned matting with windows which could be left open or
closed off effectively. Matting was used to shut the doorway, which
could be raised and extended outwards to provide welcome shade
as an awning or act as a roof for a small stall. Bamboo poles formed
the frame for these little houses, with the roof consisting of shingle
or occasionally of thatch. They looked most attractive set against
the dark green mountainside.

As our road started to climb we looked down on Lake Inle,
which lay far below us. Well-nourished cattle grazed peacefully in
lush meadows which lay between fields of maize. Many of the big
shady trees exhibited small wooded shrines fastened to their trunks.
Earthenware water butts frequently stood near, taking advantage
of the shade; these could be used by any passer-by to quench his
thirst. Finally we reached our goal: the former hill station of
Taunggyi, which boasted a lively high street. Many houses climbed
up the slope behind it. Wherever we looked we saw again the tall
spires of pagodas rising into the sky. Our hotel stood amongst trees,

fronted by a small flower bed, and formed part of a complex of three buildings. One was a marriage hall and the other, a very pleasant residential villa, was the former Residency now used for VIPs. Having deposited our belongings in our somewhat basic abode, we went into the grounds to look for the bakery members of our group had found, which sold delicious buns.

Our bus took us down town again before following a steep track which climbed between houses high up to reach the Wish Granting Pagoda, with Taunggyi – the former capital of this area – nestling down below. The view was most attractive sweeping across Shah country with Lake Inle shimmering in the distance. The pagoda itself was under repair. A group of small children appeared suddenly out of nowhere, presenting us with posies of wild flowers. We waited until the sun sank slowly behind the mountains, leaving the landscape bathed in an orange glow.

Once back in Taunggyi's high street we left the bus and joined the throng of people wandering up and down. The multitude and variety of small stores intrigued us, as did the long queues outside the cinema. Two fiery dragons guarded the prayer hall, where bamboo matting lay on the floor and Buddha's shrine stood on a platform facing the entrance. Along the walls stood glass cabinets displaying an assortment of statuettes, artificial flowers, vases, trinkets and even medals. All these articles were votive offerings akin to many we have seen in tiny churches in European mountain villages.

Once the sun had disappeared, it turned cold and since there was little creature comfort in our hotel we soon retired to bed. In contrast to the stark bareness of our room, magnificent flower arrangements glowed in every dark and draughty corner.

Some of our party returned next morning to the Wish Granting Pagoda, meeting a group of nuns along the steep path who were a picture with their pink shawls thrown over their habits. A magnificent pagoda caught in the early morning sun glittered across the valley, surrounded by a circle of many glass-studded stupas. The view from the lofty height with the mist rising up into the clear sky held a charm all of its own.

Later we left Taunggyi passing the balloon-seller already stationed in the high street with his multicoloured wares mounted on a bamboo frame. Our road led across the Shah Plain past little bamboo houses set amongst palm trees, each with its own tiny

66

bridge across a small canal. In between the houses stood miniature bamboo stalls. Maize lay on the ground to dry, husks hung suspended from the eaves and were used by the poor in place of special leaves to make cheroots, their stumpy cigars. All over the Shah district everybody – particularly women – smoked these strong cigars. Men and boys shouldered their burdens suspended from either end of a pole, whilst women balanced their loads on their heads, walking erect with seeming ease and looking wonderfully regal. Leaving the main road, we turned towards Lake Inle, stopping once to visit the marvellous 17th-century Manaugn Pagoda, which stood by the roadside looking extremely romantic in its slight decay. It was still in use and contained an enormous golden Buddha who sat on a throne.

Our next stop was Yawng-hwe on the shores of the lake, a large village with an enormous temple complex. The central golden pagoda rose out of a sea of smaller ones. The whole was enclosed within a thick wall containing many niches, now empty, but no doubt each had housed a Buddha statue in bygone days. Nearby rose three more big pagodas.

Lake Inle was beautiful. The fishermen were known as 'leg rowers' since they stood in the stern of their long narrow boats on one leg, wrapping the other around a single oar. This strange technique enabled them to sail between the floating vegetation, making it possible to steer a safe course.

Two longboats were waiting for us to board. We sat on coconut matting, enjoying the glorious views around us under the brilliant sky. Many boats passed us carrying happy-looking families, who usually sheltered beneath umbrellas from the fierce rays of the sun. They always smiled and waved cheerfully. Men stood in stationary boats twirling long poles with which they skilfully scooped up mud to be deposited between stakes to enlarge the floating islands or to build new ones. Other men were engaged in collecting weeds known as *kyupaw*, the roots of which were used to anchor the mud, whilst their leaves served as fertiliser. Fishermen dipped their conical nets into the lake. Most of the local population looked happy; women and men alike wore turbans which they had fashioned casually from towelling. Water lilies grew in wild abundance, red, white and a delicate shade of mauve. Whole gardens of lilies appeared beside water hyacinths, deep purple convolvulus, irises and a white flower – not unlike a gladioli – known as 'silver flower'. A shimmering kingfisher flitted past. Each floating island was well cultivated, most of the fruit and vegetables were grown here by a tribe knows as Inthas.

Finally we visited one of the floating villages which had *chaugs* – canals – instead of streets. Much of the day-to-day activity was carried out from canoes, including marketing. But shops also traded on the island and shoppers arrived by boat to make their purchases. Some boats drew alongside us, offering us flowers, tomatoes, bananas etc. – we bought some bananas before we disembarked. Numerous pagodas stood on the island; some new, others old, some renovated, others in need of repair. The houses appeared quite large. When we visited a cheroot factory we entered a big room on the ground floor where women sat on the mud floor making cigars. Everything was done by hand; tobacco was mixed with the bark of the tamarind tree. A special leaf was being used, and a filter was skilfully slipped into place before the leaf was wrapped around the mixture and fastened with a special glue. The ends were neatly trimmed. We bought some to bring back as presents although I did not know whether our gift would be welcomed or not. Chicken scratched around the house. Then our boat took us along to visit the weavers. Looms lay idle in the big room downstairs since the weavers were having their lunch. A baby lay peacefully asleep in a Moses basket, which hung on a large hook suspended from from the ceiling. Steep steps led upstairs to the combined sales and living quarter where women of three generations sat on the floor whilst two of the young ones displayed their wares. Nearly everybody in our party bought one or more of the attractive Shah shoulder bags, which were actually used by the men on the island. Charming photographs of family groups and school photographs had been fastened on the glass of the cabinet in which the merchandise was kept neatly stacked on shelves. The cupboard beneath the shelves served as storage space for bedrolls during the day. A plastic walker for the toddler stood in the corner. A bedroom leading off the living room also served as a sales room and contained a double bed with pink covers under a pink mosquito net. The kitchen too led off the main room, which was spotlessly clean, with a stone hearth and big iron pots. 'Shah tea', a special pink brew with an unusual taste, was served in dainty china bowls and they also offered us roasted beans and pickled leaves.

Our last visit took us to Phau Pagoda. The approach led as usual through the bazaar, which was particularly lively. People stared at us quite openly, inviting us to look at their goods and buy and asking us to join them at the low tables sheltering below bamboo roofs and try their specialities, such as *tophu kyaw* – fried bean curd. Many brightly coloured Shah shoulder bags and conical straw hats (resembling the coolie hats of Indonesia) were proffered for sale. The pagoda contained five precious images covered by gold leaf, which looked quite misshapen since their original outline had become distorted by the haphazard way the gold had been applied. Only men were allowed to do this in the Phaun Goaw Pagoda. The figures stood in the centre of a rectangular platform and were taken out once a year in a ceremonial barge for a special journey around the lake. These highly venerated statues had originally come from Cambodia.

Wherever we stepped on land, we were immediately surrounded by children offering water lilies, joss sticks, and lucky owls for sale. They were bright-eyed and healthy but very scantily clad.

For lunch we returned to Yawng-hwe before setting off for Kawal, another hill station. Our way led past Manaugn Pagoda and back to the main road. Soon we begun to climb, which afforded us a panoramic view over the fertile Shah Plateau, Lake Inle and the surrounding mountains. Meadows stretched to either side of the asphalt road, silver pampas grass swayed in the breeze. Quarries appeared from time to time along the road, usually with a column left standing in the centre. I was unable to ascertain the reason for this custom; the columns seemed to resemble the Hindu lingam which we had seen in similar places. High above the lake we stopped to walk around a bamboo village where all houses had been built entirely of bamboo: bamboo matting hung over bamboo poles. Like the Pied Piper of Hamelin we were followed by a crowd of children. In fact the whole village turned out to look at us. Wooden carts with enormous wheels stood waiting for bullocks to be harnessed between shafts.

Finally we reached Kawal, 4,330 feet above sea level amidst pine woods. The Kawal Hotel stood above the village, looking like an English country house seen from the distance, but here the comparison ended since it had been sadly neglected and was very sparsely furnished. The staff, however, were extremely friendly. Our room was huge, with bare floorboards, two wooden beds, a small crude table, a dressing table and one chair. The light was very dim since one bulb was missing. To be able to look out of the window across the village with its shimmering pagoda and glance up to the tree-covered mountains, we had to remove the curtains bodily. Towels and toilet paper were hidden in a drawer. The washroom held a basin, shower and loo. Once the shower had been turned on, the entire room became awash. The only place which provided a modicum of comfort in the whole place was the bar.

We decided to go for a walk in the woods and wandered across a meadow and over a small bridge past a single-track railway line. The whole area gave the impression of a holiday resort and had it not been for the poinsettias, cacti and frangipani, and the orchids growing wild in the woods, we could have been anywhere in the mountainous regions of Europe. Darkness descended early, when we realised that we had lost our way. Walking boldly up to one of the houses, we knocked and, pointing to the Kawal Hotel in the far distance, indicated to two girls that this was the place we were trying to reach. Laughingly they came with us, chattering all the way in their native tongue as if we could understand. They took us across fields, through apple and pear orchards, with some of the apple trees covered in blossom, until we reached the little bridge near our hotel again. Back in our room, we could not work the temperamental shower but fortunately found a very willing Indian just outside our door who – accompanied by a youth – stepped fully clothed under the shower to demonstrate how it worked. Predictably he got soaked but good-naturedly he and his young mate just laughed. Dinner was served attentively at long tables in a bare room. Once again beautiful floral arrangements stood on the mantelpiece and brightened dark corners dispelling all gloom.

As soon as it got dark the temperature dropped considerably. Unfortunately, our hot water bottle had sprung a leak and when we asked for an extra blanket we were informed to apply to 'Mr Anthony', who would oblige. Eventually we tracked the elusive man down, who was in fact the helpful Indian who had got soaked, and as far as we were able to ascertain he was the only 'working member' of the staff, which meant that he was therefore much in demand and difficult to locate. Not only did we get our extra blankets, he also produced a spare electric bulb and finally fixed the shower.

The ground was covered by white frost next morning when we woke, but the sun rose quickly, dispersing the frost speedily. It rapidly became hot. The local driver, proud of his town, took us for a long drive around the countryside through lovely pine woods where orchids had seeded themselves in the meadows and on host trees, past a Roman Catholic boarding school and a modern Government Technical Institute amidst the pines. Many European-looking bungalows stood scattered through the woods. Finally we reached the market, which 'rotated' and came to Kawal every fifth day. It was here where the various hill tribes foregathered to sell and buy. A young man who spoke English well attached himself to us almost immediately. He was twenty-two years old, a part-time student who taught part-time at a private school. In turn he introduced us to his friends, his girlfriend's aunt and her friend, his friend's mother and finally to his own mother, who sat amongst her various goods, toothpaste, soap, torches, etc. He told us the names of different vegetables and herbs. Before we visited the pagoda with its glittering top he introduced us to his teacher, his wife and small child. The pagoda was being restored. Our guide pointed to another decorated building opposite, which served as prayer hall. All the boys were friendly and eager to talk to us, not minding being asked questions and questioning us in return. Their leading questions inevitably were: 'Are you married? What do you do?' Almost always one of the questions was: 'Are you Christian?' and when we replied 'No', telling them that we were Jewish, the conversation became rather involved. Having received our guide's address and the request to write to him, we parted company and continued to stroll around on our own, intrigued by the interesting faces around us. For us it was impossible to distinguish between the various tribes, neither their features nor their apparel were of any help to us. A young woman smilingly presented me with a rose. When she saw me struggling to tuck it into my short hair she took a slide out of her shining tresses to fasten the bud into my greying curls. At a junk stall which sold bits of metal, glass and all manner of broken pieces, we bought three charming opium weights which we discovered amongst the rubbish. They were in the shape of cockerels, made of brass and quite delightful to look at. Since it was customary to haggle about the price we did likewise, though this was quite alien to us.

Returning from our pleasant morning outing, we had time to relax in the sunshine before our early lunch, after which we drove back the way we had come to Meho Airport for our flight to

71

Mandalay. The flight was on time, which was quite unusual in Burma. All we had to do was walk on with our hand luggage and claim one of the unnumbered seats amongst the forty-four. On our way down from Kawal we had passed families sitting on the ground outside their little houses and eating their meals off low tables, whilst cattle munched peacefully close by. Beehives stood in neat rows, pink buffaloes ploughed the fields, but we saw neither goat nor sheep.

Our flight took us across Shah High Plateau and over a teak forest which was extremely dense and without any path as far as we could see from the air, nor did we discover any trace of habitation. Leaving this thickly-wooded area behind us, we found ourselves above an open fertile plain with many fields. Soon we looked down on the mighty Irrawaddy River, the Bridge of Ava and the pagoda-studded Hill of Sagaing before we landed roughly but safely in Mandalay.

Mandalay appeared to be clean and prosperous, laid out on a grid system with wide asphalt roads and the remains of the Royal Palace in its centre. To reach the Mandalay Hotel we drove straight into town, skirting around the peaceful moat which ran completely round the thick crenellated palace walls. The hotel, fronted by lush shady gardens, looked quite splendid but unfortunately our box-like bedroom was very claustrophobic, with one tiny heavily cur-tained window facing an internal corridor. It contained the usual wooden bedsteads with the hard thin mattress laid on solid wood, and boasted a dressing table. A bathroom led off the bedroom, containing a basin, tub and loo but no hot water. The air-condition-ing was hidden away in a small dark cupboard which also served as wardrobe and concealed an old-fashioned coat stand. The room was very airless and hot. What we did not discover until later was the fact that whenever we turned the light on, the room next door was flooded in light. Having deposited our luggage and switched on the fan, we set off to see some of the sights. The first place we visited was Mahamuni Pagoda. When we arrived at this highly venerated place the sound of 'Three Green Bottles' greeted us, which seemed quite out of place amongst the barefooted pilgrims, the oxcarts and trickshaws intermingling with cars. The continuous music blasted forth from official loudspeakers. Slipping off our shoes and stock-ings, we walked along a long corridor lined by stalls selling the now familiar selection of goods. The 4-metre-high seated image of

Mahamuni – 'The Exalted Saint' – dazzled us. This very ancient statue had been cast in metal but had been transformed into a shining golden statue over the years, thanks to the cover of millions of gold leaves. As we stood spellbound, more gold leaves were being applied. Women were only permitted to look from a distance, they were not allowed to come close to the sacred figure. The pagoda had been built in 1784 to house this precious statue, but it was destroyed in 1884 by fire and the present building was of a relatively recent date.

A small pavilion in the courtyard housed six figures, three of which were lions, two were men and the last a three-headed elephant. Originally these figures had stood in Cambodia. According to legend, rubbing a specific part on one of the images will cure any affliction of the corresponding part of the pilgrim's anatomy. Stomachs and knees appeared to be highly polished. In a second pavilion close by stood two large figures shouldering a pole between them, from which hung the traditional bell-shaped Burmese gong which weighed 5 tons. On our way back to the bus we bought a lovely wooden carving of Indian design and also stopped to watch masons at work as they sat in a garden in the shade of a palm tree, chiselling away. Two young boys worked on an inscription, one did the lettering whilst the second carefully coloured the ornate script.

Our sightseeing continued through a bamboo village where houses stood on stilts, providing room for storage and shelter for the animals. Fields along our way were being ploughed, a dainty white egret sat on the back of a grey water buffalo. Approaching Ava Bridge we saw a Chinese cemetery. Children lined the roadside, offering speckled plover's eggs for sale. Before crossing the famous bridge which spans the Irrawaddy River on sixteen pylons and is well over a kilometre long, we paid toll. The bridge had been opened in 1934, was destroyed by the British to halt the Japanese advance and was not rebuilt until 1954. Beside the road it also carried a railway track whilst pedestrians crossed by ferry. Just to the left lay Thabye Dan Fort, built by the Burmese before the Anglo-Burmese Wars of the 19th century.

We drove through Sagaing, which was the capital of the independent Shah Kingdom in 1315. It lay at the foot of Sagaing Hills, which had become a sacred place for all Buddhists and was studded with many pagodas. Climbing up, we passed the temple guards – strange images, half dragons and half lions, known as *sinthas* or *chinthas.* (The name 'Chindits' is derived from these fiery guards.) As we reached the main pagoda and stood on the sweeping platform the sun begun to sink into the Irrawaddy River. A monk appeared who spoke perfect English, and boys and girls crowded around us; they were pupils of the monastery which was attached to the pagoda. Most teaching in Burma was still carried out by monks. Strange to relate, these pupils were Muslims. Once again we were presented with slips of paper bearing the boys' names and 'the address of the hardware store in the main street of Sagaing' with the message: 'Please do not forget me'. Saying goodbye to the youngsters we walked to a small pagoda which contained *nas* in its four niches. These Burmese 'spirits' had impish faces. Some members of our party gathered around the monk, who liked to air his English. Darkness had fallen by the time we returned to Mandalay along the same way as we had come. Neither bicycles nor cars bore lights.

After dinner we stepped out into the balmy air. When we reached the gate of our hotel one of the trickshaw drivers suggested taking us to the night market. It seemed a very long ride through the still night but finally we did arrive at an open place occupied by stall after stall selling *longyis*, jeans, jackets, clothing of every kind, household goods, shoes, pictures, spare parts for bicycles, drugs of every kind, radios and tape recorders. The list of articles was infinite, most being contraband brought from Bangkok. Apparently the law turned a blind eye. Food stalls offered rice cakes of varying kinds. Hot food was eaten sitting at rough tables. Fruit of every sort was on display. I was offered fried grasshopper but politely declined. Complementing the medley of colours and pungent smells was the continuous sound of music, creating an atmosphere akin to a lively fair. Smiling faces were everywhere and good temper prevailed, which added charm to the nocturnal scene. Stall holders started to pack up, dismantling even the neon strip lights. Dogs with their puppies and small children lay peacefully asleep amongst the paraphernalia of people, stalls, bicycles, trickshaws and goods. One little mite started to cry and I was handed the baby to comfort whilst mother calmly continued to pack up. Finally we returned to our patient trickshaw driver, father of eight, whose first and only fare we had been for the day. He had started work at 5 a.m. by taking up his place at the official 'Trickshaw and Tonga Stand' near the Mandalay Hotel.

When we returned to the dungeon of our room we found a spray of sweet-smelling jasmine on our pillow, and the problem of hot water was solved by a bucket of steaming hot water whenever we required one. The service was friendly and quite excellent.

Next morning found us on our way to the Palace Compound, which served as headquarters for the Army. The walls were 8 metres high and 3 metres thick at the base, tapering to 1½ metres at the top. The Palace formed a perfect square in the centre of the complex. Little was left of its former glory since it had been constructed of wood and had been destroyed by fire. Only a platform had remained, with steps leading up to it. Two rusty cannons loomed nearby. King Mindon's Mausoleum stood close to the Royal Mint, where the first coin had been minted in 1864. A collection of stone inscriptions which had belonged to King Bodawpaya had been preserved. The clock tower was still standing which used to strike the gong every three hours. A small pavilion housed a miniature model of the Palace made to scale. To see this we had to wait until the caretaker could be found. He eventually arrived with his young son, who unlocked the door. Standing inside this pavilion and looking at the intricate miniature model of the Palace with its strange names such as: 'The Middle Queen's Quarters', 'The Lily Room', the 'Lion's Throne Room', Tennyson Jesse's book *The Lacquered Lady* came to life. The empty space outside was suddenly transformed: water sounded in fountains and small streams, birds twittered in the many trees, the sun reflected all the gold and glitter of the splendid decorations of the many buildings. Most of all I could hear the happy, carefree laughter of the ladies of the court, who flitted everywhere like gaily coloured butterflies. I could almost hear the gong strike from the clock tower and yet all that was left was the great empty space with a few pathetic remnants of a glorious past within the confines of the thick wall.

Leaving the palace to continue our sightseeing, we passed Queen Victoria's clock tower standing in the centre of town from where we drove along a dusty main road to reach the small Burmese Market. Huge mountains of groundnuts lay piled up outside many of the bamboo houses which we passed. Small stalls selling fruit, fish and vegetables stood in a confined space beneath bamboo roofs which provided shelter from the fierce sun. A butcher was busily cutting up a carcass. The strong smell of spices hung in the air. Sweetmeats lay beside fried grasshoppers. Women squatted on the ground, many of them suckling their babies or carrying them in slings on their backs. The local population had arrived to do their daily marketing. Most food, once purchased, was wrapped up in leaves and tied into neat bundles. It was a lively scene, with men, women, children, dogs, and a pig or two, and monks walking calmly along proffering their begging bowls. Many of the women had swept up their shining tresses into a bun at the back of their heads and secured it with an ordinary comb which they had first used for their coiffure. I never could figure out whether this was done to use the comb as an ornament or was simply a way to keep it at hand. This market was the only place we had met so far which was a breeding ground for flies.

Our journey continued to the Irrawaddy River to visit the Buffalo Village and watch these mighty beasts at work. Only men who worked the buffaloes lived here with their families. It was incredibly poor, with children presenting a pitiful sight. Some of them were covered in sores, others were quite emaciated, with big distended bellies. One little girl carried a tiny boy in her arms whose eyes were sunken in his pinched face, his lips parched, his poor limbs like matchsticks. I felt certain that he was about to die. The children crowded around us and sang 'Frère Jacques' in French, clapping when they had finished. They accepted gratefully the little we were able to give. Silently we stood watching the scene below on the waterfront where buffaloes harnessed to wooden yokes dragged tree trunks out of the water and brought them up the steep slope. They were magnificent beasts and obviously very strong. One of them was being washed; having been well lathered, it enjoyed a swim with his master in the Irrawaddy River. Some of the buffaloes pulled heavy barrels from the quayside down to the water. There was a continuous movement up and down the waterfront.

Leaving the sad village behind, we felt distressed by what we had seen. It was the first time that we had come face to face with stark poverty and filth since we had arrived in Burma. By complete contrast we met a stream of children – only a short distance from the village – on their way to school, spotlessly clean, well-fed and with the boys wearing dark green *longyis*, the loincloth corresponding to the sarong, topped by snow-white shirts.

Our next stop was in front of some small bamboo houses, where we stepped inside to watch silk-weaving. Young women sat three to each loom, deftly weaving gaily coloured silk into intricate patterns and shunting their shuttles forwards and backwards with ease and skill without the use of a pattern. When I asked how they knew what to do, I was told that the pattern had been committed to memory. Another group of women were busy in the sun-drenched backyard: one hanging up strands of dyed silk to dry whilst another twisted silk on a frame to roll it into a suitably sized ball.

To visit the Swendandaw Kyaug Pagoda we turned from everyday life back into the royal past, since this had been part of the Palace Complex at one time and had been used by King Mindon and his Chief Queen. He had died there and after his death his son Thiban had it dismantled to be reassembled at its present site. Thiban used to come here to meditate. It bore the most intricate carvings, both inside and out, but the monastery sadly had weathered badly and hence was in a poor state. A tall monk with a little boy by his side greeted us and invited us to step inside the prayer hall, which was a big dark place. The monk's bed stood in a corner beneath a mosquito net, surrounded by books. The rest of the pillared hall was bare except for a Buddha who rose from a platform. The young boys slept on bamboo matting on the floor. The main room contained beautiful carvings with ten perfect panels showing scenes from the life of Buddha. The ceiling, which was the only part still heavily gilded, was very ornate. To my great amusement I found three clocks fastened to three carved pillars standing in one row, looking quite incongruous in this ancient building. King Mindon's highly decorated throne had been preserved in this pagoda. The bell which is always present in a Buddhist temple stood outside on a wooden platform. It is always struck with a sturdy branch by each pilgrim who comes to pay homage, like the bells which are struck by every Hindu who comes to pray in a Hindu shrine to announce his visit.

The ruins of Atumashi Kyaung, the Incomparable Monastery, stood close by. All that remained from it was a big hall with broken pillars and some fine stucco work. I saw a splendid replica of a crocodile. Cattle grazed peacefully amongst the ruins, paying no heed to its glorious past. Kuthodaw Pagoda was the next we visited; which was also known as the Central Pagoda.

The last pagoda we were shown was Kyauk Tawgyi at the foot of Mandalay Hill. A tall and lofty marble corridor lined by the usual tempting stalls led to the shrine. An enormous Buddha carved out of a single piece of rock sat within. I walked along another corridor, less well kept than the one we had come through, where I found palmists and astrologists, dogs and men lay stretched out in the sun, fast asleep. Around a neglected courtyard sat some of Buddha's disciples, the Arhats, each in a niche of his own.

This visit concluded our official sightseeing tour of Mandaly, but since there was still time left before we were due to depart I decided to walk up Mandalay Hill on my own. It proved an incredible experience which I did not regret. A covered stairway led up from the south side, a never-ending stream of people of all ages, all sizes and all nationalities went up and down the well-worn steps. Their different faces fascinated me. There were groups of young boys, groups of young girls, families and pilgrims on their own. Monks were happily climbing up and down; a group of old nuns, one of them a hunchback, were resting on a stone bench with baskets containing food by their side. Stalls sold trinkets made of ivory, whilst others offered food and drink. Tables and chairs to have a meal, or simply a rest, were set out invitingly on platforms which interrupted the arduous climb. Girls stood on top of each flight, tempting climbers to stop for soft drinks, holding a bottle in each hand. Many babies had been gently put down on the stone floor next to their mothers and were fast asleep. All along the flights of stairs were temples and shrines. I found prayer halls with strange figures made of clay; one contained a row of statues consisting of a man squatting beside a deer in one tableau, whilst the second group showed him holding a knife with the decapitated head of the deer beside his feet. The third scene depicted an emaciated woman with a fat baby at her breast. A figure of an Ascetic completed this strange group. I passed mystical beasts along my way, the famous Garuda (taken over from Hindu mythology) as well as *nas* – spirits – were present. There were of course numerous figures of Buddha and his disciples to be seen.

To rest and admire the view I sat on a stone bench before finally reaching the huge standing golden Buddha pointing with an out-stretched hand to the Palace. This image is known as Shweyattan. Legend had it that Buddha, accompanied by his disciple Ananda, climbed Mandalay Hill on one of his visits to Burma. He promised that in the 2400th year of his faith a great city would be founded at the foot of the hill. According to our calendar this corresponds to 1857, the year in which King Mindon moved his capital from Amarapura to Mandalay. The statue represented Buddha pointing to the place where the city was to be built. When I sat quietly to rest for a short while and admire the panorama, I was almost immediately surrounded by a group of smiling young boys. Suddenly an old woman joined them who looked like a witch and did not seem friendly disposed towards me, making me feel she wanted me gone. She may have objected to my scanty clothing (shorts and a cotton top) although nobody else seemed to have minded as long as my feet were bare. Rising slowly I walked clockwise round the shrine before climbing up to a platform with four *nas*, each standing at one corner with a retinue of headless figures behind them. Boys were stroking the *nas* heads tenderly. Finally I climbed up very steep steps to reach the last corridor, which took me to the very top. The view was breathtaking. The whole of Mandalay lay at my feet, nestling in the curve of the mighty Irrawaddy River with the sacred hills of Sagaing on the other bank.

A group of girls and boys joined me and chatted away in their usual friendly way. One of the boys wore red nail varnish on a long nail on the little finger of his right hand. They were students and offered me some fruit which looked like a cherry plum; it was pickled and tasted good. After a short rest I started to descend watching the fun-loving Burmese around me. Two young girls ran down the stairs swinging a little boy between them until they collapsed laughingly on a bench. Another young woman bent over her small baby boy, laughing and cooing. Many photographers stood along the way. Young ladies, before they would submit to being photographed, spent some time beautifying themselves in front of hand mirrors. An old man was preparing his meal on a stove just by the side of the stairs leading up to Mandalay Hill. Feeling exhilarated and content, I emerged at the bottom of the stairs into brilliant sunshine. Our driver had kindly arranged for one of the *tongas* to take me back. The boy rushed over to me but as soon as I had settled myself in the rickety vehicle he wanted to wait for yet another half-hour for another fare, but time was running short for me since we had to catch a plane. Seeing that there were plenty of trickshaws available, I climbed down and walked away but he ran after me, not letting go. Finally we trotted off past the Academy for Dance and Music along the familiar palace wall. It was midday and very hot, and wherever there was water people stood with old tins pouring the blessed liquid over themselves; women fully clothed, men stripped to their waist, children entirely naked. There were some wells but more often than not just puddles were made use of. Occasionally a discreet semicircular wall protected nakedness, when heads were visible above and feet below.

My driver stopped some way away from our hotel and I had a final argument about the fare before we parted, although the sun had been agreed on before we started.

Lunch was served in a room upstairs which permitted a clear view down into a big hall where preparations for a wedding feast were in full swing. The service was good, the food poor. All of us had enjoyed Mandalay and were reluctant to leave.

Patiently we sat at the airport for some time. To call it an airport was too grand a name since it consisted of just a landing strip and a bamboo hut. The little 44-seater Fokker plane arrived as scheduled and again we just walked on and took a seat. As we rose we looked down on the Irrawaddy River with rice paddies under water along its banks. Pagodas rose everywhere and we noticed that a tree grew in one corner in every field. Barren hills followed wooded ones, small habitations surrounded by fields appeared, whilst a lake shimmered in the distance, before the scene below us changed entirely, disclosing sand dunes to either side of the river. When we descended we saw that the Irrawaddy below us had split into many arms embracing a sandbank bearing neat fields. After a thirty-minute flight we had arrived at Pagan, where we landed bumpily but safely.

Pagan lies on a dry and sandy plane and presented the most amazing sight I had ever seen. The whole area of 40 square kilometres was studded with the remains of 5,000 temples. Huge imposing white temples like the Ananda and Thatbyinnyu soared high in the sky, whilst others were smaller and dainty, many of them built of red brick. Some were large, others small; some stood in groups, others on their own. Some had been reconstructed, others had been left to crumble down and decay. There stood perfect bell-shaped beehives and one in the shape of an exact pyramid.

Pagan had been the capital for two centuries, from 1044 to 1287, when Burma was going through a transition from Hinduism and Mahayana Buddhism (the Greater Vehicle) to Theravada Buddhism (the Lesser Vehicle). The Theravada belief has since become characteristic of Burma. It was King Anaurata who instituted a great programme of temples to be built. The threatened invasion from China by Kublai Khan threw the last powerful ruler of Pagan into a panic, and after a great number of temples had been torn down to build fortifications, the city was suddenly abandoned.

Just to digress, let me say a little about Buddhism. Some people think it is relatively simple to understand, others find it complicated. I suppose both views are correct: the basic principle is simple but if you delve further it becomes increasingly complex. It is said that strictly speaking it is not a religion since it is not centred on a god, it is a system of philosophy and moral code. Buddhists believe that to achieve enlightenment is the goal of every being. The Theravada or Small Vehicle holds that to achieve Nirvana (the eventual aim of every Buddhist) one must work out one's own path with diligence. The Mahayana or Great Vehicle states that their belief is sufficient to eventually carry them to salvation. Theravada Buddhism is practised in Sri Lanka, Thailand and Burma. There are some other divisions, such as Hindu-Tantric, which is practised in Tibet and Nepal, and Zen Buddhism in Japan.

Let me return to Pagan. The Thiriptysaya Hotel stood on the shores of the Irrawaddy River and consisted of square bungalows painted in rather garish colours and set on stilts amidst well-cared-for gardens which swept down to the river. The public quarters housed in a group of buildings stood in the centre of the complex on a raised platform. They comprised the foyer with the Dollar Shop, the restaurant and bar. The bungalows were each divided into four units, with every unit having its own terrace with wicker chairs and tables. Each double bedroom was fitted with air-conditioning and contained a refrigerator. A washroom with shower, basin and loo was attached. Little did we know when we settled into luxury that the main cable would break and that we would have neither light, air-conditioning nor a working refrigerator. But when we arrived everything seemed perfect and we set off to explore, thrilled to be in Pagan.

Manuha temple was the first we visited. This was built by Mahuha the captive King in 1059 AD. Three Buddha figures were supposed to be in the temple but there were only two left. The third had been badly damaged by an earthquake and had been removed to be repaired. It also contained a reclining Buddha. These great statues were confined in a small space, with the seated Buddha looking sad, whilst a smile played round the reclining Buddha's lips. This temple represented the agony and frustration of the imprisoned King, who would only be free after death when he would enter Nirvana smiling like the reclining Buddha. It was an impressive sight. Nearby stood the Nanpaya temple, which had served as Manuha's prison. It had originally been a Hindu temple, and four square pillars bearing the three-sided Brahma on each side in relief bore witness to its origin. However, Brahma was shown holding a lotus flower in his hand, the Buddhist symbol of purity. These lovely carvings were surrounded by intricate floral designs. Soft daylight filtered through the perforated stone lattice screens across the windows, which were a feature of the early temples in Pagan. Beautifully carved friezes arched above the windows.

To complete our sightseeing on this crowded day we watched the sun set over Pagan from Thatbyinnyu Temple, which was the highest of them all, rising to 201 feet above the ground. It was a magnificent building, consisting of two huge cubes, the lower one merging into the upper one with three diminishing terraces from which the graceful *Sikhara* rose. (A *sikhara* is the Indian-styled corncob finial of the temple.) This temple had only one approach leading to the main entrance, which was flanked by two highly-coloured guardians. The first flight of steps led to a circumambulatory corridor around the central mass. Climbing further up on stairs built into the thickness of the walls, we reached the top of the vestibule, from where an external flight of stairs led to the huge Buddha image on the upper floor which stood exactly at the centre of the temple. Another dark steep staircase within the massive walls took us to the upper terraces, from where a short perilous flight brought us to the base of the *sikhara*. The whole impression of this building was one of light and air in spite of its basic solid structure, which was achieved by high cubicles and slender stupas arising from the corners of the upper terraces and thanks to the two tiers of windows on each storey. Our arduous climb had been well worth it, rewarding us with a marvellous view. It seemed sheer magic to stand high above watching the sun spread its fading glory over the great plane.

I descended but could not find Ruth. It had become quite dark when I turned back into the temple to look for her, in vain. I became quite anxious when she suddenly appeared, having stopped to talk to two Americans who were studying in Singapore and had come for the permitted seven days to Burma. They intended to spend three days in Pagan but hoped to be able to return at a later date and make Mandalay their main quarter. They had carried a torch and had helped my friend to negotiate the dangerous way down in the dark. Wishing them well, we wistfully hoped to return one day to this magic place.

Near Thatbyinnyu stood a small temple known as the Tally Pagoda, which was said to have been built with one brick for every thousand used to construct its grand neighbour. It contained a gentle-looking Buddha in niches on its four sides.

The main building of the hotel greeted us with twinkling lights on our return. The standard lamps along the path connecting the bungalows were working but there was no light, air-conditioning or refrigeration in our quarters. The main buildings and the standard lights in the grounds ran on their own generator, but we did not really mind since it was hot enough to shower under tepid water and even launder our smalls, which dried in record time outside. Later we moved the small bamboo table and chairs under one of the standard lights so that we could read but had to retreat since swarms of insects gathered round the lamp and plagued us unmercifully.

It was almost too hot to sleep, therefore I rose early and stepped out into the still countryside where the chirping of the crickets seemed to be the only sound. I met Shah, a member of our group, and we wandered across fields in companionable silence. Spellbound we stood still, drinking in the wondrous sights of red brick buildings, some squat and massive, others slender and tall, some complete, others decaying or destroyed. The two brilliant temples, Thatbyinnyu of the night before and Ananda, which we were to see later in the day, stood out in their shimmering whiteness and their size. I loved the warm red brick buildings which glowed bathed by the rising sun. Silently we walked towards a big red brick pagoda towering in perfect symmetry up into the sky. Later we were told that this was the last to have been built. Finally we approached a small village where men were busily shovelling earth, digging ditches and harnessing oxen to sturdy wooden carts which pulled heavy loads and also conveyed big barrels full with water to every site where heavy physical work was in progress. Reluctantly we turned back to our hotel.

Our sightseeing continued after breakfast when we first visited the Shwezigon Pagoda, whose golden dome was visible from afar. Workmen were busily engaged in erecting bamboo buildings outside the temple since the Great Shwezigon Festival was about to begin, when literally thousands of pilgrims come to celebrate. It had astonished us before how rapidly the Burmese erected buildings and equally speedily dismantled them without leaving a trace.

Again we walked along the covered approach with stalls to either side. This time puppets were very much in evidence in every shape and size. For the first time we were asked furtively whether we wanted to buy rubies or other precious stones but having been warned that these might be fakes we declined, although they seemed to be 'chips' rather than fakes. The main pagoda was a solid cylindrical structure arising from three terraces. Bamboo scaffolding hung with bamboo matting partially obscured the golden bell-shaped dome. The pagoda was being renovated. Staircases placed at the centre on each side led up to the terraces and were guarded by fierce-looking animals. Equally forbidding images stood guard at each corner, but unfortunately because of the work in progress the staircases were closed. Niches on each side housed 4-metre-high Buddha statues carved in wood in Gupta style. The first one stood in the attitude of Protector. Shwezigon consisted of a vast complex of smaller temples and shrines grouped around the main pagoda. Near one of them stood a splendid statue of a horse, whilst a small temple adjacent to a stagnant tank contained a statue of Buddha with 'the jackfruit hair', which is the style I usually refer to as 'Buddha with his woolly hat'; this style dated back to the 9th until the 13th century. In another corner stood a modern shrine, resembling a sea grotto, where Buddha sat surrounded by blue waves from which numerous sea monsters reared their ugly heads. I found a small shed to the north-west of the main platform containing 37 *nas* images, which looked like impish pixies, some wearing benign expressions; others were quite grotesque, sprouting six arms; one of them looked African, with full lips. I also discovered a square pillar on either side of the eastern approach bearing Mon inscriptions.

From the Shwezigon we drove to the white Ananda Temple, which had been built in 1091 and was meant to 'represent the endless wisdom of Buddha'. Tradition had it that it had been constructed according to a plan furnished by Indian monks based on their cave temples in the Himalayas. The whole complex was meant to symbolise the mighty mountains. The ground plan, with its four vestibules lined by the usual numerous stalls, resembled a perfect Greek cross. The temple was seven storey high, six of them square and flat, each diminishing in size, lending the whole building a pyramidal shape. The seventh, which was meant to emulate the cell of a Hindu or Jain temple, formed a mitre and was crowned by a gilded HTI. In the centre of the cube stood the four Buddhas which have appeared in the present world. Two – one of them facing north, the other south – came originally from Cambodia. The other two had been destroyed by fire and replaced by a glass mosaic. Shrines to either side of the Buddha in the western sanctum contained life-sized figures of the founder of the temple, King Kyanzittha, and his primate Shin Acra Haw. Terracotta tiles which decorated the base and the receding terraces depicted the Jataka (the life of Buddha), and scenes from Hindu mythology.

The day we spent in Pagan happened to coincide with a holiday, which meant that pilgrims were all around us visiting the little shrines, where some were engaged in worship whilst others rested peacefully. Some visitors were preparing their meals in the resting pavilions, whilst others had their palms read or consulted astrologists. A woodcarver was at work in one of the pavilions; from him we bought a delightful figure of a lama with his fan and begging bowl which, though carved quite simply, was very lifelike and appealing. Having a short time at our disposal we visited the charming local museum housed nearby in two pavilions. One of them was open-sided and contained a wealth of statues, mainly Buddhas. A collection of stone slabs which had been found in the vicinity and were inscribed in different languages stood around the courtyard. They were also religious records. The second building housed an excellent selection of artefacts dating back to palaeolithic times up to the decline of Pagan.

So that anyone who wished to take photographs could do so, we returned once more to Thatbyinnyu Temple. I wandered off to climb Shwegugyi Temple, built in 1311. This elegant temple stood on a high brick platform. Both the hall and surrounding corridor had open doorways and open windows freely admitting light and air. The stucco carvings around windows, doors, on plinths and cornices were extremely fine and beautiful. The little bell on the HTI tinkled merrily in the slight breeze. On my way back I cast a quick glance at the Thandawyga Image, an enormous seated Buddha carved of greenish sandstone inside a small brick temple which stood surrounded by a low wall. Although this statue had been badly damaged by an earthquake it had retained its compelling gaze.

The Dhammayangi Temple was the very last we visited. It had been built on a similar plan to the Ananda Temple but was constructed of brick. The building as a whole appeared massive. Only the outer corridors were accessible; they displayed the finest brickwork in Pagan. The lofty arches which drew our gaze upwards were reminiscent of Gothic architecture. The many shrines bore traces of most fascinating murals of elephants, Buddhas, palaces etc. Splendid statues stood distributed in corridors and niches. This last temple formed a memorable end to a most incredible collection of treasures from the past. It was quite difficult to leave Pagan.

Before lunch we paid one more call: to see a lacquer factory in a nearby village. This is a very intricate process, starting with a frame consisting of bamboo. In first-class lacquer-ware this is the only part made from bamboo. Horsehair and donkey hair are wound round this frame, which is covered by lacquer. Lacquer is derived from the kusum tree. The article is allowed to dry and after several days it is sanded down using rice husks. A second coating of lacquer is then applied. This process is repeated various times until finally the article is engraved and painted before being polished to remove paint from everywhere except the engravings. Multicoloured ware is produced by repeating engraving, painting, polishing – the number of times corresponding to the number of colours being used. It may take five to six months to complete one high-quality article. We saw the engraving, painting, polishing of bowls, trays and other articles. The salesroom occupied part of the upstairs living quarters, whilst workrooms were located downstairs. A bed stood in the living quarters with an umbrella hooked over the headboard and a motorcycle propped up behind it. A lacquered wardrobe (a fine example of the elegant ware), low tables and low chairs completed the furniture. Tea was served from the traditional square teapot with the handle on top, which was kept warm in a well-padded octagonal box. Sugar candy of unrefined sugar with a nutty flavour was offered. Before leaving we looked for three small tiered bowls with a handle but could not find what we wanted. Later, however, we managed to locate one in the Dollar Shop back at the hotel. This shop (as in Russia) was only for tourists and goods had to be paid for in foreign currency. We also bought a small picture of two graceful dancers engraved in gold on black background.

Driving to the airport I was again impressed by the variety of shapes of the temples. Some were perfect bells, some were fashioned using concentric rings diminishing in size, some were decorated with lotus leaves, others with lozenges. Bells were crowned with tapering HTIs. There were perfect pyramids, corn-cobs, cubes. Pagan must be paradise for art students and architects alike.

The little airport lay sleepily in the sun. I sat on a wooden seat built around a shady tree where sweet-smelling pink and white oleander grew nearby. Our plane was late. I did not care, I felt at peace with the world; it seemed as if time stood still and I did not want it to move on.

As we rose into the air we were able to cast a last glance down on Pagan nestling in the bend of the Irrawaddy River and we could say goodbye to all its pagodas. The sun set as we climbed high above the clouds. Suddenly we ran into a storm which buffeted our small plane in the angry sky. It was entirely dark when we landed in Rangoon to spend our last night once more in the Inya Lake Hotel. The night was incredibly hot and sticky as we drove through the lively town where traffic was still busy and buses crowded to overflowing. Some of the pagodas were outlined by electric bulbs.

Our last supper proved a near disaster since no tables were available for our party. Finally trestle tables were set up, with some of us helping. The lobster was underdone and tough, the stodgy pudding had been boiled too long. This mattered little to Ruth and myself but some members in our group were up in arms. Before we retired to bed we repacked. I slept little and watched lightning pierce the sky. Stepping out onto our balcony, I looked up at the moon and listened to the infernal noise of millions of crows who used the big tree just outside our room as a twice-nightly meeting place. Day began and found us ready to spend our last morning in town.

Sharing a taxi with another couple in our party, we drove down town. Our driver was a pleasant man with Chinese features who told us that he was Roman Catholic. He pointed out the Pagoda of Mirrors as we passed, the Cathedral of Holy Trinity with its college, the large Hospital for Tuberculosis and a smaller Ophthalmic Hospital. When we remarked on a big building tiered like a Chinese pagoda near our hotel, he told us that this had been built by a rich Chinese as a private house but would probably be converted into a hotel in the near future. Our drive took us past another big building, which carried the strange message: 'The Research Organisation under the Auspices of Ministry number two', whatever this may mean.

On this morning we approached the Shwedagon Pagoda from a different direction and became aware of the small golden pagoda which pointed the way to it and stood next to the *sinthas*, the guardian beasts. Sparrows twittered away in their cages, waiting to be set free on a special festive day. Talking to our driver, we learnt that the price of petrol was cheap but rationed and he only received three gallons a day; if he required more he had to pay threefold on the black market and queue all night for it.

Returning to the Bogyoke Market, we bought a tape of Burmese music and some lacquer-ware and were advised to use brass polish on it to clean the shinning lacquer and varnish the gold to prevent it from lifting up. We had planned to visit the museum but it was closed; instead we spent some time in the Chinese Market, situated in the Chinese quarter, where bamboo poles stretched across narrow lanes festooned with washing. The market was crowded and very busy. All goods had been imported from China. Here we bought some Chinese slippers before returning to our hotel to sit at the pool, enjoying a cool drink of fresh lime and soda. Lunch, served early, was neither better nor worse than any other meal we had had in the Inya Lake Hotel.

Back at Rangoon Airport, we found to our amazement that there were no problems, no hassle, no prolonged waiting when leaving the country. No questions were asked, no currency checked, no receipt demanded, no forms to be filled in and not even a single piece of luggage opened and searched.

The short flight back to Bangkok by Thai Air passed quickly since we were busy keeping Shah engaged in conversation. She was terrified of flying, having survived a crash many years ago when she was pregnant. Exactly the same meal as we had had on our flight out was served at 6 p.m. In Bangkok we had to wait a few hours for our connection (as scheduled), but time once again passed quickly. First we looked at the shops, where the sales girls appeared jaded and listless, next we bought drinks at a horrendous price. Shah, staggered at this, later purchased a whole bottle of brandy in the duty-free shop at the same cost as our two drinks – which we all shared. At this point in time when we were soon to part and each go our own way, the group amazingly drew closer. Suddenly I missed my glasses and everybody seemed concerned, offering helpful advice. They were found in the plane we had arrived on from Rangoon and handed back to me, (without glasses I cannot write or read and feel entirely lost.)

A group of young people appeared who were to have flown to Burma on Air Bangladesh but had been left stranded at Bangkok Airport for the past two days. Although we were unable to help we felt extremely sorry for their misfortune; they seemed a bunch of nice people. Formerly strangers, a common disaster had knitted them into a group of close friends. They took turns to take care of a small fair-haired child.

Finally we boarded our plane and settled down to face our long flight home. Dinner was served – rice, for a change! The crew was jolly and attentive, the captain informative. After four hours we arrived in Delhi, where the crew changed whilst we had to remain on board. On our next lap to Dubai we were offered another meal. Flames of the oil refinery pierced the dark sky and Dubai's lights twinkled brightly below us when we landed at 2 a.m. local time. The airport was crowded but we know it very well and quickly made our way to the duty-free shop to buy drinks and a camera without much delay. Unfortunately the service was poor, with the salesman looking extremely bored and almost unwilling to part with his goods and very reluctant to show us any cameras. Back on board, our journey continued and presently the captain announced that Rhodes was in sight and that soon we would land in Athens. I had written a little, slept for a short while, eaten, and talked at great length to my neighbour, a young man from Los Angeles who was with our group. Whilst on our trip we had hardly conversed but on the very last part of our journey I could barely stem the flow.

There was trouble with one door when we were about to leave Athens, which meant that we had to sit on the tarmac for a further hour. Passengers occupying seats near the awkward door had to move during take-off and later when we landed.

The sun had climbed up high into the sky whilst we had sat waiting and shone on the golden domes of a nearby Greek Orthodox church. Ships bobbed up and down on the choppy sea as we circled over Piraeus Harbour. Flying over the docks, we looked down on the many ships anchored in neat rows then flew on above the densely populated area along the rugged coast. Mist covered most of Yugoslavia, mountains rose only as dim ghosts, but better luck greeted us as we crossed the Austrian Alps before rising high above Germany to land finally in Amsterdam, where we had to rush from one end of the airport to the other to catch the waiting plane. Watching our luggage being loaded, we spotted that the lock was broken on one of our cases.

The flight across the Channel was quick, with nothing to see until London lay below us along the Thames before we landed smoothly at Heathrow. In our anxiety to report the damaged case we left one bag behind but recovered it next day. Our journey had taken almost thirty hours, only half of which had been spent in the air; the rest had been taken up by waiting patiently, therefore we felt tired and weary when we reached home, yet tremendously elated by the experience we had had.

TIBET AT LAST

Beijing – Tibet – Leshan – Kunming

November 1985

Beijing

Here we are in Beijing on the second evening of our second visit to China. Our first one was in 1981 when we followed the Silk Road, this time we have come mainly to see Tibet as much as permitted.

It was a beautiful day when we left England. Frost covered the ground and transformed the bare trees. Night had fallen by the time we touched down in Sharjah on the Persian Gulf, having had a short stop in Zurich. Sharjah was a pretty airport, quite modern and built in Islamic style. All shopkeepers were Indian and carried on a brisk trade since our Chinese fellow travellers were avid customers who bought in large quantities. Even at this late hour it was a lively and colourful scene with turbaned Pakistanis waiting patiently and Arabs in flowing robes gliding past.

As we took off again we looked down on the sparkling town with brilliant lights along a straight road and saw two oil wells burning brightly in the inky sky.

Soon a pink glow appeared on the horizon, whilst stars still sparkled above in the dark firmament. When daylight broke we looked down on valleys cleaving the bare flanks of majestic mountains which were powdered with light snow. A new day had begun and the sun dazzled us with its bright glare. Desert lay below us, with the sand rippling like the sea owing to the winds which swept across the empty space. Mountain range after mountain range loomed up devoid of any sign of water or life, interrupted by more sandy desert. A sandstorm blew up clearly visible from the air, after which we flew over snow-capped mountains for a short distance before we found ourselves again over desert ringed by mountains entirely covered by snow. Small streams forged their way bravely through sands, a railway track appeared with valiant attempts at cultivation to either side, but soon the picture changed and we flew over many fields where houses lay scattered in between. The sun shone brilliantly onto a network of roads before more habitations became visible. Finally we were told to fasten our seatbelts as we descended over gentle hills with dwellings in the upper regions followed by dark mountain ranges separated by valleys. Our plane rose once more to clear some higher peaks, then we glimpsed a broad river shimmering in the distance. Neat fields surrounded many villages, and straight roads were lined by tall poplars. For the first time we saw a sealed road. Rice paddies glistened in the sun, gardens and some green crops became visible; up to then the entire landscape had been brown. It was the soft green of winter barley we saw but when we touched down at last, parched earth lay once more around the airport.

The plane had been full, with some English and Americans beside a group of Chinese gentlemen in city suits. They had been to a conference in Birmingham for two weeks, sponsored by Barclay's Bank, and had presented Ruth with a commemoration coin bearing a picture of the Great Wall on one side and 'Tec Barclay' on the other.

At Beijing Airport we met some members of our party. Finally we found our courier, Helen, and were introduced to our Chinese guide Zhiana, a pleasant friendly girl who lived with her parents and younger sister in a two-bedroom flat in the centre of Beijing. She had been waiting for two years for a one-bedroom flat so that she could get married. Her fiancé worked for a computer firm in Japan, returning home once every two months. She herself had worked in the fields outside Beijing during the Cultural Revolution when she was a teenager. It had been hard work, with little food, but she considered herself fortunate since she had been able to see her parents once every six months. She had learned English at school, from radio and from books and was now not only a guide for Beijing but also 'a National Guide'.

After we had arrived and joined up with two fellow travellers and met Helen and Zhiana, we had collected our luggage without much delay and climbed on our minibus to be taken to our hotel. Alas, (unlike in 1981 when we had stayed in the Beijing Hotel in the city centre,) this time we were near the airport in a new (opened in 1982) hotel called Yen Xian, where only tourists stayed. Driving along dusty straight roads, we noticed that street sweepers wore white surgeon's hats, masks and white gloves. Bicycles were still very much in evidence and none of them bore lights. A fair number of motorcycles with sidecars were on the road and the number of cars had increased on the busy roads compared to the last time we were here. Smallholdings along the way grew mainly Chinese cabbage. Later, in town we saw mountains of it in every market, every street stall, heaps of it piled up on the pavement. Old and young with shopping bags and the many-purpose bamboo pram bought enormous quantities of this winter vegetable since it was cheap and could be stored on wooden planks outside windows or on balconies which were already brimful with every conceivable item. It would have to last through the coming winter months and would be stir-fried for consumption.

Our hotel this time stood in a wilderness, with the Lido Hotel close by, both of them still under construction as part of a large complex with a sports ground, shops and other facilities. Whilst our hotel was only used for organised tours, the Lido catered for businessmen, mostly from Japan. Once installed in our room on the sixth floor, we explored and found the usual hall with stalls on the second floor whilst numerous shops were accommodated on the ground floor as well as various restaurants, tea and coffee shops and a swimming pool. The bank, however, was closed until 5 p.m., therefore we went to the Lido Hotel to change some traveller's cheques into tourist money. When we were here before, nobody wanted to take tourist money which was called 'funny money', but now everybody appeared to be anxious to have it.

Time passed quickly and after a short rest we all met up to go to dine. One more traveller had joined our group; Pat, an Australian lady who worked in the Foreign Service and was stationed in Japan. She had been an accountant and later an economic analyst; prior to all this she had been a teacher. It did not really matter since we never made any close contact but learned that she had been twice married, was childless and travelled a good bit. Next day we met the remaining members of our party, two American couples: Ed and Ruby and their friends Dr and Mrs Hart, who were quite a remarkable couple since he was blind and had a paralysed left hand due to war injuries received in the South Pacific. His wife had been a nurse and had stood by him, helping him through his medical studies. He worked as a psychiatrist in a penal institution and walked the wards on his own, otherwise his wife was 'his eyes'. All this we learned from Ed, who was an outgoing person, unlike his friends, who never conversed with us.

It was still dark when I woke on our first morning; condensation ran down the windows since the air-conditioning did not work. However, when we tried to warm our room only cold air came through the machine. Flasks with hot water had been provided in each room, as well as fragrant jasmine tea and pretty cups with lids, therefore we could at least warm ourselves with a hot drink. All night long we had dimly heard the continuous noise of machinery on the building site close by. Factories worked three shifts and were never closed, whilst offices had a rest day on Sunday. Most shops stayed open seven days a week, with every employee working an eight hour shift with one day off a week, rest days were staggered.

On the first morning, as on all following ones whilst we were in Beijing, a voice boomed over a loudspeaker outside in the street at 6.30 a.m. This lady probably issued instructions for the daily morning exercise, but we only saw two lonely men out in the misty cold performing their morning routine.

After a very chaotic buffet breakfast in a very crowded breakfast room we drove through the misty autumn morning to the Great Wall. Where formerly one good road had taken us there this time a dual carriage way coped with the enormous numbers of coaches which came every day to this ancient site. Last time the clouds had never lifted and it had rained, this time the sun broke through the early morning mist and we spent a glorious bright morning walking along this fantastic wall amongst big crowds. Most of them were Chinese, some tourists themselves from outside the mainland but nevertheless Chinese. There was a sprinkling of Caucasian faces, Americans, Germans, a few French, some Swiss, some Swedes. Many of the Chinese visitors stopped us to ask us to take their photographs with their own cameras. Our guide frequently uttered the same request. Much of the wall had been restored; we walked as far as we could and stood looking at more of the wall along the wooded crest of the hills.

From here we drove to the famous Ming Tombs, stopping first to have lunch since meal times are early throughout China. As customary, we sat at a round table and were served with numerous vegetable dishes, rice, soup, fish or meat preceded by some tit-bits. Beer or soft drinks were always included; some of our party asked for tea. Meals were simple and basically always the same. If we had taken Chinese breakfast we would have eaten the same food three times a day!

Walking into the dining hall, we passed through the usual array of shops with large quantities of the same merchandise. Some stalls stood at the roadside and every time a car passed by, a cloud of dust settled on the goods.

Since all the members of our party had been to China before and had visited the Ming Tombs, we walked to the Ding Ling Tomb. This was not a tomb at all but a beautiful display of all the artefacts which had been found in Ding Ling's tomb. Stepping through an ornate gate, we passed a Temple of Longevity with the usual emblem of the tortoise, as well as the dragon symbolising long life holding up the roof. In the exhibition hall itself we saw crowns, swords, dresses, uniforms, jewellery, ornaments, seals, gold bars and beautiful brocades lovingly displayed. To return to our coach we walked along the 'Animal Way', where one normally commences the visit to the Ming Tombs. Once again we marvelled at the intricate carvings, the clever expressions on both the real and mythical beasts. Stonemasons were busily working away to fashion new surrounds for each statue to prevent visitors from climbing up.

Later we were taken down town to the International Club to watch a song and dance show. Unfortunately we were late and the performance had started, but what we did see was very good. Girls sang traditional songs with sweet, pleasing voices, and the various ethnic musical instruments intrigued us since they were alien to us. The dancing was excellent, particularly two dances: one where a fisherman played a goldfish and the second a very expressive dance of a seagull. It was not only the dancing but also the miming which was highly polished.

Next morning it was again misty when we woke. Our first stop was the well-known Tiananmen Square in the centre of the city, where tourists mingled with the local population crowding this open space. Long orderly queues had already formed to visit Mao Zedong's mausoleum. In absolute silence we too filed four abreast past his embalmed remains lying in a glass sarcophagus. As tourists, we were privileged and did not have to wait, getting preference over the Chinese. The mausoleum had been built by volunteers in 1976 and was visited daily by thousands between the hours of 8 and 11 a.m. An obelisk erected in memory to the People's Heroes stands in the middle of the square.

Having done our 'duty' we felt free to mingle with the crowd. Men squatted in small groups, talking or gambling; little knots of people congregated around tables. Public photographers touted for business, standing beneath gaily striped umbrellas at these tables, and found many takers.

Little children who had been left in the charge of two young ladies whilst their parents paid homage to Mao Zedong were most delightful to watch. They did not wear nappies, instead their trousers had slits. Everybody, small or grown-up, wore trousers, we hardly ever saw a woman in a skirt.

Mao Zedong's large picture still dominated the square, looking sternly down from the massive red gate which led into the Forbidden City. The Imperial Palace or Forbidden City stands surrounded by a moat with picturesque little old houses on its side and willows dipping their branches into the still water.

Once again we stood in the huge courtyard on the fifteen layers of stone which had been laid in criss-cross fashion on top of each other to prevent anyone from tunnelling a secret passage beneath the Forbidden City. This time we could only look into the temples and halls; we could no longer walk through the buildings to look at the ornate tall columns, to admire the coffered ceilings or to stand in amazement at the vast collection of treasures within.

The whole complex is very difficult to describe. Again I was intrigued by the colourful roofs with their lovely little figures at each corner. Only the Emperor was allowed to use the colour gold. Red, yellow, blue and green were also used, each colour signifying something of importance: air, water, earth, sky.

This time we visited the Clock Museum, which had only been open for the past two years and displayed the Emperor's collection of mechanical clocks, starting with French, English and German and finishing with Chinese models. Most were incredibly ornate and the timepiece itself seemed almost incidental, a means to show off extravagant workmanship and expensive materials.

For the first time we also saw the Courtyard of the Concubines, where again we felt overwhelmed by the wealth of jewels, ivory and carvings. The third new experience was the Hall of Jewellery, which as the name proclaims exhibited the jewels of the Empress.

It was most enjoyable to be able to amble leisurely in pleasant sunshine and to realise that most visitors were actually Chinese.

Lunch was taken in a big eating hall – for tourists only – near the Temple of Happiness, which we visited in the afternoon. It is a delightful complex, where the predominant colour is blue. It still seemed a happy place: children played and balloons were sent up into the sky and sang until they shrank and floated gently down onto the stony ground.

Before we returned to our hotel we drove back down town again to visit one of the Friendship Stores, which was a vast building with very comprehensive merchandise including 'Moslem meat' in the food hall.

That night we dined down town in a special restaurant to sample Peking duck and Mongolian hotpot. It was of course a typical tourist place, which was obvious when we approached and saw the vast number of waiting coaches outside. But the food was excellent, washed down by sweet Chinese wine followed by fierce Chinese spirits. We had some delicious walnuts and watched fascinated the way the Mongolian hotpot was prepared at the table. Thinly sliced meat, shredded cabbage and noodles were quickly cooked in boiling water in a special pot set over a charcoal fire.

A grey, melancholy morning greeted us next day. Breakfast was even more chaotic than on the previous morning, therefore none of us minded leaving the hotel for good. Once more we drove into town past little houses standing in their secluded courtyards between the high-rise flats festooned with laundry. Laundry also hung on the branches of the trees which lined the streets or was suspended on lines between them. Regretfully we sped past the old Lama Temple to return to the Friendship Store, where everybody bought 'provisions', before we strolled down the road past some flats which looked as if they were attached to embassies. The local population were doing their daily shopping in small free markets. It was strange to see little boys wearing soldiers' caps. Traffic was dense but buses, trolleybuses, lorries, taxis and a few private cars with hordes of bicycles on special lanes flowed smoothly along. Every taxi carried a feather duster on its rear window ledge.

Our schedule included a visit to the Summer Palace, which is a pleasant place on a sunny day with its big artificial lake. Since all of us had been there before, it would have been nicer to visit a museum or the old Lama Temple instead of wandering through the private gardens of the last Empress on this very dreary day. But this was impossible; flexibility was an unknown concept. Once again we saw her private theatre with the stage and costumes well maintained and again walked along the long corridor, taking delight at the Watteau-like pictures painted on the beams. This time we had an opportunity to climb up the slopes above the lake to reach the Pavilion, as all local visitors seemed to do. For lunch we stopped in one of the many enormous eating halls which were part of a big shopping complex.

After lunch we drove to the airport to board our plane to Chengdu. The airport was crowded, mainly with soldiers waiting to board the plane. There was no conscription in China, we were told; the Army was made up of volunteers, but these got fewer and fewer as time went on. Passports had to be produced in lieu of identity cards (every Chinese who worked carried an identity card), and all tourists sat at the rear of the plane. Pretty girls in blue trouser suits donned frilly aprons to serve cartons of kiwi fruit (made in Sweden) and presented each passenger with a small box of candies, as well as a key ring with a globe of the world attached, before lunch, whilst piped music almost lulled us to sleep.

It was dark by the time we arrived in Chengdu, when it started to rain. Our guide, who was a little man, greeted us with the words: 'Hurry up, we are late for dinner since we have to drive into the city to a restaurant where they are waiting for us.' Saying this, he whisked us into town along a straight tree-lined road. Bicycles still had no lights, whilst oddly enough buses and lorries drove with dimmed lights, turning them up into a blinding glare whenever two vehicles met. Inside the city our guide gave us a running commentary on all the buildings, which we could no longer see. Leaving the wide avenue, we drove through narrow little streets into the old town to the restaurant. As usual we climbed upstairs along a staircase festooned with chrysanthemums in full bloom. Alas the place looked grimy, the food was not very good, and it was too late for tea.

Our hotel was called the Jing Yang Hotel and was enormous, but we had no time to explore. Apart from the fact that harmless insects scuttled around in our bedroom, our cases had been misdirected to another hotel and it took considerable time before they arrived, it did not take us long to organise ourselves and leave them ready packed outside our room before we retired to bed.

We had arrived in the dark and left before daybreak, but life was already stirring. Cars, lorries and the never absent bicycles were on the move, whilst some people were jogging. The airport was crowded, mainly with soldiers and their families. Little babies cocooned in padded blankets were tied to their mothers' backs. The waiting room was bare, with stone floors and nasty plastic chairs, with one attractive bamboo settee for VIPs standing in a side room.

Tibet

Our plane took off just after 7 a.m. and first flew over fertile countryside. The Province of Sichuan, with Chengdu as its capital, is renowned for its agreeable climate, which supports lush vegetation. As we rose quickly high above a sea of clouds, whole snow-covered mountain ranges popped through the thick white blanket, bathed in the morning sun. The clouds disappeared, disclosing an entire panorama of seemingly never-ending mountains covered by eternal snow. Once again our view was blotted out and we concentrated on food. The night before we had already received a luncheon box in our hotel which we 'sorted out' leaving most of its contents in our room. Once we were high up in the air we were handed a second box, preceded by kiwi juice and followed by tea at a later stage.

Finally we descended and flew across wide valleys with bare mountains; gone was the snow. Roads, fields, houses, and a wide river with sandbanks appeared. Flat-roofed complexes lay scattered below us. The wings almost dipped into the blue water of the river before we landed at Lhasa Airport just after nine a.m. The sky was blue but slightly cloudy, the air was crystal clear. Having walked slowly to our waiting bus we were soon on our way to Lhasa, which was a two-hour drive round a mountain range. It started to snow very gently. Driving along, we saw first a yak-skin boat crossing the river and later a horseman fording the stream. To stretch our legs and admire a rock painting, we stopped at a lake. The crude painting representing the Bhudda Avalokitesvara, a Bodhisattva (which means 'the Buddha to Be') who came from India, where Buddhism commenced, was perfectly reflected in the clear waters.

I find Buddhism extremely difficult to understand. In spite of the fact that I tried to read the late Christmas Humphreys' *Buddhism, an Introduction and Guide*, I have not been able to come to grips with the subject.

It had stopped snowing when we stood in the clear air and we felt awed by the magnificent stillness around us. At a road junction we turned north, forsaking the road which led on to Xigaze, Tibet's second town. Our road followed the River Lhasa, which begins just as a mountain stream but joins with others before entering India, where it becomes the mighty Brahmaputra.

Everybody had heard about the Potala Palace, everybody had seen photographs of the Potala Palace, we all had dreamt of the Potala Palace, but nothing could have prepared us for the actual visual impact on this cold, clear winter's day. It stood before us in all its glory: the warm dark red central palace flanked by pure white buildings, crowned by golden roofs glittering in the brilliant sun. It rose in perfect symmetry astride its hill against the background of high protecting mountains.

Having 'recovered', we proceeded to Guesthouse Number Two which stood outside town. A long drive took us through a compound with many bungalows placed neatly in rows and occupied by Chinese soldiers. Further along was the guesthouse, in big grounds. Bungalows painted in bright ochre stood to either side of the drive. One served as souvenir shop, another as general store and post office, a third proclaimed proudly 'The International Club'. The remaining bungalows were for the staff. Passing the 'dining hall' we arrived at our 'villa', which was built from solid grey stone and consisted of three parts: two units containing three interconnecting bedrooms to either side of a draughty corridor. One bathroom with a Western toilet stood at one end and also housed a temperamental shower (which we did not discover until later). A primitive washroom with 'Mohammed's Footsteps' (as we called the hole with foot imprints either side) was available outside. Two pleasant and very willing young girls acted as our room attendants. Shelves had been built around the walls of the bedrooms but no provision had been made to hang up clothes. Radiators had been fitted in every room but they did not work. During the day it was gloriously warm and invigorating under the brilliant blue sky, but when the sun went down it became bitterly cold. Lights inevitably went out, and once the electricity failed there was no hot water. All we could do was go to bed to keep warm. An artificial potted poinsettia decorated our room.

Next morning we drove into Lhasa. It is a curious town, with many new buildings. A new guesthouse was being erected on the outskirts and had been scheduled to open in the autumn we were there, but building was still in progress. Nearby stood a very luxurious-looking new hotel which had been open but was closed again to rectify some structural faults (so we were told, but we actually thought that a Chinese delegation had taken up residence and therefore it was closed to tourists). Opposite stood the Palace of Culture, an imposing building, modern in style.

How can anybody describe the Potala? To appreciate this unique place, one has to be there and mount the worn steps under the incredibly brilliant blue sky in this crystal-clear air amongst the stream of devout Tibetan pilgrims wrapped in their ankle-length greasy fur-lined yak coats, which are always handed down along the line. I have no doubt that the Tibetans are the dirtiest people I have ever seen, but it is humbling and very moving to be part of this scene and we felt privileged to be amongst the pilgrims in this, to them, so sacred place. An imposing gate protected by various fierce-looking statues led into the first courtyard, from where we climbed up innumerable stairs to countless courtyards, saw small private apartments of the Dalai Lama and his court, stood in amazement in the large Hall of the Sutra, which is the library containing all the canons. These were printed on long strips of parchment, bound into books between wooden covers and lovingly wrapped in rich brocade. In the Funerary Hall we stood overawed by the fantastic funerary pagodas, all made of gilded bronze studded with precious or semiprecious stones; some of them were even overlaid with gold leaf.

Failing to find the guide allotted to our group, we attached ourselves to another English party, who had an excellent Tibetan lady guide speaking perfect English. We followed her from terrace to terrace, then she led us into a room which housed a model of the funeral ritual made in semi-precious stone. Here was the sacred mountain which actually rises behind Sera Monastery (which unfortunately we did not see) where the corpses are taken to be dismembered, the bones cleaned of all flesh. The meat is chopped up to be fed to the vultures who wait patiently and watchfully throughout this procedure. Models of men dismembering the deceased, the vultures, the mountain, trees and rivers had all been made to scale but many of the models had fallen down, having been disturbed by rats.

One visit to the Potala was not sufficient to be able to absorb everything and to take in all the intricate carvings, the fascinating murals, the interesting statues, the brilliant *thangkas*. Whatever we did miss on our short visit, it still left us with a deep impression.

In a small pavilion specially set aside for visitors to rest and sip tea, we made a brief stop before returning to our guesthouse, where we met up with our local guide in the afternoon. He was a strange little man who told us later that he came from a noble Tibetan family and had been sent, accompanied by his manservant, to Darjeeling to be educated at St Joseph College. It had taken seventeen days to reach Darjeeling. At some stage he had taught but now was a guide, unfortunately not a very good one, but it seemed that in both China and Tibet good guides were rare.

By midday the weather was absolutely brilliant, with the sun streaming into our room. Since we had time we went to explore the general store to buy some postcards, which to my great surprise all reached their destination in a reasonable time. Here we met guests from the other 'villas', most of them were elderly Americans with an incredible zest for life. They were dressed in fur coats, fur-lined boots, wore bonnets, earmuffs, carried muffs and had been into Lhasa to buy hot water bottles. An interesting Dutch couple who were well-travelled and were doing this trip independently, advised us to visit Korea if we were interested in Buddhism. We did follow their advice in 1987. China had actually opened her doors to independent travellers three years prior to our visit to Tibet. Many lonely travellers we had talked to had told us that it was easy enough to find accommodation but it was extremely frustrating to get connections. All one needed was 'plenty of patience and plenty of time'.

In the afternoon we returned to the city to visit the Jokhang Temple which stands in the centre. The open square in front of its gates was packed with a seething mass of humanity, most of them devout pilgrims. It was quite a feat to make our way to the entrance since pilgrims approaching the temple prostrated themselves on

102

dirty sacking; men, women and children alike appeared to be completely oblivious of anything and everything around them, concentrating on touching the hard ground with their foreheads again and again. But there were not many pilgrims inside when we walked up the narrow staircase past a monk chanting his beads. Frequently I gave the Tibetan greeting, poking my tongue out, which was usually reciprocated.

Again I cannot give a detailed description of this ancient temple where we climbed from sunny courtyard to sunny courtyard until we stood as high as we could go, dazzled by the golden roofs, puzzled by the Garuda, since this is the mystic bird sacred to the Hindus, overawed by the fierce dragons and monsters, which protected the temple and warded off the evil spirits. Some intricate carvings on beams and pediments were very beautiful. Here we entered many halls and admired many treasures; in the main hall, which was bedecked with beautiful brocade, stood the large gilded bronze statue of Sakyamuni Buddha flanked by two figures. One of the monks in the temple wanted us to record his chanting but unfortunately none of us had a tape recorder since it was cumbersome enough to be lumbered with cameras etc. The frescoes – many of them blackened by the golden lamps – were fascinating and we stood in admiration before them. Each of the many side chapels contained a statue, such as that of Guanyin, the God of Compassion, with his eleven faces and four arms.

After the silence and tranquillity of the temples it seemed strange to emerge into the bright sunlight again and join once more the seething throng of people on the square. Many offered us trinkets to buy but we doubted that any of them were real semi-precious stone and rather suspected that they were made of coloured glass or possibly plastic.

After visiting Jokhang we strolled through the narrow lanes of the old town which surround the temple and form the market area. It proved quite difficult to proceed amongst the dense crowd of people buying and selling, men carrying carcasses on their backs or enormous loads of wood or other commodities. Women often glared at us and shied away.

Finally we called at the post office for some stamps and waited at a street corner for our coach to pick us up, watching the world go by. Suddenly whilst standing in the sunshine I felt cold and shivery and by the time we reached our villa I really was not feeling well.

103

The blind doctor and his wife had felt poorly since we touched down in Tibet and they as well as their friends returned to Chengdu as soon as they were able to get a flight. The rest of the party did not fare too badly, two had slight oedema, slight headaches and just minimal shortness of breath.

In the small hours of the morning I felt sick and stepped out into the cold starlit night. Frost covered the ground and adorned the bare branches. It began to snow slightly. Everything was perfectly still, the air was as clear as champagne.

When we left next morning it was still dark although we could make out ghostly shapes around us. A little tree bedecked with prayer flags suddenly loomed up through the mist. The sun rose behind us since we were travelling due west. Pink hues formed a halo around the top of the mountains which stood majestically before us.

I missed most of the journey, feeling sick, aching all over and running a temperature, but I remember seeing some geysers shooting up into the air. Later we had to stop at a river and wait for the ferry in the company of many pilgrims, some of whom were on foot, others in crowded trucks. Another bus also stood waiting at the river's edge. Since buses have precedence on ferries, our landrover followed the bus. It was, however, a tight squeeze and quite a feat to get the vehicles on. All the passengers had to alight. Once we arrived safety on the other side, I snuggled thankfully back into my corner. I faintly remember a fisherman coming up to our vehicle carrying two trout freshly caught, which our young driver bought. Apart from this I do not recollect anything more until we actually stopped outside our hotel in Xigaze, which had a very imposing entrance hall. Having climbed up many stairs and walked along endless passages I was glad to be able to sink into a very comfortable bed, where I – regretfully – spent the two nights and one day of our stay because I had quite severe backache, headache and fever but no shortness of breath (oxygen was available in both hotels). A young American doctor (we had given her and her friend a lift from Lhasa since their transport had not turned up) came to see me and thought I had an infection and all I required was warmth, rest and plenty of fluids. Our accountant – the only other English member in our group – came to the rescue and gave us a packet of tomato soup. Ever since that time we never travel without packets of soup. The room was comfortable, a small radiator in the bathroom provided adequate heat.

The rest of our party went off next day to visit the old monastery of Tashi-Laya, built in 1417. Xigaze is the seat of the Panchen Lama, the second in charge, head of the yellow sect. Ruth was impressed by this ancient monastery, where the remaining few monks continued the tradition of cooking rice in a large cauldron for the whole community. Later they went to a carpet factory on the outskirts of town where the Tibetans were highly amused when Ruth drew out a handkerchief to blow her nose. Tibetans spat freely and used thumb and middle finger to clear their noses. Ruth bought a small rug to add to our collection from various lands we had visited.

In the meantime I dozed on and off throughout the day. A maid appeared but beat a hasty retreat when she saw me in bed. I heard continuous chanting below the window from sunrise until after sundown, stopping at midday when everybody downed tools. It came from a group of workers digging a reservoir next to the hotel.

When we were due to leave next morning, the whole of the hotel lay deserted and it was extremely difficult to find the staff and rouse them from their sleep. But eventually they surfaced and served us tea and bread in the big draughty barn of a dismal dining room with dirty tablecloths. Apparently the meals had been very poor and, sadly – although the hotel had only been open for two months – it had already fallen into a sorry state of disrepair. The solar heating system was broken, hence there was no hot water, and the light failed just as we were ready to leave our rooms and carry our luggage along the long corridors and down the many stairs, since service was almost non-existent and even tea and bread had been offered with bad grace. It was just before seven o'clock when we finally left. Life had not as yet begun, apart from the dogs who had howled on and off right through the night.

It was another cold morning, with hoar frost on every stone, on every blade of grass and on every branch. Once daylight broke, life commenced; donkeys pulling small carts met us along our way, men and women strode briskly in the crisp morning air. The road ran between fields. Water was plentiful, with streams and rivers full of fish and a number of birds nearby. The sun rose quite suddenly, almost blinding us since we were driving due east.

The few isolated villages which we passed were surrounded by mud brick walls. The bricks had been made by mixing mud with straw, which was poured into simple wooden frames and left to dry in the hot sun. Splendid mountain ranges, looking as if they had been carved by human hand, towered above us. Our way led through a wide valley followed by a sandy desert. Frost covered the inside of our windows and mist rose in the distance whilst we continued travelling through 'emptiness', a vast expanse of land without human life and with very scant animal population.

After some time we reached an area which was slowly coming to life, where smoke rose from flat-roofed houses, and where a woman walked across a field carrying a wicker basket on her back full of yak dung which she would shape into cakes and dry in the sun for use as fuel at a later date. The sun shone brilliantly on the bare sculptured mountains in front of us, reflecting off a river where a lonely boat forged its way across. As we had been advised we all wore masks to protect ourselves from the dust.

Herds of yaks filed through what looked like a lunar landscape. The herdsmen drove their cattle each morning to fresh pastures, returning to their homesteads at night. Usually they rode ahead of their herd, looking out for new feeding grounds. Many black goats nibbled daintily on everything in sight, but we saw very few sheep.

It was half past nine when we reached the ferry, but we could not see the ferryman although many pilgrims had already assembled and were waiting to cross. They had climbed down from their trucks and moved about to keep warm. Their faces were quite remarkable, their skins weathered by the cold and winds. Every one of them was wrapped in their yak-skin coat, which was often edged with colourful borders. Heavy silver ornaments and silver studs hung from leather straps which dangled down from their ragged cummerbunds. Their headgear was very varied, from caps of any shape to fur hats and bonnets. Small children were precariously – almost hanging upside down – tucked into the roomy pouch of their mother's grubby coat. At last the ferryman arrived. The thin air almost took our breath away as we stepped out of our landrover. Returning to the warmth of our vehicle, we continued through a stony wilderness where a herd of yaks, followed by goats and sheep, nimbly picked their way between the stones.

Mountains after mountains stretched in front of us as far as our eyes could see, covered by small tufts of vegetation and a few tough

106

shrubs. The sky was brilliantly blue with just a wisp of snowy-white clouds hovering above a bare mountain, whilst a thin band of snow outlined the saddle of another one.

After crossing a bridge, we started to climb and reached farm-steads surrounded by fields where some trees struggled bravely to stay upright. Men and women were already hard at work in their fields. Further along, small rivers were covered with ice, where whole caravans of yaks belonging to nomads filed along on the opposite bank. Each of the mighty beasts carried a colourful saddlebag but only a few herdsmen accompanied the large herd. It made us wonder whether these were a small advance party of nomads looking for new pastures. A little bit further on we passed black tents belonging to them.

Farmers threshed their grain standing on a board harnessed to a patient yak, whilst the women performed the winnowing by hand. Fishermen had stepped outside their tent to admire a new boat which lay nearby. Small rodents appeared and disappeared into their little holes; these were *pykels*, mountain hares.

The road rose steeply to reach Dungula Pass, 17,400 feet high which was marked by a prayer flag, from where we had a splendid view. As we continued our journey we passed a shepherd sitting on the ground carefully stitching his carpetbag, which served him well to transport yak dung, wood and any other commodity. Later we crossed a stony high plateau where majestic snow-clad peaks rose up, forming a stark contrast to the rocky bareness of the remaining terrain. The scenery as we reached Shan La Pass (16,700 feet) was magnificent and awe-inspiring. It was midday by then and many people were on the move. On the other side of the pass we encountered another high plateau, where pilgrims lined the road-side waiting for the Panchen Lama to come. He lived in Beijing and nobody knew when (if at all) he would arrive, but these pilgrims had infinite patience.

At the first geyser we left the road and drove right into the complex to picnic between glasshouses in which peppers, tomatoes, potatoes and other vegetables grew. An enormous plastic solar dome overshadowed all else by its mere size. Nobody challenged us; in fact, apart from a family of puppies, we only saw one woman, washing her clothes. The water which gushed forth was boiling and smelled faintly of sulphur. There were more geysers as we drove on. When we traversed another stony wilderness we passed a mule grazing near an isolated tent and saw many saddlebags lined up neatly in a row along a nearby riverbank.

A clear-edged mountain group covered entirely with snow was framed at either side by rocky giants. Suddenly we saw brand new bicycles lying at the roadside. They belonged to a group of men engaged in building a canal close to a big community which spilled down a mountain slope. Terraced fields surrounded this village. Farmers were winnowing grain further along close to another village, which was festooned with prayer flags. When we neared it, a snow-covered mountain range towered up into the brilliantly blue sky; a bare rock in front of it looked like a giant elephant lying on its side. The mountains to either side were thrown up in most fantastic folds and convolutions, with rocks tinted an unusual shade of red.

Reaching a wide valley surrounded by bare rocky mountains, we approached Lhasa, where more prosperous-looking farms appeared and women and men stood at the wayside busily knitting, whilst others counted their beads as they walked along. Willow trees lined the banks and surrounded the farms.

It had taken eleven hours of a glorious drive to reach Guesthouse Number Two. Our young driver had astounded us with his skill. We had noticed that drivers appeared to be careful and none seemed to be aggressive. Back at the guesthouse, we changed our room to be near the inside bathroom now that our party had shrunk, since the outside bathroom had become extremely malodorous when the electricity failed and it was no longer possible to flush the toilet. It took us time and effort to make our delightful room attendant understand that we would like her to change the bed linen in which other members of our party had slept two days ago. When she had understood she willingly obliged, refusing a small gift.

It did not take us long to settle back into this friendly place where nobody locked anything and everybody seemed pleasant and helpful. The outsized thermos flasks were always readily refilled with boiling hot water, enabling us to make fresh tea in the lovely china cups with lids.

Our last day in Lhasa dawned. It was so bitterly cold that I could not feel my fingers and ice flowers adorned the windows, but the sky was again incredibly blue, transforming the cold wintry scene into a strange fairytale picture. After breakfast we drove out to Drepung Monastery, which was known as 'Mountain of Rice' since it lay heaped up on a cliff. Near the entrance stood the Temple of the Oracle, a small gold-roofed building. Many dogs enjoyed the sunshine, basking against the wall of the monastery. Once again we joined the throng of devout pilgrims who carried their rancid butter with them in jars to use to float the lighted tapers on the fat. Stonecutters sat on the steps, carving attractive lettering on slates.

Again we climbed from terrace to terrace, up through narrow lanes where monks and pilgrims lived in close company with their livestock. The view from the main terrace in front of the Great Hall was magnificent, with the sun shimmering on dazzling golden roofs, shining on the golden emblems and being reflected off the impressive golden towers standing to either side. An old monk took us inside, where banners, shields, bows and arrows and uniforms hung suspended high above from tall columns which held up the lofty roof. The walls were covered by lovely frescoes, and many beautiful statues of Bodhisattvas stood in niches around the big hall. Following the pilgrims, we climbed up to the Maitreya Hall, where the devout first rang an enormous bell which hung from a massive beam to announce their coming before they paid homage to the statue of the Maitreya. It was here that the funerary pagodas of the second, third and fourth Dalai Lama were kept. Funeral pagodas were not built at the Potola until the death of the fifth Dalai Lama.

Halls leading off the Great Hall contained frescoes and statues. There was almost too much to be able to take in all in on one visit. A narrow passage led us to a white *chorten*. Here I got really cross with our young Chinese national guide, who did not adhere to the rules of any Buddhist shrine to walk clockwise around it. When I mentioned it to her she just laughed, saying, 'I am not a Buddhist.'

The last place we visited was the Big Hall of the Monks, which was an enormous lofty place with red cushions on the floor where they congregated for their chants and prayer sessions.

Reluctantly we left to return to our guesthouse. By then it was midday and very warm and beautiful. Nothing ever happened between noon and 3 p.m., hence we rested, read and wrote cards.

In the afternoon we visited Norboling Park, which used to be the Dalai Lama's summer palace set in a big park. It was a relatively modern building of no particular significance apart from the Dalai Lama's private quarters, which had been opened to the public. His personal belongings, such as the hand-operated gramophone and also his tiled bathroom with a western toilet, were on show. In his mother's room hung a painting of the Dalai Lama and his brother. The throne in the Audience Hall and the 'Cycle of Life' depicted on its wall were very impressive.

From a special pavilion which stood tucked away behind a quiet courtyard where birds in small cages hung suspended from the walls chirped away, he used to watch theatre performances laid on for him in the grounds.

In one corner of the park was a small zoo where one section contained different species of deer in bleak sunken enclosures, whilst species of cats and small bears were confined to very tiny cages.

On our way back, we stopped once more to visit the Hall of Cultures which was actually a conference centre with a number of vast halls, rest rooms etc. built around a cool and pleasant courtyard with many plants.

I was glad to return to 'base' since I had not fully recovered and had hardly eaten anything and was beginning to feel weak, but I did make an effort to go into the dining hall at night. It was extremely crowded with large Chinese parties but the girls who served remained smiling, pleasant and helpful.

Once again electricity failed but fortunately we had packed our main luggage, which had preceded us to the airport in the morning, and had therefore only our hand luggage to contend with.

The nights were magic, with many stars and with the moon 'hanging upside down' in the inky sky. Having an early start next day, we soon retired to bed and I slept well until 5 a.m. It was cold but not frosty when we walked across to the dining hall, where we were the only party. The young girl who served us lay fast asleep on a settee beneath a picture of the Potola on the wall. She woke, smiled and looked after us cheerfully.

It took one hour and a half driving through the dark to reach the airport along the same road as we had come. Even in the semi-darkness we were able to see dimly the reflection of the saint in the lake. The airport was crowded, mostly with Army personnel and their families going on leave accompanied by mountains of luggage. Again we had to show our passports in lieu of identity cards. Having passed the security check, we waited in a large dreary hall from where I watched the sun rise over the mountains.

Finally we queued for a considerable time for the bus which took us out to the plane. We sat for two more hours inside the crowded plane on the tarmac since Chengdu was fogbound. It was very hot, stuffy and smelly. The stewardess handed us a lunch box and kiwi juice again. The plane was airborne at twelve o'clock and took us across beautiful mountains with a few settlements in wide valleys. In places the mountains exhibited a purple hue. Sand and more sand followed, until we could see clear green water and a few fields. Further along, mountains were sprinkled with snow but this scene gave way to an entirely snowbound landscape with frozen lakes. Looking down, we wondered how man or beast could survive in the forbidding, awesome wilderness. Clouds blotted everything out below us but parted again to show us rugged peaks covered by snow and ice. The stern panorama was breathtakingly beautiful but quite terrifying, with snow, glaciers, craggy mountain tops and ravines. It seemed as if we could see the mysterious footprints of the Abominable Snowman on the deadly white carpet below us.

Narrow valleys appeared, with green slopes falling down to fast-flowing streams, and we thought we could detect some houses. Craggy peaks struggled through deep blankets of snow, whilst clouds sailed majestically above it all in brilliant sunshine. For a short while all was obscured once more until the sky reverted to its brilliant blue again and we looked down on brown mountains sprinkled with snow with rivers forging their path between them. Rocky terrain with frozen lakes became visible before the sun blazed down on bare mountains with slopes covered by green trees but no sign of habitation, no path, no houses, then suddenly I saw a wide valley enclosed by lower mountains with rivers and a village surrounded by fields. A thick blanket of mist swam between rocky peaks; the sun had suddenly vanished, leaving a white sea below us. Finally we flew through dense fog and could barely see the wings of our plane as we descended slowly to land safely at Chengdu at one o'clock.

Tibet – enchantment or disappointment? I do not know. I had read so much before we came. I felt sad to have seen an old culture almost entirely destroyed, extinct – particularly Lhasa seemed to me a melancholic city. Perhaps one day we shall return, perhaps we shall be able to travel by road from Kathmandu and spend more time in this mysterious country.

Back in Chengdu, stepping out into the warm misty atmosphere with gentle rain falling down on us, Tibet with its crystal-clear air, its brilliant blue sky, its cold, cold nights, seemed quite unreal, like a dream. Gone was the stark barren landscape replaced by fertile well-irrigated land, where all work, however, was still carried out by hand. Water was drawn up from the irrigation canals by buckets, which were then slung at either end of a pole and carried across one shoulder to the field, where a giant ladle was used to water the crops. Men and women patiently hoed the fields. One old lady sat on a low stool carefully planting lettuce in a straight row. Sugar cane, radishes and cabbages were all sold at the roadside and meat hung suspended from large hooks from trees. The road into town ran straight between fields, with trees to either side. As always, we encountered hordes of bicycles; some even had trailers attached, whilst others carried deep wicker panniers to either side filled to the brim with all kind of things. As we approached the town, we passed farmsteads and finally blocks of high-rise flats.

The same guide who always seemed to be in a hurry had met us at the airport and once again regaled us with a running commentary about the buildings on either side of the wide avenue leading into the city. A good deal of construction was in progress, including one building scheduled to serve as an American Embassy. Since 15th October – when diplomatic relations between China and the USA had been re-established – a hotel was used in its place. Laundry festooned each window in the high-rise blocks of flats, and trick-shaws mingled with the vast numbers of bicycles as well as trolley buses. On our way to the central square, which was dominated by a statue of Chairman Mao, we passed the new stadium. Strange to relate, our guide had no comment to make about Mao. Turning off the broad road took us into narrow lanes of the old town where we found stores selling every conceivable merchandise; we saw book-stores, free markets, bazaars and wooden two-storey buildings. Again, time had come to have a meal and we returned to the same place with the trailing chrysanthemums where we had fared badly last time. However, a special feast had been laid on for us to make up for our previous meal.

We drove out into a suburb to visit a silk embroidery factory. In the showroom, we admired the finished articles, ranging from simple embroidered scarves and ties to most elaborate pictures, some of which were double-sided with different designs on either side. Upstairs in the workrooms we were aghast at the primitive conditions these young girls worked under. These were just 'concrete boxes' with poor light from a naked electric bulb where they sat hunched over frames, stitching away at the most intricate and exquisite designs. Although we stood quite close to watch, we still do not know how on earth they managed to produce two different pictures on two side simultaneously. Some of the pieces took two years to complete. To see an exhibition of paintings, we crossed the peaceful Water Garden and bought a picture, not a traditional one but painted in 'naïve' style. From here we were taken to a brocade factory but work had stopped for the day. According to our guide, electricity had failed but we had a suspicion that it was done to halt production since too much merchandise was available. Again we were amazed at the primitive conditions which prevailed and looked in astonishment at the old-fashioned handlooms.

It was a melancholic November day when we drove back to the Jing Jiang Hotel, seeing many bicycles with special bamboo seats for children, both in front and at the back. The hotel was an imposing building standing in tranquil gardens, with large shopping arcades on the ground floor and enormous restaurants (serving indifferent food). The toilets amused us since they had 'stable doors' just covering the midriff of the unsuspecting user. The hotel was an interesting place to stay since it appeared to be the meeting point for independent travellers, with a continuous stream of people coming and going, arriving or arranging for their departure. The single travellers formed a 'fraternity' and often joined up for part of the way or just for a meal.

Finally we retired to 'an upgraded room', which meant we had a television and a refrigerator, neither of which we used, but we did appreciate the fact that there were no insects sharing the accommodation with us. It was still dark at eight o'clock in the morning when we left in a mini-coach for the station. Two Swedish travellers whose taxi had not arrived, which was not an unusual occurrence and constituted the hazard of travelling independently, were getting anxious, hence we offered them a lift. It was easy to talk to the younger of the two, who sat next to me. He had travelled through China with his sister for some time. She was a student of agriculture at Uppsala whilst he had just finished high school and hoped to follow her to the same course at university. They had parted company – she had gone to Tibet and Nepal – but they had planned to meet up for Christmas in Hong Kong. He had just received a letter from his parents and remarked rather wistfully: 'It is good to know all is well at home'. Since our party was booked in 'soft seats' on the train and the Swedes had tickets in the 'hard seat' compartment, where they would have to sit up on hard wooden seats all night, we parted company at the station. Our 'soft seat' meant that we had a compartment with four berths and travelled in comfort.

The train passed through countryside shrouded in mist, past field after neat field where green vegetables were grown. Homesteads stood nearby, some tenements rose close to the rail track, and canals ran straight as a die through the countryside. Rice paddies, bamboo groves and sugarcane plantations became dimly visible through the mist, and we saw ducks and black pigs; a man stood on a board harnessed to a waterbuffalo ploughing his field. Terraces were planted with tea. The whole landscape looked very neat and tidy and, as we had remarked before, all work was done by hand. Little houses with convex red tiles looked very attractive.

At eleven o'clock we arrived at Emoi station, where we left the train to drive through the countryside in warm sunshine. The mist had gone. For a short while we mingled with the crowd in the free market and looked around us. Pigs lashed to a cart were trundled along for sale, rushes used to thatch roofs lay ready in bundles to be purchased, freshly slaughtered meat hung on trees, the medicine man sat on the ground dispensing his potions. On many stalls cooks using bamboo cooking containers had started to prepare food which looked and smelled most enticing. A big paper wheel decorated in gay colours was carried at the head of a procession. This signified the opening of a new business. People stared at us, some were delighted when we took photographs and posed happily, others shied away. A man sitting beneath a tree which bore a mirror was being shaved, in fact he was being relieved of all his hair.

Leshan

The time had come to continue our journey by road past terraced fields and haystacks. We saw a big bamboo waterwheel at the side of the river, and for the first time we encountered a plantation of lovely maple trees. There were not many banana groves along our way. Factory chimneys belonging to brickworks appeared and we passed the kilns and also lime kilns. As we entered Leshan children

114

were just coming home from school. This bustling little town lies on the bank of the broad River Min and had been closed to tourists until 1979. The local population seemed extremely friendly, smiled easily and appeared very outgoing, standing in groups chatting or walking along knitting and talking to their companions.

Accommodation had been booked in the one and only hotel, which stood at the end of the town overlooking the river. Our room was typically Chinese, with a television which had been lovingly hidden beneath a red velvet cover. The hotel was being extended, a new wing was being added with lifts and all modern comforts, but at the time we visited we had to negotiate a builder's yard and find our way precariously over planks, avoiding cables and other pitfalls, to reach our room. The eating hall and a small shop lay tucked behind the new wing. As I said before, all work was done by hand; road repairs were carried out by pickaxe, shovel and crowbar. Big red granite blocks were lifted in a cradle fashioned from rope by six men who chanted in unison as they trotted along shouldering their massive load. Girls smilingly carried heavy burdens in baskets on their backs or transported them suspended from poles across their shoulders.

We went out to buy a bottle of white wine. The shops appeared well stocked. All shopkeepers slept at the back of their open fronted shacks. A quilt maker carried on his trade in the middle of town. This was quite fascinating and we stopped to watch, realising that we were being watched in turn by most of the local inhabitants. On our way back to join our group for a trip across the River Min to see the Big Buddha, the Dafu, hewn out of the red cliff, we saw that everybody used rag mops to clean the floors.

The Dafu stands 390 feet high and was begun in 713 by a Buddhist monk by the name of Haitong in the hope that the Buddha's watchful eye would subdue the swift current of the confluent of three rivers and protect the boatmen. Dafu did help since the surplus of the rock from the sculpting filled the hollow at the foot of the cliff which had sucked so many to their certain death before.

The boat was full, with many Chinese and a few groups of minorities in their colourful costumes with very distinctive features. Looking back from the boat as we crossed the wide river, we realised the size of Leshan and also saw that part of it was modern, but most of it was old with beautiful tiled roofs and decorative gables. As we neared the red cliffs of Jai Ding we recognised Hindu gods and little genies carved out of the rock. Steps and tunnels stood out quite clearly, with many people climbing like ants up them. Suddenly we came face to face with the Buddha himself, who stood in a recess, feet firmly planted on the rock and looking sternly straight ahead. Tourists were scrambling over his feet or standing on them in groups to be photographed. Our boat stood still in midstream for quite a while so that we could watch the spectacle and observe the crafts around us before we anchored some miles downstream. Some of us elected to follow our local guide to climb up through bamboo forests to the top of the cliff. Soon we lost count of the number of steps which led up but we were not alone since many people were on their way up or down. At almost every turning point of the twisting path with its many stairs stood a stall selling cheap trinkets, fruit, nuts or soft drinks. Apart from these there were also many photographers, complete with horses and the costumes of the minorities, touting for business, and also rifle ranges. Zhina bought mandarins, ashanti nuts and tried her hand at rifle shooting, and in the end could not resist the temptation to purchase trinkets for herself and for presents. The whole atmosphere of this path was akin to a fair or an amusement arcade extending up the side of the cliff. Finally we visited some temples in which a few poorly clad monks were engaged in sweeping the forecourt. A mat lay on the ground in front of the Buddha image and many of the young Chinese visitors paid homage, kneeling down on it.

A coach with the rest of our party stood waiting to take us back to the boat.

At the hotel we had persuaded a kind member of the staff to put our bottle of white Chinese wine into the refrigerator for our evening meal. It was quite palatable and we therefore decided to buy some more for our forthcoming train journey. It was fun to walk back into town, popping into one little shop after another in search of the same wine. In the end we had to compromise after some complicated negotiations, helped by a young man who was very anxious to practise his English and then walked back with us, telling us that he was a tax collector and had taught himself English from books and the radio. His English was limited but we parted best of friends. Back at the hotel we met a young American, passing each other on a plank, who had travelled on his own and thought China most exciting. He was a minister's son. All the travellers we met were anxious to see and to learn about China; they were keen young people, none of them were drop-outs.

One thing disturbed me during our short stay, namely the fact that many people in Leshan seemed to be suffering with eye disease, but I had no opportunity to find out more.

When we left next day on a grey and misty morning, the town was already bustling with life. On our way back to Emoi station we stopped at a silk factory but this (like the brocade factory) was also not working because of lack of electricity and all the workforce had been given a 'day of rest'. We boarded the same train going south on which we had travelled from Chengdu the day before, to continue our journey to Kunming. Again we had the privilege of using 'soft beds'. The journey was lovely, taking us along a wide river which had been dammed further along for a big electricity plant. Logs floated down it. The line had only been recently built and went through 340 tunnels and many picturesque gorges. The sky was blue again, the earth red. Terraces climbed up steep inclines in narrow valleys, villages looked neat and tidy, graveyards appeared from to time to time seemingly in nowhere, and snow-capped mountains towered above the rural scene. Some of the houses along the way had bamboo matting as walls. Our train stopped now and again at small stations. Most of the population belonged to one or the other of the many minorities and were extremely friendly. One man asked us: 'England? London? Hampstead?'

As our journey continued we saw maize hung up beneath the eaves to dry. The countryside was green and lush, water cascaded down the sides of the mountains and was channelled into conduits to irrigate the fields. Many people were busily working on the land, others walked along the railway tracks or on the road.

A friendly staff served lunch in the dining car and, surprisingly, hot food was really hot, which seemed a great rarity in China. After lunch we left the picturesque gorges behind and travelled on through hilly, well-irrigated countryside with the occasional snow-capped peak still visible. Again we were impressed how well-cultivated the land was and how neat it looked with its fields and rice paddies and many goats. The setting sun reflected warmly on the red soil and work continued until all daylight had gone.

In our journey we only saw one Chinese lady smartly dressed. She was on the train and looked well-groomed and elegant in a smart grey dress and high boots.

I slept fitfully until dawn broke, when we were still travelling through rich countryside with well-cultivated fields where crops were rotated to the maximum efficiency. Fir trees with their deep green branches contrasted with the red earth. People were already at work, out in the fields and firing a kiln.

Breakfast was Chinese-style: hot milk, hard-boiled eggs, small pieces of cold meat, jam sandwiches, noodle soup and tea. Whilst having our first meal of the day we were passing through open countryside along a wide river where the kaleidoscope of vegetables amazed us.

Kunming

After 9 a.m. we arrived in Kunming, 'City of Eternal Spring', where a female railway guard directed the alighting passengers using a megaphone. Our group waited in the big square outside the station for our local guide and soon we were on our way through this thriving city where trees with flowers dripping honey lined the streets which took us to the Grenhill Park Hotel, opposite the big park of the same name. This was an extremely comfortable, well-run hotel which was geared to receive VIPs, and we were proudly told that Henry Kissinger and his wife had stayed here in Suite 206 recently.

Kunming is the capital of Yunnan, one of the most southerly provinces of China. Of the 54 minorities who live in China, 23 are found in Yunnan.

Once settled in our pleasant room and having ascertained that hot water was restricted to certain hours, we walked out into the sunny day, smiling at the notice 'No Spitting, no Littering'. Passing a parking lot for bicycles, we saw that they all carried licensed number plates and again most of them were fitted with bamboo seats for children. Men played ludo or enjoyed a game of mah-jong along the pavement, whilst we joined a children's game in which we spun a hand around a circle painted on a board showing various animals around its periphery. One man supervised the game, whilst his partner made replicas of the animal depicted out of spun sugar.

118

Each player received the spun sugar animal corresponding to the one the hand had pointed to when it came to rest.

Having had our game, we joined the many families in the big park with its numerous trees and flowering shrubs, its pleasure gardens, ponds with boats, children's playgrounds, bridges over streams, teahouses and little shops. A large number of minorities in their colourful dress enjoyed this lovely day, making this place even more interesting for us. It was sad to see a group of old ladies with crippled feet who had come from a home to listen to a concert specially performed for them. They all were dressed alike in blue trousers and Mao jackets. Young women sat in the sun busily knitting whilst fathers looked after the little ones.

After lunch we drove to the north of this active, busy town, passing through the narrow lanes between little houses and past the oldest temple in the ancient quarters. Smoke billowed forth from the numerous eating places and from many shops. The old houses had unusually shaped roofs and once again we were amazed at the large quantity of things people were able to cram on their small balconies. Outside town lay fields again, and grain had been strewn on the road, waiting for traffic to do the threshing. Small carts were harnessed to small horses which are a special mountain breed found only in Yunnan. Our goal was the Golden Temple, where we joined the crowd of local families and followed them through three elaborate gates guarded by mystical beasts which resembled unicorns. Sun streamed through the trees which surrounded the temple as we climbed up the marble steps past a fierce stone lion standing to either side. Two small children played happily on these ferocious-looking beasts. The little temple stood on a marble terrace, the pillars were cast of bronze, the beams of gilded wood, whilst the roof with its delightful figures on each corner was covered by copper scales which gleamed in the brilliant sunlight like pure gold. A Han prostrated himself in front of the Buddha as we watched silently. Incense burnt in the temple, permeating it with its heady scent. Lovely stone carvings of garlands of plants and beasts adorned the graceful building. The oldest known camellia tree, planted four hundred years ago, stood beneath an ancient iron flag. A wishing well with a dolphin, jaws wide open, attracted big crowds. As we strolled on we found an archway which led into a well-tended garden where pot plants were arranged around the base of trees and shrubs. Continuing through pine woods uphill brought us to the bell tower, which we ascended to see the big bell and to admire the panorama of Kunming City across the wooded hill. An art exhibition had been mounted on the ground floor and once again we bought a picture; this time a portrait of a minority girl in her traditional costume.

Back in town, we drove through busy streets where we got off to stroll about on our own, poking into a 'store' which was full of cheap goods, walking through lively streets lined by many stalls, all selling clothes. Finally we stopped at the Flower and Bird Market, which as the name implies sold birds, bulbs, plants and cut flowers. Although it was only small, trade was extremely brisk. An old lady guarded the bicycles which had been neatly parked in an allotted space near by. The inevitable food stall was busy as usual.

Later that evening we were taken to the Kunming Hotel to see a film about the province of Yunnan. The hotel was enormous and was being partly rebuilt. The hall where the film was shown was huge and freezing cold. Apart from our small party there were only about a dozen tourists in this cavernous place. Unfortunately it was a very poor film in every respect.

Yet another misty morning greeted us when we set off to drive through town (south this time) to visit the Stone Forest. People were performing their traditional exercises everywhere in a most distinct and deliberate manner, without hurry, without any awareness of life around them. Outside the hotel sat a group of Sani ladies (one of the minorities of the province) in their bright embroidered costumes, offering colourful little purses for sale. Bicyclists used their special tracks, riding along with their little ones tied to their backs, almost entirely obscured by blankets. Kunming struck us as a clean town with a profusion of flowers: black-eyed Susan, zinnias, dahlias and hydrangeas added colour to the busy scene.

In China, as it was in Russia, all housing was State-owned, for which everybody paid 8% of their salary (I think it was 5% in the USSR). In Kunming there were very few private cars, if any at all.

Out of town we saw men and women patiently hoeing their fields, irrigating their vegetable patches, carrying their cabbages and cauliflowers to market on wooden trays which looked like large replicas of the copper pans used formerly on weighing scales. Yunnan is a very fertile province, with orchards of pears, peaches, plums and apples and super vegetables of every kind.

Women sat on the ground carefully picking corn kernels off the cob one by one by hand. A market along the road sold only crude furniture, all made in exactly the same style and colour. Further along, big panniers specially made for bicycles were offered for sale. From time to time we passed villages, in some of which a tiered pagoda rose over the roofs of the little houses.

Our road ascended between fir and eucalyptus trees to reach a ridge and continued parallel to a narrow-gauge rail track. This was the French-Sino Railway originally built by the French to connect China with Vietnam, which lies close by. It had been finished in 1902 but of course these days it terminates at the border.

Our coach stopped at a guesthouse above a large man-made lake where we were offered tea or a soft drink and as many walnuts as we could or wished to eat. We had to crack them ourselves in a rather ingenious way: the nut was placed snugly into a hollow which had been gouged out from a thick piece of wood and hit with a small wooden mallet. This simple device actually worked very well. Having had our fill, we continued down rugged mountains into a wide fertile valley, passing through a large village where a hydro-electric plant dominated the scene. Some of the houses were thatched, whilst others had been built of mud bricks reinforced by straw. The road rose again at the end of the valley and we looked down on a bare stretch with some murky ponds, whilst terraced fields climbed up the steep incline above us. In the villages, we saw pumpkins drying on shelves above doorways and corn on the cob strung up below the eaves, whilst peppers lay on flat roofs or on the ground to dry. Haystacks stood in the fields. Before we entered a narrow gorge with lush vegetation we passed many ponds. The Army was on the move, which slowed down our progress in this narrow confine. Men and women alike were busily quarrying and collecting gravel along the roadside. Isolated graves stood amid the high grass on the mountainside along the narrow gorge which finally opened up into a landscape of fields on either side of a tranquil river, where white lime kilns looked picturesque along its banks. The road climbed up once again leaving the river glistening in the sun sneaking through rich earth below us. A herd of buffaloes looked quite precarious grazing on the steep slopes. We had reached the highest point of our journey and followed a winding road with trees to either side which were well limed, and past lakes through a very fertile high plateau where lotus flowers were specially grown in paddies. Every village seemed to have a pond as its central point. Finally we arrived at the hotel in the Stone Forest.

Some 270 million years ago a thick limestone layer formed at the bottom of the sea. When this was thrust up to become land, rain water seeped through the rock and opened up the sharp fissures which remained visible in the Stone Forest. It covered an area of 27,000 hectares but only 80 were accessible. From the distance these grey pinnacles set amongst green trees looked exactly like a sinister forest. The paths were well marked and led through narrow gullies and up steps cut into the rock to clearings, many of which were occupied by the inevitable photographer with horses and an array of tribal costumes. The stones were weirdly shaped: there were groups resembling linen folds, a giant crocodile opened its jaws wide, a pair of doves kissed lovingly and a perfect elephant stood clearly silhouetted high above. A castle reached high up to the sky and we also came across more well-defined statues of animals.

Before we left we strolled down to the lake, where Sanis had put up their stalls displaying purses, scarves, aprons etc. They are a subgroup of the Yi tribe and have their own language, their own script, believe in animalism and continue to practise both polygamy and polyandry.

When we drove back at the end of the day, people were still working in the fields. The delightful carts drawn by the little horses jingled gaily with their bells as they trotted along serving as taxis. Work was still proceeding at some building sites within the city when we got back after six o'clock. Big hoardings advertising sundry wares always depicted demure European damsels; we never saw one with a Chinese face.

Yet another misty morning greeted us when we journeyed west of town to visit the Western Mountains. The road rose steeply through beautiful pine forests looking down on Lake Dian Chi, the sixth largest inland lake in China, graced by many boats and numerous fishing nets. Beginning our climb, we passed through the Dragon Gate, a stone arch which brought us face to face with three enormous plaster gods guarding the mountain. One had three eyes, whilst the other two held mirrors in their hands to ward off the evil spirits. Following all the other tourists along the narrow path above the lake, we climbed up many steps to visit the caves which one monk had patiently decorated with wall paintings. It had taken him seventy-five years to complete and when he reached the end of his life's work the tip of the paintbrush fell off in the last cave. He was so distraught that he threw himself over the cliff in his disappointment. There were four caves, all rather crude and garish to our eyes. The blue God of Water and the red God of Fire guarded the entrance. In one of the caves stood the four heavenly guardians: the God of Disaster and Fire, the God of Protection and Rain, the God of Change and Thunder and the God of Light and Wind. In another one stood a goddess symbolising fertility. The last cave contained the sea and Buddha's disciples.

The main bulk of the tourists returned the same way as we had come but a few intrepid folk went on and we joined them. The number markedly declined as the path became steeper and stonier, crossing paths which led down. We bravely soldiered on when we were joined by a young American chemist from California who worked for the well-known firm of Syntex. He was on his own; having saved up his holiday from the previous year, he was spending two months exploring China. Before he had embarked on this adventure he had tried to learn the rudiments of Chinese, but travelling on one's own becomes lonely and sightseeing sterile. Since nothing can disguise the fact that we are 'foreigners', this creates an easy bond between fellow Caucasians and contact is usually quickly established.

Leaving the trees behind, we laboured up through alpine flora, finding gentian growing, and observed strange rock formations. It was pleasant to see and hear birds again, which we had missed since returning from Tibet. Finally our path petered out and we took a trail pointing downhill. First we passed three young Chinese sitting amongst the shrubs deeply engrossed in a game of dice. They are known as great gamblers. Then we passed two maidens, but they shied away from us when they realised that we wanted to take a photograph of them in their splendid colourful costume. Finally we met the young Swedish boy whom we had given a lift in Leshan coming up the slope. It did not even seem strange to meet again up on the Western Mountains. He was able to point us in the right direction and we finally reached our mini-coach to set off for our way to the lake, stopping twice to visit two temples from the Yuan period: Huatins and Taihua. Both stood in tranquil gardens with still waters in their forecourts and both were Zen temples. The Heavenly General faced Buddha in the main temple, which represented the Heavenly Palace. They believe in the Trinity of the

Buddha of the Present, the Buddha of the Past and the Buddha to Come. Buddha in the Zen temple always sits on the lotus blossom, which although it grows in mud is pure. This symbolises man, who lives in the mud of suffering but can rise above it by giving up all worldly trappings to become pure like the lotus. Only Lamaism, as in Tibet, Ladakh, Nepal and Bhutan, has a human representation. Our guide informed us that each of Buddha's fingers is of specific significance, denoting love, hate etc.

But enough of Buddhism, which I find very involved and complicated. Let us return to the Western Mountains and Lake Dian Chi, first of all to the two Zen temples, in one of which stood five hundred Arhat clay figures representing Buddha's five hundred disciples. The story has it that Buddha sat under the pipal tree preaching, but only a few disciples were present, when suddenly five hundred bats descended from the tree to listen to his words. In their eagerness they bent down too near the fire and fell into it. Immensely moved, Buddha transformed them by reincarnation into his five hundred disciples. These figures were life-size and superbly realistic depicting fat jolly men, thin sad ones, some were rich, others poor. A merchant with his wares stood next to a farmer seated on his ass. Some of the statues were quite grotesque, such as one with an elongated arm. I believe that the best of these five hundred Arhat are to be found in the Bamboo Temple to the north of Kunming, attributed to the same sculptor, Li Guang from Sichuan. Alas, we never saw that temple.

Leaving all temples behind, we spent the next few hours cruising on the lake and looking up to the Western Mountains with their thickly wooded slopes, which are also known as 'The Sleeping Beauty', and with some imagination we were able to visualise a reclining woman whose tresses floated down into the blue waters of Dian Chi. The boats on this lake looked like sinister pirate craft with their square sails, one or two or three hoisted into the air. Some carried heavy cargoes of gravel, whilst on others fishermen were pulling in their nets. Laundry fluttered in the breeze, suspended between two masts. As we neared the shore a speedboat shattered the tranquil scene.

On our way back to town we were caught up in a traffic jam. As there were few railway lines, everything was transported by road. Apart from the heavy lorries, the Army seemed to be once more on the move. Near Kunming outcrops of craggy mountains formed a dramatic background to the lush green fields.

Before reaching our hotel we stopped to visit the free market and also searched for a mosque. In the 13th century the Mongols had taken the town. When Marco Polo visited Kunming he was amazed to find that 'some worshipped Mohammet, others idols and some were Christians (Nestorians as in the South of India).' We did not find the mosque since it had been razed to the ground. The Islamic population had shrunk; there were not many left to worship, and in fact we saw no mosque at all.

Most of the people in the busy market were either Han Chinese or one of the many minorities, and the majority were very friendly, with a ready smile. Large selections of fresh vegetables, freshly killed meat and enormous mountains of bean curd were displayed for sale.

Back at the hotel we met the young American chemist in our dining room. He shared a room with another traveller in a special block belonging to our hotel, standing well-hidden at the back. Most of the large hotels had some kind of dormitory accommodation with communal washrooms and showers where guests could just book the bed and take potluck with whom they shared. He had come alone to have a meal and was asked to share a table with an English woman on her own who forthwith clung to him. In the meantime – before she appeared on the scene – we had arranged to visit the night market together. It was impossible to shake her off. She never stopped talking and told us that she lived in Hong Kong, where she taught English, which was very lucrative, that she was divorced and had two grown-up children. Eighteen months ago she had remarried a drummer and they had set out to visit India, where he had fallen ill. She had sent him back to his parents in England and was now on her own. For a short while I managed to escape from her and wandered between the stalls with the American, who wanted to buy some provisions for a long journey which he had planned to start the next day. At one stall he was given the wrong change; since he was conversant with Chinese, he stood firm and without much ado received the correct sum, whilst I (presumably the stallholder thought we were travelling together) was presented with a hard-boiled egg. No doubt this was a practical way to say 'sorry' without losing face. There was little else to see since we had come too late. This market was primarily for the local population to buy their food and also to eat cheaply in the open, where food was speedily cooked over fierce charcoal fires.

In vain did we try to find somewhere to have coffee, soft drinks or an ice-cream. Everything lay in darkness, firmly closed. There was nothing else for us to do but walk back to our hotel and wish our two companions 'safe journey' as we parted company.

Rain woke us next morning, when we were told that the plane scheduled to take us to Guangzhou (Canton) was delayed. We had to wait to be issued with luncheon boxes before we were taken to the Municipal Museum, where we spent an enjoyable hour seeing a charming exhibition of the twenty-three minorities of Yunnan which showed costumes, jewellery, crafts and utensils, demonstrating their customs and rituals, festivals etc.

When we arrived at the airport we found that there was a further delay. Only two planes sat forlorn on the tarmac, nothing at all happened, inactivity prevailed. In contrast to the emptiness outside on the airfield, the airport was crowded with an interesting collection of passengers. A French party had been waiting for twenty-four hours, a party of Austrian businessmen had calmly settled down to play cards. Most of the fraternity of independent travellers were Scandinavians. A charming Swede, who lived in Denmark and was a freelance theatre costume designer, told us that he had worked hard for years, never taking a holiday, until he suddenly felt that he had come to a standstill. He needed to refresh himself and revitalise in order to remain creative. To do this he had decided to take a few months off from his work and travel the Orient. To us he appeared very much alive and we found him stimulating to talk to. He had joined up with a retired Danish teacher and they hoped to get their plane in time to pick up a boat to take them down the Yangtze River.

Having shared our lunch boxes with the Swede and his companion, we finally took off after a four-and-a-half-hour wait. Casting a last glance on the neat vegetable plots, the canals, straight roads and pink villages, we left Yunnan and flew across a lake near Nanning, which is the capital of the autonomous region of Guangxi. We looked down on a winding river, ponds and fields. Strange volcanic peaks were followed by a range of low hills. Buffaloes stood near a waterhole. At 4 p.m. we landed at Anning, where we waited in the warm and humid sparse transit lounge. Wet face flannels and tepid tea were offered to us to refresh ourselves. When we continued we flew over flat fertile countryside with many lakes and strangely shaped outcrops of rocks before rising high above the clouds. Fifty minutes later, descending over even ground we landed at Guangzhou.

Unfortunately we saw little of this bustling town. Its big airport, exhibiting numerous hoardings advertising luxury hotels, modern stores, modern machinery etc. seemed positively to ooze an atmosphere of prosperity. A waiting coach swept us through the city amongst the throng of dense traffic. Tall modern buildings towered above old staid houses with their now so familiar balconies crammed to overflowing with a large variety of goods. A bridge across the broad Pearl River took us to Shamian Island, which used to be the British and French Concession. Our last night in China was spent in the most sumptuous hotel I have ever come across. A waterfall cascaded from a great height down to the ground in the main hall, to be caught in a pool surrounded by lush vegetation and with a pavilion poised romantically on a rock. Our meal – sorry to say – was meagre and indifferently served.

When we had first arrived we had toured around the various shops and changed our remaining yuans in the busy hotel bank before dinner, as advised by our guide, which we regretted afterwards since we were still hungry when we strolled out into the warm dark night along the canal, which was a true lovers' lane. Crossing the bridge brought us into a poor district with humble, crumbling dwellings and murky lanes full of decaying garbage. Pools of light issued from the numerous eating houses and fell on uneven pavements, where we picked our way carefully between rough low tables at which people sat on equally low benches eating out of small bowls. Poor people settled down for the night along the waterfront. Our intention had been to describe a circle and return to the island via the second bridge. This, however, was under repair and since there was no footpath available, only a very busy road, we retraced out steps to cross the first bridge again and walked along the peaceful wide roads of the former Concessions. Looking up, we saw the quiet gracious buildings which used to house the British and French in the last century. Some of these patrician buildings had been converted into rooming houses but most of them were still well-kept and served as offices or schools. Shady trees lined the streets.

Morning started early in Guangzhou; people were bustling about like millions of busy little ants. Fathers were taking their little ones to nurseries and schools. The inevitable bicycles with licence plates stood neatly parked in official parking lots. Looking across the city from our hotel window high above, we noticed brilliant splashes of bougainvillaea and hibiscus in full bloom, as well as other shrubs and various kinds of flowering trees. A woman in a white wide-brimmed hat swept the street. Laundry which seemed never absent from any scene, fluttered between trees.

On our drive to the railway station we noticed that vegetable plots had given way to high-rise blocks. Our train to Hong Kong was waiting as we arrived. It was furnished with adjustable seats, giving us an opportunity to watch the scenery in front and at the back. A trolley came trundling through the open carriage with tea and other beverages.

The journey took us through lush countryside where palm trees flourished and gardens were ablaze with flowers. Once again we were impressed by the intense cultivation. Corn was being cut by a foot-operated machine and tied by hand into neat bundles to be stacked in orderly fashion. Young papayas, mangoes and oranges grew here and oleander bushes were in full bloom. Waterbuffaloes lumbered along, pulling or carrying heavy loads. Building was done using bamboo trunks slung together to form scaffolding, window frames were constructed on site.

It was yet another grey, dull, misty day when we passed a mining village and crossed a wide river carrying many barges. The vegetable plots were small since this made it easier to rotate the crops. Suddenly we saw the first tractor, but threshed grain was still being transported in baskets suspended at the ends of a pole across one shoulder (or both). A few graves clustered together in between fields, before we passed slowly through the last town in China, with a preponderance of modern high-rise buildings. At this point all toilets throughout the train were firmly locked until we had crossed the frontier, where we encountered more modern buildings towering high into the sky but also saw shacks huddled in between them.

The day remained grey and wet as we continued by road. The first double-decker bus came into view when we approached the harbour of Hong Kong. Mist shrouded the boats as well as the famous Peak. Finally we arrived at the Lee Garden Hotel, which stands in the north of the island. A note from our New Zealand friends whom we had met on our first trip to China in 1981 and had not seen since then – awaited us. They had lived in Hong Kong for the past fourteen years, where he lectured in Asiatic Science at the University and where she was University Librarian. Before we strolled around this vibrant, vital city with its many people and its many shops we arranged to meet them for an evening meal. It was an entirely different world from the China we had just left. People were slender, not squat, well-groomed and extremely smartly dressed.

Brian told us later when we met for a hilarious and stimulating evening when conversation never flagged, that until a short time ago the Hong Kongese had identified themselves with China; only quite recently had they developed their own quite unique style. He mostly taught women and found them intelligent and bright; both our friends felt that they related much more easier to the East than to the West.

Hong Kong comes positively to life at night, with all districts ablaze with coloured lights; shops are open, business is brisk, eating houses are full and people are about until the small hours.

Next morning we wandered out to pick up a bus to take us to Stanley Market, in the bay of the same name which lies in the south of the island. It was interesting to travel right across to see the fantastic amount of building in progress, to skirt the wooded Peak, to look down on the sea. Stanley Market had been originally opened for British soldiers who had little money to spend. It was full of reasonably priced merchandise and we had a lovely time buying odds and ends.

Before we left for the airport we rested in our room. Hong Kong airport seemed to lie almost in the centre of town. Our departure was delayed but we made up for lost time, arriving at Gatwick earlier than we were due. The plane had stopped at Dubai, which we found markedly changed; the shops looked smarter and the service was more attentive than in the past.

Full of vivid impressions, we arrived home to remember all we had seen and experienced and think about a life so very different from our own.

THE ART OF MAKING HAPPY

Sri-Lanka or Serendip

February 1986

Dawn was breaking over the island as we descended through a turbulent sky. Discreet lights appeared and a boat became clearly visible in the sea below before we flew across lagoons and inland over lush countryside.

Our flight from Heathrow had been slightly delayed and it was midday by the time we rose into a heavy sky. A tepid sun filtered through the clouds onto the countryside blanketed in snow. But soon we travelled in perfect sunshine high above a white carpet of clouds until we landed smoothly at Zurich, to find ourselves back in winter again, with snowflakes dancing around our stationary plane. Skimming over the wintry scene, we rose again above the clouds to continue in brilliant sunshine. From time to time mountain tops appeared to pop out of the sea of white clouds or a plane forged its path ahead below us, leaving a long silver trail behind. Another plane suddenly soared above us when a pink line appeared at the top of the clouds, heralding the approaching dusk.

Dubai greeted us with its many twinkling lights when we touched down, but we barely had time to stretch our legs in this nowadays very sophisticated airport before we were recalled for the final lap of our journey.

When we left the airport in Negombo we stepped straight from winter into the tropics since a dense forest of palm trees surrounded us. Passing the entrance to the lagoons, we followed the old Dutch Canal through part of Negombo. Hordes of prim-looking young women, each clutching a small parcel, streamed out of the station and were joined by more maidens emerging from small houses

131

tucked amongst the palm trees; probably they were all on their way to work in a nearby factory, carrying their lunch with them.

On our way to Brown Beach Hotel, where we were to rest on our first day, we passed many Catholic churches and Catholic shrines. The population had been converted to Catholicism by the Portuguese in the 15th century. Many had adopted Portuguese names such as Da Silva and Perera and had remained faithful to their new faith.

True to its name, Brown Beach Hotel stood on the beach, which was pure sand which stretched for miles. Fishermen, black as in the south of India and known as *karava*, were out at sea in their dugout outrigger canoes, called *oruva*. Their front sails were large and square, with a small triangular one hoisted behind.

After a splendid barbecue dinner, we walked along the road past closed hotels on the seaward side and numerous tourist shops on the other side – waiting in vain for trade. One young man told us: 'Mrs Thatcher is signing off'; he had heard the news of a forthcoming election on the radio and this was his interpretation.

Next morning it was bliss to have an early morning swim in the warm Indian Ocean since in the morning the sea was relatively calm; by the evening it had become rough and big rollers threatened to knock me about.

Our sightseeing started by exploring Negombo, where we visited a number of singularly uninspiring Roman Catholic churches, beginning with St Sebastian, the largest on the island, built in 1874–1922. It was a Jesuit church with few pews and open confessionals. Outside stood two bells; a new one had just been delivered, cast in India. The church stood on a large sand-covered courtyard surrounded by small houses, one of which served as a Sunday school. Cows had settled comfortably in a shady corner. The next visit was to an equally nondescript church, the Church of Beatitude. It seemed strange that all figures and painting showed only white-skinned saints.

A visit to the remains of the Dutch Fort followed, which formed the entrance to a prison where six hundred prisoners were kept. Our guide told us that there were fifteen prisons in all on the island. It seemed a somewhat strange introduction to a place so full of history to commence with inconsequential sights and unimportant information; however, we were prepared at this point to reserve judgement.

The next place we were taken to was the fishing harbour, where we spent a short time looking at the catamarans, which were cleverly constructed by slinging two trunks together to form a platform. Boatmen knelt on this, using short rudders or poles in shallow water, whilst the *oruvas* served in deeper water and out in the open sea. Young men usually greeted us with the familiar 'Good morning, mother' because of our greying hair.

The fish market, which we saw next, was not bustling with activity since it was Sunday and all fishing had stopped for the day. Some fish of varying kinds, from mackerel to shark, hung suspended drying in the sun. From here we continued to the tranquil lagoon, after which we crossed the Dutch Canal once again where fishermen sat mending their nets. It was a peaceful sight.

Finally we called at a Buddhist temple which was being restored. A smiling monk showed us around, explaining the crude wall paintings which depicted Buddha's life. Incorporated in Buddhism on the island were Siva and Ganesh, the two well-known Hindu deities, easily recognised: Siva the Protector with a third eye and a second pair of arms and Ganesh with his elephant head. The temple formed part of a complex; in one ornate building decorated with elephants' heads, monks and pupils lived, whilst a heavily decorated pavilion was used to celebrate festivals. Pupils were having a lesson in their school hall.

By the time we returned to our hotel it was too hot to do anything apart from swimming and relaxing.

The next day started badly, with an overcast sky, no time for a swim and no bus in sight at the appointed time. To utilise the time we strolled to the bank to exchange some traveller's cheques, but even after this very lengthy transaction there still was no sign of any vehicle. Some considerable time later we were told that the road to Colombo had been closed owing to a fire in a factory. Finally our bus did arrive and we drove on the now familiar road through this busy, bustling town and past the airport. On our way we saw attractive bungalows set in lush gardens beneath lofty palm trees as well as poor shacks clustered together along the riverbank and near the railway track.

Arriving in Colombo, we were taken straight to the Archaeological Museum past the Green Park. The museum was housed in a pleasing white building surrounded by well-kept grass, with a very old banyan tree in its grounds.

Unfortunately, the rooms containing the earliest periods were closed. There were some very mediocre presents from foreign countries on display. The 16th- and 17th-century carvings in wood and ivory and articles fashioned in brass were attractive, and we were intrigued by sundry exhibits like spectacles in elaborately carved cases and the delightful 'ear picks' consisting of tiny dainty spoons with delicately carved handles.

Moonstones were entirely new to us. These were semicircular carved stones used as doorsteps to every temple. There were numerous statues of Buddha and, strangely, a superb collection of artefacts from Moen Jodara, Pakistan.

There was just enough time left to cast a quick look at paintings done by travellers in bygone days to see how they imagined these strange lands to be. Paintings on cloth were extremely attractive and we also admired some very fine murals before we had to leave.

Our drive took us along Beira Lake on Slave Island, where formerly the Dutch kept slaves securely enclaved since the surrounding waters were heavily infested with sharks. From here we crossed over to the area known as The Fort. Nothing had remained of this erstwhile bastion, it had become a very busy district with the Lighthouse clock tower serving as a landmark. Sweeping past the President's House with his guard in their splendid scarlet uniform standing smartly to attention we drove towards the former busy Passenger Harbour, now lying idle. At the Taprobane Hotel, known in bygone days as The Grand Hotel, we made a short halt. Alas its grandeur had gone with the passing of the passenger ships which used to bring people to the island.

Having completed our official sightseeing tour, we set off on our own to look for Pettah, the bazaar quarter. A thin Singhalese gentleman appointed himself as our guide and led us into the bustling district. He showed us the Jami-ul-Alfar Mosque, which was quite startling with its clear red and white brick façade amongst the rather drab grey and brown buildings which contained shops. Inside the small courtyard we saw the devout men at their ablutions but were not permitted to venture further into the prayer hall.

Continuing with our visit, we hailed a motorised trickshaw. Narrowly missing cars, barely failing to knock bicyclists off their steeds and only just managing to miss numerous motorbicycles by a hair's breadth, we rushed along our perilous path to the Kayman's

Gate, which was no longer a gate but merely a stone belfry. At the Shanhjgavla Temple with its typical tall *gopura* (entrance gate) covered by garishly coloured figures visible from far afield, we halted. Inside we were shown the Hindu trinity of Siva, Vishnu and Brahma, but were told that the shrine guarded by Ganesh and Scanda – Siva and Parvati's sons – was not open until 6 p.m. However, we were permitted to glance through a grille to admire the shimmering golden figure within. The priest played a little tune on the large ceremonial drum before we left.

Our next stop was at a Buddhist temple. This was again a complex surrounding a shady courtyard. The monks were resting in a cool hall to one side, whilst children were having their lessons in a hall opposite. Between these two buildings and facing the entrance stood the temple, which was a modern building erected on the site of an ancient one. Inside, around the whole length of the walls, stood enormous figures depicting Buddha's life. A statue of Buddha seated on the lotus occupied the middle of the room. The ceiling was completely covered by meaningful symbolic paintings. As always there was the Cycle of Life, shown in figures along an arch. Below its apex stood the parents at their wedding, then the babe was born and appeared at the bottom of the arch to the left. Above the baby was the boy playing with a hoop (in the previous temple he had played with a cricket bat), at the apex he had grown into a man and was now getting married himself. Next he was shown with his son and then he moved slowly down the arch as an old man with a stick, to end life finally – opposite where his life had begun – as a dying man.

To complete our visit to the city we joined our party again to drive past the handsome Assembly Hall (Parliament) and along the promenade parallel to the Galle Face Green, on which the British used to hold their horse races, past new hotels and the charming old Galle Face Hotel, which looked comfortably old-fashioned poised on its superb vantage point overlooking the unbroken sweep of the Indian Ocean.

Along the Beira Lake we stopped to see the modern Simanalaka, a Buddhist hall built out above the lake, which was a gift from Bhutan. A group of devout girls sat in front of a statue of the reclining Buddha placed on a marble platform which was connected to the hall, they seemed entirely oblivious to life around them.

Exquisite zodiac signs were embossed in copper, forming a frieze around a white *dagoba*. 'Dagoba' means relic house and is equivalent to *chorten* in Tibet and stupa in other Buddhist countries.

Further along the road we visited the Gangarmaya Bhikku Training Centre. This school had a wonderful façade showing the life of Buddha on large vertical panels with longitudinal rows of elephants, dwarfs and other Buddhist emblems between them. A starving Buddha was most impressive. The temple itself had the usual Jataka displayed in larger-than-life figures. Again, here was the story of man, from cradle to grave, along the arch of life. Above this sat Buddha protected by the Makra – the Monster – with a guardian to either side and two snakes terminating at the zenith of the arch in a fearful mask designed to keep all evil away.

The prayer hall was raised and gleamed with highly polished brass reflected in golden mirrors. Women were busy, some preparing little oil lamps, cleaning and refilling them, whilst others wound leaves around fruit ready to be tendered as offerings. A large elephant was led into the courtyard to be prepared for the big Elephant Procession, which was due to take place on 25th February and commenced from this temple.

A Dutch church which we passed announced the time of service in both English and Tamil. Little seemed to have remained from the past foreign occupations of the island. The Portuguese had left their faith and names along the west coasts, the Dutch their canals and remnants of forts along the west and south coast, the British some colonial buildings as well as the red pillar box and driving on the left.

Most of the churches we had seen had no architectural value. Usually the clock tower stood on its own. In contrast to the churches, the Memorial Hall of Independence, with the statue of Senanayka, their first President, in front, was a very fine building in true Singhalese style.

At the white town hall, which bore architectural similarities to the American Capitol, we stopped where a snake charmer sat on the grass outside demonstrating his art. Opposite the town hall loomed an impressive statue of Buddha.

Finally we passed a universal burial ground which received Christians, Hindus, Buddhists and Muslims alike; we had noticed that churches and temples stood side by side, Buddhist shrines frequently faced garishly painted Christian chapels, and the silver domes of St Lucian's Cathedral shimmered amongst the medley of churches, Buddhist shrines, Hindu temples and mosques.

Once more we stopped before leaving the city to have a look at the Bandaranaika Memorial International Conference Hall, a pleasing building which had been a gift from the Republic of China. A large Buddha stood opposite, a replica of the Aukana Buddha, which we would visit later.

Crossing a different bridge we left Colombo, meeting the road which we had taken into town in the morning. Along our way we had seen Montessori Kindergarten complexes and Catholic churches. Lessons were frequently given out-of-doors.

On our journey back to our hotel we passed the site of the fire which had started at 3 a.m. and had continued for nine hours. One man had been killed by a lorry. There was little to see. This is all we were told, nobody seemed to know whether it had been an accident or arson.

Next morning we travelled north. Wood-fired tile works lined the road. Clay articles which had been fired yesterday had taken their place with mountains of pots heaped up along the roadside. Butchers were carrying on their trade in wooden booths. It was impossible to tell whether a house was just a house or also served as a shop.

At Mahawewa we stopped to visit a batik factory, which was a peaceful place set amongst flowers and shrubs. Apart from the main designer, only girls worked there and everything was done by hand. There was no noise from whirring machines. Chemicals from Germany were mixed with vegetable dyes. Each girl worked on one article, following the whole process through, except for two girls: one who designed freehand onto pre-washed cotton at the start and the seamstress who made up the garments or embellished the fabric with gold or silver thread at the end. Old-fashioned Singer sewing machines were used by hand. Tea and coffee were offered graciously before we left.

The first rice paddies we passed were dry and many dainty egrets were picking up grains left behind from the harvest. Bungalows had given way to huts with coconut matting forming walls and coconut fronds roofs. Cows and goats grazed peacefully in the dry paddies. Travelling through the coconut groves, we saw coconut fibres being twisted by hand into string and rope. Here we stopped to watch toddy being tapped. Quite ingeniously, the toddy man who performed this task shinned up the tall trunk using coconut shells tied to the tree as a foothold. He looked wild, with his mop of unruly hair, wearing only a loincloth and having his primitive tools tucked in a wooden box strapped round his waist. With a wooden hammer which looked like a cudgel, he tapped the stem where the flowers had been, then cut thin slices out of it with a sharp machete-like knife which allowed the sap to flow. The sap dripped into a black pot. Nimbly he walked from one tree to the other along two ropes. The foaming milky liquid was presented to us in a coconut shell. The taste is quite difficult to describe. When subsequently boiled and distilled, the sap is marketed as potent arak. The same tree was tapped two or three times a day for four months, after which it was left to rest for eight months.

At Madampe we looked at the crude statue of the Riderless Horse. Legend has it that the rider did not pay homage to the god in the nearby shrine as he was passing. His horse reared into the air and threw him. Picking himself up, he vowed that if he survived he would build a monument to honour and appease the deity. Now every passing traveller pays tribute at the shrine.

Crossing the Deduru Oya (*oya* means river) we drove near a Hindu *karava* settlement. The village *kovil* (temple) was dedicated to the goddess Draupadi, and worship to her included an annual fire-walking festival. For eighteen days pilgrims adhered strictly to a vegetarian diet. Each day a temple official read a passage from the Buddhist Jataka to them to give them strength for their ordeal. The close intermingling of Buddhist concepts and Hindu mythology had become very obvious to us. In this area was also the Roman Catholic church which was the site of a pilgrimage during the Feast of St Anne on 26th July. Even Muslims came to worship the Virgin Mary's mother, whom they called Hannah Bibi.

As we drove through the countryside the huts along the river-banks became poorer. In some parts makeshift hovels served as temporary homes for migrant coconut pickers. Pigs and even a speckled deer roamed amongst the dwellings.

A subtle change took place as we travelled along: it became less lush – we had entered the dry zone. Skirting Mundal Lake, we found ourselves in savannah country and saw termite hives for the first time. A little boy returned with a water pot from the well, women picked nits out of each other's hair, one woman suckled her baby. Shrimp baskets hung from trees to dry before they were used again. Marrows grew on roofs. It was a different scene.

When we reached Puttalam Lagoon the coconut palms had disappeared and were displaced by bananas. In Puttalam town we passed the President's Residency and the Judge's Residency before stopping at the rest house for lunch. A pomegranate tree bore fruit, and a snake charmer tried hard – but in vain – to attract our attention.

After Puttalam we turned inland. Every drop of water, whether in rivers, pools or wells, was well used. Children were soaped and washed in the nude, older boys lathered themselves, loincloth and all. Ladies submerged themselves into the water fully clad in their saris.

Rice paddies were still with us, where egrets surrounded scarecrows. Tabrova Wewa (*wewa* means tank or artificial lake) was covered with water lilies. Boys in a boat held up fishes they had caught for us to see and admire. Herons, cormorants and other birds abounded on and around the lake. Huts in this area were made of a frame of sticks filled with red mud bricks and covered by a thatched roof of palm fronds. The earth was red, big boulders lay strewn about. Goats nibbled happily at anything within their reach. Water hyacinth produced vivid splashes of mauve amongst the fresh green of the young rice. Equally startling was the red colour of chillies drying in the sun. Further along hung tobacco leaves strung up to dry. A smithy stood by the roadside before we passed a hospital, which consisted of dirty bedsteads sheltering beneath a roof, where a large number of patients lay huddled together and surrounded by their families, who were there to take care of them. It was a sorry sight.

Suddenly we ran across our first roadblock. Up to then we had only been stopped briefly, once by a soldier with a gun. However, we did not have to halt for long before we were on our way again, when we saw windmills with the notice: 'Energy and Waterworks'. The landscape grew greener and appeared more fertile and lush as we approached Anuradhapura, but the Army became very much in evidence, guarding roadblocks.

On our way to Tissa Wewa Rest House we saw a *dagoba* which was under restoration and therefore obscured by bamboo scaffolding. The rest house was undiluted Somerset Maugham, standing in lush grounds with grey monkeys climbing up the many trees, birds making peculiar noises during the day and crickets chirping once daylight had faded, and fireflies flitting through the velvet sky. The rest house, which constituted the main building, contained the public rooms. An old-fashioned His Master's Voice gramophone stood on the heavy oak sideboard between silver meat covers. It occupied the place of honour, but did not work. The ornate wall clock was never wound in case the spring wore out. Comfortable cane chairs and a Victorian settee stood outside our room on the open veranda. Little pink lizards had a lovely time inside the big glass bowl which served as a lampshade. Pink mosquito netting enveloped our beds.

As soon as we had settled in we set off on foot along irrigation channels through the green valley to the Tissa Wewa, which was probably the oldest artificial lake in Sri Lanka. From here we walked on marshy ground to the former pleasure gardens of the kings, accompanied by a retinue of children. The garden covered some four hundred acres, where great boulders lay scattered about, many of which used to be crowned by summer houses. Since only temples were built of stone, nothing survived from any of the other buildings. Two royal pools had been skilfully designed using the huge boulders as a background, with exquisite carvings of reliefs of elephants on their surface. Water from the tank filtered through stone channels over dancing elephants into the upper pool which fed the lower one. Further along stood the Isurumuniya Rock temple at the side of a square tank – which was under repair –with delightful carvings visible to either side: a lovely elephant and the rain god, to mention only two. A very old Buddha sculptured out of rock and covered by gold leaf sat on his lotus flower in a cave, flanked by two guardians which had been carved out of sandalwood and were of a later date.

To see the famous sculpture of 'The Lovers' we went into the newly-built small but most attractive museum. This sculpture was quite 'explicit', with the woman seated on the man's lap and lifting a warning finger, probably to manifest her coyness, but the man nevertheless proceeds. It was thought that the figures represented Saliya, King Dutugemunu's son, and the low-class milkmaiden whom he loved. Some jolly dwarfs and a group of the royal family, King Dutugemunu and his wife, were most enchanting. The king was flanked by Saliya on one side and the milkmaid, Asokamal, on the other. She, not being of royal blood, was much smaller in size. A servant held a fan above the king's head.

To admire the view we climbed up on top of the rock and saw

the silver bell of the Jetavanarama Dagoba shimmering in the distance. Finally we visited the New Hall to see the reclining Buddha and were told that if Buddha lies with his eyes closed, he is asleep; if, however, his eyelids are lowered but the eyes not fully closed he has reached Nirvana. This reclining Buddha had reached Nirvana. The walls were entirely covered by scenes from Buddha's life, the Jataka. The sun was just setting: we therefore walked along Tissa Wewa to admire the spectacle over the still waters, which formed a fitting end to an exciting day.

After dinner a magician and his little daughter performed for us. The ten-year-old displayed remarkable acrobatic skill.

Our next day commenced with a visit to the Archaeological Museum, where the first room contained Buddha images. An early one from northern India showed many folds flowing down his robe, whilst a later one from southern India only demonstrated a single one. Both had been carved in granite, both were meditating with hands held horizontal. When teaching, both hands were held up; when blessing only the right was held up, whilst the left rested in his lap. When Buddha sleeps his eyes are closed and his feet lie close together. When he has reached Nirvana (as we saw yesterday) his eyes are open, his feet in step. Buddhas were sculptured in limestone, in granite, in rose quartz, alabaster, marble, wood, silver and ivory. Having admired Buddhas in limestone, granite and rose quartz, we continued to see other sculptures. The Herostoa showed the hero killing his enemy, who, when dying, with his last breath vanquished him with two spears. However, the hero rose, whilst the evil sank below. This sculpture was Japanese and was the only Buddhist one I had ever seen which actually depicted a warlike scene. The female figure, symbolising fertility, and dwarfs, dancers and many other figures were on display. The Nestorian cross was here as well as the Hindu sculpture of the man cutting his own throat as sacrifice to Kali.

One section represented the Iron Age, with large iron ewers used for ablutions before prayers, and hammers, nails and chisels exactly the same shape as we use nowadays. The Hindu Trident, symbolising water, fire and air, stood next to the tray which held the powder for the *Tikka*, the holy sign upon the forehead of every devout Hindu. Three fingers are used to make the three lines which again stand for water, fire and air. Swords were exhibited as well as farm implements.

Next we saw the replica of the inner chamber of a *dagoba*. The walls inside the chamber were covered with delicate paintings. *Dagobas* were built of clay bricks and the sites from which the clay had been dug were left to collect rainwater to become useful reservoirs.

Buddha sat beneath the sacred Bo tree gaining enlightenment. A halo formed by all colours of the rainbow surrounded him, hence the colours of the rainbow constitute the Buddhist flag. Next to Buddha sat the Hindu gods with their respective 'vehicles': such as Nandi the Bull, Garuda the Eagle, the Peacock etc. The moonstone at the entrance to a Buddhist temple usually depicted elephants, horses, lions and bulls in concentric half-circles; but not so in moonstones found in Polonnaruwa, which was a Hindu settlement, where the bull, being a vehicle of God in Hindu mythology, was sacred – not to be stepped on – and was therefore missing. Buddhism is considered a philosophy, whilst Hinduism ranks as religion. In Sri Lanka we found the two incredibly closely entwined.

Figurines, pots, coins and other artefacts had been found in the harbour. They came from Greece, Persia, China and Arabia, indicating that trade had flourished with countries far across the oceans.

There were precious stones enclosed in rock crystal, collections of bead-necklaces, bangles made from conch shells and a vast array of other jewellery. These articles had all been found inside a relic chamber. Metal neck and ankle rings on display were used by dancers to produce noise when moving in their graceful way. Writing was done on palm leaves with a pin dipped in powder. Singhalese script is derived from Brahmin Sanskrit, whilst Tamil script looks distinctly different.

Amongst a collection of coins we saw the very first which had been 'stamped'. An Indian coin bore the portrait of Lakshmi, Vishnu's wife, the Goddess of Wealth. There were Roman and Arabian coins as well as 'exchange money' in the form of silver hoops, which were used like our modern traveller's cheques. Kuwela, the God of Wealth, was shown on early medieval coins. Chinese coins had holes in the centre so that they could be strung up and worn around the neck for easy transportation.

A collection of Hindu gods cast in bronze contained Siva dancing the Cosmic Dance. His four arms denoted power. He held a flame in one hand, a drum in another, and danced on the evil foe whilst four musicians played.

A figure of a very beautiful woman looked incredibly sad. Legend had it that because of her great beauty she was being constantly pursued and found no peace. She prayed to become ugly, her wish was granted and a second sculpture showed her ugly but with a smile on her face, looking happy and content and playing the cymbals. Siva's Lingam was well displayed.

Before the figure of Buddha became the symbol of Buddhism three different emblems were accepted: first the bo tree, secondly the *dagoba* and thirdly Buddha's footprint. Buddha's footprint was one of the exhibits in the museum.

An ingenious clay pot for boiled rice stood in a deep dish which when filled with charcoal and lit kept it warm. Fine examples of water pots, burial pots, clay pipes like the hubble-bubble (to keep the smoke cool) had been collected, as well as numerous clay tiles.

Out in the grounds we admired the clever 'safe boxes', which consisted of square stone boxes divided into many compartments. When full of valuables they were closed with a heavy stone lid and buried in the relic chambers. They also had evolved 'urinals' in ancient times, where one squatted over a hole in a stone slab beneath which were three interconnected clay pots which acted as a septic tank. The first contained sand, the second charcoal, the third lime. The third pot had an outlet. To defecate, people squatted over the 'squatting plate'. They also had a 'bidet stone', which was eighteen hundred years old.

The dragon balustrade led up to every temple. The dragon was a mystical beast compiled of parts from eight animals: a lion's foot, a crocodile's teeth, a serpent's tongue, an elephant's trunk, a wild boar's tusk, the body of a fish, monkey's eyes and a peacock's tail.

Having enjoyed the museum, we commenced our tour of the actual site of this ancient capital. One of the most important features of any settlement was the provision of water. Tanks had many uses since water was very precious. Humans used them to wash and bath, animals to quench their thirst and keep cool, after which the water was conducted via irrigation channels to the well-cultivated paddies where rice was grown. The rainy season only lasted three months (October, November and December); water therefore had to last for the remaining nine months.

The Ruwanwell Dagoba, built by King Dutugemunu in the third century BC, was the first *dagoba* we visited. The base consisted of 336 elephants forming a wall, the pinnacle was of solid bronze and

143

supported a crystal – a gift from Burma. This *dagoba* had been restored fifty years ago, when Dutugemunu's original water bubble shape had been entirely regained. Legend had it that the King lay dying before the building had been completed. He called his brother, to tell him about his anguish that he might not see it finished. His brother set to work, and using bamboo which he covered with white cotton, he achieved the appearance of completion. Dutugemunu saw his shrine completed and died a happy man.

Lanka Rama Dagoba – built in the shape of a bronze bowl – was the next we visited. The shape of the *dagoba* had evolved from a triangle to a bronze bowl, through a water bubble to a lotus bud, to finally reach the elegant shape of a bell.

The next *dagoba* was the Thuparama, the oldest in Anuradhapura, built in the third century BC and containing Buddha's right collar bone. This too had been reconstructed. Originally all *dagobas* were protected by conical wooden roofs carried on stone pillars. The wood had long perished but some of the pillars still remained. Thuparama Dagoba when first built had been triangular in shape, resembling a heap of rice, and was referred to as 'Paddy Heap'. Originally simply fashioned from earth, its present form was of a perfect bell. From the raised platform of the Thuparama Dagoba we could see a trough which used to stand outside the hospital and when filled with oil soothed the sick. Here still stood the base of many smaller *dagobas* around the main one which were the relic houses of the high monks, whilst the ashes of the lower monks were enshrined in smaller *dagobas* which stood in one row in the shadow of the big one.

The tallest of them all was the Jetavanarama Dagoba, built in the third century by Mahasewa, which stood in the centre of Anuradhapura, whilst one on each cardinal corner of the city were aptly called Southern, Northern, Western and Eastern Dagoba. Since it had been restored the Jetavanarama Dagoba soared in shimmering silver glory, crowned by a crystal finial – which had been a gift from Burma – into the sky.

In the Temple of the Tooth Relic, near the Abhayagiri Complex, we found a most beautiful moonstone. Every moonstone showed a border of elephants, symbolising birth, followed by a border of horses, which stood for old age, succeeded by a border of lions, which meant sickness, finally completed by a border of bulls symbolising death. The semicircles were surrounded by flames since the dead were devoured by fire, whilst the inner circle next to the animals showed a garland of twisting vine, signifying the ups and downs of life, good days followed by bad days. This was succeeded by a semicircle of ducks; ducks stood for cleanliness, which meant that each person had to keep themselves clean to reach the last circle, the lotus flower, which represented Nirvana.

Every temple was flanked by a guardian to either side of the moonstone, each of whom was protected by a cobra and also carried a pot of flowers in his hand for good luck. One or two dwarfs were seen at their feet to carry the weight of the dead up to Nirvana. Apart from the moonstone and guardians, every temple had the dragon balustrade – which we had seen in the morning – leading up to the entrance. Both the moonstone and the guardian had undergone some evolution throughout the ages. The moonstone underwent four phases. The first stone was entirely plain, shaped like a half-moon. Next the lotus flower appeared, followed by the animals and vine. The semicircle of flames was added, and finally the ducks were inserted between the garlands and the lotus flower. Similarly the guardians evolved from plain guard stones. Then a flower appeared, followed by the guardians themselves. Eventually the carving became more elaborate and finally the dwarfs were added.

The best moonstone we saw was in the Mahasane Palace near the Abhayagiri Complex. The granite foundation still stood but the remaining part had disappeared since it had been built of teak. Heavens opened and big raindrops drenched us on our way to the palace, but the sun soon reappeared and dried us remarkably quickly.

The Abhayagiri Dagoba soared up into the sky as a grassy mound on a red brick base carrying a broken pinnacle on its top. This made a splendid foil to the shimmering dome of the restored Jetavanarama.

All that remained of the Northern Dagoba was a base with overgrown bricks on top. The Western Dagoba was under reconstruction. The largest of them all was the Eastern Dagoba which was the highest in the world, and this too was renovated. In former days all *dagobas* were built of red brick and whitewashed, signifying purity.

Next we visited the Samadh Buddha. This immense limestone Buddha sitting in the meditating posture dated from the fourth century AD and wore his robe in a single fold. Full face he looked stern, but observed from either side he smiled benignly and serenely, having attained enlightenment.

The most sacred spot of all Anuradhapura was the Sri Maha Bodhi, which was the famous bo tree brought to Sri Lanka by Princess Sangamitta, sister of Mahinda, who had brought Buddhism to Sri Lanka. It is the oldest authentic tree in the world and has been guarded for over two thousand years. Only a slender branch had remained, standing on a platform well supported by an iron crutch. The frail branch was overshadowed by a younger, bigger bo tree. The leaf of it when folded at the base resembles the shape of a *dagoba*. In the courtyard stood some of the oldest moonstones, which were quite plain, whilst on the platform next to the bo tree rose a small temple, which was modern and quite simple. A table laden with flowers which had been artistically arranged stood in front of Buddha's statue. We intended to return later for puja, the service.

As we drove on we passed the Citadel, which was being excavated, and continued past the enormous Eastern Dagoba, which consisted of fifty layers of bricks on a foundation of granite and limestone. Finally we reached the Brazen Palace, which in fact was the biggest monastery and had originally consisted of nine storeys housing nine hundred monks. It was later destroyed and rebuilt with seven storeys for seven hundred monks. All that was left was the foundation and the pillars which had carried the first floor.

The Southern Dagoba was also being restored and all we could see was the handsome stepped foundation. Treasures found in the relic chamber had been removed to be exhibited in the museum.

Our last visit was to the Twin Pools, which were only used by the monks, who sat on a step scooping water into a bronze bowl to minimise pollution. When the water became dirty the outlet was opened to direct it into the rice fields. All water was conducted from the city by sub-channels into pipes leading to the reservoir to be filtered before it was stored. The pipes opened at the bottom of a deep chamber for sediment to settle and from here the water was conveyed by channels running at the top of the first chamber into a second chamber, which was filled with sand. Clean water flowed into the reservoir.

The Twin Pools were peaceful, with turtles swimming about. It was safeguarded by a stone Naga, the Water God. This was the end of our visit to the ancient site of the Royal City of Anuradhapura.

Nothing had been planned for the afternoon. We joined a lady in our party and hired a taxi to take us to the Western Monastery, which stood to the west of the Abhayeguri Complex and was the remains of fourteen forest hermitages built from the 6th to the 9th century. It was a peaceful place, set amongst meadows beneath shady trees. Only the basic ground plan could be seen. The principal part consisted of two raised platforms connected by a huge monolith. The first was open to the sky, the second, which was on a higher level, still bore the stone columns which once upon a time had supported the wooden roof. The entrance was easily defined, with stone beds either side. The only decorations left were on the urinals situated in a corridor which encircled the complex. Whilst I strolled from one monastery to another, the other two had followed the driver inside one of the mud houses, which were red and thatched with palm fronds. It was divided into two parts, one serving as sleeping quarters, the other as living accommodation. It was sparsely furnished, with some blackened pots and pans in one corner of the living room and a crude bedstead in the other room.

Further along the road our taxi ran out of petrol. Whilst our driver went off to get some, we strolled along the road. Cheeky children rushed out of the mud huts, asking to be photographed. We took many photographs and later posted copies of them all back to Sri Lanka. Our driver returned on the back of a bicycle with a can of petrol and took us into New Anuradhapura, which was poor, dirty and smelly, with open sewers, but people were extremely friendly and smiled easily. Generally they were of slender build with clear smooth skin but very poor teeth. Here we tasted *thambili* for the first time. This was the sweet liquid contained in the brightly orange skinned coconut. The top was sliced open with a sharp knife and the contents drunk out of the shell. It seemed too sweet for our taste.

Satisfied with our afternoon, we returned to our rest house for a short while until it was time to walk to the temple for the service. It had been here in this very temple that three Tamil terrorists had mowed down and killed a hundred worshippers on 14th May last year, 1985.

As unobtrusively as possible, we sat down on the cool floor.

147

Some young girls were bringing their offerings and started to pray. People came and people went. Many sat motionless in the lotus position with eyes closed, whilst others prostrated themselves. A lady, who carried a little girl beautifully dressed in a pretty white party dress, told us that it was the little one's first birthday and that was why she had come. Later her fourteen-year-old daughter and nine-year-old son joined her; a servant girl carried the offering, consisting of a basket full of lotus blossoms.

A group of saffron-clad monks, their right shoulders bare arrived drumming and chanting, which could be heard as they approached. The high priest positioned himself in front of the Buddha image behind the offering table and chanted, supported by the congregation, whilst 'the birthday child' crawled happily on the floor. When it all finished we walked slowly back under the dark sky engulfed in warm air. Poor people were just settling down for the night outside the temple around a small fire.

Our next trip to the wildlife reserve was cancelled because of unrest, which altered our programme, and we set off to visit the sacred Mountain of Mihintale. Our way led through New Anuradhapura and out into the lush countryside. Old and young alike were immersing themselves in the irrigation canals, soaping themselves with 'best Lifebuoy soap' and laundering their clothes. The washing was spread out on the ground to dry. Cows were frequently tied into pairs on long ropes, buffaloes stood almost always with forelegs to forelegs tethered together to prevent them taking flight into the jungle. Strange to relate, in Sri Lanka we never heard the term 'rainforest' – it was always referred to as jungle. A notice proclaimed: 'Guesthouse for Economical Accommodation'. Once again we came up against a roadblock. Further along we passed a teak plantation. A woman spread rice on the road so that the cars would separate the husk from the grain. Girls sat on the ground plaiting dry palm fronds into mats. When we arrived at Mihintale we were immediately besieged by young boys. This happened wherever we stopped unless there were official guides on the site. Each boy selected a tourist and nothing could shake these self-appointed guides off. Finally everybody gave in, willing to pay for this service at the end. More trying was the never ending chorus of: 'school pens, bon-bons, rupees' and the ever-outstretched hands.

Legend had it that in the year 247 King Devanapiya Tissa of Anuradhapura was deer-hunting in the Forest of Mihintale when with arrow poised he followed a deer into the thicket. However, his hand was stayed when the deer suddenly spoke to him with a human voice, posing him a riddle to test him. The King solved the riddle and the deer transformed itself into Mahinda, the son of the great Buddhist King Ashoka of India, and thus converted the King Devanapiya Tissa of Anuradhapura and established Buddhism in Sri Lanka.

Before we commenced to climb the 1,840 granite slab steps, we quickly looked at the remains of the hospital at the bottom of the sacred hill. None of us counted the steps but in fact they did not seem so formidable as we ascended. Having climbed up the first flight, we branched off to our right to reach Kantakacetiya, a ruined *dagoba* with some lovely sculptures of dwarfs, geese and other figures. I went off with my guide to scramble over rocks to inspect some natural caves, which contained faint traces of colour on their walls, where monks, hermits I presume, used to live. Returning down the same steps we then continued our straight path up until we deviated once again to see Sinah Pokuna, a small pool surmounted by a rampant lion. A few steps further up and we found ourselves on a plateau where formerly a monastery stood on two levels. We had entered the monk's assembly hall, from where we looked down into the refectory with two huge stone troughs which used to be kept filled with rice by lay followers. Round mounds within the complex were the tombs of the departed monks. Here we found a complete snakeskin amidst the high grass; it must have been recently shed, but we found no trace of the reptile itself.

The next flight of steps brought us to the place where Mahinda had met the King and where a *dagoba* had been built to commemorate this important event. Close by rose the statue of the King on the exact spot where he had stood transfixed when the deer addressed him in a human voice. Three Buddhas were encased behind glass: a golden one from Burma was flanked on either side by a marble one from Nepal. A saffron tree grew behind the *dagoba*. It was called Amabasthale Dagoba (meaning 'mango tree') and from its bark the saffron dye for the monks' robe was derived. To reach the top of the smooth boulder on which Mahinda was said to have preached or meditated or both, we climbed up some perilous footholds on sheer rock. It was known as 'Mahinda's Bed', from where we had a superb view. My young guide would not let go of me. It was extremely windy and I felt unsafe on top of the

149

rock, but once we had climbed down to the Amabasthale Dagoba I felt safe again.

Having recovered my breath, I tackled the last flight of steps to reach the Maha Seya Dagoba, which was said to enshrine a single hair of Buddha. A large reclining figure of Buddha who had reached Nirvana lay in the temple. From here we looked to the highest point of Mihintale, which was said to have served as repository.

Returning to the Amabasthale Dagoba again we followed an overgrown trail which led through dense thicket to a smooth slab on top of a bolder protected by an overhanging rock forming a roof where Mahinda is said to have waited for the King.

Our final decent led via the Naga Pokuna, a silent pool where monks used to bath watched by the Naga, the hooded cobra, carved in rock above the waters. It was evidently still being used, judging by the telltale wrapper of the Lifebuoy soap at the side of it.

On our journey back we saw many children returning from school, mostly on foot, occasionally on bicycles which inevitably carried more than one passenger. A rice paddy was being ploughed by two buffaloes, with the ploughman knee deep in mud.

Back at the rest house, we were received by a beautiful saried lady who had taken over from the manager. He had gone on leave that morning.

Later we drove to the second rest house, which lay on the shores of Nuwara Wewa, to have a swim in the pool. That night we tasted buffalo curd topped by coconut treacle, both of which I found quite delicious.

Next morning we had an early start but our hostess was up to greet us with a smile and supervised our breakfast offering us 'hoopers' to taste. These were paper-thin pancakes made from rice flour. First we were served an 'egg hooper', followed by a plain one. We were shown how this one was usually eaten: marmalade was spread on it and a finger banana was added before it was rolled up and daintily picked up by hand to be enjoyed. Intrigued by this to us new dish, we asked to be shown the kitchen. Special round-bottomed small iron pans were used to cook each hooper over the fierce heat of a calor gas ring. The pan was oiled, coated with a thin layer of batter, placed over the hot flame and skilfully rotated, removed from the heat, then covered by a lid for a few minutes before being gently peeled off onto a plate. At another table a cook was grating coconut on a special coconut grater which consisted of a many bladed iron cone mounted on a stand screwed to the table and worked by a handle, rather like our old-fashioned hand mincer used to be. The actual head impressed me by its useful ingenuity. A pot of curry was bubbling away on the ancient range. Curry constituted the standard breakfast for the staff. The kitchen quarters were large, airy and spotlessly clean.

Finally we bade our hostess goodbye and left for our next port of call, passing the Isurumuniyan Temple standing to one side of our road and the Vessagiriyo Caves on the opposite side. Suddenly our way was barred by the Army and we had to take a bumpy secondary road which led past a big Buddha to our right and a large Hindu temple to our left. From time to time we saw gravestones among lush vegetation and wondered about the role of 'graves' when the normal custom of disposal of the dead was cremation. Much later when we passed traces of a recent cremation we were told that the 'light ashes' were dispersed with a fan to all corners of the globe whilst the remaining ashes were scooped up into a pot and buried. A board or stone with the name of the departed was placed above the pot. Sandalwood, which was the most expensive of all woods, was only used for the cremations of monks.

Wagons piled high with various loads jogged along, their coachmen protected by a wooden roof which projected forward above them. The lush vegetation had been replaced by cacti growing between big boulders in the sandy soil. Our road criss-crossed the unprotected rail track several times with never a train in sight. As we reached a big tank a giant lizard lay sunning itself in the road. It 'posed' for us for quite a while. Later a mongoose crossed our path, and of all the many colourful birds we saw flitting past, the kingfisher was the most brilliant. Buffaloes stood or lay in the water to keep cool. Coconut shells had been placed on the road waiting to be crushed to powder for use in various ways. Coconut shells were (not in powder, of course) carved into utensils or simply served as bowls when halved, or was used as firewood and also to protect the roots of tender saplings and preserve all available moisture. Tall scaffoldings with platforms rose on the side of the road, on which most remarkable lifelike figures stood, acting as scarecrows to keep elephants away. Men mounted these platforms at dusk to keep watch for the beasts. When we made a short stop, a young woman invited us to see her home, which was a mud hut divided into two rooms. Doors and windows were open to the sky.

151

A fire was smouldering in a sunken pit in one corner with a few blackened pots nearby on the floor. A crude bedstead stood in the bedroom. She was engaged in pounding rice, using a thick straight stick which fitted into the partially hollowed-out cavity of a tree trunk. She scooped up the powdered rice into a flat dish woven from coconut fronds which she tossed skilfully into the air to free the rice from the husk. Next to the hut stood a boulder with a flat shiny surface on which a big stone lay ready to ground red pepper which had been drying in the hot sun.

Just after Kala Wewa we left the secondary road to follow a track to see the magnificent 39-foot-high standing Buddha of Aukana, which had been carved out of the rock in the 5th century AD. *Aukana* means sun-eating. This impressive statue is supposed to be best seen at dawn when the first rays light up the finely sculptured figure as it stands with both arms raised shoulder high, the left hand lightly resting on the right shoulder. The robe fell in amazingly soft-looking folds, creating a flowing, almost diaphanous impression. The statue remained attached to the rock. It was protected by a brick shelter which had – we were told – caused considerable controversy. Our Queen had visited this sacred spot in 1981 and a photograph of Her Majesty hung prominently displayed in the office near the entrance.

Retracing our route as far as Kala Wewa, we soon reached a major road on which we speeded along to our final goal, Parakrama Wewa. Humans shared this large expanse of water with animals. At one end above the tank stood a rest house where the Queen had stayed, but we drove on to the far end to a second one. The position was beautiful but the rest house was dirty and the service poor.

As soon as we had settled we set off to explore the ruins of the second capital, the ancient city of Polonnaruwa. This was a most romantic site, set amongst shady trees and high meadows. First we admired Pothgul Vehera statue, which was a superb figure of a man, looking most lifelike, holding either a book or a rope. Some authorities said that this was the statue of the Indian religious teacher Agastaya, an open book in his hands; others maintained that this was King Parakramabahu the First (1153–1186) firmly clasping the rope of kingship. Whoever he may be he was truly beautiful to see. Walking across lush meadows brought us to the remains of a round building standing on a platform which was the Pothgul Vehera, the Southern Monastery, a hollow *dagoba* which used to serve as a library. Some of the original plaster with traces of colour was still visible. The reading rooms used to be covered with wooden roofs, but only the supporting columns had remained standing. Four solid *dagobas*, one in each corner of the surrounding platform, contained the remains of important monks.

Next we drove into the Royal City to visit the palace, which used to have seven storeys. The ground floor consisted of fifty rooms but all we could see were the remains of massive walls, certainly strong enough to support so many floors. Holes in these walls had anchored the wooden beams which carried the floors above. We entered and stepped into the enormous Audience Hall surrounded by many cell-like smaller rooms which were thought to have served as guardrooms. The thick walls were brick built and lined with plaster which consisted of lime and sand. The ceilings had been supported by wooden pillars. Near the official quarters were the ruins of the King's private departments.

It was peaceful to wander across the wild meadows, where we saw an extraordinary tree which consisted of four varieties: palm, bo, oleosa and aregusta – to reach the council chamber, which had a delightful frieze of elephants around its base. Each one had been carved in a different pose. Above them ran a band of laughing dwarfs. A moonstone lay at the bottom of the two flights of steps which led up to the chamber. Only the stone columns still soared into the sky, the wooden roof had long since disappeared, and each of these pillars bore the name of the minister who sat close by. Near this building moss-covered stone stairs led down into the large stepped royal bath, where the crocodile still held its jaw open but no water gushed forth anymore. The royal bath had been built from brick on the outside and stone inside and changing rooms had been provided at one side. Underground conduits had fed the pool from Parakrama Samudra, an inland sea, and water from it was finally used to irrigate the land.

On our way to Siva Devala, a Hindu temple, we passed the septic tank. Siva Devala was in almost perfect condition with Siva's lingam in the innermost room. The base of the building was built of stone with brick above. This temple was seven hundred years old.

The next building we visited was the Latha-Mandapaya, the Flowerscroll Hall, where the King listened to the chanting of the monks. It consisted of a lattice stone fence imitating a wooden one surrounding a courtyard with a small *dagoba* in its centre. This little *dagoba* had stone pillars in the shape of lotus stalks bearing unopened flower buds. Nearby stood the Maitreya (Buddha to Come) on a raised terrace.

The Two Relic Terrace, which comprised two beautiful temples standing opposite each other, was our next port of call. These had been built at different times by different kings. The Matagage, the Temple of the Tooth Relic, had been built in the 12th century and contained three statues of Buddha, all standing upright. Although they were somewhat weathered they still were extremely imposing in their regal posture. Opposite stood the oldest building of Polonnaruwa, built in the 7th century: the remains of the circular Vatodage, where the moonstones were most distinct, with the bull missing since a strong Hindu influence prevailed, but the remaining emblems were there, with each semicircular stone carrying the same design: the outermost band showed the flames which like life itself will become extinguished, the next showed ducks for purity, followed by elephants for birth, with horses symbolising old age, succeeded by lions, which denoted sickness, the twisting of the garlands of the vines meaning the ups and downs of life and finally the lotus standing for Nirvana. Four entrances situated at the cardinal points led into the temple where a seated Buddha faced each of them. Here lay the finest guard stones to be found in Polonnaruwa.

Nearby stood the thousand-year-old statue of Buddha. His robe was simple, without any folds, and curls were absent from his head. Not far from this remarkable statue was another surprise in store for us: The Galpota or Stonebook, which was 26 feet long and 14 feet wide and had been brought here from Minintale bearing the inscription telling of King Nissaka Malla's (1187–1196) invasion of India. Next to this enormous edifice rose a strange stepped building, the Satmamal Prasada, which meant Edifice of Seven Storeys, which showed the angular stupa of Cambodia.

A city wall used to surround the entire city, but this had long since collapsed. Before leaving the Royal City we visited the Thuparama at the south-west corner, the best preserved building in Polonnaruwa. Its walls were built of brick as much as 7 feet thick and corbelled to form a vault or *gedige* and was known as 'a vaulted image house'. The main image area was in a square chamber. A large ruined Buddha stood in the inner sanctum, whilst the decoration on the external walls showed strong Hindu influence.

154

The largest *dagoba* rose outside the former city walls and was being restored by Unesco. It had formed part of the Alahana Pirivena the biggest monastic complex in Polonnaruwa. As we entered we found the monks' living quarters on a lower level, from which few steps led up to the three chapter houses with the burial mounds of the important monks nearby. A hall with many columns constituted the highest structure in Polonnaruwa and probably solemn religious rites were performed here. The abbot's throne was very prominent. All these quarters were in ruins, therefore the well-preserved Kiri Vehera Dagoba stood out as a crowning glory. *Kiri* meant milk-white and white stood for purity. Much of the original plaster was still intact. It was thought to have been built by Queen Subhadra, one of King Parakramabhu's wives. Inside were two rooms where the English archaeologist H.C.P. Bell had found a casket with nine compartments containing three precious stones.

The last *gedige* we visited was the impressive Lanka Tilaka, which meant 'The Jewel of Lanka'. This massive brick building stood 170 feet long, 60 feet wide and 58 feet high. The great nave showed traces of brilliant murals where each section told most charmingly a legend from olden times. One related the story of a rabbit surviving a fire and reaching Nirvana. Here was also the story of Buddha descending the golden ladder to preach his sermon. Three colours had been used: green, yellow and red. A gigantic headless Buddha in walking position dominated the shrine and behind the wall against which he stood was a dark passage which provided a safe home for many bats. Once again Hindu influence was marked in the exterior decoration of the building. It also contained the best-preserved dwarfs made in plaster.

Across the road from the Alahana Pirivena a path took us through lush meadows to Galvihara; which comprised four figures cut in the middle of the 12th century from a single granite wall. They could best be seen by climbing up a smooth shining granite boulder lying opposite amid the high grass which surrounded this rock shrine. They had formed part of King Parakramabahu's Northern Monastery and were most impressive.

The first Buddha, 15-feet high, was seated against a highly ornate background of pure Indian design. The second Buddha sat in lotus position beneath an umbrella in a cave surrounded by various Hindu deities such as Vishnu and Brahma. The third statue stood 20-feet high with folded arms and some authorities thought that this statue was Buddha's disciple Ananda grieving for his master who had departed to Nirvana. Last but not least was the 40-foot-long reclining figure of Buddha entering Nirvana with eyes slightly open, feet in step. It was beautifully sculptured in stone, with even a slight depression in the bolster where he rested his head and with the sun wheel symbol decorating the end of the bolster.

The royal bath, built in tiers of eight-petalled lotus blossoms, was the very last monument we visited and was extremely elegant in its simple geometrical design.

Light had faded by the time we returned to the rest house. I went for a swim in the pool and that was the end of a long and memorable day.

The air-conditioning was noisy and kept us awake, and most things did not function properly; however, to our great surprise, the dining room was efficiently run.

Lightning flashed across the firmament and next morning was cloudy as we stood at the shore of the tank watching the birds in the sky and three little piglets foraging on the ground.

Soon we were on the move once more, retracing our steps for part of the way. The roads were already wet but got worse when heavens suddenly opened; but just as it had started suddenly, so it stopped to give way to yet another hot and humid day. On our way to Parakrama Wewa on the previous day we had passed a heavy lorry which had broken down and stood in the middle of the road. It was still in the same spot but new tyres had arrived. After some time we left the road on which we had come from Anuradhapura to turn south past a lily pond and through jungle with brilliant flowers and many types of bushes and beautiful trees. Porcupines scuttled along the road, green parakeets, brilliant blue kingfishers and storks, to name but a few of our feathered friends, flitted past. A fox slunk into the undergrowth, colourful plumed jungle fowl scratched amongst the thick vegetation. Girls walked on high stilts just to earn some money by performing tricks, since we were driving through a very poor area where people had to walk for miles to collect water from the nearest well in round-bottomed clay pitchers which the women carried supporting the heavy vessel on one hip. The word 'Dates' appeared prominently painted on rocks. We were told that the Government had planned certain housing projects, aiming to complete one a year. 'Dates' referred to the completion of a new housing development.

Sigiriya, the Lion Rock fortress, loomed suddenly up on the horizon in front of us. This massive monolith of red stone rose 600 feet out of dense green jungle. It was here in the 5th century that Kasyapa, King Dhatusena's son, fortified himself after he had killed his father by incarcerating him alive. Kasyapa was the eldest son born to a concubine. His half-brother Mongallan, whose mother was the Queen, fled to India swearing revenge. When after eighteen years Mongallan marched towards Sigiriya, Kasyapa rode forth on his elephant to meet him but became bogged down in marshland. Forsaken by his troops, he drew his sword to cut his throat and, holding the bloody blade high above his head, he stuck it back into its sheath before he was sucked into his muddy grave.

Past the remains of a *dagoba* we got off our coach to climb up until we stopped beneath the Cobra-hooded Cave, so called since the projecting rock looked like a cobra's head and helped to from a natural cave. As we climbed higher, treading along the original stone slabs newly fixed into place, we saw the stone throne and opposite, on a higher level, the audience hall, which had been split off the main rock by an ingenious method. A channel had first been chiselled just large enough to take the trunk of a teak tree, which was inserted and soaked in oil. Fire was set to it and when it was blazing fiercely cold water was poured onto it, thus splitting the rock. Steps led up to the other part of the rock into which a tank had been sunk. All water had to be pumped up with the help of a wooden pump from a large tank which we could see in the distance. Once it had supplied all needs of the citadel, it was led by channels down to the palace gardens at the foot of the rock to feed the pools and fountains and finally drained into the crocodile-infested moat which lay between the inner and outer rampart entirely surrounding the rock.

All buildings in the past had been covered by wooden roofs and we could still see the keys hewn into the sheer rock into which the wooden beams had been securely fitted. Small rooms served the royal guard to watch in a cramped position over their paranoid King.

Halfway up we halted to look down on the pleasure gardens, still easily visualised even if devoid of ornamental trees and flowers. A wild tamarisk still grew amongst the other trees. Four entrances stood at the cardinal points.

Next we ascended a modern spiral staircase to be able to admire the Sigiriya Maidens, which were delightful frescoes delicately executed. A queen holding a flower was followed by a servant. Another beautiful lady carried a delicate frangipani, which was the temple flower. Nobody knew who these lovely maidens were, whether courtesans or nymphs. To see them we walked along a pathway clinging to a sheer cliff, before we descended along the spiral staircase again and continued along a gallery which was protected on the outside by a 10-feet-tall wall built of brick and lined by white plaster coated with a glaze of honey mixed with a little lime and white of an egg to give a shiny surface acting like a mirror, on which some five hundred 'damsels' painted on the rock wall used to be reflected; but only twenty-two of them have survived. Tiny graffiti which had been inscribed between the 7th and 11th centuries were engraved on the mirror. Of these 685 had been deciphered and were published in 1956. Looking across from this gallery we saw a huge rock rising out of the dense jungle; looking like a lumbering elephant. Out of another rock two thrones had been carved, one for the King the other for his Queen.

As we climbed higher our self-appointed guide pointed to the 'balancing rock', which appeared to be most precariously poised, threatening to crash down on any unexpected foe. The path which we were following used to be protected by a wooden canopy but all we could see was the channel which had acted as a drain above the roof to divert the rainwater. The King used to be carried up to the top of the rock. Our steep narrow path ended on a large flat grassy platform where a gigantic brick lion used to crouch as if emerging from its den. Only his enormous paws remained where formerly an entrance had led up to the summit through the gaping jaws ascending an enclosed flight of 1,200 steps. The steps were interrupted by platforms. A few stone slabs between the huge paws were all that was left, followed by a short flight of open iron steps, which we climbed up before we scrambled as best we could across the rock, using any grooves or footholds we could see cut in the rock. At last we stood on top of Sigiriya on the grassy summit where once a palace covering four acres had risen into the sky. All we could see was the ground plan of big buildings and an enormous rock pool facing east towards the jungle, which even today is still full of wild beasts. There was a magnificent smooth throne carved out of rock with a tiny cave below it for the guard to stand. It was too small for the guard to sit or lie and if the unfortunate man dropped off to sleep during his twenty-four hours on duty, he was doomed to fall to his certain death. The descent was quite easy, and the climb had been well worth the effort for the superb views alone.

After a walk in the gardens, which were reminiscent of Versailles in their geometrical layout with pools and fountains which could still be traced, we continued our journey south, stopping at a simple rest house for lunch. Having mastered the intricacy of ordering food, it had become easy for us to refuse the full menu and order 'short eats' such as 'cheese toast' or fresh fruit, lime or tea, which was all we required.

It was sticky and oppressive as we climbed up a huge sloping rock 300 feet above the village of Dambulla to visit five temples of the Raja Maha Vihara. The caves' history dated back to the 2nd or 1st century BC, when King Valagam Bahg took refuge here after having been driven from Anuradhapura by invading armies. When he regained his throne he transformed these caves into magnificent temples. Suddenly heavens opened and torrential rains poured down, forcing us to seek refuge in the last of them, accompanied by cheeky grey monkeys. Later kings had added more adornments, therefore statues of Buddha abounded, forty-eight in all, including a 50-foot-long reclining Buddha. But there were also statues of Vishnu and Siva from the 13th century and some of the King. Every inch of walls and ceilings was covered by frescoes showing scenes from Buddha's life and events from Singhalese history.

Finally the deluge abated and gingerly we threaded our way down, trying to avoid puddles and rivulets. Alas rain followed us along to the fertile district where spices and herbs were grown. These gardens were all Government owned. When we stopped to visit one of them we were handed umbrellas to protect us whilst we wandered around. We were given a short talk and offered a glass of spiced tea before walking through the demonstration garden, where we were shown the bitter oranges used for marmalade or essence, and the coffee plant with its small white flowers. Coffee in Sri Lanka is bitter. It is known as Arabian coffee and has a high caffeine content. They also grew two varieties of pineapple, the small bitter one was used like the bitter oranges, the large long one was juicy and was eaten. The vanilla pod, we were told, was derived from an orchid which bore two flowers, male and female, and had to be artificially pollinated to produce the long bean. Pepper is a creeper; to obtain white pepper it is boiled to remove the skin and to obtain black pepper the plant is dried in the sun whilst still green.

Cinnamon is derived from the bark of a tree, carefully lifted off in thin sheets and rolled into the well-known sticks. Ginger is derived from a tall plant. Jackfruit, reaching enormous size, grows on a tree. It ripens in four months, when it is eaten as fruit but before it is ripe it is boiled and consumed as a vegetable. Cacao beans are the stones of a big fleshy fruit which in Sri Lanka is only grown for home consumption. Finally we learned that curry powder is a mixture of three herbs: chilli powder, mustard seed and curry leaf. Before we left we bought some spices.

Leaving the herb and spice gardens behind, we passed some lime kilns before we got caught up in traffic as we approached Kandy. It was dark when our coach skirted the lake to reach Hotel Suisse, where we stayed. It started to rain again and we had to abandon all thoughts of a walk along Kandy Lake but allowed ourselves the luxury of the old-fashioned hotel: a bathtub with hot water, beds opened for us, pink mosquito netting artistically draped, sweet-smelling frangipani blossom placed on our pillows and a balcony to sit on, contentedly looking out on the lake until it was time to dine.

Next morning we drove above the lake, past many pleasant houses set into the hillside, some of which were private villas, others guest houses or hotels, some were old, others new. Many new buildings crowned the wooded hills which encircled the town. From here we looked down on the lake, which was man-made purely for pleasure; it never was used to irrigate the district nor did it act as reservoir.

Driving down past the busy bustling market we noticed many Victorian buildings before we reached the modern University Town set amongst beautiful trees. Particularly splendid specimens of *Ficus benjamin* grew there. Above the River Mahaweli, opposite the University Town and set on the hillside, stood a mosque, a church and a Buddhist temple next to each other in perfect harmony.

The next few hours we spent around the enormous Botanical Garden, first on a short guided tour, then a stroll around on our own. Kandy Botanical Garden is the largest in Sri Lanka and known for its large variety of plants and trees. Our guided tour started in the Spice Garden, past a lovely mahogany tree (an import from South America), leading us to an allspice tree, cinnamon tree, ginger tree and nutmeg tree. Our guide showed us the bay rum tree from Venezuela, which is used to manufacture bay rum lemon shampoo. The camphor tree is a native of China and Japan and the

160

pungent oil is derived from its bark. Before strolling on to another part of the garden we admired the lovely orange flower of the Ashoka tree. The batik plant derived its name from the pattern of its leaves. It grew near the striking bird of paradise flower (which belongs to the banana family and comes from Hawaii). The balloon plant, true to its name, had numerous green balloons festooning its branches. I saw a chameleon and a lizard basking in the sun. Busy Lizzies grew in gay abundance in a kaleidoscope of colours side by side with many of our ordinary garden flowers. A small pond outside the Orchid House was covered with tiny white water lilies aptly called 'Water Snowflakes'. The Orchid House was sadly disappointing. Orchids in their natural habitat grow on trees, taking their nourishment from the air, not from their host, therefore they are not parasites. Out in the garden we saw some small orchids which had been grown in soil and at the other end of the scale the giant orchid tree also bloomed here. It came from Malaysia and only bloomed every seven years. In the Palm Garden we saw the native tree, the fruit of which is used for jelly, sugar candy and treacle, the sap of the flowers for toddy and arak. Java's almond trees with their weirdly shaped gigantic roots which grew above ground gave us welcomed shade as we strolled on to reach the West Indian cabbage palms, whose foliage is used for salads. Nearby we stood in amazement looking at a tree covered by fruit bats hanging upside down. They feed on a special citrus fruit and normally only fly at night since they are unable to see in daylight (hence the saying: 'as blind as a bat'). Something must have disturbed them and roused them from their normal sleep since they certainly flew for us in brilliant sunshine. As we continued our leisurely walk we saw the Venezuelan rose, the lilies from Cana and the touch-me-not-mimosa, which covered the ground. If its leaves are touched they fold up. Many splendid tulip trees were in full bloom. The enormous rain tree – native from Venezuela again – was most impressive in its mere size.

One part of the garden had been specially designated for VIPs to plant trees. Here we met a party of pretty young ladies in their gay saris beneath colourful shades, looking like brilliant butterflies. They clustered around me eagerly and were happy to answer questions, telling me that they were third-year art students and had another year to complete their course. It was their turn to ask questions, which were: 'Where is your husband? How many chil-

161

dren have you got?' When I said I was not married they broke into a chorus bewailing my fate: 'Oh, we are so sorry, so sorry, why not?' It was quite touching.

To complete our visit we walked past the giant bamboo by the river. For three months it grows one foot each day, then it slows down. When it stops growing it turns yellow and dies. Finally we stood in the shade of an enormous banyan tree which was 125 years old

Left to our own devices we decided to take a bus back to town and caught a crowded local one. Much to the amusement of the other passengers, when proffering our money for the tickets we mistook the driver's head shaking for meaning 'No' having forgotten that in the East shaking the head from side to side actually denotes 'Yes'. In fact when we reached the terminus and asked for directions to the Orient Hotel, the kind bus driver offered to take us there in the bus, which we politely declined.

To start our wanderings in town we first walked through the busy market looking at stalls but found it quite hard to shake off the boys offering their wares. A lady in our party had joined us and entertained us with stories. She had at one time worked at Kew Gardens and when we had been in the Botanical Gardens she had pointed out the tree the late Sir George Taylor, Director or Curator of Kew, had planted. She knew his housekeeper, who had no good word to say about this very highly respected man. When we passed a Methodist church where smiling young girls sat in the cool hall, our companion told us that she had known the Reverend B. and his sorely-tried wife. He had preached in this church, enjoying the ladies since he was 'partial to the pleasure of the flesh'.

As we walked on we noticed the Bake House, a well-frequented eating place, and the old-fashioned Queen's Hotel with its shimmering dome up above and cool arcades sheltering shops down below.

Walking along the lake we cast a glance across to the pleasure island on which the last King had kept his harem. Near the lake stood the Old Empire Hotel in its rather neglected garden with a wistful air of bygone gracious days. Our way led past the Temple of the Tooth Relic to the Arts and Craft Centre, which formed part of an attractive modern complex. Not many artists or craftsmen were actually working when we called. One man sat cross-legged on the veranda working on small lacquered boxes, another was weaving with fine coconut fibres, three men were hammering brass in united rhythm, sitting in the shade of another veranda at the back of the building overlooking a stage on which young girls were rehearsing a dance.

From here we returned to the Temple of the Tooth Relic, past the National Museum housed in the former Queen's Palace situated on a hill. The temple was entirely surrounded by a moat in which a snake wriggled its sinuous way. Off came our shoes and hats before we climbed up to the imposing entrance. The famous Relic of the Tooth, which no one ever sees, was kept in a 400-year-old two-storeyed sanctuary in the centre of the inner courtyard. The delicate wood carvings and exquisite paintings were most delightful. The walls of the shrine were entirely covered with murals, many of which were being restored, and each little scene deserved to be studied in detail and enjoyed on its own. One charming picture showed nine ladies forming an elephant, signifying the nine months of pregnancy.

There was also the now familiar story of the white rabbit which had sacrificed its life for Buddha by jumping into the fire and was shown in the moon having reached Nirvana. Two vignettes were almost Egyptian in their stylised concept of body and limbs topped by smiling round faces.

A big ornate door led up to the council chamber and to a shrine containing a golden Buddha from Burma. Two Iraqi soldiers stood to either side of this shrine, posing to be photographed. Finally we ascended a flight of wooden steps to the upper gallery to admire the imposing carved door, flanked at either side by elephant tusks, behind which the famous 'Tooth Relic' was kept. Casting our glance outside, we saw the many-columned audience hall where the last King had resigned his kingship and surrendered to the British. Kandy was the fourth and the last of the Island's Royal Cities. The Independence Hall in Colombo was an exact replica of the audience hall in Kandy.

As we stood on the gallery and looked towards the big bell, a present from Japan, surrounded by many oil lamps waiting to be lit as a prelude to the service, a young man close to us muttered: 'British were bad, bad. They destroyed so much.' It was the first time that we had heard this sentiment uttered but it surely must, from time to time, pass through the minds of many.

Opposite the Temple of the Tooth stood the temple complex of Pattini Devala, almost entirely surrounded by a high wall. The

163

shrine itself was the second oldest building in Kandy. It served now as a Buddhist monastery, with three shrines and a lovely cool modern building for the monks which contained a central shady courtyard round a pool. Restoration of the old part was in progress. It had originally been a Hindu temple and much of the sculpture showed Hindu influence.

A young man beckoned us to step inside one of the temples, containing a large crude Buddha reclining contentedly. Well-fed dogs played in the large courtyard.

It was extremely hot in the brilliant sunshine as we wandered through the dusty streets and past the handsome former King's Palace, now containing the Archaeological Museum, to find the Vishnu Devala, the most important Hindu temple, which stood behind the Natha Devala – the oldest temple in Sri Lanka – on the slope of a hill. It was a peaceful place, with numerous shrines decorated with coarse figures painted in garish colours, childlike in concept but very interesting to see. All the temples stood on platforms which were accessible up steep flights of steps.

After this visit we decided to head back to our hotel and walked past the big Anglican church of St Paul. Architecturally it was of no interest, but what intrigued me was the close proximity of Buddhist, Christian and Hindu places of worship. A minaret rose in the distance.

Glancing through narrow doorways into secluded courtyards which were surrounded by dilapidated houses with broken wooden balconies, we saw notices and realised that it was here that solicitors and lawyers had their offices. Nearby stood the Headman's Hall, a shabby replica of the audience hall, where feeble old men clad in rags sat on stony ground. It proved impossible for us to glean any information about this building.

Finally we hired a rowing boat to be gently transported across the lake to our hotel. A cool pool beckoned to me for a quick swim.

Later we all drove down town back to the Temple of the Tooth Relic to join the throng of worshippers for the evening service and the opening of the relic chamber. Our group stood in front of the big Japanese bell, which was surrounded by a myriad of flickering lights. Nearby – a sad sign of modern times – stood a soldier, rifle in hand. The temple was crowded with old and young, and groups of schoolgirls dressed in white stood politely aside for us. Every worshipper carried a fresh flower, either a lotus or a frangipani

164

blossom, in their hand. Only freshly cut flowers were used, to symbolise life since flowers like life itself will wither away and die. The flowers were most artistically and entirely simply arranged on the offering tables in front of the shrine. The delicate fragrance of the frangipani flowers mingled with the strong smell of the incense sticks which, having been lit, permeated the air. Alas I never caught even a glimpse of the golden casket, the outermost of seven in the shape of a *dagoba*, in which the tooth was kept, since too many people crowded around the now opened door of the shrine. The drumming and blowing of a flutelike instrument had heralded the coming of the monks who preceded the high priest. He unlocked the heavy door and, once this had been done, chanting commenced.

A side shrine near the Burmese Buddha was opened and we were able to see the most precious Buddhas in the temple, which were kept behind glass. One was made of pure gold, one had been carved from rock crystal and the third one was a miniature (3 inches by 2 inches) emerald carving.

To conclude our full day we went to watch some Kandyan dancing. Each performance started with a plaintive sound on the conch shell. The music which followed was rather monotonous to our ears, played on drums by hand or using a drumstick shaped like a hoop fixed to a handle at a right angle. The dancing was brilliant, costumes and make-up excellent. Most of the dances were ritual, usually performed as temple dances at festivals. Particularly impressive was the Mask Dance with fearful-looking masks and rolling eyes and long tresses of hair. There was also a classical dance of the Wild Tatooed Veddha (the indigenous tribe of the island) Hunter. Another dance was a fierce tribal one performed by two men wearing elaborate silver headdresses, heavy bangles on arms and legs and silver ornaments on their chest. A gentle dance of maidens sowing and reaping provided a contrast. Two fierce warriors danced a fire-dance using two torches each, which they moved over their own naked flesh without searing their skin. Finally three of them danced on red-hot embers without marking their soles.

Back at the hotel we helped ourselves freely from a large buffet table before retiring to our lovely room, where once again mosquito nets had been daintily arranged over the turned-back clean linen, and fresh sweet-smelling frangipani blossoms had been placed on our pillows.

Two cooks – one in a white turban, the other in a funny chef's hat – presided over breakfast next morning, cooking eggs whichever way guests desired. The previous morning only one cook had been there but he appeared to be able to fry, scramble and boil eggs and toss omelettes all at the same time.

Mist was slowly rising from the lake as we followed the road along its shore. Pelicans sat on branches of a tree close by. Life had commenced, children were on their way to school with sexes strictly segregated: girls assembled in one forecourt, boys in another. Both stood to attention in a straight row before they marched or performed exercises.

We passed a home for the elderly and drove through the Muslim district, encountering many mosques and men in turbans. Following a railway line without encountering a train, we watched groups of people walking along the track – this had become a common sight. After crossing the Mahaweli River we reached Gampola, where we started to climb along a road with a poor surface and many potholes, which wound and twisted up the hillside through tea plantations. A butcher displayed carcasses under a flimsy roof. A mosque stood to one side, a *dagoba* to the other before we arrived at Pusjelawa, with its open drains and closed cinema giving the appearance of a frontier town. From time to time we saw lifelike scarecrows protecting the densely planted tea gardens, which were surrounded by miniature hedges. Down in the valley lay well-tended rice paddies. Temples which we passed presented a mixture of Hindu and Buddhist architecture and wherever there were temples there were churches too. Numerous waterfalls cascaded down the mountainside. Sadly, many of the large numbers of beggars we saw were blind.

A little boy clasping a bunch of flowers in his hands panted up the steep slope to get in front of us (whilst the bus followed the hairpin bends) so that he could offer us his colourful collection. He did this various times without success until we finally succumbed and gave him money and took the flowers, but he asked for them back. Content, he stayed behind, firmly clutching his trophy and waited for the next bus.

At last we arrived at Labookellis Tea Plantation, where we were offered a cup of tea and shown the processing of it. On our way up we had seen the women picking the fragrant leaves and had watched them come down the steep incline carrying their baskets on their backs and using long staffs to avoid slipping along the narrow path. After a bell sounded they stopped and waited patiently by the side of the road until they had all assembled. A man who was obviously in charge gave a sign, whereupon they marched in single file to the nearby station to have their loads weighed and receive their pay.

By midday we had arrived at the former hill station of Nuwara Eliya. After having skirted the town and passed the General's Mansion, we climbed up to the Hill Club, an incongruous pseudo-Tudor mansion standing high up in its own grounds in Sri Lanka's beautiful hills. It was so very British that it seemed unreal, both outside and in, with its splendid library furbished with comfortable leather armchairs, big desks, books galore, magazines and newspapers. Two bars were available, one proclaiming that it catered 'For men only' whilst the second stated it was a 'Mixed Bar'. Snooker and Billiards could be played indoors, whilst fishing and riding could be pursued outdoors. The big cosy drawing room lay next to the elegant wood-panelled dining room where we dined by candle-light, waited upon by uniformed waiters wearing white gloves and presenting a very miserable meat pie on a silver platter. Later, as the day drew to an end, a large log fire was lit and the countryside shut out by soft velvet curtains.

When we walked into town we found it dusty and dirty beyond belief. There was a very British-looking post office and a 'Victoria Park', but there was nowhere clean and wholesome for us to eat a snack for lunch, therefore we walked back to the Hill Club and went next door to the even grander Grand Hotel to have a 'short bite' in the coffee shop.

Later we set off for a walk into the hills. I wanted to get to the top of Mount Pedro, the highest peak, but we missed our way and followed a stream which led us past a trout hatchery into thick woodland. Later we learned that no civilian was permitted to climb Mount Pedro without a special police permit, and in any case soon after our return it began to rain.

It was pleasant to find our beds turned down and hot water bottles placed between fine linen sheets. An almighty thunderstorm raged outside whilst we were warm and snug in our beds.

Next morning we passed the lake, saw the golf club and many ponies before we left this strange place where we had seen abysmal poverty in the grimy hot town and splendid villas in well-tended shady gardens up above. The poorest of all the people there were probably the Veddhas, the last of the indigenous population.

Our journey took us through a fertile district with terraced tea gardens and lush vegetable plots. Flowers in brilliant colours grew in wild profusion. There were hollyhocks, delphiniums, French marigolds, roses, dahlias and many more growing in the gardens, under exotic trees. Wild flowers lined the road, beautiful morning glory, the deep orange blossoms of the tulip tree, the snow-white trumpets of the trumpet tree; poinsettias grew as trees. The morning mist lifted and the sun broke through, glistening on the rice paddies which stood under water in the valley below. An ancient Ford Prefect jogged along the road; we also encountered many Morris Minors on our journey

The views were superb, the road poor. Attempts had obviously been made to fill in the numerous holes. Bricks were being made by simply pouring yellow clay into wooden shapes which were subsequently baked in adjacent kilns. Sand was being collected from the nearby river-bed by hand.

Our road climbed up once again and we looked down on a fertile valley where fruit and vegetables of every kind grew. Stalls all along our way displayed vegetables which were frequently bartered for goods, like coconut, which came on lorries from other districts. At Bandarawella we stopped at a rest house. Bandawella was a thriving, clean town with many hotels and guesthouses. Here we saw children playing volleyball on a sports ground, whilst adults played cricket nearby.

At a beautiful place called Ella we stopped once again to look down through a gap between the mountains to see a panorama of mountain range after mountain range fading away into the distant sea. Below Ella Gap the impressive Ella waterfall cascaded over rocks into a clear cool pool.

Down in the valley, we drove through rubber plantations, where children beseeched us to buy little hard rubber balls. Dainty white egrets perched in wet rice paddies which were surrounded by low mud walls forming a neat pattern when viewed from up above. Once again we were back to turbaned heads.

A mongoose ran across our way and we found ourselves back in the jungle amongst palms, teak trees and other jungle vegetation. Children were returning from school.

Stalls lined the road displaying 'signs' rather than written descriptions. A weaver bird's nest (consisting of two compartments) hung from the nearby tree, denoting that this stall sold eggs and chickens, whilst a buffalo skull denoted the sale of buffalo curd and honey. Honey was actually coconut treacle. Firewood was built up into neat towers reminiscent of children's play with matchsticks. Little green limes, papaws and vegetables of all kinds were offered for sale. Finally we drove through flat open countryside with houses built of coconut matting beneath high palm trees. Here we stopped at Tissamaharama Rest House on Tissa Wewa. There was 'no room at the inn' for all of us, therefore we volunteered to be boarded out at the Lakeside Inn down the road, which had a very big dining area and an equally spacious sitting area but only five rooms and had only been open since the first of the month. Our cell-like room contained two iron beds beneath mosquito nets, a single chair, a shelf for one suitcase, one bedside table, a wall mirror with a shelf beneath it and a towel rail. A washroom with shower, basin and toilet was attached but there was no running hot water anywhere in Tissamaharama since nobody saw any need to have hot water when the temperature was always high. However, we did have the luxury of two cane chairs and a table on our porch and also a big electric fan mounted on the high ceiling.

I woke early and sat out on the porch watching life beginning to stir. Adults walked to work, children – who seemed small for their age – to school. Everybody made an early start whilst it was still relatively cool. Staff in both the rest house and in our little inn were very attentive and really charming. A tray of tea was brought to me as soon as I sat down on the porch and we felt quite sad to leave and move into the rest house with the rest of our party, where we had a proper room, well furnished, with a balcony overlooking the waters of the Tissa Wewa.

After breakfast, during which we had been watched by monkeys, surrounded by dogs and serenaded by crows, we drove to Kataragama. Before approaching this sacred complex dedicated to the God Kataragama and venerated by Buddhists, Hindus and Muslims alike, we bought a tray of offerings from one of the many stalls placed here for this purpose. Fresh fruit was prepared and arranged artistically on a flat coconut tray adorned with red garlands. Carrying the offering, we entered the sacred ground and crossed the first courtyard, before taking off our shoes to walk across the second. Passing the Ganesh Temple, we reached a wide path lined with stalls offering temple flowers for sale. At the end of this path stood the big white stupa, the Maha Devala, on top of three terraces. It is a simple building with four golden Buddhas, one at each cardinal point.

In 1948 this complex had been entirely cleared of all houses and shacks following an outbreak of typhoid. On special festive days in July and August Kataragama gets crowded with Buddhist, Hindus and Muslims from all districts who come to worship. Plans were afoot to provide rest houses, running water, sewers and other facilities for the pilgrims, who swelled to enormous crowds during this time.

Next we visited the small temple dedicated to Vishnu and Kataragama – Hindu and Buddhist deities combined under one roof. Most of the sculpture was pretty crude, but in a small glass case stood delicately carved figures of Vishnu and Kataragama; the latter with many heads.

The small museum within the grounds was our next goal. The first room contained photographs of the various excavation sites. The main building was divided into a number of little rooms, each donated in memory of a beloved spouse, a parent or benefactor. These were arranged around a central courtyard. I admired the delicate votive objects such as the small statue of Buddha found in the Kiri Vehera shrine. A *yupa* pillar stood beneath a parasol which originally used to crown every stupa but had been perfected over the years into an elaborate finial with glittering crystal which now adorned each *dagoba*.

The statue of King Dedimunda, the founder of Maha Devala, was housed in a small shrine at the foot of the main *dagoba*.

It was time to join the throng of pilgrims outside the main temple. Those bearing offerings stood to the left, the rest to the right, in orderly lines, to wait until the door was opened. Then everybody crowded inside, leaving a centre gangway clear. Our position was between a row of big ornate gilded candlesticks in front and an arcade of columns behind us with copper bells above us. Three steps led up to a bright yellow banner, which bore an enormous painting of Kataragama in vivid colours, whilst smaller, slightly less startling replicas hung to either side. A modern clock ticked away. When the clock struck a quarter to eleven, everybody who found themselves beneath a bell tugged vigorously on the rope. The ensuing din was incredible and appeared to go on and on endlessly, added to which an old man in front had begun to chant and a young man near him seemed to have been carried away by it all and he too commenced chanting and at the same time he started to twist and gyrate like one possessed. An orange carpet was rolled out in the centre gangway, a red velvet cushion was placed on a stand, drums sounded and the high priest appeared dressed all in white, which denoted purity. He carried his offering wrapped in a red velvet cloth which hung suspended from a pole placed across his shoulder. An embroidered baldachin was held above him. First he paid homage to the large Kataragama before disappearing behind the painting through a hidden door into the sanctum which only he was allowed to enter. The drumming, the ringing of the bells, the chanting continued, fortified by the crying of some of the small children who, dressed in their best, were carried in the arms of their parents. The high priest reappeared holding a bowl. He was handed the velvet cushion, with which he once more disappeared, only to reappear carrying a tray with a pile of 'milk-rice' with a lit candle in its centre. Those with offerings received a handful of rice to eat and a ladle of water to drink. A thin old man joined the congregation. He wore a loincloth and carried an orange cloth slung over his left shoulder. With his long hair and long beard he looked like a Hindu sage. When I asked our guide about him we were simply told that he was a 'Tamil'.

As we filed out through a side door into the sunshine again, we too received a handful of hot spiced rice and a ladle of water. In the little Ganesh temple which we visited next we were offered more rice and a tikka (which we politely declined).

Further along stood a small Buddhist shrine. When I asked why the big Buddha sat behind a lace curtain, I was told this was simply done to keep the dust off. In front of the offering table stood a tray set with food and drink for Buddha's lunch; a row of small Buddhas were arranged on it too. Again we saw the lovely emblem of the white rabbit facing the man in the moon, who I think represents a former king.

From this Buddhist shrine we wandered across to see the mosque, which alas was not a very attractive building and where women were not allowed to enter to see the tomb of a Muslim sage. Muslims are buried straight into the earth without any coffin within twenty-four hours of their death, whilst Buddhists are placed in a wooden coffin before they are burnt.

171

The last shrine we visited was dedicated to Kataramaga's wife. The priest who stood in front of it looked like the Tamil we had seen in the Maha Devala.

Leaving the complex, we crossed the broad Menik River, where a small boy jumped down from the high bridge for our benefit and to earn a few rupees. As in every river so also in the Menik, men and women were cleaning themselves and their clothes and enjoying a swim. On festive days pilgrims take a ritual bath in the river. Many steps led down to the water. I think that the scenes during a big festival must be as impressive as on the Gat of the Ganges in Varanasi.

Finally we returned the way we had come, where the lotus blossoms which had been open on the pond before the sun gathered momentum were now closed, and where a brilliant red British letter box stood out amongst the lush green vegetation. On our way we encountered many inns, guest houses and simple hotels. Back at our hotel we elected to stay behind whilst the rest of the party went to a nearby nature reserve – where incidentally they were almost charged by an elephant. For some time we sat on our balcony until a storm blew up, making the palm leaves sound like rain. The sky suddenly darkened, the tank became shrouded in mist and a tremendous thunderstorm broke out, followed by torrential rain. It stopped as suddenly as it had commenced and we decided to go out for a walk along the towpath, following the swollen river to a nearby white *dagoba* which formed part of a complex with a school where monks were being instructed. Buses passed us which tried carefully to avoid the deep puddles, people cheerfully rode through the wet on bicycles or waded through them on foot. Having dutifully walked clockwise around the *dagoba* – having noticed a poor demented youth curled up on a stone slab nearby muttering to himself – we followed a path through rice paddies which led us to the Sangran Giri, an old *dagoba* standing amongst tall palm trees with a few small mud houses skilfully thatched with palm fronds tucked beneath them. This *dagoba* was being restored and we could see the stepped brick foundation crowned by a grassy mount. The moonstone was there and the guard stone, both weathered by time and climate but clearly visible. Stone pillars were still standing to form the four porches at the cardinal points. Slowly we strolled back past the poor boy still muttering away on his slab. Youngsters stood on the bridge in small groups, men were swimming, lathering

172

themselves in the high waters of the river. A cow with three legs and a stump stood in the meadow but seemed to be coping well. For a little while following the storm there was no electricity in the whole village. Arriving back in our room we found a friendly pink lizard catching insects.

At breakfast next morning a frangipani blossom lay tucked into each napkin and as we were leaving each lady was presented with a gardenia to bid us good speed on our way.

Our journey commenced along the banks of the Tissa Wewa through familiar settings of little houses tucked away in lush vegetation. Children were on their way to school, adults on their way to work. A peacock sat up in a tree, we saw tobacco, maize and rice being grown and passed eucalyptus and mimosa trees. Land clearing was in progress, possibly intended for a housing project. The countryside was flat; in places it was scrubland. Soon we turned south towards the sea, and outside Hambantota we saw saltpans. Most inhabitants in this area were Muslims, descendants of Malaysians who had first been imported by the Dutch and later by the British. They were fishermen, farmers and saltpan workers.

At our next stop we were able to buy some delicious buffalo curd in attractive clay pots and coconut treacle 'honey', was sold by weight in ingenious bottles made from coconut bark. Alas the one we got burst in our full case on our way back to London and made an awful sticky mess. Apart from the 'honey' we also purchased a bottle of arak to take home. It makes a pleasant drink when diluted with fresh lime or pineapple juice.

Many small carts pulled by patient buffalo were piled so high with coconuts or other commodities that we could no longer see the vehicle under the great load. Strings with tiny flags made from coconut leaf wafted in the breeze across our road, denoting a wedding or cremation. Yellow flags appeared and lined our route until they terminated at the ground within a monastery complex where a monk's cremation was being prepared.

Before we reached Tangalla, a sheer rock with a white *dagoba* on top suddenly appeared between trees. Tangalla boasted lovely beaches and clear waters and had many Dutch houses, two Dutch kirks and a mosque. All along this southern coast lay sandy bay after sandy bay. Old women sat in shallow water, washing coconut shells; we were back amongst coconuts once more. Women walked along the roadside balancing enormous jackfruits on their heads.

173

Dondra, through which we passed rapidly, was an important religious centre. Then we saw the lighthouse which denotes the most southerly point of the island where the sea stretches unfettered across to Antarctica. Little huts made from coconut matting stood beneath coconut palms along silver sands. At Ruhuna we were impressed by the attractive modern complex of the new university; at Matare Rest House we called a halt. This was an old fortified town where part of the original rampart still remained, as well as the later Star Fort within the city, which was being used as library and bore the coat of arms of the Dutch Governor above its entrance.

To see the Weherahena Temple Complex we left the coast and drove inland. The oldest part dated back two hundred years but a hundred years ago another part was added outside and underground and adorned with the most grotesque religious cartoons. The latest addition had been made about sixty years ago, consisting of an enormous statue of Buddha, about the ugliest and almost obscene sculpture I have ever seen, and yet in the courtyard stood an exquisite bronze statue of a monk.

A bridge at Merissa was festooned with fish laid out to dry in the scorching sun. Outriggers reappeared in the sweeping bay of Weligama where we saw fishermen on stilts for the first time. They actually perched on crossbars which were attached to tall poles and were firmly wedged into the sand below the water. Miserable shacks were followed by attractive bungalows. Women sat on the ground teasing coconut fibres which lay in large heaps by the roadside; these were used to stuff mattresses. Further along, women were spinning coconut fibres. The coconut palm certainly is a very versatile tree and used to its utmost. A little boy held up a civet cat for us to see – it looked like a wolf cub to me. On a sandy beach of Unavantua we saw fishermen in tents made from coconut matting and some of them were spreading their nets out with tender care.

The old Dutch fort of Galle – which means stone – rose in the distance. As we approached it we passed a Montessori nursery, a vegetable market and a fish market, and saw a whole pile of old shoes heaped up at the side of the road for sale. The Dutch Navy was in town, two busloads of young blond men stood outside the Orient Hotel, next to the Dutch church. The Orient Hotel was a comfortable Dutch colonial mansion with lofty cool rooms, tiled floors, quaint bedrooms and a very attractive secluded garden.

Galle was a pleasant town though neglected and derelict in parts. Near the ramparts and lighthouse stood a *dagoba* outside a church. Further along we found a Hindu temple, a mosque and a Buddhist temple all in close proximity. The Army sat in tattered tents near the old city gate, trying to recruit young men.

As we continued, the sun filtered through the palm groves, forming patterns on the lush undergrowth. The blue sea lay shimmering beyond the golden beach. Small houses nestled between the vivid green vegetation under brilliant blue sky. For me, this picture of blue sky, shimmering clear waters, golden sand and little huts in luxurious vegetation beneath coconut palms distils the essence of Sri Lanka.

Cows ambled along the road, glass-bottomed boats lay waiting to take customers out to see the coral reefs. Further along we passed through an area with strange pagoda-like buildings, made from coconut matting, which served as workshops, stores or simply helped to protect workers, who were building, from the relentless sun.

At Ambalagoda, which was well-known for its mask-carving, we stopped to visit the Master Carver Ariyapala. Sadly, he was partially blind, but his son carried on the tradition of the craft and the designs, carving the demon masks used for ritual dances. These were hand-carved, carefully painted in brilliant colours and lacquered. A young Italian boy was learning the craft. I found these masks quite horrendous; many of them represented diseases and were used for exorcism.

Past Ambalangoda we saw Muslim cemeteries side by side with Buddhist prayer flags. In Alutgama – wedged between the resort of Bentona and Beruwala Beach – we passed big fish markets and big fruit markets, and saw much leather-wear on sale.

In the next bay fishermen were bringing in their nets, chanting whilst they were hauling in their catch. This was done twice a day and took one and a half hours to complete. Two boats watched that the nets were not fouled by treacherous rocks and a third one lay out at sea at the end of the net.

It began to rain at Mangona. Then we passed through small villages which used to be fishing villages but had become beach resorts. Near a mosque which was being restored we saw Muslim women, heads modestly covered, wearing colourful saris. As we approached Kalutara, a white *dagoba* dominated the scene. It was

175

a very beautiful modern building and did not serve as a reliquary but was hollow and painted inside.

Suddenly a tropical storm broke out, which made it very difficult to see out of our bus, but I did notice that the 'Urban Council' had moved into a splendid building at Panadura, that Moratuwa had a Christian church and some fine houses surrounded by mean little ones and Buddha standing close by another church. In Basil Trading Centre, Pfizer, Glaxo and Singer Sewing Machines each had factories and offices. Suddenly a red London bus loomed up in front of us and on this stretch of our journey we saw for the first time a sign on a building with 'Jehovah's Witness' on it.

After a long and hot drive we arrived at Mount Lavinia Hotel, which stands 11 miles south of the centre of Colombo on the ocean. This former residence of the British Governor is an imposing building with a large cool marble hall. With its pool on the terrace overlooking the ocean, its private beach, shops and numerous elegant reception rooms, a coffee shop and ballroom, we found it all very overwhelming. All bedrooms had balconies facing the sea. Far out lay an oil rig, sailing boats, motorboats, water-skiers and windsurfers were out on the clear water, and the beach swept to either side of the hotel as far as the eye could see. The ocean was rough and treacherous with many jagged rocks and dangerous undercurrents.

Our first day in this lap of utter luxury we spent mostly at the side of the pool until the breeze became too strong. When we stepped out on our balcony early in the morning, a fishing boat was pulled ashore and later we watched elderly men earnestly doing exercises on the beach.

In the late afternoon we walked out of the grounds and were immediately besieged by a horde of children chanting the well-known chorus: 'Pen, bon-bon, money', but we remained firm, refusing their request, offering instead to take their photographs. Having done so, we asked them for a name and address so that we could mail them a copy. They led us through an overgrown garden to a complex of mean little houses and took us into one of them, into a dark dingy room which had been divided into living and sleeping quarters. Father painstakingly wrote out his name and address and we took our leave, to stroll on. We passed a large sports ground where schoolgirls were receiving prizes. One group wore kilts and glengarries. Houses along the road had seen better days. On the main road we saw a 'Pudding Shop' next to an 'Express Cleaners' whose doorway was festooned with pineapples. The sign of 'Mastercarver' lured us into an Aladdin's cave where we bought two lovely masks carved from golden jackwood. One of them represented King Parakramabahu the First.

Satisfied with our walk, we turned back to the sea past nice villas, hotels, restaurants and clubs until we reached the beach. Here we found many hotels with their private stretch of golden sand. Finally we walked along some rocks where lovers sat beneath umbrellas shielding them from the scorching sun and from stares. Back at the hotel that night we had a barbecue on the terrace looking out to sea which was quite excellent.

A Singhalese couple I had known for many years picked us up next morning in their brand new Japanese car to take us to their home. On our way we stopped at a temple which had a *dagoba*, and yet in the main shrine of the complex we found the usual mixture of Hindu and Buddhist mythology. The worshippers paid homage to Buddha in the front porch, before bringing their offerings, requests and thanks to one of the Hindu gods seated in individual shrines at the back of the temple. Gertrude explained once again that pure Buddhism is not a religion but a philosophy stating, 'Man alone is responsible for his Fate.' Buddha had preached tolerance and one of his principles was: 'Thou shall not kill', therefore until quite recently the Army had not been trained to fight but merely played a ceremonial part.

They took us along poor roads teeming with traffic, past colourful markets, to their home, which was a tranquil oasis on this hot humid day and consisted of a cool bungalow hidden behind trees standing in its own large grounds. The front garden, with sweet-smelling flowers, was neatly kept, whilst the rest was jungle where coffee, pineapple, jackfruit, mango etc. – all they wanted – grew. The cesspool was far from the house. A small tank served the family for a dip, a wash or a swim.

A niece who had recently married in a register office was staying with Gertrude until a Singhalese wedding could be arranged, which was a most elaborate affair and the responsibility of the bride's family, whilst when the newly-weds returned from their honeymoon it was the bridegroom's turn to give a house-warming and homecoming party.

177

Their eldest son, his pregnant wife and their little son were also living temporarily with their parents until he had built a house in the grounds.

It was good to be able to talk and ask questions. They told us that once again Sri Lanka grew sufficient rice for its own need. After Independence all schooling was taught in Singhalese, replacing English, but this had been reversed again. Medical treatment was free but of poor standard with overcrowded hospitals, therefore anybody who could afford to pay sought private treatment. Herbal medicine was widely practised since most people were suspicious of modern drugs and also it was much cheaper. As far as the Tamil question was concerned, this was a very complicated issue since there were actually three factions of Tamils who did not agree amongst themselves: they were the original settlers from India in the arid north, the later immigrants who had migrated to the fertile north-east of the island and the poor workers imported by the British to work the tea plantations. Initially it had started as an economic question since the Tamils held most of the key positions in the Civil Service and the professions, and after Independence the Singhalese no longer accepted this situation; also the Tamils demanded more fertile land. The whole issue had been stirred up into a religious and ethnic question in spite of the fact that for centuries Tamils and Singhalese had lived peacefully side by side.

When we said farewell to our hosts they presented us with a parcel of special tea and a large pineapple. The rest of the day we spent again at the pool and in the evening we had a memorable fish barbecue on the terrace under the velvet sky. The heat of the day had abated by then and a pleasant breeze wafted across from the rough sea. Soon the time had come for us to leave for the airport. Our journey took us back to Colombo. Outside the town our coach was stopped for speeding, which apparently was a very common procedure, but all went well and we arrived at the airport in time. General confusion seemed to reign there, but finally we boarded and took off half an hour late. For once, we were unable to leave the plane at Dubai.

It was a long flight. Cold air blew in through the vents. After daylight broke we flew above the clouds and did not know where we were until the captain announced that we were approaching Zurich, where it was snowing and the temperature had dropped to five degrees below zero. Greyness engulfed us as we slowly descended and found that thick snow covered the airfield. There was a thirty-minute delay for the de-icing equipment to be available but this became considerably longer. A job which normally takes twenty minutes took one hour and twenty minutes instead. Snow-ploughs were in continuous operation. Finally, after three hours' delay, we were airborne once more and rose above the thick clouds into blue sky and sun. Visibility was lost again, when we descended. Once we were able to gain clear vision again we saw a sprinkling of snow covering the countryside before we reached terra firma at the end of yet another memorable journey.

SACRED MOUNTAINS, TEMPLES AND TALES

South Korea

April 1987

It was extremely difficult in 1987 to find a tour operator going to Korea. Our last hope was a small botanical-orientated tour operator. With great doubts we contacted him to ask whether he only concentrated on plants. He laughed and reassured us that he did not intend to forgo any temples or any other interesting sights.

We left London on a bright spring morning and whilst waiting on the runway watched Concorde rise into the air gracefully like a bird. Once we were airborne we crossed the Channel, saw France's coast clearly below us and soon descended through a sea of clouds to land in Paris since it was here where we had to pick up the Korean plane. At that time Britain had no diplomatic connection with Seoul.

We walked past an avenue of tempting shops as we went from one part of the airport to another to board our plane. Unfortunately we could not get a window seat and were obliged to catch a view whenever we could manage. Our journey continued in bright sunshine all along the way. From time to time we glimpsed an eerie landscape covered by snow or sharply etched peaks alternating in other areas with flat countryside showing faint outlines of fields, shrouded by a still white blanket of snow. After eight hours in the air, having eaten at peculiar times, we reached Alaska. Snow-capped mountains surrounded the airfield as we landed bumpily at Anchorage. The transit lounge was one lively shopping arcade with expensive merchandise. It was pleasant to be able to step out on the observation platform and to feel the fresh cool air on our faces.

The temperature was 30 degrees Fahrenheit, but it was sunny and bright. Soon – with a new crew on board – we were airborne again.

Time passed very quickly and ceased to matter whilst we slept, ate, watched a film and a short feature documentary about Korea until we landed at 4.30 p.m. local time on 22nd April in Seoul. All along our flight we had travelled in brilliant sunshine during the day, but Seoul greeted us with rain. Grey and dull, was our first impression of this city.

It was pleasant to sit comfortably in our hotel room sipping an aperitif and nibbling nuts at the end of our first day, having enjoyed our first private sauna (in a very antiquated 'machine' in our bathroom). The hotel stood south of the River Han in a new suburb of this ever-growing town. The streets were busy with a continuous stream of cars, buses and taxis in large numbers. Almost all cars were fitted with most elaborate seat covers and with a pleated arrangement along the rear window ledge. Some of these covers were quilted, others were made of brocade, whilst some of the drivers' seats were bedecked with wooden beads. Boxes of tissues were equally artistically disguised and proudly displayed in the centre of the back window. Women drivers seemed to be missing in this dense traffic. All cars were spotlessly clean and all drivers wore white cotton gloves; in fact nearly every manual task was performed wearing gloves: street sweepers used rubber gloves extending up to the elbow, garbage collectors did likewise, as did all other people engaged in dirty jobs.

First thing that morning we went for a walk round the block and were amazed at the cleanliness of the streets, the well-cared-for villas with pleasant gardens, many of them with roofs of traditional design. Wherever possible, plants grew. Trees, usually conifers, thrived on roofs, stood on balconies, were placed outside front doors. Bedding plants grown in plastic troughs added colour every-where. There were innumerable small shops and eating places. An enormous church with twin towers which was under reconstruction loomed up on a hill behind our hotel. Wherever we looked were hotels.

To start our sightseeing tour we had to join the dense traffic on the busy broad avenue which led across the River Han to Kwangh-wanoon Gate, one of the original nine gates which used to pierce the city walls. Only five had remained, looking attractive with their unique traditional roofs.

Our first visit was to the National Museum housed in a handsome building, built by the Japanese. Here we spent only one hour, to see some of the important exhibits such as the golden treasures found in tombs from the Silla period, silver and bronze from the Kaya era, and superb celadon ceramics from Koryo Kingdom, which cannot be reproduced since nobody has been able to achieve exactly the same soft green-grey colour. In olden times the temperature which was necessary in order to fire the clay to this lovely hue was tested by the potter against his hand. When we return to Seoul again, we hope to pay a longer visit to the museum. As we left, hordes of children streamed into the building as well as groups of very old men, some with wispy beards, leaning heavily on sticks, all clad in their traditional apparel.

From here we made our way to Changduk Palace, where at set times tours were conducted by English-, Japanese- or Korean-speaking guides. Everything in this country seemed very orderly. Changduk Palace ranked as Seoul's best preserved palace. It was originally built in 1405, burnt down in 1592 and was rebuilt in 1611. As in China, all palaces had originally been built of wood on stone foundations and surrounded by thick stone walls. The whole complex was very charming, with its hipped roof curving towards heaven, guarded by clay animals at each corner. All roofs had been constructed on true and false rafters. The latter were purely ornamental in the shape of dragons. The whole architecture was reminiscent of Chinese, but less elaborate, more rustic and more restful to the eye. There was the usual central pathway solely for the royal couple, flanked on either side by ramps serving the rest of the royal court to reach the audience chamber. One old building was covered by dark blue tiles. This was the royal colour and this too cannot be reproduced these days. The King was called 'Dragon' and sat on the Dragon Throne. Every building bore a dragon on its roof except the King's private apartments: one dragon could not be superimposed upon another.

The courtyards were tranquil and serene beneath the shady trees. All buildings were kept warm by under-floor heating. Their brick chimneys stood apart. During the winter months the lattice windows, which were covered with white paper, were turned into 'double windows' by sliding wooden shutters across. During the hot summer months doors were suspended horizontally along the ceiling on large hooks and sun blinds were let down. The last descen-

183

dent of the Yi Dynasty – an old prince and his equally ancient wife – still lived in a small palace within the complex.

To reach the gate to the Secret Garden we passed the hospital. The gardens covered a huge area behind the palace complex and used to be closed to the public, having been created solely for the use of the royal family and their intimate friends. Entering through the Gate of Longevity, made from one massive stone without a join, we entered this 'paradise' where trees abounded. Here the King could fish in a lotus pond from a small pavilion built on its shore or he could read in a library erected above the lake or, if he wished, throw a party for his friends in a hall on the first floor of the library, or conduct examinations in the examination hall. Admiring the flowering trees set amongst the conifers and other deciduous trees, we continued to stroll leisurely until we reached the 'Dragon Tree', a gnarled Chinese pine with roots shaped like dragons about to ascend to heaven which was said to be 700 years old. To return to our coach we walked along the now empty palace moat, past the oldest of the stone bridges which spanned it, which we had crossed at the beginning of our visit. From the Secret Garden we drove to the only bell tower which still remained standing. During the Yi Dynasty the bell tolled to announce the nightly curfew. Although it has stopped tolling, curfew remained from midnight until 4 a.m. until quite recently. Sharon – our very charming guide – told us that one day when she was out with a European friend and the siren shrilled (it had replaced the bell), she was astounded at her companion's amazement and disbelief since in her innocence Sharon had assumed that curfew existed all over the world. When telling this story she laughed about herself; her marked sense of humour was one of the features which endeared her to us.

For our first Korean meal we were taken to a small restaurant which stood well tucked away. We took off our shoes before we sat on cushions around a low table. The floor was covered with yellow oiled paper, and spotlessly clean. There was under-floor heating. It was a very dark place with small cubicles and discreet side rooms screened by curtains for privacy. Numerous small dishes were served beginning with a little bowl of soup and another of rice for each person. Chopsticks and a spoon were the implements to be used. Food was highly spiced with onions and garlic freely used. I must confess I am not very keen on Korean food. Usually the meal was accompanied by roasted barley tea – this time it was rice tea – neither China nor Indian tea were ever offered. In our hotel, which was a 'Korean inn' with a restaurant attached, we had coffee for our breakfast. One of the men in our party had great difficulties to manipulate the chopsticks. Without much ado one of the girls who served us knelt down beside Victor, gently took the chopsticks out of his big, clumsy hands and fed him daintily with titbits. Incidentally we had met both Victor and his friend Francis in Peru many years ago.

To continue our sightseeing tour we drove through Seoul to the Pugak Skyway which led through foreign quarters to Pugak-San above the city. Since this was a military zone near the American Army Station, no pedestrian was allowed in the area; it could only be approached by bus or car and no vehicle was allowed to stop along the way. The view from the top was interesting since we could see the old town cradled between Nam-San (meaning South Mountain) in the south and Pugak-San (meaning North Mountain) in the north. Part of the old city wall still stood but the town had grown so enormously that all we could see were hundreds of skyscrapers towering above clusters of low traditional roofs. At Pugak-San old and young ladies in their national dress looked like gay butterflies in a kaleidoscope of brilliant colours.

Our bus took us down town again, this time to visit the East Gate Market, which was crowded with both people and merchandise. Rough benches and tables stood amidst the profusion of goods and milling crowds, and people sat there calmly eating the most extraordinary-looking food. Many of the fruits and vegetables we saw were completely unknown to us. Some sweets tempted us, we tasted them and later bought a small amount. When we admired the most elaborate arrangements of confectionery we were told that these were presented to in-laws at wedding feasts and were actually carefully selected from glossy photographs. On the floor above the street were household goods, textiles, beautiful silks, lacquered ware inlaid with mother-of-pearl and many more articles for sale. Having been completely overwhelmed by the amount and variety of goods and the huge number of people, we crossed the River Han again, passing the luxury Silla Hotel – looking most impressive – standing next to a park which was ablaze with golden forsythia and pink cherry blossoms. Our last visit was a flower market which stretched along either side of the main road, with boxes over boxes

185

of flowers in a glorious rainbow of colours outside a number of glasshouses. I had never seen such giant ranunculi before.

Later in the evening we joined forces with most of our party. in search of food. All of us opted for non-Korean food and walked along the main road, where eating places lined either side displaying their Korean dishes on plates in the window with price tags attached, looking most attractive. Leaving the main thoroughfare, we came upon a pizza house, which was large and brash with only two tables occupied. Here we settled for plain dishes. The other two parties were families with small children. They were absolutely spellbound by an incredibly noisy performance of outsized animated animals. The children had to answer questions, sing songs and recite verses before each received a prize. The performance was partly in English, partly in Korean. In spite of the din we had a splendid evening. On our way back to the hotel we passed a large number of sports grounds, tennis and golf, surrounded by high netting and also many of the well-cared-for parks, mostly planted with conifers. Newly planted trees had their trunks covered by rope to protect them until they were established.

Breakfast next morning was pure purgatory since the service – although very friendly – was very inefficient. Having waited for an hour, we were presented with cold omelettes or cold scrambled eggs, one small gas ring heated one small kettle for coffee. The ordeal over, we started our journey to the east coast.

It was a grey and misty morning as we travelled through the city to pick up the Yougdon Expressway, which was a toll road, extremely good and fast. From time to time it broadened out into wide bays which were intended to serve as helicopter pads in time of war. The area we travelled through was well-cultivated and contained many glasshouses covered by plastic sheeting to encourage the early ripening of vegetables. Apart from these there were many rice paddies and the whole district was ablaze with golden forsythia, which is indigenous to Korea and grows wild. Many magnolia trees were also in bloom.

Sharon accompanied us on our entire journey through her country. She was an extremely pleasant person, did not mind being asked questions and in her turn appeared to be interested in us and our lives, which is quite unusual since generally the local guides do not ask questions and do not seem to be interested in our culture and our background. Her obvious eagerness to hear about our country, customs etc was most refreshing and gratifying. She asked one Irish member of our party whether Ireland although a separate state belonged to England politically.

Sharon herself was born in a small place north of the capital and was one of four children but she was the only member of her family who lived in town. Having been to university to study psychology, she had been unable to find a suitable job. Knowing English and Japanese, she had become a guide eighteen months ago. Her English was quite excellent and she told us many things about her country, such as that Army service, which lasted three years, was compulsory for men when they were nineteen years old but could be deferred if they were at university. Girls were able to volunteer.

It seemed strange to us that a child when born is considered to be one year old and that everybody commences another year on New Year's Day. Thus a child born in December becomes two on the first of January. Primary schooling starts when the child reaches seven and is compulsory and free, whilst high school and university have to be paid for. As in China, rice is the staple food and their three meals a day consisted of rice with side dishes.

The mountains were still shrouded in mist as we travelled along, passing ginseng fields protected by straw roofs. Red ginseng was a State monopoly. Later we tasted Ginseng Up and found it refreshing. From time to time we saw hill tombs, which were grass-covered mounds often flanked by a column either side with a stone tablet bearing an inscription mounted between them. Buddhists believed in cremation, Confucius in ancestor worship. Choosing a beautiful position for the tomb ensured health and fortune for the family of the deceased.

Slowly the sun broke through. Once we had left Seoul well behind us, the traffic diminished, with few private cars on the highway, and we mainly met coaches and lorries. The countryside became undulated, with rice paddies lying between wooded hills and oxen ploughing the fields. Occasional small hamlets provided brilliant splashes of colour with bright red or blue roofs. Some of the roofs were corrugated iron, others were tiled. Only one group of ugly-looking flat-roofed houses built of concrete appeared.

As we climbed up a mountain road – lined by golden forsythia – wooded slopes accompanied us with fresh light green deciduous trees contrasting with the sombre tones of the conifers, whilst daphne and other flowering shrubs provided colour. Mist still veiled the distant mountain ranges. The road descended into a wide valley where a river meandered through.

Our driver drove extremely well in spite of the fact that he had collected medicine for himself from a pharmacy at the beginning of our journey, smoked incessantly and at one point opened a bottle of Ginseng Up to drink it without stopping. Once he halted, feeling anxious about a new tyre, but obviously was satisfied after he had hit it with a slender wooden mallet.

Many of the newly-built villages which we passed had numerous churches with windows framed by curtains. The large number of churches had already surprised us in Seoul.

Our road led up and down and we lunched 2,500 feet above sea level on Korean 'fast food' for the first time. The steaming hot noodle soup served in paper cups followed by ice cream were both delicious. Our journey continued downhill, negotiating many sharp bends presenting an ever-varying panorama of mountains. Roadworks were in progress but did not cause any delay. The sun reflected on an enormous brass kettle which one of the workmen was filling from a waterfall cascading down at the side of the road.

At Kangnung, which lies on the sea, we left the Yongdon Express Way to turn north. The soil was sandy, seagulls swooped down over the estuary; soon we were following the sandy beaches along the sea. Herons, or maybe they were storks, stood in the rice paddies. The topography of Korea is such that the east coast is rising whilst the west coast is sinking into the sea. Gentle hills intervened between the road and the Sea of Japan.

At Naksana we halted in a large parking lot lined by booth after booth offering souvenirs of all kinds. Enormous mountains of dried fish and dried seaweed (a great delicacy) were also on sale. A couple sat on the sandy ground patiently cleaning seaweed and stringing it up to dry in the sun. Sadly most of the beach was closed and patrolled by the Army in case a North Korean boat tried to land.

Entering through a lovely old gate, we walked up to Naksana Shrine past some phallic tombs outside the walls and continued through a peaceful orchard with flowering trees and through a second small gate protected by four fierce looking guardians. Before entering the final courtyard we admired the well-preserved oldest bell. The shrine itself contained a golden Buddha beneath many lotus-shaped lanterns hanging suspended from the ceiling in preparation for Buddha's birthday on 5th May. In spite of the many pilgrims, it was a peaceful place; they were entirely oblivious of what happened around them, prostrating themselves in front of the golden Buddha. Here we encountered monks for the first time. They wore grey coats which were quite loose, tied in front and sometimes worn over ordinary clothing, at other times they were clothed entirely in grey. Their heads were shaved but usually hidden by the traditional wide brimmed straw hat.

Leaving the shrine, we made our way to the enormous statue of Kuanyin, the Bodhisattva of Mercy and Compassion, who is the only female Bodhisattva. Crowds of school girls surrounded this fine statue who were extremely friendly and loved to talk to us and besieged us to take photographs of them with one of our party; in particular they were intrigued by Tom with his grey hair and thick grey beard, since neither grey hair nor beards are ever seen in the local population. I had never know any other nation taking so many photographs of each other. The view down pine-clad slopes across the sea was beautiful.

The last place we visited was a small pavilion looking out to sea from a promontory. Peace descended once the children, having obediently followed the command to assemble, had left.

Returning to our coach, we continued the short drive to the entrance of Mount Soraksan National Park, where we stayed in the rather luxurious new Sorak Hotel set against a background of pine woods. Our bedroom in true Korean style was spacious and had a small anteroom where we deposited our shoes in exchange for the slippers which had been provided for use in the bedroom. It was covered by oiled yellow paper and sparsely furnished, containing just two bedrolls, two small pillows filled with grain, duvets inside brocade covers, silk-covered cushions to sit on and a low table. Sitting and sleeping on the floor was partially for practical reasons to take advantage of the under-floor heating and partly as a symbol of humility.

Having settled in, we walked out into the park, which was highly organised as far as parking facilities were concerned. Crossing on a suspension bridge we ambled through the woods towards a water-fall. In a clearing stood a simple complex of souvenir stalls and eating places where we met a young Korean couple. He was a botanist, the only one in all Korea who specialised in palaeolithic pollens and grains, which meant that he worked with archaeologists dating plants and seeds found on excavation sites and reconstructed the flora of that specific era; the eating habits, skeletons of people and animals, health aspects etc. He had come to Mount Soraksan National Park to look for a species of forsythia which only grew here. Our leader, a botanist, walked ahead with him whilst I followed with the wife. They had married in New York, where her sister lived, and stayed on in Carolina and Maryland for eight years. The eldest two children were born in America. Ten years ago they returned to Korea, where two younger children were born. The children were aged thirteen, eleven, nine and seven. She herself came from a large family of five boys and two girls. Most Korean families, however, only had two children.

Although we followed a small stream we did not reach the waterfall but at least we did find a white violet with unusual feathery leaves. The young Korean couple gave us a lift back to our hotel in their car. It had been interesting to listen to the two botanists conversing with each other. The Korean botanist thought that it might be possible that he would come to Kew in September.

Our meal in the western-style restaurant was quite hilarious and we ended the day joining Frances and Victor in their room for a drink and local strawberries.

Our Korean bedding did not prove very comfortable. But tucked in the ante-room we found a refrigerator and toothbrushes, face flannels and shampoo were provided in the bathroom; everything was simple but very clean.

When on wakening I looked out of the window, the tops of the mountains were shrouded in mist but later this descended and it began to rain, steadily and relentlessly, which delayed our departure into the park. Since the weather did not improve we set forth into the woods in pouring rain, passing an enclosure with different kinds of bell-shaped stupas erected to honour illustrious Zen monks who had died. Slowly we walked through the lovely woods in which flowering prunus, wild cherry, peach and wild pear trees in full flower mingled with the dark green of the pine trees, with the light green of the larches and the various shades of deciduous trees. The going was not hard but extremely wet, as we followed along a burbling brook, crossing numerous bridges, some made of wood others of metal. A continuous throng of people were on the move, coming and going. Schools came up here, especially in the spring. Men and women of all ages, with most of the women in pantaloons of all colours and textures, families – with father usually carrying the youngest on his shoulders – all had come in spite of the rain. Soon we arrived at Shin Hungsa Temple, which, like many of the other temples, went back a long way. Originally it had been built in 625 AD but was twice destroyed by fire. (No wonder the Koreans were almost obsessive as far as fire precautions were concerned; not only did we have smoke detectors in our room, we had also been provided with smoke masks and a staunch rope.) It was finally restored in 1648. According to the painting on the indicator board, it was going to be extended into a big complex.

The first gate through which we entered was a single pillared entrance. The four fierce-looking Heavenly Kings of the Four Corners of the Compass guarded the second gate, which led into the courtyard. There the old Granite Pagoda stood in the centre, whilst the monks' sleeping quarters lay to one side, their meditation and lecture hall to the other with the temple between them. Thirty monks lived in Shin Hungsa. One of them, dressed in a padded grey coat, was our guide and showed us a hall containing a large drum and many lotus-shaped lanterns which were all used for special festivals. He also took us to a pavilion where he proudly displayed a wooden block print of the *Sutra*.

Another monk hurried along in a very elegant grey coat, a dark brown shawl draped over his left shoulder, and started chanting in front of Buddha, who stood in his shining glory flanked by Kwanswum and Taiseisi, two Bodhisattva, on either side. 'It is time for Buddha's lunch,' muttered Sharon, our guide.

The most charming vignettes, full of fun, adorned the outside walls of the buildings. They were a combination of Shaman, Taoist and Buddhist imagination. Finding traces of Shaman-Taoist iconography in a Buddhist temple was like paying protection money to a former landlord!

A very old bronze bell ensconced in its own pavilion was surrounded by a lattice fence which allowed us to peer through to admire it. The bell, as well as a giant drum, was used during special ceremonies. A modern stupa rose behind this pavilion.

Leaving Shin Hungsa Temple, we joined the stream of people wandering slowly uphill over stones and gnarled roots past 'restrooms' (toilets, which were well-advertised), eating stalls and souvenir booths. At a small mountain brook the path divided: one side led to a monastery for nuns past a small shrine where a small white statue stood entirely protected within a plastic bag; the other path led us on to the Rocking Rock, a huge boulder which could be moved when pushed at a certain angle but always returned to its original position. Schoolchildren stood here at the end of the trail, listening spellbound to the story of Ulsan Bawi, the spectacular granite boulder which bars the way out of the valley. Inside this rock lay the Keso Hermitage; a Buddhist swastika in red was carved above the entrance. Chanting issued from within as we followed the narrow corridor, which was lit by neon strip light. A young woman dressed in grey, the custodian, stood discreetly in a dark corner. Sharon prostrated herself numerous times in front of the golden Buddha. I stole a glance into the little shrine tucked behind a rock which bore exquisite paintings of the Taoist Mountain Spirit to either side of the Buddha.

Tracing our way back through the woods, we marvelled at the never ending stream of people, often singing as they walked along. They frequently greeting us cheerfully and occasionally stopped to shake hands. At one of the many eating places we halted to sample a delicious quick-fried potato cake before our final descent. Feeling very wet and cold, we luckily found a warm and cheerful eating place near the entrance to the park.

In the afternoon we took a different trail along a very picturesque gorge with most fantastic rock formations and many natural pools. The final feat consisted of crossing the clear stream, helped by a stout rope, to reach an almost vertical pink rock. A path led up through pine woods to a cave on the other side, but unfortunately this path was closed. The rain was pouring down, making us exceedingly wet, so we hurried back the way we had come. There were fewer amenities along this way than there had been on our morning walk; no women sat along the way tempting us with titbits out of their basket, nobody crossed our path – we were the only ones braving the elements.

Again the mountains were shrouded in mist and rain poured down relentlessly next morning when we set off by bus towards the coast the way we had come. Once we had reached the sea we turned north along the shore past many small fishing villages, some of which were just a collection of shabby little houses clustering in a bay. Again we were surprised to see so many Catholic churches.

The sandy beaches, however, were out of bounds, patrolled by the Army lest spies slipped across from North Korea undetected.

Curfew still existed in this 'sensitive area' from midnight until 4 a.m. Bundles of hay had been piled on concrete blocks, and wood had been stored in special block huts along the roadside in readiness to be spread across the road and lit in case of war. Although we had encountered various checkpoints, we did not have to stop at any of them and proceeded peacefully on our way through rice paddies, but Army camps still lay dotted about. Near the demilitarised zone numerous grass-covered tombs appeared. Soon we left the coast turning inland through rural scenes with farmsteads, fields, small orchards and more rice paddies.

When we had reached the end of the road, our journey had taken us right round Mount Sorak. Even though it was still raining and very cold, we were ready to walk up the valley along an easy path following the 'stream of hundred pools'. Rain stopped after a while and it turned into a lovely sunny day under a blue sky. The rock formation was quite incredible, particularly beneath the clear green waters where white veins made pretty patterns. Some of the rocks were beautifully curved by water pressure over many years, others had been shaped into terraces where little pools had collected on each step, making up the hundred pools which gave the river its name. Above the valley towered cliffs and mountains, slopes covered by fir trees and rhododendrons. Pretty plants sprang out of sheer rock. Finally we caught sight of our goal on the other side of the river: Paekdam Sa Temple (Temple of Hundred Pools). A very makeshift bridge led across which we negotiated with faint heart, balancing precariously. A new stone bridge was being built.

Two monks lived in the temple. A third one, in a patched grey coat and wearing the usual flat-brimmed straw hat arrived whilst we were there; he was 'a wandering monk', we were told. Passing through the gate, we entered the courtyard in which a simple stone pagoda marked the centre. The monks' kitchen, with a beautiful black iron grate, and their library were housed in a building on the right, whilst another one to the left served as sleeping quarters and for meditation. This was equipped with under-floor heating since the winters must be very cold. (It had been only 8 degrees fahrenheit when we started off that morning.) Facing us stood the temple which had been burnt down various times and renamed numerous times in order to change its ill luck and finally moved from a polluted area to a clean one. Since the first location had been used for hunts, it was thought that the blood from the animals had soiled the holy ground and displeased Buddha. The original Buddha statue and the wall paintings had, however, been saved and were very old indeed. A bell and wooden gong stood outside the temple. To admire Buddha we stepped inside where the wall paintings, amazingly fresh in colour, once again showed Shamanistic influence. There was also a most extraordinary array of small seated figures placed on silk cushions to either side of Buddha, representing his disciples. One had a moustache, another clutched a swan and yet another one held a fish close to his body, and all of them had Buddha's large ears with elongated lobes. A lovely bronze bell stood in the corner. I strolled up to peep into a small shrine standing tucked behind the main temple in a meadow and discovered a most delightful painting of the Mountain Spirit, a typical Shaman emblem. Near this shrine a young man was busily searching the ground. He showed me the little green plant he was collecting and simply called it 'mountain vegetable'.

One of the monks provided a most welcome cup of coffee, gladly accepted since it was still very cold. As always, a glass of fresh clear water was also offered.

Apart from the two monks, a family with two children also lived in the temple complex. The man was busily laying a water pipe and fixing a tap in the kitchen whilst the woman was lagging the pipes. On a raised platform behind the kitchen stood a collection of jars of all sizes; they served as storage, the smaller ones containing soya paste whilst the larger ones were used for the famous *Kimchi*, which constituted their winter vegetable. At the end of the autumn, cabbage was shredded and packed tightly into the stone jars in brine with spices, onion and pepper before being buried in the ground and left to ferment. *Kimchi* was used by everybody all through Korea.

When we traversed the frail bridge again, we met a party of young men taking shelter under an arch of the stone bridge which was being constructed. They had climbed over the top of Mount Sorak from the other side and been caught in a snowstorm, which had soaked them down to their skins. They were drying out by a fire and beckoned us to join them to warm ourselves. Three soldiers joined us and grilled tiny dried fish over the open fire. Feeling restored, we wandered down a narrow path to the newly built 'inn', which proved to be quite simple, greeting us with a large log fire and offering some provisions. Pondering what to buy from the limited selection, we decided on a packet of biscuits and a tin of chopped meat. With four climbers who had just arrived, we exchanged some biscuits for chocolates. They also offered to boil some water for us on their Primus stove to make coffee but unfortunately it refused to work.

When we walked back along the stream the way we had come, we were able to admire the splendid scenery in sunshine. Very few people crossed our path but we met two Korean nuns in full habit and some Army jeeps passed by. There were some 'restrooms' along this way and we noticed a public urinal without doors next to a more discreet ladies' toilet. Stalls and eating places were entirely absent in this part of the forest.

The coach took us back the same way we had come, negotiating many sharp bends, driving uphill into a wide valley which was extremely fertile and where all work was still done entirely by hand. Special wooden frames were used to dry fish. Wooden huts on stilts stood at regular intervals along the road, containing logs to be used to obstruct roads in order to stem the advance of any invader. When we reached the sea again, it was deep blue and less rough than before. Seaweed hung drying in the sun. The road turned inland again and rose up into the mountains when we suddenly saw two enormous new buildings in the far distance set amongst dark pine woods flanking a big pleasure wheel. Finally we dropped down to Sorak Dong, a new resort complex with gay red, blue and green roofs topping the white buildings, which sparkled in the bright sunshine.

Our last morning at Sorak greeted us with brilliant sunshine and a cloudless blue sky, allowing for the first time a perfect view of the majestic peaks around us. On our return the previous evening we had tried to get up to Mount Sorak's peak but had been too late, the last cable car had left when we arrived at the station. On this lovely morning we fared better when we walked along to the station to join the throng of chattering local people waiting for the next cable car. Riding up over the lovely woods, enjoying the panorama, we looked out far across the sea, which lay in the distance at the end of the valley. Once we had reached the top we clambered up to one of the peaks. The wind rose and tugged fiercely at us. There were crowds of people around us; all except our party were Koreans. Women of all ages in their wide pantaloons climbed nimbly over rocks like agile monkeys. When we went back to the cable car station a whole carload of honeymoon couples arrived. Only a few of the brides wore traditional costumes, which were pink. But all the others wore pink blouses embroidered with pearls, carried white handbags and wore high heeled white shoes. Men were in city suits. I only saw one bridegroom in traditional dress of pink brocade pantaloons topped by a colourful waistcoat beneath a short fitted jacket with toggles which terminated in twenty Zen-shaped amber beads.

Leaving Soraksan National Park we drove down to the sea past the tall figure of the Bodhisattva of Mercy of Naksana again. Two parachutes descended over a field, struggling against the strong winds, heat haze covered the mountains, rice was ripening beneath plastic cloches. At Yang Yang, which was a sizeable town, we turned away from the coast, climbed up through wooded slopes past a little shrine standing at the foot of terraced fields and came upon a collection of new houses looking most attractive, built in traditional style, with the ever present *kimchi* jars standing close by.

Leaving the fields behind us, we followed a steep road upwards through woods before plunging down into a gorge which led into a valley with a few small farmsteads surrounded by fields. At the end of this valley we entered Soraksan National Park again, where we saw pretty white birch trees covered in new delicate green leaves. At Osaek we began to climb steeply again through dramatic scenery. Many of the trees were still bare and only a few pine trees provided dark green colour. Very occasionally a brilliant splash of pinky-mauve rhododendrons appeared at most unexpected places: they grew on top of rock chimneys or sprang from almost vertical cliffs. Some pine trees also arose precariously out of sheer rock. Low bamboo formed part of the undergrowth and stony pinnacles loomed up in weird shapes. This fantastic road took us to Hangye-Ryong Pass, 3,000 feet above sea level. I have never seen so many coaches parked in one place anywhere as on this superb spot high up in the sky.

After a brief stop to admire the view, we continued on Highway 44 which plunged down into a wide valley with a stony river-bed and past a large military camp. Most of the houses here had gaily coloured roofs, some of which were slate, others corrugated tin. After the big town of Wongfong we encountered a large number of military checkpoints but did not have to stop at any of them. Fields

196

and rice paddies lay everywhere. Inse struck us as a shanty town. To our surprise we realised that babies were tucked inside special aprons, slung on mothers' backs.

Climbing out of the wide valley we reached a high plateau with farmsteads amidst fields. We saw chicken coops for the first time, and fir trees which had been newly planted. The scenery remained remarkable as we continued to travel high above sea level, where forsythia lined the road and fruit trees were in blossom and young poplar trees were slowly coming into leaf. Soyang Lake, a man-made lake, reminded us of a Scottish loch.

For lunch we stopped at a place which was obviously fully equipped to cope with many coaches. A crowd of male students in a uniform consisting of coloured trousers and tops had also halted here. They were university students on their way to a compulsory training course in martial arts in the demilitarised zone. This had been decreed by the Government to let students see 'reality' since they had not experienced war, and was also designed for them to use up surplus energy in order to forestall unrest and demonstrations.

For the first time we drank ginseng; up to then we had only tasted 'Ginseng Up'. Ginseng certainly had an earthy tang related to its origin from a root.

Behind the building of this rest station, women sat on the ground busily inserting tree mushroom spores into holes which men had drilled into oak logs. The holes were sealed with a small plastic disc, the logs covered with black tarred netting and left to germinate. Nobody minded our inquisitive stares, they gave us samples to take home to dry and use. Mushrooms of all kinds were a great speciality in Korea.

The busy highway was mainly used by coaches and lorries; we hardly saw any cars. Returning from Soraksan National Park to Seoul we took the southern route, whilst on our way up we had travelled along the Yougdon Expressway.

Rice paddies stretched as far as the foot of the surrounding slopes many of which were being reforested. Prosperous farms appeared, with wood stacked up like our old-fashioned haystacks, with ginseng plantations nearby. An Army convoy passed us. The mountains were still with us in the distance in the early afternoon when we reached Hong-Chon, where the wide main street was lined with shops. Outside town high-rise flats dwarfed the traditional roofs, towering above farmsteads and rice paddies. After Yang-Logwan we followed a willow tree avenue where pale green leafed branches dipped low down onto the road, succeeded by poplars. Barley fields were well-advanced and we saw an enormous modern red brick church standing in the midst of one. There were few birds along our route, though we had watched the antics of a small wagtail at breakfast and had seen jays in the woods. Men carried heavy loads on wooden frames shaped to fit the contours of their backs. Some things were transported in open woven bamboo baskets, and bicycles were fitted with tall frames behind their seats to hold substantial loads.

Gone were the high mountains, instead we saw an isolated vineyard growing low vines. For the first time we followed along a railway track, which led us past the Paradise Hotel, a modern complex where a large windmill turned in the breeze. Black and white cows grazed on the slopes, whilst men were busy in the fields. Small children with satchels strapped to their backs came home from school at 3 p.m.

Still following the railway to our left, we were accompanied by the broad Namhan Gang River to our right, whilst lovely gentle wooded hills were all around us. A man lay fast asleep, his head resting against a grass covered ancestral tomb. Melons were offered for sale along the road, which was the first time we had encountered them.

As we neared Seoul traffic built up. Black and white cows and black goats still grazed peacefully near large brickworks as we passed through a dusty industrial town.

A four-lane road ran through the busy town of Kuri, still framed by gentle slopes covered by pear orchards, then suddenly we found ourselves back in Seoul again. This time we had arrived on a sunny day. As we drove past the university we saw an open market near the river, young trees lined the roads, which contained traditional houses with their lovely hipped roofs. To call at an enormous 'Cultural Centre', which contained a bank, a post office and a large bookshop, we continued into the centre of town. In fact we made a beeline to the bookshop, which we found in the basement of a shopping arcade brimming with activity. Here we bought a lovely, well-illustrated book on Korean culture and a general book about the country, with excellent photographs. Glue was provided in the tiny post office to stick on stamps and seal envelopes since neither were self-adhesive.

Having completed our 'business', we waited outside the American Embassy (as it happened) for our coach to return. When we tried to take a photograph from here of the National Museum standing against a background of mountains (which would have made a splendid picture) and a foreground of lovely flowers, we were politely but nevertheless very firmly stopped by two soldiers. Before entering the Embassy all cars were halted; boot, engine and undercarriage were all tested with a metal detector before the gate was opened for them to proceed. One man walking past was stopped and had to show his identity card.

Once again we were amazed at the profusion of flowers; large pansies, double pinkish mauve rhododendrons and other flowers and trees were everywhere. Mature trees, with their roots surrounded by a ball of earth contained in sacking, stood ready to be planted. Our coach took us past the lovely South Gate – which rated as 'National Treasure number one' (I do not know how many National Treasures existed in the whole country) – across the River Han and back to our Golden Castle Hotel again.

Having settled into our previous rooms, we tried to find the attractive looking 'Pizzeria Coffee House' which we had spotted in the residential quarters behind our hotel on our first morning in Seoul, but were quite unable to locate it. All we could find were night watchmen sitting in little huts which bore flashing red lights on their roofs. There were people about, but although we asked, nobody seemed to know. Back we trotted to the main road again. First we descended down some stairs but only found men in the place and the hostess gave us an odd stare! Retreating hastily, we wandered on and found a splendid restaurant where the food was quite excellent, the service superb with many bows and 'Yes mams'.

Brilliant sunshine greeted us next morning. When we drove through the already busy town we saw little tots in cheerful brightly coloured uniforms, all with hats or gay caps, being ferried in big coaches to nurseries. We continued on our way to visit the impressive Olympic Complex, which although it was a modern building had managed to incorporate the traditional curved lines. To our great surprise large numbers of old people (many in their traditional costumes) had also arrived to visit this enormous complex. Again we found that they loved to take photographs of each other. It seemed strange to us that they also liked physical contact, liked to touch. A party of handicapped youngsters had also come, each led tenderly by an adult. The actual stadium was huge and was being used for concerts prior to the Olympic Games.

Our journey continued past tall flats, each with a glassed-in balcony festooned with laundry and containing the inevitable *kimchi* and soya paste jars. Soya paste was also left to ferment and apparently the taste improved with keeping. Herbs were also stored and some were kept for five to seven years before use. A small fruit market displayed its wares on the pavement. Finally we left town on a busy expressway, on which we had to pay a toll. Wooded slopes, splashes of forsythia, rice paddies, glasshouses, cloches were back again, frequently plastic sheeting was used to cover seeds. A foundry which we passed at great speed was well known since it had cast Yi Sun-Sin, Korea's 16th-century hero, whose statue we had seen near the town hall in Seoul.

Our journey took us along a highway with four lanes in either direction, with car behind car as far as we could see. At a tree nursery we left it to visit the Korean Folk Village, which had been created in 1974 to preserve the vanishing culture, not merely for the tourists but primarily for future generations.

Again I have never seen so many coaches in one place, never seen so many people visiting one location. There were large groups of children of all ages: tiny tots with satchels on their backs containing their lunch, all wearing the same cotton hats, whilst bigger children carried mats resembling our beach mats and also their lunch. Later they all sat, the bigger ones took their shoes off before they settled on their mats, the little ones sat on the grass, all in orderly groups, none of them made any undue noise. The meals were packed in dishes and quite elaborate. They left no paper or morsel of food behind when they had finished their meal. It was very impressive.

The village itself was delightful, with thatched houses, farmsteads, rich merchants' houses, mansions, a doctor's surgery, artisan's dwellings and a magistrate's house with prison attached. The buildings were from different districts. Totem poles serving to keep away the evil spirit from the village stood at the entrance. Sharon knew these from her childhood. Many of the articles we saw displayed she had grown up with and used herself when she was small. Under-

200

floor heating used to serve for both heating and cooking in the past. Paper was being made as we stood and watched. It seemed a very tedious and complicated process, using the bark from mulberry trees. Craftsmen were carving, working in brass and demonstrating various skills. Spellbound, we watched dancers, who were all male; some used dumb-bell-shaped drums. Some had huge pom-poms on their hats, whilst others again had gay streamers fastened to their headgear and a third group displayed plumes wired to their head cover. Streamers and plumes were used as an integral part of the dance by being twisted, twirled and turned. Men were also walking on tightrope – there was almost too much to watch and see. In the shop, which had exquisite articles to sell, we bought a charming little silk screen with a hand-embroidered picture of children before we had a typical Korean lunch: a barbecue of tender beef served with various side dishes all washed down with rice wine.

Our journey continued through flat, fertile, well-cultivated countryside, with orchards, rice paddies and vineyards. Mountains loomed up in the distance, wooded hills were back again. Good food, rice wine and warm sunshine compounded to make all of us sleepy.

At Osaka Resting Place we halted. These resting places were quite amazing since they were geared to cope with millions of people most efficiently. Apart from petrol stations and toilets, they always offered food, both to eat on the premises and to take away. At times the facilities were quite simple, at others they were quite sophisticated, with restaurants, coffee bars, vending machines, ice cream parlours etc., but they were always spotlessly clean, with friendly service.

Soon we left the highway and, following a curvy mountain road, rose high up to a plateau from which we could see majestic mountain ranges in the distance. Again we passed one of the many enormous churches and noticed the presence of the *kimchi* jar at every house. Men ploughed their fields following their oxen, ginseng grew here and was usually protected by straw or tarred black netting. After Miwon we dropped down into another wide valley, then drove through a narrow wooded one which led us into a wide basin where the modern town of Poun dominated the scene. Climbing up again, we continued through woods alternating with rice paddies, skirted a reservoir and rose up into the mountains to reach Malti Pass, which presented us with lovely views and sur-

201

rounded us with flowering trees and flowering shrubs. After passing Korea's most important pine we entered Sognisan National Park. This old pine, called Chon-Ipium, which means 'Cabinet Minister', according to legend lifted its branches in respect to King Yi Bego (1456–1468) when he passed with his entourage. The humble pine's politeness was rewarded by the flattered King by elevating it to the rank of Cabinet Minister!

At the Tourist Hotel, which stood at the end of Sognisan village, we checked in. Its impressive entrance hall proclaimed all its amenities: restaurants, coffee shops, nightclub, beauty parlour, swimming pool, shop etc. The swimming pool lay empty and our rooms were quite simple, although this time we had beds to sleep in, not *doles* (rooms with under floor heating and futons on the floor). To our surprise toothbrushes and razors were always provided, at least in all the hotels we stayed at.

To visit one of Korea's oldest temples, Popju-Sa, we walked into the park. Once almost all the other tourists had streamed out of the woods, perfect peace descended. Popju-Sa was a large complex containing many structures apart from the usual temple. Many well-preserved stele made of stone which had weathered through the years stood scattered throughout the woods. To enter the courtyard we strolled through two gates, the second one guarded by the fierce looking Kings of the Four Corners of the Compass. A famous cement Buddha, the largest in Korea, was being demolished to be replaced by a replica in bronze. Here we found a most graceful five-storey wooden pagoda with the story of Buddha painted around its walls inside and with a thousand little white figures of Buddha carefully arranged at the base of a big Buddha statue. An 8th-century granite lantern supported by two exquisitely carved lions and a very old ablution trough in the shape of a lotus, as well as another very old lantern showing faint traces of carving, were all within the compound. Near the entrance stood an enormous iron rice pot in which in the 8th century during the Silla period, when the Kings of the Songdong Dynasty reigned, rice for three thousand people was cooked.

Just as we slipped into a temple, candles and joss sticks were being lit. In this temple we admired the very expressive faces of Buddha's disciples lining the walls. The building was double-roofed, with crossbars most ingeniously supporting the second roof. The carvings and painting on the beams were quite exquisite. Once again I managed to peep into the small Shamanistic shrine with its Mountain Spirit riding on the tiger. Next to the pagoda stood an open pavilion protecting a big bronze bell and a cloud and fish which hung suspended from the roof, as well as a drum which stood next to the bell. We did not have to wait long for the twice-daily ceremony, comprising the beating of the drum, the ringing of the bell and the beating of both the cloud and fish, which symbolised the beginning of the day and the ending of it. Everything in Buddhism is symbolic. The fish stands for all creatures in water, the cloud symbolises air and all creatures within, the bell and drum stand for earth and fire. The ceremony was first performed by a monk in a grey coat with his brown shawl thrown over his left shoulder, followed by a novice in black. Both, of course, had shaven heads. The 150 monks who remained at Popju-Sa lived in a compound close by. Many other halls stood in the complex but we made our way slowly to a rock where a serene-looking flat-faced Buddha sitting on a chair had been carved on its smooth surface. A pagoda rose from the top of this huge boulder, guarding Buddha. Two monks had arrived with a blue canvas bag to collect the offerings from a wooden box below the rock.

As we continued on our way we watched men erecting a large wooden board in the courtyard to display a giant painting in honour of Buddha's birthday. Strolling leisurely through the woods, we walked past more stupas standing beneath shady trees until we found ourselves in a tranquil courtyard lying on the river bank with carefully tended flowers everywhere. We realised that we had intruded into the private quarters of the monks. Hastily we withdrew and made our way back to the hotel.

However many people may be walking in these woods, however gaudy the stalls may be near our hotel, with dodgem cars and other fairground trappings nearby, the temples in these woods were of such great magic that we were able to forget all else and only felt the incredible serenity pervading this sacred place set amidst the mountains in woods – which nothing was able to disrupt or spoil.

Next morning a group of Japanese tourists were busily performing their daily exercises in front of our hotel when I first stepped outside. They counted aloud and stretched and jumped in perfect unison, all dressed in identical jumpsuits. Leaving them to their pursuit, we set off to climb the Munsand-Dae Rock on Mount Sogri, which stands at the height of 3,000 feet. Already at eight o'clock in the morning a steady stream of children were marching past the hotel. They had emerged from the village – we were unwittingly caught up in amongst a girls' school. (Sexes were still very strictly segregated, marriages were still being arranged.) Since we had to watch our step to make our way between the throng of children who surged around us, we saw nothing of the river which we were walking alongside. The girls were good-natured, inquisitive and very friendly, but it was quite a sobering thought to see all these children and young people organised into well disciplined groups, ready to be used as perfect machinery for anyone – good or bad – strong enough to hold the authority and power. Individuality and all free thought appeared to be entirely missing.

At the first rest house we were able to part from the girls by deciding to take the right fork through the woods to reach Chon-vanbong (the peak) since the bulk of the girls were taking the left fork. For some time peace, perfect peace reigned as we strolled through the woods on a superb day with the sun filtering through the trees and tiny blue gentians, brilliantly blue dwarf irises and blue and white violets as well as various flowering shrubs delighting us on our way. We crossed countless brooks along bridges cast in cement to simulate logs or balanced from stepping stone to stepping stone. At the third rest house we stopped for a drink. Bottles of soft drink and soya milk lay cooling in a trough filled with clear spring water. Here I drank wine made from the bark of a tree, which tasted of herbs and quinine. Bottles containing snakes stood next to flagons of rice wine on crude shelves. Potato cakes were being fried.

Our path became more difficult with over eight hundred steps to climb. To add to all hazard, a horde of children descended at the same time as we were trying to ascend. The views along the way were magnificent; in one clearing we looked into a valley framed by high peaks. At last we climbed up metal steps to reach the crowded peak. Seven hundred boys had arrived! Every spring and summer, schoolchildren from all over Korea were taken to climb this sacred mountain. They stayed in the area for two or three days, sleeping in hostels in the village. To our surprise there were very few adults supervising them; the teacher carried a whistle and megaphone.

After a short rest we traversed the smooth rock and picked up a narrow path which led uphill and downhill. Steps had been hewn into the rocks at some places, at other parts it was just a steep incline we had to cope with. Finally we crossed the ridge of Mount Sogri, where we stopped to refresh ourselves with a drink at a very grimy hut. The woman who served us carried her baby tucked into a padded apron on her back. Flies buzzed around.

After a five-hour climb we negotiated the last metal staircase, which brought us face to face with Munsand-Dae Rock. At the rest house they served 'instant noodles' in a paper cup, which was very acceptable after our strenuous exercise. Climbing up metal stairs to the ultimate top of the rock, from where the view across mountains and valleys, with weirdly shaped rocks rising into the blue sky and fir trees springing out of cracks, was unforgettable. The air was crystal clear but it was very hot. Sadly the beautiful scene was marred by litter and dirt, which seemed so very strange compared with the built-up areas we had seen, where all had been spotlessly clean. To reach the Korean-style toilet we had to pass the urinals, where the stench almost knocked us back. The toilets were incredibly soiled; water was not available. In stark contrast, just below the toilets lay a helicopter pad and we watched one landing and taking off again.

Many old women and men, bent and frequently with markedly bowed legs, clad in traditional dress and wearing rubber-soled shoes with upturned toes, slowly climbed up the rock, some of them carrying their bags on their heads. It was a fascinating sight. Young people wore jeans, whilst the older generation were in their silk pantaloons. Sharon was surprised that some women in our party wore skirts. The Koreans seemed to be a nation of hikers and even the old people were very nimble on their feet. We even saw a group of young blind people – each led solicitously by a sighted adult – up in the mountains.

Our descent was quite tedious, we slipped and slithered down the sandy soil made even smoother by the many youngsters who had 'tobogganed' down before us. We had to watch every step not to trip over gnarled roots or jagged rocks. Once, we halted to taste delicious liquid yoghurt cooled in a clear stream. Before reaching the end of our trail I joined three members of our party to follow a sign saying 'Hermitage 0.1 km'. Walking through woods brought us out into a sunny clearing, then we climbed up to a small plateau with well-tended fields and recently planted fruit trees to a temple built in traditional style but with double windows in metal frames.

Two pairs of shoes and a plate of peanuts had been left on the terrace but there was no sign of anyone being about. The chimney which served the under-floor heating was set apart and we also found a television aerial between shrubs behind the building. Once again I climbed up, to the small Shaman temple which clung to a rock, to see the painting of the Mountain Spirit on the tiger. I also found a most unusual centrepiece painted in black.

It took three more hours to reach the end of our journey and as we were leaving the woods another stream of more people entered to begin their climb to the rock.

After a short rest we wandered down the main street of the village, looking at a row of shops all selling the same merchandise. Numerous eating places stood between the stalls. Mushrooms, the local speciality, in all shapes and all sizes were everywhere offered for sale. Children played computer games in amusement arcades; computer games were certainly popular – we had noticed them in some of the hotels too.

This road actually did not lead to the village, the village proper lay on the other side of the river. Ruth explored it the next day and found it to be very poor. Everywhere some kind of alcoholic drink, from bark, from roots, from almost anything, was being brewed and freely imbibed.

It was less bright next day when I woke before 6 a.m. to make tea. Voltage in the mountains was low, 110 to 125, but fortunately I always travel with a spare element, and using two at the same time speeded up the process considerably and therefore I was ready for breakfast at seven o'clock. Sharon had suggested to meet for an early start so as to miss the hordes, though some groups were already on their way to visit Popju-Sa temple when six of us started our adventure.

Cherry trees had been recently planted and were reflected in the clear water of the river which we followed on our way to a hermitage. Woods had been sadly denuded and intense reforestation had begun all over Korea; 80% of all necessary wood was now being imported.

The first resting place which we passed looked charming with a flowering cherry tree next to a traditional building. At the second resting place we crossed the river on a bridge which looked as if it had been constructed of tree trunks, but once again the 'logs' were cast in cement.

Nobody else was in the woods when we forged our way through dense forest with delightful glimpses of rocks, trees, flowering shrubs and high peaks in the distance. After some time we reached the hermitage, which, being a place of importance was well marked. The signs were in Korean script with Chinese lettering beneath it on one side and in English on the other. Great controversy reigned in Korea as to whether Chinese script should be taught in schools or not. Past history is intimately linked with Chinese culture, therefore Chinese script had a role to play in understanding Korean history and culture.

A well-weathered stone Buddha standing on a rock greeted us as we approached the hermitage. The hermit, a jolly, round-faced man in a padded garment, was prostrating himself in front of a beautiful Buddha with a curly cap, flanked by two statues with oriental-looking headgear.

Around the corner stood the *kimchi* jars surrounded by the usual array of smaller jars, whilst around the other side, facing the beautiful view across the forest and valley towards the mighty peaks – incongruous to see – stood a smart director's chair! A somewhat dilapidated shrine could be reached by climbing up perilous steps hewn into the rock and safeguarded by a rickety rail. Having completed his prostrations, the hermit rose to greet us, beaming all over his good-natured face, obviously delighted to see us. He had lived in the hermitage these past seven years; students, especially those engaged in studying law, often came before their final examinations to be able to study in this atmosphere of peace. They paid for their keep. Two students were spending their time at the hermitage the day we called. Four years ago the monk had become paralysed but had refused all medical treatment, deciding to follow Buddha's teaching, which meant to 'clear his mind through numerous prostrations each day'. He had made an almost complete recovery. He invited us for lunch but we had to decline regretfully. It was a wonderfully peaceful place.

On our way back we watched a dark brown squirrel with a white belly and a bushy tail jumping gracefully from branch to branch. Earlier we had seen a black woodpecker climbing up a tree trunk and also managed a close look at a cuckoo flying through the woods. We went in search of another hermitage, which, however, we failed to find, ending up at an abyss, having battled our way through dense woods along a tough trail. But we were gratified since we found a little dark blue gentian with four bells on one stem and also established that the dwarf iris had roots not a corm. Retracing our steps we came upon a tortoise with a stele on its back, which indicated 'Royal Remains' when found in woods. (Incidentally, as in China, both the tortoise and crane are symbols of longevity.) Once more we battled along a trail covered by leaves and scrambled across a brook, only to find that the path petered out. Eventually we called it a day and returned to our hotel.

Whilst in the thick forest we had not met a soul but once we had reached the lodge, the hordes were there again, many of them carrying transistors. Families had settled themselves comfortably to cook *bulgari* (beef barbecue) on small Primus stoves, others were keeping cool sitting on rocks in the middle of the stream and eating their picnic, whilst a group of old men in their traditional clothes sat on the grass enjoying their food. Yellow and white ribbons tied to trees exhorted visitors to take their rubbish home, so as not to harm the forest.

It started to rain soon after we got back and was raining heavily when we left after lunch. On our way to Matli Pass again, we stopped at the 'Ministerial Pine' to visit the nearby museum but found it closed. Skirting the reservoir we reached the wide basin between Poun and Sangju via Kwa-Gun. (Gun means village). After Oxchon-Gun the road rose, fields covered the slopes stretching up to the woods. Many attractive picnic places lined the road and flowers were everywhere: beds of pansies and beds of azaleas had been planted. It was still raining when we drove down into another valley and I was beginning to feel sleepy after our morning's hike.

Finally we reached Expressway Number One, which linked Seoul with Pusan. Mountains were hidden by mist. The vegetation was lush and very green, with many pink blossoms between leafy trees. As we neared Kim Chow we noticed heavy rolling stock on the railway line. Kim Chow was a big sprawling town situated at the foot of wooded hills. Kumi was another sizeable town which we passed and had many modern flat-roofed buildings, numerous ugly high-rise blocks of flats and a large modern church but few traditional houses. Everything looked very grey.

In pouring rain we journeyed on crossing the brown River Nakton Gan just after Waegwan, where we left the Expressway Number One, passing Taegu, which was Korea's fourth largest city and important for its textile industry. Driving through miles and miles of agricultural countryside, it was hard to believe that only 30% of the population now farm the land; it used to be 80%.

Our journey continued on an expressway again. Barley was standing high as we passed village after village with tree-lined streets and large churches. Our road climbed up into mountains again, featuring many sharp bends, and we looked down on a broad river-bed full of stones, before we entered a forest to reach our goal: Kaysan National Park. It was still raining heavily when we parked beside many coaches. Since our driver flatly refused to take us to our *yokwan* (inn), there was nothing else for us to do but wearily walk through the heavy rain up to the inn where we arrived soaked to the skin. The rooms were primitive but nobody minded, particularly after we had all shared a meal in a small Chinese restaurant accompanied by Korean wine. We all prayed for the rain to stop.

The rain had stopped and it was warm when I slipped out into the village next morning. Schoolgirls streamed out of the hotel next door to us on their way to visit Hainsa Temple, shops were opening, the stone floors of restaurants and bars as well as the pavements were being mopped, flowerpots were placed outside shops to greet the new day. Music sounded, heralding the dustmen, who worked protected by masks and wearing rubber gloves with long gauntlets. The day was bright and became very hot (in pleasing contrast to the past days) when we set off to visit the famous Hainsa Temple. Walking down the street past the bus terminal, we joined large groups of adults and schoolchildren as well as tiny tots. The little ones were on their way to school, the older ones on the way to the temple. Women squatted on the ground weeding the lawn by hand.

The way to Hainsa led uphill past an enormous shopping complex before entering the forest. Near the entrance stood a group of stele, one of which was very old, with a weathered turtle carrying a stele on its back. Rubbish bins were either cast in cement looking like hollowed-out tree trunks or made of simulated bronze to look like dainty ancient incense burners. Before reaching the first gate – which was a single one – we passed a resting place which had an enormous variety of souvenirs for sale. The second gate, a double one, showed the four Devas painted on wood; usually these were placed there not as paintings but as outsized figures. A very old pagoda and an ancient lantern dominated the main courtyard as well as the pavilion, protecting the four emblems of drum, fish, bell

209

and cloud necessary for the twice-daily ritual – at 3.30 a.m. and 6.30 p.m. – to signify the beginning and the end of each day.

Hainsa was an enormous complex of many temples. A large hall stood to one side of the first courtyard, in which Buddha and his two Bodhisattvas sat on their lotus flowers in golden splendour at one end of this vast building, whilst the other end served as storeroom for lanterns, flags, baldachins and for a huge white elephant. The white elephant commemorated the dream Buddha's mother dreamt before her son was born. A monk was busy inside the hall, whilst outside a young man was spraying a pole which carried a lotus. These preparations were for Buddha's birthday celebrations.

Most delightful Shamanistic shrines with fierce paintings and many lively carvings were present in the temple complex. Charming, delicate pictures adorned the outside walls of the other temples, which told stories of Buddha's life before he became Buddha. Sharon had a wealth of legends to tell; one was of Buddha as a boy searching for truth. On his way he met an ugly monster and asked this terrifying creature whether it knew the truth. On being told that the monster did, he begged to be enlightened. The monster replied that he could only oblige if he could devour the boy. Truth to a Buddhist is more important than life itself, therefore we saw the boy, having climbed up a tree in sheer terror of the monster, flying through the air into the monster's jaws. The monster, however, did not gobble him up but told him the truth. Another set of pictures told the story of the boy who was sent far from home to learn wisdom. He became homesick and ran back to his mother who loved him dearly, but after the first rapturous greeting she became stern and told him that he had been sent away to learn and that she would test him to see whether he had worked hard enough. She extinguished the fire and made him write whilst she baked a cake in the dark. Her cake was perfect, the child's calligraphy was not, therefore his mother sent him back to continue his studies; in later life he became the most famous calligrapher.

To either side of the first courtyard lay the quarters for the 120 to 150 monks secluded behind walls. One of their buildings was being refurbished. Their living quarters were tranquil, surrounded by well-tended gardens. I peeped into their kitchen and saw an enormous black range. Chanting began, indicating that the monks were offering Buddha his daily meal, which sometimes consisted of a bowl of rice, at other times it was just a bowl of pure water.

Water had always to be pure so as not to displease the Mountain Spirit and make him angry. Cleanliness, like truth, is all important to every Buddhist.

Very steep steps led up to the building specially designed to house the famous *Triptikata*. This is an enormous collection of wood blocks, inscribed on both sides, giving the entire laws as taught by Buddha, the complete rules as preached by him and the explanation to both his laws and his rules written by a famous monk, hence the name of '*Triptikata*'. It constituted an extremely impressive reference library. Housed in a simple wooden building, it was entirely safe from vermin, rot or any other threat since the construction was absolutely perfect with its 'natural ventilation system'. A monk – with each tooth outlined in silver – told us that neither bird, rat nor chipmunk ever slipped through the wide-open slats of wood. A complete *Triptikata* in print lay enshrined in rich brocade behind glass above the entrance.

In the last courtyard stood two more buildings containing wood blocks of poetry and fables. Even the large number of visitors did not detract from the peaceful atmosphere which prevailed and made it pure joy to wander around. Whilst I was just doing this, three ladies waylaid me and asked me my age; I did the same, which caused much laughter.

Unfortunately, the museum was closed and equally sadly there was no time to climb up Mount Kaya to see the Buddha carved in rock. Instead we strolled into the surrounding cool woods past many bird boxes and mistletoe high up in the trees and numerous hermitages scattered around the temple. Having climbed some steep steps, we watched workmen constructing a new building in traditional style. The beautiful windows were covered with glass instead of paper as it had been the custom in olden times. A second door slid inside the first to give double protection (a prototype of our modern double glazing). Sharon told us that in former days the bride spent her first night in her own home. She was dressed in many layers and when night came her husband had to undress her, whilst the wedding guests crowded outside the windows, wetting the paper to be able to see through until the bridegroom extinguished the fire as a signal for everybody to withdraw. Sharon's mother had still followed this custom when she was married. Above this new house stood the hermitage, which had been built into a rock bearing a small temple. A tiny statue of Buddha guarded it from a nearby rock. I smiled when I discovered a brand new washing machine waiting to be plumbed in, which stood next to the traditional *kimchi* jars.

I was intrigued by the monks' clothing: some wore wide pantaloons caught at the ankles to fit snugly, others wore pants generously wide as far as the knees then fitting tightly round the lower legs, like jodhpurs. In this temple novices were clad in dark brown; we had previously seen them in black. Reluctantly we left this enchanted place but stopped before we reached our *yokwan* to taste the dark bitter juice pressed from a special root found in these mountains.

Sitting in the sun surrounded by many Koreans, we ate our lunch as they did. People seemed to eat just anywhere when the time was right, therefore we did not feel uncomfortable or self-conscious as we might have done. One party even settled down on the pavement for their meal.

The beautiful sunshine allowed us to admire the lovely scenery as we drove through the forest; it had been obscured by mist and rain the previous day when we had driven through on our way up to Kaysan. Three tiny tots walked unconcernedly along the road hand in hand and with satchels strapped to their backs. Children seemed perfectly safe along the open road, cars and lorries would slow down and gently hoot. Tremendous celebrations were held on a child's first birthday since few used to survive at all. Similar festivities were still taking place when a person turned sixty since few reached this age.

Passing through a tollgate got us back to the expressway again. We climbed up into hills surrounded by fields as far as the eye could see, backed by densely wooded hills. The sun beat down but everything looked fresh and green after the torrential rains. Shortly after we had driven past some traditional houses, a satellite station rose up at the foot of a hill outside Taegu surrounded by rice paddies. Reaching the Seoul–Pusan road we proceeded due west through yet more fields, this time of onions, barley and rape, past well-cared-for orchards. Then we saw a large coal tip loom up in front of us, the first we had come across. A tractor with a gaily striped sunshade hoisted above was being used in a field. Near Taegu big petrol storage tanks rose up, shining silvery against the dark green of the wooded hills. High meadows protected many

212

grave mounds; boys fished in an invitingly cool-looking reservoir outside Yong-Chon; a ridge of high mountains rose in front of us.

Beautiful flowerbeds set amidst green lawns lined the approach to Kyongju, the ancient capital of the Silla Kingdom of the 5th century, which had been declared a Museum City. Big colourful pansies grew in stone troughs beside beds with delicate rhododendrons and azaleas in lovely shades. From time to time we caught a glimpse of attractive old villages enclosed by thick walls with gates akin to the first gate leading into a temple. Doors stood open, revealing courtyards surrounded by buildings on all four sides, where old men sat contentedly in the hot sun, smoking their long pipes and dreaming away.

The road led past the National Museum and the Chomsongdae which is the oldest astronomical observatory in the Orient. The 29-foot-high tower had been based on a 17-foot square base built of twelve rectangular stones, one for every month of the year. Twelve levels of stone led up to a square window which faced south. Twelve further layers of stone tapered to the top, which terminated with two square stone slabs whose corners corresponded to the cardinal points of the compass. Altogether 365 stones had been used in the construction of this cylindrical-shaped tower. It was thought that a ladder must have been used for the astronomer to climb up to the square window to gain access.

Since there were hundreds of coaches parked both at the National Museum and at the Chomsongdae, we drove on to visit Anajii, which used to be a park with an artificial lake, man-made hills and palaces solely used for royal banquets and festivals. It represented the very first landscaped garden. The lake, known as the Duck and Goose Lake, had been excavated and many treasures had been unearthed before it was skilfully restored, with three islands cultivated with lovely shrubs. Ducks and geese had been put back and the replica of a wooden boat lay anchored in the clear water, where carp abounded. Three pavilions had been re-erected; the largest, called Immaejon, stood at the water's edge, a smaller one rose further along whilst the third one contained a scale model of Anajii during King Mumu's time (AD 674). Photographs of some of the artefacts found at the bottom of the lake were displayed. The whole park with its many flowering trees and shrubs was most delightful.

213

From here we continued to visit Pan Wolsone, a small artificial fortress in the vicinity, which used to be entirely surrounded by a moat. The Royal Palace stood nearby but only traces of the base covered by grass had remained, as well as the ingeniously well-preserved 'ice house', the Sokpiggo, with its arched granite roof, three ventilating chimneys and the sloping floor to collect the melted ice, which had been constructed in AD 506 and still felt cold as we descended down three well-worn steps to peer through a grille.

The time had come to drive to our *yokwan*, which stood down town and had been recently built but had neither lift nor parking place. Here we had the usual *ondol* (under floor heating), a tiny bathtub, and were issued with minute towels. I guessed that all Koreans are very small.

Having walked through a busy market, where we again marvelled at the large quantities of the selfsame articles, we arrived at a department store where business was still brisk. Taking the lift, we reached the restaurant on the fifth floor, where we sat round the typical large circular table with a revolving centrepiece and dined in true Chinese style in a private room, having a very jolly time. On our way back we were amazed at the number of shops still open since it was ten o'clock; to our great surprise we also found two 'English bakeries'. Our tour leader stopped to get new glasses, a transaction which proved both efficient and inexpensive, and he was able to collect them one and a half hours later.

In a new coach with a new driver, who had arrived promptly at 8.30 a.m. from Pusan, we started early the following morning.

The sky was overcast but it was dry. Even though it was Saturday, children were on their way to school. Traffic wardens with whistles controlled pedestrian crossings down town since it was really quite dangerous to attempt to cross; vehicles did not appear to stop for pedestrians. As we drove out of town along tree-lined roads with rice paddies to either side, we passed old villages again where men still used oxen to plough their fields, where pear and cherry orchards were in bloom. Mist swirled around the lovely landscape as we drove past Pulguksa Temple up to Tosokuram Grotto, a man-made grotto on the ridge of Ohasam Mountain 2,500 feet above sea level. Unfortunately our view was restricted by mist, but the flowers, the variety of trees and the flowering shrubs were pure magic. Terraced rice paddies descended down into the valleys between woods. The grotto consisted of a square antechamber symbolising the Earth and an arched main room symbolising Heaven, set in a 'Garden of Eden', with an abundance of trees and shrubs and a large variety of rhododendrons and azaleas which grew in the most delicate shades of pink side by side with the deepest purple and red hues. Box had been neatly trimmed to form hedges. Double-blossom ornamental cherry trees were everywhere around us, vying with maple trees of all shapes, colours and sizes. Magnolia in full bloom bore blossoms from pure white through a full range to almost black. Fragrant viburnum grew wild in the woods, magenta-coloured peonies caught our eyes and proud deodors stood along the road. It was a place of enchantment.

The grotto itself had been air-conditioned and closed off behind a glass wall. Although we could get a clear view of the superb white statue of Sakyamuni Buddha and were impressed by it, we were unable to appreciate the noble architecture of the grotto built into the rock, nor could we do justice to the Goddess of Mercy – Avalokitesvara – with her eleven heads, thousand arms and thousand eyes on the palms of her hands, who stood behind the seated Buddha, nor could we see the ten disciples and the eight important Bodhisattvas cavorting around Buddha. We could only dimly perceive eight generals carved in stone, representing the eight classes of being, two guardians in fighting posture and four devas stamping on little threatening demons in the anteroom. Devout pilgrims placed money into a box to buy incense sticks, which they lit. It was incredibly peaceful in the woods above the sea and fortunately we had avoided the hordes of visitors who came walking up as we descended. Our coach took us to Pulguksa Temple. This whole area, the grotto and temple, had been declared a national park and any new house had to be built in traditional style.

Pulguksa Temple was set amidst the most wondrous garden, with streams and ponds spanned by bridges. Some very ancient trees spread their branches protectively over new ones. Whenever saplings were planted, rope was tightly wound around their trunks to prevent evaporation and they were always supported by three stout stakes forming a triangle, with the tree as apex. This method seemed so efficient and much simpler than the one stake we use at home. 'Pulguksa' means 'Temple of Buddhaland' and is the oldest temple in Korea, consisting of many buildings. In spite of the large number of visitors, it maintained an atmosphere of absolute serenity and it was delightful to wander beneath the trees, cross bridges over streams and ponds, peer into shrines, look into this temple, climb from one courtyard on steep stone steps to yet another one. The central double-tiered staircase used to lead the pilgrims up to the main temple but it had become too fragile and had to be closed, which meant that we had to walk round it. This staircase formed the very oldest part in the whole complex and consisted of thirty-three steps representing the thirty-three skyworlds. Thirty-three strokes were used to beat in the day and to complete it.

In front of the main temple in the terraced courtyard stood two great pagodas from the Silla era; one was of complicated structure where no mortar had been used. Inside a niche on its left side sat a tiny growling lion on a lotus pedestal. This was the 'Many Treasured Buddha's Guardian'. In the second, simpler pagoda a *sari* (holy relic) of a very revered priest had been discovered in the second storey: the gilt-bronze pavilion-shaped box contained silver *sutra* plates, a gold and copper *sari* box, *sutra* wood blocks and an incense burner wrapped in silk embroidered with many jewels. It was thought to have been placed in the pagoda in AD 706.

Beautifully preserved Sanskrit inscriptions adorned the front of the altar in the big hall, which had been used originally for Zen practice. In another temple we admired a wall painting of the Goddess of Mercy, whilst in the Shamanistic temple a monk was chanting, preparing Buddha's meal, which meant of course that I was unable to take a photograph of the most fascinating clay figures seated on silk cushions on either side of Buddha. Priests marched briskly in a row from their quarters across the courtyard to perform a special service.

As we were leaving this heavenly place, which was bustling with activity in preparation for Buddha's birthday, we saw a snake peacefully curled up on a hedge, enjoying the sunshine. Our last visit was the shop, where we managed to get a tape of the monks' chanting and some charming postcards. As we walked back to our coach, big raindrops started to fall and the rain gathered momentum as we drove along to the Royal Tombs, the Kwaenung, thought to be the grave of King Wongsong from the 8th century AD. It lay peacefully amongst old pines, with six statues lining either side – reminiscent of the approach to the Ming Tombs outside Beijing. The first pair looked like grim soldiers with western features, the second like civilian guards with oriental faces. A pair of lions completed the statues along the way which led to the big grass-covered tomb. The base of the tumulus was surrounded by the twelve zodiac figures which stood for years, not for months. Wherever we looked in and around this ancient city, we saw grass-covered tumuli, most of which had not been excavated since Korea had not got the means to take care of all its artefacts.

By lunchtime it was raining hard but this was a good time to visit the National Museum in order to avoid crowds. This beautiful complex was set in a landscaped park with many of its treasures tastefully displayed out of doors, but because of the torrential rains we only stopped to see the 23-ton 'Emille', one of the largest and most resonant of all bells in the world, after which the museum had been named. Legend had it that a small child fell into the molten mass when it was being cast and called '*Emille, Emille*', which means 'Mummy'. The bell had scalloped edges, scenes of four *asparas* (angels) had been embossed on it between delicate grasses.

The museum was divided into three parts: the main part consisted of prehistoric finds, which mainly comprised exhibits from Silla's Buddhist heritage. There were sculptures in clay and stone, most beautifully decorated roof tiles with dragons, turtles, the mystical phoenix, lotus petals etc. *Sari* bottles and *sari* caskets in various shapes and in a profusion of materials were displayed. Buddhas large and small, in stone, ivory, wood or precious metal, were well represented, as well as vases and vessels in every form and every size, made of all kinds of material.

The second hall housed the amazing royal treasures of gold diadems, gold caps, gold belts adorned with many precious and semi-precious stones.

The last hall contained mainly treasures found below Anapjii Lake.

There were some visitors in the museum besides our party, we noticed a group of deaf and dumb people who used the sign language to communicate, but all the students had left and it was peaceful and quiet in the lofty halls.

When we sprinted into the Tumuli Park to see the only tomb open to the public we got drenched again. It was also known as the Tomb of the Flying Horse, where the famous painting on birch wood, used as a mudguard, had been found. We had just seen it in the second hall, as well as all the exquisite golden jewellery, beads, girdle, ceremonial sword, earthenware vessels and a magnificent crown. Here we were able to appreciate the construction of the

217

tumulus, which consisted of a square wooden chamber surrounded by a stone wall which had been built without mortar, topped by more stones and finally completely covered by earth heaped up to make it into a perfectly round mound. The place where the wooden coffin had stood, the spot where all the jewellery had been found and the position in which the casket containing earthenware goods had been discovered were all pointed out to us.

Finally we visited the Silla kiln where fifteen craftsmen reproduced pottery from ancient times. Glaze had not been known in those bygone days but a shiny finish could be obtained by controlling temperature and airflow. Pottery was either grey or, at a higher temperature, it became red. We bought the zodiac figure of a horse and also purchased a replica of a little house with a chimney. These little houses were actually still used as water droppers for calligraphy.

When we returned to our *yokwan* the flags above the entrance looked as bedraggled as we did. Up at the Songnisan Hotel each flag had been carefully wrapped into a plastic cover when it had started to rain. To get dry, we made ourselves as comfortable as we could, and rolled up our bedding to support our backs against the wall whilst sitting on the brocade cushions provided. It was, however, no small feat for us – unaccustomed as we were to sit on the floor and use a low table. Our wet clothing dried quickly, spread out on the heated floor.

That evening we all drove out of town to the Bomun Lake Development, a holiday complex situated around an artificial lake containing not just one but three five-star hotels and all amenities expected in such a place, including a 'swan boat' to cross the lake.

To eat *bulgari* and to watch folk dancing at the same time, we were ushered into a big hall. Neither the food nor the performance was particularly good. Afterwards we called in at the palatial Tokyo Hotel to change some money and to see how the rich Japanese spend their holidays! Fortunately the rain had stopped by the time we returned to our *yokwan*, therefore we decided to walk to the English bakery for coffee and cake. Coffee was served in a small flask with cups arranged on a tray which had actually been collected from another shop further along the road. The cake looked like a coconut cake, but was 'pure dough'. Whilst in the bakery we noticed that many families lived at the back of their little shops.

The next day started grey and cold. Nothing had been planned, we were left to our own devices, therefore we decided to buy some shoes in the market. It was easy enough to find a large covered market which sold fresh and cooked food and every conceivable kind of merchandise, and we found what we wanted without any difficulties.

Later, when we left Kyongju, the sky brightened and the sun broke through. Before finally saying goodbye to this lovely city we drove to the outskirts to visit the 200 year old village of Chioe, where the descendants of the original lord of the manor still lived. Azaleas, rhododendrons and flowering cherry trees provided a blaze of colour everywhere. Around the village lay well-tended fields, early cucumber and courgettes grew protected in plastic greenhouses. In between the fields rose tumuli of former kings and queens. Excavations were in progress. A woman walked calmly between the ancient graves on her way to the stream, carrying her washing and a wooden washing stick. Nearby stood a well-known Japanese restaurant built on the site of a former royal palace. The gardens, with a pond, gnarled pine and an enormous magenta coloured peony tree, were quite magnificent.

To see the Rae-Ei (the Three Standing Buddhas), dating back to the 6th century AD, we drove through woods at the foot of Mount Namsam. Standing sheltered beneath ancient trees, they were well-weathered but looked very benign, especially the large Buddha in the centre, who bore a smile and showed deep dimples in his cheeks. The sun filtered through the tall trees highlighting the delicate mauve colour of the wisteria which had entwined itself amongst the dark green pines. Feverish activity prevailed in a small temple nearby where everybody seemed to be busily engaged in covering an enormous frame to make a lantern for Buddha's birthday.

Our very final visit in Kyongju was to P'osok-Chong (Abalone Stone Pavillion). Here beneath shady trees lay a stone channel in the shape of an abalone, which is a sea creature. This was the idyllic place where the King used to entertain his guests and where wine cups were sent to float along the water whilst courtiers recited poems. Sadly, in this so-peaceful place the Silla Kingdom ended in 926 when the King was slain and his blood mixed with the clear water of the Abalone channel.

Rejoining the expressway again, we left Kyongju. Beautiful mountains loomed up; the sun streamed through the windows of our coach, sending me to sleep. Almost halfway between Kyongju and Pusa lay the old temple of Tongdo-Sa set amidst pine woods, the largest temple in Korea. Walking along a clear mountain stream which leapt merrily over large boulders, we joined many families who had come out to spend the fine sunny Sunday afternoon here. Some enjoyed their picnic spread out on a rock in the stream, others had erected small tents on the bank to cook their meal. All along the way food was offered, with low tables and chairs standing under majestic pines inviting visitors to sit down. Stone pagodas stood in the shade, stele in the woods, many inscriptions were visible on rocks. A man was kicking a little grey owl which must have fallen out of its nest until we told him to stop, and one member of our party picked it up and placed it under a tree in the woods. All of us hoped it would manage to survive.

Near the entrance to the temple stood a fine carving of the founder, a monk by the name of Cha-Jang. Legend had it that he journeyed to China to find the 'truth' to save his nation. Whilst in China he had a visitation from a holy apparition who gave him relics of the Buddha: his yellow robe, his skeleton and his teeth. Returning to his native land, he founded Tongdo, which means: 'Salvation of the World through Mastery of Truth'. The relics have been preserved within the temple inside a beautiful pagoda.

A lovely old arched stone bridge spanned the river near the first gate. The temple was pure joy to behold, with its buildings mellowed to muted, gentle tones. Since none of the painting had been restored, the intricate architecture was much more apparent. The beautiful main hall was devoid of all statues since 'the Truth needed no figures to be represented'. The ceiling was quite outstanding, with the three flowers of Korea – the peony, the chrysanthemum and the rose of Sharon – embossed on it. Many of the beams and wooden pillars were uneven in girth having been left in their natural shape, some were twisted, others arched, just as nature had intended them to be. There were numerous temples, some of which, however, were closed. One of them, devoted to the founder, displayed his portrait behind the altar. The lovely Rice Bowl Pagoda, which, true to its name carried a rice bowl on its column, was magnificent. A pond lay in a secluded corner near the Rice Bowl Pagoda, spanned by a graceful bridge; it was here that one of the nine dragons lived. The other eight dragons had been killed by

Cha-Jang, the founder of the temple, and to placate the ninth the bridge had been built.

In the middle of a well-tended garden stood the Sari Pagoda containing the precious relics of Buddha. It was quite difficult to leave this enchanting place which had so much to offer, there were so many exquisite paintings to see – one which I particularly liked was painted in soft shades of blue showing a boat carrying souls to paradise.

From Tongdo-Sa we drove the short distance to the port of Pusan, which was Korea's second biggest town. The drive was most pleasant, through mountain scenery where I noticed irrigation channels for the first time, before we reached the City Expressway, which took us into Pusan past many modern buildings, high-rise flats and large churches but barely any traditional roofs apart from temples, many with blue tiles. Temples were always built in traditional style. Pusan was bustling with activity, building seemed to be going on everywhere.

Our *yokwan* stood near the docks in a very dusty district, but inside it was spotlessly clean and our tiny bathtub was lined with a dainty green mosaic. The owner asked me – when I came down into the entrance hall – my age and guessed correctly within a year. I realised that Koreans always greet first, then ask how you were, where you come from and, finally, your age. I do not know why age is so important to them.

Again we all went out for a Chinese meal together and, as before, true to Chinese custom, we were shown into a private room where we sat at a round table. After our meal we walked in the still warm evening down to the docks along uneven pavements where we had to watch our step. The town continued to be very lively, with many people about and a fair amount of traffic on the roads, which had to be crossed via overhead bridges. The city appeared to fan out from the harbour in all directions and millions of lights climbed up the sides of the surrounding mountains, whilst the brilliant lights of the high Pusan towers marked the centre.

Walking around the block before breakfast the following morning we saw trees on every available rooftop. Shops were being opened to be swept and cleaned, pavements washed down and flowerpots placed outside shops and eating places. The large number of coffee houses quite amazed us. Steps led up to a different level of Pusan but we had no more time to explore any further since we had to return for our breakfast, which we took at the top of the big Ferry Hotel in a private room which looked like a conference room with long tables and many chairs. Two winches, one at either end, stood ready in case of fire.

A splendid morning was spent seeing some sights in this vibrant city. First we joined the dense traffic to climb up to Dragon Park, where next to a flower clock stood the imposing statue of Admiral Yi, who slew the Japanese. Behind him rose the high Observatory Tower from a platform which supported an amusement arcade, where a party of elderly women cackled outside the Chamber of Horrors. It also housed an aquarium and many other diversions. A lift whisked us up to the Observation Chamber, from where we had a magnificent view over the big town with its imposing hotels, its many schools (children seemed to line up in the school yards as if on parade grounds) and its enormous harbour serving many ships. Photography was allowed from the platform on which the tower stood but not from the top.

Driving down again, we were impressed by the profusion of camellias growing to either side of the road which took us down town again to the busy harbour. Most of the vehicles on the congested roads were either large buses with single seats to either side or taxis; parking was the same problem as in any other bustling town. Women sat cheerfully wherever there was space on the side of the road on a heap of earth or perched on a pile of bricks, offering their wares. The fish market was a beehive of activity where women shod in rubber boots, clad in rubber aprons and wearing long rubber gloves extending right up to their elbows, did all the work. It was spotlessly clean, with clear water running continuously with not a single fly to be seen. Many of the fish and crustaceans were alive, others were expertly gutted, cut up and bagged or artistically arranged in piles. Most of the fish I could not name, many looked ugly, some were enormous monsters leering at us. Out on the quay fishermen were busy getting their boats ready or bringing in their catch. Further along was the general market and, finally, we reached the spice and herb market where herbalists sold moleskins and skeletons of small fish and birds as well as herbs. Rejoining our coach we drove along the beautiful coastline where dark green woods fringed the blue sea and where we passed the Ocean University, situated on an island connected to the mainland by a causeway. This was the only Ocean University in the world.

A splendid road with wisteria tumbling over the side led up to T'ae Jongdae Park, which lies on the tip of the peninsula jutting out into the sea. King Muyol of Silla, who unified the Three Kingdoms in AD 668, used to spend his leisure time at this beautiful spot. Many visitors had arrived before us and once again we noticed that Koreans will use any place to have a picnic.

Our last visit was to the UN Cemetery. Sixteen nations fought in the Korean War and it was the first (and hopefully the last time) that UN forces fought in combat. Each country had its own plot beneath its national flag. Some countries, for instance France, had requested that their dead rest in their own soil, hence their spaces – still with a flag flying above – lay empty. The whole cemetery was beautifully kept and very moving in its simplicity, therefore we were amazed to find honeymoon couples posing for photographs beneath trees growing near the graves. A group of tiny tots came to have their picnic close by.

This completed our visit to Pusan and we drove to the airport for our flight to the Isle of Cheju. Our short journey took us above the south coast before flying across the South Sea to this subtropical island.

A coach stood waiting for us to take us from the north coast, where we had landed, to the south coast of Cheju, travelling past orange groves surrounded by pines; but growing citrus fruit was no longer profitable, therefore bananas and pineapples had been culti-vated during the last year to replace them. Brilliant golden rape fields interrupted the luscious green, hence we were surprised to see that all wide river-beds were full of stones but dry. Grassy tombs rose up, surrounded by low walls which had been built to protect the graves from the native horses which roamed about. The animals were small but very sturdy; sadly they had dwindled in number and been classed as a protected species. Well-nourished cows grazed in the lush meadows, which seemed strange since we had neither seen fresh milk nor butter, usually we had been served with dried milk or soya powder and margarine. The glasshouses we passed were full of bananas and pineapples. Bicycles had four bars reaching from the seat down to the body of the machine. Whether this was to make the bicycle more steady to be able to cope with the high winds which prevailed on the island, I do not know.

On the south coast of the island we stopped at Sogwipo, the second city of the Cheju, where we once again stayed in a simple *yokwan*, sleeping on the floor. Going for a walk on our own, we found the hilly little town quite delightful as we first made our way down to the sea, stopping a woman who was pushing a heavy barrow laden with pineapples uphill, to buy a small one. In spite of the hard work she seemed cheerful enough. A man pushed a cart laden with sprats. Houses were small and low, some old, others new, but all of them stood in colourful gardens. The old buildings were thatched. The thatch was held down by iron hoops because of the fierce winds which buffet the island. Two sayings were in common use: 'What the island has is plenty of women, winds and stones', and 'What the island has not got are beggars, gates and thieves'. Instead of gates two bars were used. In former days their number was three, since when all three were used it meant that the owner was away, two meant that he was home but did not want visitors to call, one indicated that the owner was in residence and happy to receive guests.

Small shops were brimful with souvenirs, and cleaners and tailors were still working although it was getting late. Most families lived at the back of their shops and even the smallest hovel and the meanest *yokwan* possessed a television screen; we saw children watching a cartoon. Children looked fresh and healthy and played happily in the street, skipping tirelessly, laughing and dancing, singing merrily. From up above we looked down on the lovely setting of beautifully landscaped gardens along the shore, with the promenade sweeping around the bay, where a ferry was crossing the blue sea. The time had come to return and meet up with the rest of our party to go out to dine. All of us had decided to eat fish 'western style' in an elegant looking restaurant, but the waiter did not understand what we wanted. However, after waiting a very long time, succulent bream with vegetables and chips was produced and enjoyed by all.

Throughout the night we had heard chanting in honour of Buddha's birthday. All of us rose early, ready packed to leave this delightful place. Life had already begun to stir, with shops being opened to be cleaned and streets being swept at 6 a.m.

Our drive up to Mount Halla – the volcano which dominates the island – took us along a scenic route through fresh looking dark green woods rich with varying vegetation. We caught a glimpse now

224

and then of the coastline, the black basalt contrasting with the blue of the sea. A few small islands rose out of the brilliant waters. Leaving all habitation behind, we climbed higher and stopped one hour later to begin our tedious ascent, scrambling through dense forests, mostly of leafy trees interspersed with a few pines. In the dense woods stood the 'Virtuous Tree'. Legend had it that once upon a time famine raged through the island and a faithful maidservant climbed through these woods looking for acorns to sustain her master and his family. Overcome by weariness and weakness from lack of food, she fell asleep beneath the tree. When she awoke she found herself beneath a mountain of acorns. Scooping them all up, she saved her master and his family. Whenever famine struck again the faithful maid collected acorns from this tree.

With great relief and pleasure we emerged from this sinister wood to breathe in the clear mountain air, and walk on springy ground amidst meadows ablaze with clumps of azaleas in flower, catching a hazy view of Sogwipo far below us. Two grave mounds stood in splendid isolation, surrounded by black stone walls. Primula grew here as well as pale blue gentian and other alpine flowers. The dark volcanic earth was damp and water stood in some of the hollows of the volcanic rock, yet some of the riverbeds and small mountain streams were dry. A few of us soldiered up the steep incline to reach the saddle, others stopped for a rest or turned back along the way we had come. Crowds of young Koreans – some carrying transistors – had arrived, when we started we had been the only party. Up on the ridge we could look northwards down onto the town of Cheju. I was the only one anxious to continue up to the crater, which we had not even seen, but since no one else wished to go we all turned back, picking our way carefully over big roots and treacherous stones.

Driving on, heading north, we stopped briefly to admire the statue of the 'Mother of the Island' standing amongst a sea of flowers and carrying her water jug and her special basket on her back. Soon we reached Chin-Jeju (New Cheju) and settled in our *yokwan* before strolling out down the main street lined with shops bursting with souvenirs. A coach stopped, disgorging a load of honeymoon couples who descended on these shops. After passing many hotels we finally reached a lovely park with a shop close by selling orchids.

Some of our party went to see the Lantern Ceremony in a

beautiful temple in the old town. Many lanterns in the shape of the lotus flower hung suspended in the forecourt and had already been lit. A monk was chanting but unfortunately only a handful of worshippers had assembled inside the temple, which was a fairly new building with exquisite carvings. All the brass shone brightly, reflecting the lanterns, and birthday gifts of fruit and vegetables for Buddha had been artistically arranged. Cheju had only a few temples and, apart from the happy brides, we had seen few people in traditional dress.

Later we strolled across from our *yokwan* to the imposing Grand Hotel where a steady stream of guests still kept on arriving and milling around in the sumptuous lobby, which was all marble with glittering lights reflected in the fountain playing in the centre. It also housed an arcade of elegant shops, coffee bars, cocktail lounges, sauna, swimming pool and various restaurants. A glass cage lift whisked us up to the restaurant on the 16th floor, which was the beautifully appointed Skyway (western style) Restaurant. One honeymoon couple had as much trouble trying to use a knife and fork as we had experienced in trying to eat with chopsticks! As we left, even in the dark, honeymoon couples were still posing round the fountain to have their photographs taken.

Next morning, when we woke on a beautiful day, we found that all the other members of our party felt ill, but most of them – however feeble they felt – joined the day's outing. Cheju was a delightful green island with a central massif and golden beaches fringing the blue sea. The scene was pastoral, intensely cultivated with rich fields, with cattle grazing contentedly in lush meadows, plump chickens in every yard and black goats nibbling at whatever they could find to their taste in the land of plenty. Goat's milk was held to be beneficial to any woman having just given birth, to restore her complexion.

At the Cheju Suk Won we stopped to see this special collection of shapes which nature had sculptured in stone and wood, beautifully displayed beneath trees. This had been donated to the public by the collector fifteen years ago and all articles exhibited had apt names. 'Grandfather' was very prominent, who was a somewhat grotesque figure carved of grey volcanic stone. In olden days a pair of 'Grandfathers' used to stand at every crossroad to keep the evil spirit away. The 'Mother of the Island' was also represented here, with her special basket on her back and carrying the water jug.

Korean women on the mainland balance their loads on their heads, but because of the high winds which sweep across the island women of Cheju carry theirs – like the Mother of the Island – on their backs. The three bars which used to replace gates were here, as well as the double grindstone to grind grain by hand and the hand press to press the oil from golden rape. A delightful legend was carved in stone which told of a couple who were deeply in love and married, surrounded by rejoicing members of their families and friends. They were poor, hardworking and very devout Buddhists but remained childless. They prayed and prayed that their union would be blessed, then the husband dreamt that their wish would be fulfilled. Soon the wife became pregnant and gave birth to twins, a boy and a girl. The husband worked harder than ever and grew rich but he changed and became mean, forsook his wife, took a mistress with wavy hair and embarked on riotous living, whilst his wife found herself with child again and became very sad but prayed for her husband to return to her. At the same time he dreamt the same terrible dream night after night for seven consecutive nights, which made him realise that he had done wrong; he mended his ways, returned to his wife to live with her happily ever after. This story was extremely charmingly displayed in one tableau after another.

Our next visit was to the 'Folk Village', which was an old village consisting of an extraordinary mixture of some well-maintained houses demonstrating the ancient way of village life and other houses still occupied with families carrying on their normal lives regardless of prying eyes, whilst quite a number stood forsaken and derelict.

In olden times two slabs of stones with a slit between them and placed over a privy in a pigsty served as a toilet. The pigs, being scavengers, disposed of the waste, the leaves of a nearby parsimony tree served as paper and a stout stick kept close by was used to keep the pigs away. From farmyard to farmyard we went peering into dark kitchens and into living quarters. Each complex lay surrounded by a stone wall built of volcanic rock; all houses were thatched and single-storeyed, grouped round a courtyard. Simple implements were displayed, many of which – such as the water pitcher, which was used as a musical instrument, and the baskets carried by the women – were still in daily use. The kitchens frequently stood separate from the living quarters because of the danger of fire. According to ancient custom, when the eldest son got married he and his bride took over the living quarters and the parents moved into an annex at the other side of the kitchen. Dried dung on its own was used as fuel, when mixed with straw it served to build walls. This was a very poor village, just growing barley and rape and was partially supported by the Government. The few stalls we saw only sold honey at high prices. Women were taught bee keeping in a small hall which we found tucked away in a corner of the village. I followed some chanting, which led me into a courtyard where three women were preparing Buddha's lunch. Actually we had not seen a temple but what impressed us was the fact that however poor the villagers were, they all tended their delightful gardens in some secluded corner.

From here we drove to the beach, to a small bay which lay empty near a greenhouse full of banana palms. Here the fragile members of our party could rest in the shade of pine trees in sheltered depressions in the volcanic rock which were filled with soft sand, whilst we walked along to the beach to watch the women divers. These women, completely enveloped in rubber suits with flippers, but without snorkels or goggles dived when the tide was out to collect shrimps and other delicacies in their baskets strapped to their backs. They worked underwater for hours on end; we heard their gay laughter as they called to each other. Walking past one small hut where square baskets containing all their belongings neatly arranged stood outside the open door, we reached a second hut, standing on a promontory of black rock, which was obviously used to store nets, hooks and baskets, and saw the remaining ashes of a big fire in the centre of the room.

After this peaceful interlude we drove to the Sunrise Mountain Rock – Song San Ilchubong – a curious volcanic cone which can be scaled and where the view is said to be magnificent. However, this lovely place was so overcrowded that we did not join the throng climbing up the narrow trail, looking like busy ants. Horses were for hire to trot along a course on the grassy slope but we were satisfied to wander past souvenir stalls, ice-cream stands and eating places to a splendid viewing point from where we could look down into the bay. Two diving women had just climbed up, still in their gear, and started to sell sea cucumbers. One of them looked quite elderly, the other one had a plump young face.

Women on the island wore dark pantaloons and bonnets, which

they usually tied down with a kerchief, whilst the ladies on the mainland were clad in either pastel or vibrant hues.

Our journey continued until we reached the lovely Nutmeg Forest, which lay completely deserted – we were the only visitors. The nutmeg which gave the forest its name was entirely different to the one we knew, it was a very old species of Japanese pine and its bark was used for medicinal purpose. The forest was pure magic in its stillness, with the sun dappling through the thickness of the varied vegetation. When we found a bench in a clearing we stopped to eat our lunch – at peace with the world – before walking on over springy ground. Coming out of the forest, we passed a splendid playground with wooden swings and climbing frames.

Unfortunately the rest of our party were very languid and loath to explore further. We therefore just visited a mushroom farm before calling it a day. Having already seen the process, it was really of little interest to wander through glasshouses full of oak logs containing holes for the spores. Few mushrooms were actually to be seen. Each log was used for five years before being discarded.

On our way back to our *yokwan* we suddenly realised that rice paddies were missing, rice had to be imported from the mainland. Rape was being grown on the island for oil. Taxis stood parked at all kinds of locations, waiting for honeymoon couples who frequently had their photographs framed by golden rape. Grave mounds stood scattered about, usually these were single, occasionally we saw family graves but one slope in the distance appeared to serve as graveyard. Sometimes the mounds bore a stele carrying an inscription.

Cheju was an extraordinary island. It had only five-hundred thousand inhabitants but boasted five universities.

In the late afternoon we pottered across to the Grand Hotel to look at the elegant shops and wandered down the busy streets again, stopping to purchase a grip to accommodate all the extras we had acquired. Then we found another splendid hotel, the Cheju Royal Hotel, set in beautiful gardens. Later we returned to dine there, western style. On the way we saw for the first time a woman drive a car.

The road to the airport was lined with camphor trees. The modern airport was quite splendid and efficient and soon we were airborne, flying parallel to the coast and looking down on well-cultivated fields, seeing brilliant red and blue roofs on low white

229

houses set amidst lush green countryside. Leaving the beautiful bays behind, we swept out to sea, casting a last glance back at the lovely silhouette of Mount Halla. Reaching the west coast of the mainland, we turned inland and were surprised at the mountainous character of the peninsula. We passed a sizeable town (I do not know which one) before looking down on mountains, valleys, rivers and roads. Another city lay below us, surrounded by fields, with a road sneaking between more cultivated land. Three rivers joined near another town. Field lay close to field, resembling a giant patchwork quilt, with a broad river forming a glittering border. Mountains reappeared, another big river was making its way to the sea. Once again we flew out over the water and looked down on neatly laid out harbours with boats and tankers along the quay and liners out in the sea, before we flew over sandbanks and turned inland again over terraced rice paddies nestling in valleys between densely wooded hills, then reached flat countryside with well-irrigated rice paddies to land at Seoul. At passport control and customs sexes were strictly segregated for personal security checks. This procedure occurred whenever we arrived or left. Photography was strictly forbidden at the airport.

As we speeded along we appreciated the beautifully landscaped approach to the city which lay shrouded in haze – heat or pollution, I did not know which. The well-cared-for flowerbeds, the lovely flowering trees and fresh leafed willows were a joy to see. In complete contrast stood row upon row of soul-destroying blocks of flats at the side of the road. The green between these grey concrete monsters offered a slight relief. A quaintly shaped tree surrounded by a blaze of colour from a clump of azaleas stretched its branches across the road as if pleading to be taken note of and to be praised for its beauty.

Many cars sped on numerous roads in all directions. We passed the impressive domed Houses of Parliament, with well-trimmed grass verges. It had surprised us to see women squatting down cutting grass by hand with small sickles; we never saw a lawnmower anywhere in our travels through Korea.

Soon we found ourselves back at the Golden Castle Hotel, where the young manager greeted us with a warm smile, solicitous for our every need. As before we occupied room 211 with the somewhat primitive sauna installed in the bathroom. Sharon, our super guide, had thoughtfully arranged for the coach which had met us at the airport to wait in order to take six of us down town to the American shopping centre of It Aewon, which was a broad avenue lined with shops catering for western tourists. The wide pavements were packed with people and we saw more western faces in a short space of time than we had seen throughout our entire stay in Korea. There were some very intriguing people around us, some strange couples reminding us of characters out of Somerset Maugham's stories. Shopkeepers touted for business promising 'special price' as we wandered in and out of shops, buying in some, just looking around in others. To rest and to refresh ourselves we sat outside an authentic American Wendy-Bar, enjoying the sun. American servicemen, most of them in mufti, appeared to be relaxed as they bantered good-naturedly with the local population. Sharon had told us that Korea had three television networks: one for the general public, one purely aimed at adult education and the third one for the Americans. After our rest we parted from Sharon and four of us continued on our way, the other couple having left us some time before. In utter amazement we mingled with the enormous crowd of shoppers.

Trade was very brisk around us and when we had had enough we headed for the 'Shuttle Service' which was a courtesy bus provided by the big hotels to take shoppers to the centre of the city. It took us through attractive quarters with impressive modern buildings, fountains, statues and squares and streets teeming with people. It was quite easy, having left the bus, to find a subway, which was stunningly furbished with marble halls and spotlessly clean, with no graffiti to be seen. The system was simple since it was colour-coded and all we had to do was to follow the colour plainly marked on the ground on the platforms and painted on the grey coaches. There was a flat rate for the tickets, which had to be fed into a machine to gain access and exit. Carriages had single seats to either side and the floor was being cleaned by two women as we rode along. Our journey took us to Tong Dae Mun, the East Gate Market, which was a most amazing place with the entire area consisting of shop after shop with merchandise piled from floor to ceiling and spilling out over pavements, up stairs, along bridges which spanned across the busy streets and down the stairs on the other side, covering every available space with goods. There were areas selling only shoes, shoes inside the market hall on every floor, shoes outside on pavements, nothing but shoes everywhere. I do not think that there existed sufficient number of feet to wear them all! The same applied to towels, linen and other articles. It was impossible to buy just one pair of socks, these were always in bundles of five or ten.

When we ventured inside the covered part we found it chock-a-block with both merchandise and people. Day in, day out, these poor sales people worked in artificial light without a breath of fresh air for long hours. Some of them looked extremely languid and lethargic. We too were beginning to wilt and decided to return to our hotel. Finding our way successfully to a subway, we sat in comfort on the circle train taking the longer ride to Yoksan station rather than having to change twice. Everyone we encountered proved helpful and kind; people in the subway offered us their seats, and if we hesitated in the street somebody would come along offering to help. When Ruth, feeling weary whilst we waited for the bus, sat down on the ground a shopkeeper rushed out with a piece of cardboard for her to sit on. However, when we emerged from the subway at Yoksan station we lost our bearings and had a long way to walk back to the hotel.

Much later we ventured out again to try to find a suitable venue to eat. Beverly Hill Hotel, the first hotel we found with a western grill room was dark and too noisy for us and we fled. The next hotel had a beautiful approach ablaze with colours of most glorious hues. Big expensive-looking cars swept up to the entrance. Although we found a super buffet on the top floor we decided the menu was too big for our appetites and descended to the western grill room where we dined well although a lonely Indian gentleman was the only other guest there.

The last day dawned promising to be hot and sunny again when we packed for the last time. Fortunately we were able to keep our rooms until the time of our departure to the airport.

By subway we went down town and found Tuksu Palace tucked away, forming an oasis in this big bustling town. Initially it had been built as a royal villa but was used as a palace during the first two tumultuous decades of this century and became associated with much of the historical intrigue surrounding the demise of the Ti Dynasty at the hands of the Japanese.

Apart from the delightful palaces, pavilions, shrines etc. built in traditional style, there were two solid Renaissance stone buildings complete with Ionic and Corinthian columns, the work of a British

232

architect. They formerly housed the museum of modern art but quite recently this had been moved to a specially-designed complex outside town. As we entered through the lovely first gate, serenity and peace enveloped us; a pond with fountains playing lay in the centre, surrounded by pergolas with wisteria cascading over them. Groups of azaleas and flowering trees grew everywhere as well as a superb chestnut tree which was in full bloom. Steps led through a gate along a processional path across a stone terrace to the Throne Room. The throne stood in front of a painting of the sun and the moon, and a writhing dragon picked out in shimmering gold decorated the centre of the coffered ceiling. One corner of the garden housed a very old bell near the first 'water clock', which consisted of three bowls on a high platform and of two bowls working a mechanism turning the columns which struck the hours. Sadly the mechanism had been lost. The clock had been invented by the versatile wise King Sejong (1410–1550), whose statue stood in the grounds. There was plenty of time for us to walk around, to look and to absorb the atmosphere of this unique place which lay in the shadow of modern buildings, many of them luxury hotels. Over its brow appeared an unusual Italiniate building with a square belfry, which was the Anglican cathedral. Strangely the contrast did not detract but somehow enhanced the loveliness of Tuksu.

Turning from the sublime to the ridiculous, we made our way to the South Gate Market – passing the lovely South Gate, or Nawdaemun. This lively market was mainly in the open and not as enormous as the East Gate one. The barrow boys were yelling lustily, whilst cripples pushed their barrows along. In a narrow side lane food was being freshly cooked, fish was being grilled over charcoal, various pots simmered on hot bricks. Here we purchased our sweetmeats and in the open market we bought pairs of rubber gloves with long gauntlets as well as white cotton gloves and a pair of pantaloons for myself. Fruit was artistically arranged. Prices varied, but whilst merchandise seemed cheap, food appeared dear.

Since we had neither time nor any space left to purchase more we hastened back to South Gate and found our way from there to the Kybo Office Building, admiring the modern architecture set against the background of the mountains surrounding the town. Diving down into the enormous bookstore which occupied the basement of this tall building we browsed through books before choosing a delightful one of Korean fairytales. I hoped that reading them might help me to gather some insight into the Korean mind. Whilst in the store we also purchased a lovely illustrated book of 'schools' (temples) which will be a pleasure to look at again and again. After a snack in one of the many bars on a floor containing only eating places (there was also the main post office and a bank in the building), we found our way through subways where many vendors had spread their wares on the ground and across squares and busy streets, back to the station. Again we were offered seats in the crowded carriage and a lady immediately spoke to me in English, telling me that she had lived for seven years in America. Many people, particularly the older generation proudly wore buttonholes of roses or carnations, men wore red silk ties. This was in honour of 'Mother's and Father's Day'. Frequently the older women whilst chatting to me would stroke my arms; presumably they were unaccustomed to see bare forearms.

As arranged, I met Sharon at the hotel to hear about the Buddhist concept of confession. Although she spoke excellent English it was not always easy for her to find the right phrase to convey exactly what she meant to say. Often she used her hands in a fascinating way to emphasise a point. She told me that Buddha taught five basic commandments:

1. Thou shalt not kill.
2. Thou shalt not steal.
3. Thou shalt not have affairs outside marriage.
4. Thou shalt not tell an untruth.
5. Thou shalt not drink intoxicating liquor.

Sharon tried to illustrate confession, which she called 'knowing the truth', with a story. A monk was visited by a well-to-do widow who had come to pray, which often led to a prolonged stay. Whilst staying there she fell in love with the monk, who, however, rejected her. Saddened and humiliated, she decided to throw herself over the cliffs to her certain death. She told the monk about her decision. In order not to break the first commandment, he relented, but having broken the third he felt deeply troubled and journeyed forth to seek advice from a highly educated monk. Prostrating himself, he told his story. After some deliberation he was told that he had freed himself of guilt by having come and told his story, thus he had come to know the truth. My interpretation was that the monk had taken time and trouble to think through his problem, he had made a deliberate decision not only to embark upon the journey but also to tell the truth, however painful it might be. Thus it enabled him to unburden himself and get rid of his feeling of guilt.

For some time we talked about conflicts and spiritual values. She often felt that being a tour guide frequently caused problems and she felt threatened. In fact she had met an American tourist and had fallen in love with him and he had returned to Korea for two years to teach. She had not told her parents but had taken him home with a group of other friends, but unfortunately her parents had not liked him. This made her very uncertain about the future. At the time of our talk she was prepared to join him in America but in a subsequent sad letter she indicated that he had terminated their relationship on a further visit.

The time had come for us to leave. The young manager insisted on taking a photograph of us all before we boarded the coach to drive out to the airport and enjoy a last look at this handsome town. An unusual instrument was being used at the roadside: a handle with a broom on one end, a sturdy shovel on the other, which we thought simple and very practical.

General confusion reigned when we arrived at the airport since our travel agent when booking our return journey had not allowed for the international stipulated time decreed to transfer luggage when changing planes and we were told that we would have to take a later plane from Paris to London.

We left Korea at night just before 8 p.m. and arrived at Anchorage at 10 a.m. It looked dreary, with not a vestige of green on the ground. As we landed we caught a glimpse of Mount McKinley, Alaska's mighty peak, and after take-off we saw the snow-covered Rocky Mountains with rivers forging their way through icy grounds before we dropped off to sleep, only to find on wakening more snow on the ground and ice on the windows.

Finally a faint rosy glow appeared in the east whilst the moon still hung in the sky in the west. It seemed a long and tedious flight. The sun rose over the ocean as we approached Paris. The journey across the Channel was short, flying high above the clouds. Spring greeted us on our arrival home, back from a memorable journey to the land of temples and flowers.

THREE COUNTRIES RECOVERING

Laos, Cambodia, Vietnam

January 1992

Laos via Bangkong

As always before a journey excitement and anticipation prevented sleep. Early in the morning we joined the amazing volume of traffic streaming out of London and were driven to the airport in plenty of time to check in dutifully three hours before take off. Time passed quickly. It was our first flight on Qantas and from the time we checked in with our modest luggage until the end of our journey the service was friendly, relaxed and cheerful. It was nice to hear Australian accents again and to see fresh, smiling faces. Everything seemed so easy, boarding the plane, settling into our seats with plenty of legroom, receiving socks, earplugs and eyeshades, earphones – all aimed to make our long flight as comfortable as possible. There was only a slight delay, which the captain utilised to tell us our flightpath.

Once we were airborne, details of height, speed, outside temperature, flying time and location appeared on a screen, alternating with maps showing us our route. Soon we crossed the Channel to Belgium, passed an airbus near Munich, and flew over Austria, which lay shrouded in clouds. As we crossed the Bosphorus near Istanbul the sky darkened and night descended. Lights twinkled below us; probably we were flying above Ankara by then. Between watching two films we passed over Teheran. Although tired, sleep escaped us and we were wide awake when we flew across India, seeing both Delhi and Bombay coming up on the screen, and followed the path across the Bay of Bengal to Rangoon. It was still dark when we started to descend. The sky turned pink above a blanket of clouds. Once we had passed through these we saw some isolated groups of lights below us. It became light enough to distinguish rice paddies, irrigation canals and a wide river surrounding Bangkok.

Rows of neat houses greeted us before we touched down on the huge airport, where we walked along seemingly never-ending corridors; walking, since most of the moving corridors were out of action. Now and again a frail-looking cleaning lady had abandoned her mop or broom and sat fast asleep, huddled in a heap propped up against a wall. Waiting in one of the many queues to have our passports checked seemed an eternity. I had forgotten how incredibly long every transaction takes in the East. Two little boys played happily with their toy trains on the smooth shining floor whilst a pretty little girl danced, humming contentedly to herself. This provided slight relief and brought smiles to most faces.

Finally we were able to claim our luggage and walked out into the hall, where almost immediately an official tour hostess bore down on us, asking us whether we had booked a hotel and transport. We gave her the name of the hotel we had booked and she phoned to check, only to be told that nothing had been reserved in our name and in any case they were full, in spite of the fact that we had received written confirmation. Quickly, without giving us time to think, the tour hostess proposed a 'deal' consisting of bed and breakfast in a hotel and transport to and from the airport, with a half-day city tour thrown in; all this at a reasonable price. The only drawback was that the Metro Palace Hotel stood in a shopping area away from the centre of the city, not in the Old Town or near the river. But knowing that hotels in Bangkok are always full (since many travellers stop over on their way to or from Australia) we were content. Arrived at the hotel, we were first given a room with a double bed. At the third time of asking to change to a twin-bedded room we were successful and all seemed well. But later, having enjoyed the luxury of a hot bath, when pulling out the plug the bathroom was flooded. Help was summoned, but in spite of many feeble attempts to clear the outflow with a hand pump, the situation remained unchanged during the time we were there and no doubt afterwards.

Before we could finally relax we had yet another hurdle to cross:

Ruth's visa to Laos had been wrongly dated and we were instructed to contact a lady in a special travel office. It was extremely difficult to make anyone understand that we required transport to this office, which was a good distance from our hotel. Finally we got one of the young receptionists to write down the name and address of the office in Thai script. A taxi asked an exorbitant amount, a *tuk-tuk* (the open sided three wheelers which whiz through town giving excellent and cheap service) was summoned and a price was agreed. No sooner had we turned into a narrow lane round the corner from our hotel when the driver stopped and offered to combine the journey with sightseeing for a higher sum and when we said firmly 'no' he refused to take us any further. With the help of an American who happened to be standing outside our hotel, we managed to find another *tuk-tuk* which took us through wide streets and narrow lanes teeming with a tremendous volume of traffic until finally we arrived at our destination.

Bangkok is a large city in which many of the old Thai houses have been replaced by soulless modern blocks. Skyscrapers have risen up, a profusion of offices, hotels, fantastic trade centres and shopping malls have taken over where formerly little wooden houses stood; but shacks still stand along the river and along the road, offering almost any commodity from plastic articles to delicate garlands of sweet-smelling flowers. Food is still cooked and eaten in the street. A 'happy smile' painted on a board, denoting a dentist, and other telling signs still abound.

In a vast modern marble building where the computerised lift whisked us up to the fourteenth floor we found the travel office. Finally we were able to make ourselves understood and found that three more photographs were needed for a new visa to be issued. Accompanied by a member of the staff, we walked a fair distance along the main road to the photographer's shop, which was a dingy room with a number of desks where four girls languished. Successful at last, we returned to the office, where we were promised that the visa would be sent to the hotel next day.

Our mission completed, we managed to find another *tuk-tuk* without any further ado (although the journey seemed at times more hazardous than before) to take us back.

As I looked out from our room at the sixth floor on the sunbaked scene I saw a few small houses huddled together in a square with green trees scattered about, with a low rusty apartment block

239

beneath a corrugated roof nearby. Both the mean little houses and the poor apartment block were overshadowed by modern skyscrapers. On one corner rose a tenement block festooned with washing on each balcony, whilst silver foil covered some of the windows.

Presently we set off on a three-temple tour as promised by the tour hostess. Our guide offered to show us two temples, that of the Golden Buddha and of the Reclining Buddha, but we were able to persuade him to also take us to see the Marble Temple.

The Golden Buddha Temple, the Sukhotai Tramit, was the first we visited. It housed the biggest Buddha statue cast in solid gold and is seven hundred years old. Initially the figure had been completely covered by cement and only in 1955, on moving it to its present place had the cement cracked, revealing the golden image. Fragments of cement were displayed in a glass case near the side of the statue. He sat in the position known as 'Conquering or Resisting Mara' (evil). His legs were crossed, his right hand rested lightly on his right thigh pointing towards the earth, whilst his left hand – palm upwards – lay across his body. His face with its classical features looked serene and the gold covering the statue was so brilliant that it almost obscured the outline. Opposite the entrance stood a shrine dedicated to the late abbot who had taken part in the construction of the temple. He too was shown in the sitting position, covered in gold leaf, with fine sensitive features. Every temple is part of a complex surrounded by a wall.

Our next stop was the temple of the Reclining Buddha, the Wat Po, which is the oldest temple in Bangkok. This was quite dazzling, consisting of ninety-one *chedis* which are pointed dome-shaped stupas containing relics of Buddha, and four *viharas* (halls) in addition to the *bot*, the main shrine. The remaining buildings comprised the impressive library, the monks' quarters and a plain crematorium with a hall in which the bodies were kept for four days before cremation. Above every temple rises the tall column which disguises the chimney of the crematorium and is visible from far afield. The ashes of the departed are deposited in an urn, to be kept in the temple or taken home; or they may be scattered on a river or placed near the mouth of a river, when great care has to be taken not to let them lie on a riverbank lest somebody coming to wash or bathe inadvertently steps on them, thus disturbing the spirit of the dead.

Throughout the Wat Po enchanting groups of plants, rocks and delightful figures of men and beasts formed focal points. Apart from jolly figures of large ponderous mandarins, solid effigies of Marco Polo stood around. These Chinese statues had originally served as ballast for ships trading between the two countries. The *chedis* were profusely decorated in a variety of styles, from relatively plain carvings to glittering inlay of coloured glass, gold leaf or mother-of-pearl. The most elaborate ones were the four main *chedis* dedicated to the four Rama Kings. An enormous golden lingam, which was much venerated by women anxious to bear a child, stood in a prominent position.

Looking at the profusion of buildings, statues and decorations, I was once more struck how intricately Buddhist and Hindu mythology are interwoven. The great Hindu epic of the *Ramayana* is known in Buddhism as Ramakien and frequently performed; the main characters are often depicted in Hindu as well as in Buddhist temples.

Doors and window shutters were particularly handsome in the main temple, consisting of teak wood covered by filigree design in gold. The Reclining Buddha himself was quite overawing to behold, with his head supported by one slender hand and resting on a stone pillow inlaid with mother-of-pearl. The soles of his feet bore his 108 auspicious signs, adorned with shimmering mother-of-pearl. The figure had been made of brick which had been covered by layers of lacquer and plaster and finally bedecked with gold leaf. Along one side of the shrine stood 108 bronze bowls, into which worshippers dropped one satong (the smallest currency) for luck. Wat Po is considered Bangkok's university, where the principles of art, religion, science and literature are being taught. In addition visitors can also have their hands read and their stars foretold. Both the Traditional Medical Practitioner Society and the Traditional Thai School for Massage have their headquarters here.

The last temple we visited was the Marble Temple, or Wat Benchambophit standing in a beautifully peaceful garden where graceful bridges spanned a little canal which demarcated the temple from the monks' quarters; stone benches invited us to rest under the shady trees. The temple itself had only been built in the early 20th century. The courtyards were made of Carrara marble. An interesting collection of Buddha statues was displayed, including a model of the Starving Buddha which we had seen in the museum of Lahore. Buddha's gestures were intriguing, particularly one with

241

one hand raised, begging his relative to stop fighting. Both hands raised meant that Buddha was calming the ocean. Both of these figures were standing, whilst Resisting Mara (another favourite attitude) showed Buddha seated cross-legged. Two figures presented him walking.

Tired but pleased with our first day, we returned to our hotel, driving along the grounds of Chitralada Palace, which stood surrounded by klongs (canals). Along our drive we saw women, sheltered from the fierce heat beneath straw hats, engaged in sweeping the streets and working on building sites. Vendors pedalled along pulling all kinds and all sizes of merchandise behind their bicycles; we even saw them conveying a complete kitchen in this manner. Women and men alike carried their loads – seemingly effortless – in baskets suspended from either end of a wooden yoke which was placed across their left shoulder. Monks with their begging bowls stood patiently in a line to receive rice from a woman, a task which was to earn the giver merit and at the same time served to provide the monks with one of their twice-daily bowl of rice.

Before retiring to our beds we took a light snack in the coffee shop of the hotel when we suddenly realised that neither of us had slept for thirty-six hours.

Refreshed after a night's sleep, we were eager to start the day. Having made a list of places we wished to see, we asked one of the charming young ladies at the reception desk to transcribe it into Thai script. We hailed a *tuk-tuk* and proceeded first to the Bovornivet Temple. To avoid repetition of the experience the previous day, we first agreed the fare before joining the dense stream of traffic. However, not far from our hotel our driver stopped in a side turning and tried with all the power of persuasion at his command to cajole us to visit some shops on our way. When we steadfastly refused he got out of his vehicle and declined to drive further but hailed another *tuk-tuk*. He did not ask for any money, simply instructed the driver where we wanted to go and informed him of the sum we had agreed on for the journey. Having transferred, we continued at an erratic tempo, sometimes stopping for a considerable time in the heavy traffic, at other times hurtling along at breakneck speed whilst we hung on for dear life. At no time did anyone display impatience, everybody just sat and waited patiently. To tell the truth we quite enjoyed the hustle and bustle around us when we had to wait in the dense traffic.

To our great surprise we actually reached our goal – the Wat Bovornivet – safe and sound. This large complex with its shady trees, waterways and numerous buildings behind thick walls appeared like an oasis of tranquillity and peace in this pulsating metropolis. A sign 'School for those going Abroad' pointed to one of the houses. Outside the monks' quarters hung saffron robes strung neatly along a line. Dogs, cats, hens, cockerels and turtles enjoyed the sun and shade, birds in bamboo cages hung on the wall – these are released on 'auspicious days' earning their owners merit in the next world. Visitors were allowed to feed the turtles. Inside the *bot* (shrine) were two golden seated Buddhas, whilst a smaller image cast in bronze stood in front, celebrating the liberation of the country in 1257 from Khmer rule. The murals were most unusual and very charming, depicting foreigners in Thailand: American missionaries were shown disembarking, the English at horse racing, the Germans prospecting for minerals.

There were few visitors in this secluded place. Two girls from Brisbane who had stopped off en route to Europe chatted to us for a little while whilst an American couple asked us the name of the temple.

Leaving the Wat Bovornivet, we made our way on foot, stopping frequently to ask directions. Just before we reached Lak Muang – the City Pillar Shrine – we crossed the Klong Bangkok Yai and passed vendors selling amulets. This delightful temple was quite small and as usual surrounded by a wall. In an open-sided hall Thai dancing was being performed, followed by a play, 'to amuse the spirits'. Next to this hall stood a stall selling food with a place to rest adjacent to it. Another pavilion housed a number of lingams garlanded with flowers which were gifts from the women who came to pray to conceive a child. Pilgrims were able to purchase offerings from a stall nearby. Lotus buds, orchids and many other flowers were on sale, as well as incense sticks. Offerings were always most artistically presented, frequently arranged on flat baskets. On a long table a variety of cooked food such as pig's heads, roasted chickens and grilled fish was displayed on banana leaves. I am not certain whether this display was meant for pilgrims to eat or intended as offerings. The shrine itself was quite small and, as always, stood raised on a podium reached along cool marble steps. It was octagonal in shape, with doors and window shutters beautifully decorated with gold leaf tracing on the outside and a single colourful figure on the inside of the wooden shutters. Descending white marble steps, we reached the altar, which stood in the centre. Buddha surrounded by flowers and golden vessels, incense sticks and offerings resided here. Lak Muang was said to be inhabited by the spirit which protects Bangkok. Rama the First placed a stone pillar in the centre of the original Hindu temple to mark 'the city's soul', conforming to the Hindu custom of installing a lingam in the middle of any temple dedicated to Siva.

To return to more mundane matters, toilets were near the entrance. These (as usual) consisted of 'Mohammed's footsteps'. When we joined the short queue we were immediately directed to the last 'little room' in the row which was dry, whilst the remaining ones, although clean, were flooded with water overflowing from a bucket placed beneath a dripping tap. All the Thai ladies in their saris with open-thonged sandals either stepped into the water or skilfully across it to the raised platform.

To reach the enormous complex of the Grand Palace we had to cross the very busy street, which was quite a feat. Soldiers stood guard at the big gate. The grounds remained open to the public all day but the ticket office closed for two hours at midday. Fortunately we were just in time to obtain the tickets and were also handed a small booklet to show the way. Everything seemed very well organised and all we had to do was to follow the plan in the book, which also gave brief descriptions of the main treasures. It is a huge place; in fact it is a walled city. The marked way led to the famous Temple of the Emerald Buddha, the Wat Phra Keo. The shrine itself, standing on a raised platform, is magnificent. A pillared ambulatory surrounds the main shrine, which is covered by the traditional colourful stepped roof. Every inch of wall, pillars, shutters and eaves shimmered and glittered with gold, mother-of-pearl and glass in hues of reds, blues and gold. A frieze of small golden figures ran along the building, mythical golden figures stood in front of the entrance. To enter the shrine we had to ascend the narrow marble steps. Having slipped off our shoes we sat obediently on the cool floor, taking care to tuck our feet discreetly below us since to point the soles of your feet towards the altar is highly irreverent and not allowed. The Emerald Buddha, a small figure made of green jade, sat high up on an elaborate golden altar. He (as it is customary with all Buddha images) was clothed in his seasonal cloak, which was changed three times a year to correspond with

244

summer, winter and the rainy months. This important figure was flanked on either side by large mirrors in heavy golden frames. Screens decorated with beautiful pictures of flowers and animals, inlaid with mother-of-pearl, were also surrounded by ornate golden frames. The walls were entirely covered by murals depicting the life of Buddha, beginning with his birth and continuing his story clockwise around the shrine.

On our way out we admired the doors, exquisitely inlaid with mother-of-pearl and when we finally emerged we stood rooted to the spot, dazzled by the general view, taking note of the eight stupas all of the same design but in different delicate colours which rose up behind the elegant stepped roofs in front of us. To the left of the Wat Phra Keo stood three pagodas on a raised terrace, one of them the Royal Pantheon. These three pagodas reflect the changing centres of Buddhism. An enormous golden one built in 19th-century Sri Lankan style housed Buddha's ashes. The middle one was the Phra Mondop (the library), built by Rama the Second in Thai style in the 18th century. It had superb mother-of-pearl doors and shutters and splendid golden *nagas* (snakes) forming the balustrades on either side of the marble steps which led up to the doors. These *nagas* terminated in human- and dragon-headed claws held vertically. Behind the Pantheon stood an impressive stone model of Angkor Wat, contrasting sharply in its severe plainness with the glittering décor which surrounded it. The Phra Mondop (the library) intrigued us, with the gabled roof of its *vihara* (hall) decorated with tiles and porcelain flowers.

The whole courtyard was surrounded by galleries which showed fabulous murals depicting the *Ramakien*. These paintings were beautifully maintained and all gold was repainted every five years. One scene was being restored whilst we watched.

Apart from the main monuments mentioned, there were many more wonderful things to see. On the terrace where the three stupas stood, delightful statues – half man, half animal – known as *kinnara* were scattered about, as well as shaped trees in attractive porcelain pots. Set near a bell tower in Khmer style we saw a group of elephants with smooth shining heads; since elephants denote strength (the kings rode into battle on the backs of the mighty beasts), parents bring their children here and walk three times round the group, rubbing the elephant's heads to bring strength to their little ones. A beautiful statue of a black hermit – the Patron of Medicine – sat on a pedestal near the exit which led out of the temple complex to the remaining part of the Grand Palace and took us first into the audience hall of Amarinda, with its throne surmounted by a canopy of nine tiers of white cloth. This throne stood in front of a golden boat-shaped altar. The hall's wooden ceiling, painted with golden emblems on a red background divided into compartments by black and golden beams, added to the beauty of the well-proportioned building. Geometrical patterns in gold on a red background covered every inch of wall space. The audience hall of Amarinda formed part of Mahamentien complex, where all buildings were interconnected and stood within a wall. The style of these houses and pavilions was relatively simple, with brilliantly white walls and heavily carved window surrounds beneath the stepped green roofs, edged with red.

Strolling along slowly, we were able to feast our eyes on the profusion of buildings in Thai style and admire the flowers and bonsai trees grown in attractive china pots which bore delicate landscape scenes. Some of these pots were filled with water with lotus flowers gently floating on the surface. Walking between well-kept lawns led us to the Palace, which was guarded by soldiers who with their smooth beardless faces looked almost too young to be in uniform. The Palace was T-shaped, with a longer horizontal part. At the junction of the two arms an ornate gilded tiered finial rose above the many-stepped green roof which again was outlined in red. The long façade was almost plain, with simple arches, but gold glittered on the corner gables.

Adjacent to the Palace lay the Dusit group of buildings, where we were allowed to enter the audience hall containing a throne of mother-of-pearl beneath the usual nine-tiered canopy denoting that it was used by the lawfully crowned king. Two large mirrors in heavy gold frames stood against the back wall. A delicate Tree of Life had its place beside the throne. A simple throne placed to one side was used by the King to receive ordinary people, whilst the elite had their audience in front of the central throne. Walking to the back of the building, we found a charming corner with a group of trees growing out of an artificial mound made of rocks. Stone animals, a horse, a pig and a cow, had been placed on a ledge in front of a small pond where a bench invited us to rest and contemplate the scene around us. Elaborate shrines rose up contrasting sharply in their glittering glory with the simplicity of this corner, high above the walls to either side with narrow stone steps leading up to them.

Continuing our sightseeing, we paid a short visit to the Wat Phra Keo Museum, where we saw bones from dinosaurs, ancient tools and fragments of old buildings in various rooms downstairs. Visitors had to take off their shoes to climb upstairs to admire the offerings made to the Emerald Buddha. One room contained glass bowls and vases in all shapes and sizes, whilst simple and elaborate thrones stood in some of the other rooms. One of the displays consisted of a very plain altar where a chair had been placed in front. My enquiries revealed that this was meant for the teacher, a role sometimes taken by the King himself. In another room a collection of miniature Buddhas made from silver, ivory, wood and rock crystal – all exquisitely carved – was displayed.

After we left the Grand Palace, which had certainly lived up to its name, we skirted Sanam Luang Park, an open grassy space where trees provided a welcome protection from the scorching sun, to reach another wide and busy thoroughfare which brought us to the university. Continuing our leisurely walk, we found ourselves soon near the banks of the river in the middle of a lively, colourful fruit and vegetable market. With slight difficulties we managed to locate Wat Mahatat in a dusty road amongst dilapidated houses. Following a monk into the complex, we walked through the monks' living quarters until we gained entrance to the main courtyard, where a young novice approached us, eager to show us around. He opened a door leading to the *bot*. A gallery surrounding the courtyard contained effigies of Buddha on pedestals. These served as cremation urns, with each pedestal bearing a photograph and particulars of the deceased. Monks came to this peaceful courtyard to meditate since Wat Mahatat was known as a famous meditation centre. Our young guide was anxious for us to see all the urns but as all Buddhas were identical we preferred to go and see the *bot* which was relatively simple but, like all temples, lofty with a high ceiling. The outside walls were yellow. At the side of the altar stood an interesting collection of miniature Buddhas. Three men were comfortably ensconced on the floor, whilst a monk stretched himself luxuriously behind a desk. This little group gave the shrine a relaxed, homely atmosphere.

Having thanked the novice we stepped through the thick wooden door into a second courtyard. A babble of voices drifted through the windows of a large house in which monks sat cross-legged on the floor, engaged in earnest discussion. A second big building housed their sleeping quarters, whilst a smaller house between these two was the famous library of *Wat Mahatat*, where monks sat at long tables, deeply concentrating, to study Buddha's laws.

Since we were anxious to reach Vimanek Palace before 3 p.m. (the time when the ticket office closed) we left and walked out into the busy street, where it did not take too long to hail a *tuk-tuk*. Once again we pointed out our destination in Thai script on my little list and once again we agreed on the sum to pay before we started on our journey. It puzzled me how the drivers decided on the price since only too often they did not know the way, but even if the drive should prove longer than anticipated they still adhered to the agreed sum and always refused a tip. Our poor old driver asked passers-by many times and had to retrieve his way frequently before finally arriving at the zoo, which stood close to the Palace. Here he asked a soldier standing on guard who would not budge from the spot where he stood. Our driver simply mounted the pavement to get close to the motionless figure and found that we had actually reached our goal and were able to enter the gate with five minutes to spare.

It was a large compound with various buildings where we first walked along a canal spanned by a dainty bridge, with a very handsome green wooden building to one side of the water and a number of whitewashed houses beyond. We never were able to learn what the green house contained but ascertained that the whitewashed buildings housed a picture gallery, offices and conference halls. Everywhere were lovely colourful flowers and big shady trees.

The mansion itself, which stood behind a wall in a beautiful garden, was a teak building which had been erected in Victorian times as a summer palace for the King. It had been recently restored and opened by Queen Sirikit as a museum displaying the royal family's memorabilia. It was of pleasing design, built around a courtyard with an artificial lake. An octagonal tower which contained three floors presented a striking feature. First we were ushered into a small snack bar, where we had to wait for an English-speaking guided tour.

It was interesting to wander from room to room to hear about the royal family, who appeared to be well loved by the people. The

King and Queen were held in high esteem and the present royal couple – like the King's parents before – are involved in many projects to further the well-being of their people. There were photographs, ivory articles, china collections, tortoiseshell boxes, enamelled items, musical instruments, thrones, weapons, paintings, letters and books. The King's bathroom, next to his bedroom, and his workroom with a collection of typewriters were shown to us. The bathroom contained a tin tub and a toilet which was the first inside loo in Thailand. His sitting room and the Queen's quarters were both housed in the octagonal tower and were light and airy, with many windows opening out on the inner courtyard and looking across the lake towards the guesthouse on the distant bank. With great pride we were shown the King's telescope in a special room. The entire palace was beautifully kept, with highly polished teak floors in every room. It was interesting to learn that women used to wear their hair as short as the men until Rama the First returned from his first European tour and introduced many western ways; amongst them he gave permission for women to let their hair grow. He was the King of *The King and I* fame, and Anna Leonowen's family still own a factory in Bangkok. The whole place was enchanting and we wandered around the pleasant grounds before we picked up another *tuk-tuk*. Once again the driver lost his way and we ended up at Bangkok Palace Hotel instead of our modest Metro Palace Hotel, but the doorman put us right and we returned safely to our abode.

After a brief rest we walked the short distance to the Indra Hotel (where we had stayed on a previous visit some years ago) to dine in the coffee shop. Afterwards we strolled along the busy main road lined with many stalls selling a profusion of merchandise. Before retiring to bed we booked a trip for the following day to Ayutthaya, the ancient capital.

Next morning we had an early start. Unfortunately neither of us had slept very much and poor Ruth had suffered acute discomfort following the pleasure of eating an enormous banana split the night before, but forgoing her breakfast, she bravely rose. Walking along the now familiar way to the end of our narrow lane, we passed a Baptist nursery and also took note of the many spirit shrines which stood in gardens and courtyards, on balconies and roofs. In between apartment and office blocks lay building sites where work commenced early in the morning and continued late into the night by artificial light. Oblivious of all the activity around her, a woman had pitched her home on a building site, hung her laundry on a line and was calmly preparing her breakfast as we passed. Men and women were already at work on machines in small factories; a board announced the forthcoming building of a shopping mall. The narrow lane widened slightly, sufficiently for stalls to appear on one side. Each stallholder was already busily preparing and cooking food either over charcoal grills or in deep bubbling fat. A shrine in the middle of the main road, which was already thronged with heavy traffic, was being dismantled.

Finally we arrived at the Indra Hotel. Here we had to wait in the large marble hall – which resembled a lively railway station – for our guide, who was fifteen minutes late. He led us to a minibus where a young Japanese couple were the only passengers, in which we drove to different hotels to collect other tourists, comprising two Buddhist nuns and their disciple, a young English couple and a Swiss man with his Canadian wife. Our drive led through town to the Chinese Quarter, where life had already begun, with housewives eagerly shopping in the street markets. Near the Sheraton and Orion Hotel we drew to a halt and transferred to a waiting coach. A mixed party of twenty-five set off for the journey up country to Ayutthaya, the ancient capital. Fifteen years ago we had made the same trip and remembered the peaceful countryside of green rice paddies and palm trees with the mist rising slowly over the waterways where silent fishermen sat patiently along the banks. Things had changed; where formerly the dusty roads had been empty of traffic, now the enormous volume of vehicles of all kinds impeded our progress, forcing us at times to a complete standstill. It took a long time to leave the city behind and even longer to reach the open countryside. Growth had taken over and surrounding villages had merged with Bangkok. When we did reach the open country, we could no longer see the soft green of the rice paddies since wherever we looked new developments had been or were being built or new projects were being advertised on large hoardings.

At Ayutthaya the road followed where formerly the walls surrounding the huge palace had stood. This had been known as Wang Luang and had been entirely destroyed by the Burmese in the mid-18th century. It had been the capital for 417 years, ruled by 33 kings of various dynasties. Now only some red bricks from the original foundation lay scattered throughout the vast grounds.

Great grey *prangs* (stupas or tower) loomed up in all directions. Our bus parked outside the Wat Phra Sri Sarpet, the former Royal Chapel, which looked new with its brilliant white walls beneath the stepped roof, the gable adorned with shimmering gold, doors and windows richly carved. Cats and dogs abounded but did not appear to belong to anyone. Although thin and ill-kempt, with many of the dogs almost entirely denuded of hair, they were docile and took no notice of us. Adjacent to the *wat* lay the enormous burial ground of the kings. Three Sri Lankan-styled *chedis* containing the ashes of the Ayutthaya kings stood on a terrace. Climbing up to the terrace we looked across this vast palace ground before walking around it to look at what was left. Remnants of brick walls, some broken columns, headless Buddha statues (some of them still revered, with yellow scarves draped across their mutilated bodies) lay strewn about. Along the wall opposite the three royal *chedis* rose the remains of 108 pagodas. Next we stepped into the Wat Phra Sri Sarpet, which, like Wat Phra Keo in Bangkok, was the private chapel of the King and hence no monastery had been attached to this temple. Unfortunately the enormous Buddha was just being cleaned in preparation for Queen Sirikit's 60th birthday and was hidden from view, so we had to content ourselves with admiring the many Buddha heads poised on pedestals which contained ashes and lined one entire side of the building. Smaller shrines stood at the foot of the tall Buddha and were well honoured, judging by the large amount of gold leaves applied to the Buddha images and the various offerings in the form of beautifully arranged flowers, fruit, and lighted candles, as well as sweet-smelling incense sticks deposited around them. On our way to our next site we caught tantalising glimpses of more ruins of ancient *wats* and *prangs* which made us want to spend more time in this ancient city.

Driving around a huge pagoda which stood in the middle of the road we arrived at the Wat Yai Chai Mongkol, which was a well-cared-for temple built by King U-Thong in 1357 for meditation. Little wooden houses on stilts stood in the shade of some magnificent trees. Here the monks lived to meditate. Each tree along the way to the *bot* carried a board displaying a saying or exhortation for the monks walking slowly along to absorb and learn, such as (quoting one example): 'Conquer a liar with the truth'. In spite of many visitors, including a group of giggling schoolgirls, it remained a peaceful place and nothing detracted from its serene atmosphere.

251

In 1592 King Naresuan of Siam seated on an elephant defeated the Burmese invaders killing their crown prince in single-handed combat. In memory of this victory he built a massive pagoda, which towered over the whole complex. First we were led behind a wall to gaze in amazement at the vast gleaming white statue of a reclining Buddha. Inside the shrine a large mural commemorated King Naresuan's victory showing him in battle seated on his elephant.

An enormous pagoda rose behind the *wat*, which I climbed, along a narrow staircase. From a terrace high above we had a magnificent view over the countryside with many *prangs* and pagodas framed by lush vegetation. The *bot* with a large seated Buddha facing the pagoda, lay beneath me, gilded Buddhas sat along the four walls of the courtyard, gleaming in the fierce sunlight. Everywhere were flowers; a nursery where they were grown was tucked in one corner behind the pagoda. In fact we had passed quite a number of nurseries on our way.

From Wat Yai Chai Mongkol we continued our tour to the Bang Pa-In, the Royal Summer Palace, which had been originally constructed in the 17th century but was rebuilt in the 19th century by King Chulalongkorn. It consisted of many small palaces built in different European styles standing amidst beautiful flowers with orchids tumbling out of coconut shells fastened to each tree and bougainvillaea spilling in riotous colours over large china pots. Here we saw the old bo or peepal tree, which was over three hundred years old and came as sapling from India, beneath which the King used to sit to meditate. A canal ran through the grounds, opening up into an artificial lake with a man-made island bearing a beautiful typical Thai pavilion. Behind this lake lay the King's apartments, built like Versailles and nowadays used for State occasions. Beside these buildings stood an Italian-style pavilion, whilst further along we admired a Swiss Palace which looked as if built of light and dark green wood. In fact it had originally been constructed in wood but burnt down four years ago and had since been rebuilt in brick painted to simulate wood. On a small island jutting out into the lake we saw the observatory, but this, as well as the Chinese Pavilion, was entirely obscured by green netting. Both buildings were being renovated in preparation for the Queen's birthday and were therefore closed to the public. On our way back we looked across to the remains of a windmill which in the past used to pump water from the river into the canal.

To embark on our return journey to Bangkok, we made our way to the River Chao Phraya, which embraces Ayutthaya on its southern and western side, whilst the Lopburi River flows to its northern boundary and the Pasak River, completing the circumference, to the east. Our journey back, as on our previous visit, was extremely pleasant, drifting down the wide river in which lotus flowers popped up and down (alas without blossoms) and barges fully laden with a variety of goods chugged past. One was full of sand, another one bore Pepsi-Cola; whole strings of junks were being dragged along by motorboats. Entire families lived on some of these simple crafts. We sailed past isolated shacks and houses built on stilts and many temples, some of which we were told were very old and of great importance. Villages came into view, one of which produced pottery which we saw being loaded onto boats to be taken to the markets in Bangkok. People in this village (so we learnt) were descendants of the Mon people who had come to Thailand from China centuries ago. New buildings and factories appeared as we neared the city and finally Bangkok arose in front of us through a haze of polluted air. Klongs joined the river, where people lived in wooden houses, in shacks or on boats, most of which were festooned with washing as well as with flowers grown in old tins or storage jars. As we approached Bangkok we had a splendid view of the glittering royal barges, the Grand Palace and Wat Arun, the Temple of the Dawn, standing opposite the royal abode.

In the course of our tour we had become more familiar with our fellow travellers and exchanged experiences. The young Swiss man managed a four-star hotel near Zurich and had been travelling with his Canadian wife around Thailand for the past month. They had spent one night with an isolated hill tribe in the north of the country in a place so remote that it had taken them the best part of a day travelling by train, by boat, by elephant and finally on foot to reach it. Not surprisingly, the conditions in the tribal village were extremely primitive. An American from New Jersey was in Bangkok on business. It was his first visit to Thailand but, having worked in the East – he had been in China for the past three years and finally left without achieving any conclusion to his deal – he was accustomed to the slow way in which things were done. Transactions proceeded at snail's pace but were inevitably accompanied by good manners and by plenty of smiles. I also spoke to the lady who had come with the two nuns. They wore their saffron robes over trousers, had their heads shaven and used coolie hats to provide protection from the sun. They both had very healthy appetites and ate large quantities of the food provided for us on the boat. The lady, who called herself their 'disciple', came from Kuala Lumpur and spoke perfect English, having studied at Oxford. All her children had been educated in England, the boys had been to Marlborough College before going up to Oxford. She herself visited England every year to meet up with her college friends and had recently retired from an important administrative job in the Government.

Finally we disembarked at a big shopping centre called River City, where we walked through the cool hall with its splashing fountain and elegant shops and where, even though it was now January, Father Christmas was still in evidence. Here we boarded a minibus which took us through town on a long and tedious journey back to Indra Hotel in dense traffic that barely moved. Walking back through the narrow lanes, we saw building work still going on and men and women still beavering away in dingy rooms at their machines, where we had seen them when we started our day.

When we set off early next day to visit the National Museum, we were amazed to find that the rubbish which had littered the streets the night before had already been collected and the streets had already been swept clean. Once again it took a couple of attempts to find a *tuk-tuk* driver who knew the way and charged a reasonable fare (I am convinced that they quote the first figure which comes into their heads). The driver told us that the museum did not open until 11 a.m.; my guide book said 9.30 a.m., whilst in fact it opened at 9 a.m. We politely declined his offer to take us shopping, whereupon he raced almost in a straight line at breakneck speed along the main street.

The National Museum is housed in a former palace, and well planned. A beautiful Thai pavilion stands near the entrance. In the prehistoric pavilion, where we started, the exhibits were clearly annotated in English, with some quaint phrasing. Going through room after room, we traced the history and development of the country from ancient to modern times. Before stepping into the

254

Red House, which had been the real home of the princesses and was built of wood in Thai style, we visited a relocated temple. There was also a temporary exhibition of uniforms, which showed traditional costumes, later followed by ensembles displaying distinctly European influences, though the Thais are very proud of the fact that their country has never been colonised. This is reflected in the modern name of Thailand, 'Free Land' – instead of Siam; Bangkok means 'City of Angels' and an angel is its emblem.

We learnt that Bangkok had the first tram in the world.

The museum contained a wealth of treasures, with articles in pure gold or ivory, or inlaid with mother-of-pearl, as well as collections of weapons, thrones and royal carriages used for special occasions such as coronations or royal cremations. Delightful puppets, masks and toys of all kinds, as well as beautiful china and delicate silverware, were on display. The elaborate elephant seats on which the kings used to ride into battle – later used in ceremonial processions – fascinated us. Interesting sculptures from different epochs and different regions were well exhibited and showed the many styles in which Buddha had been presented. There were a large number of Hindu gods and goddesses represented, since Hinduism had preceded Buddhism and some aspect of Hindu religion has been absorbed into Buddhism. Unfortunately the textile department was closed, but after almost four hours we had reached saturation point. It was midday by then and very hot, which made us rest for a short while in the simple snack bar, where we enjoyed a bowl of delicious noodle soup cooked in Chinese style.

Our next port was Jim Thompson's House. Jim Thompson was an America who had been in Bangkok during the war, serving in the OSS, and returned to settle in the city. He revived the silk industry and put Thai silk on the world map. He re-erected six wooden Thai houses along a klong and furnished them exquisitely in Thai style. Sadly he disappeared without a trace whilst holidaying in the Cameroons in 1967. Since he was divorced and had no children, he left everything to a nephew, who converted the property into a foundation and opened it to the public. The revenue helps to preserve the house and the rest of the money goes to a school for the blind. The re-erected houses have been slightly adapted to modern life and stand in a shady garden amidst dense foliage, which was extremely pleasant on a hot day. A charming young lady with an excellent command of English took us round, pointing out the fine china, ceramics and paintings as we wandered from room to room.

Because of the intense heat we decided not to visit any other place and walked slowly back to our hotel. Soon we reached the main thoroughfare and recognised now familiar landmarks – such as a shopping mall housed in a modern building called Hollywood Street, where earlier we had seen a Christmas tree in the courtyard. It had now disappeared, leaving a naked skeleton of a tree made in wire in its place, but it had looked exactly like a beautiful fir tree when it was covered. In fact we had noticed that all topiary in the East was not made by cutting plants into shape but by training the growing evergreen over a wire frame.

The rest of the day we spent relaxing by the pool in our hotel and later we went out to dine, lingering on our way to look at the merchandise on the street stalls spilling over onto the pavements and out into the street. There was the same profusion of goods in the shopping arcade housed in the Indra Hotel, and it made us wonder who actually buys this vast amount of varied merchandise. In the Indra Hotel we sat next to a couple from Brisbane and started talking to them, then the diners on the two adjacent tables joined in; they too came from Australia.

That night we found a big ugly-looking beetle climbing up the hand towel and waving its long antenna menacingly at me. I gently closed the door until the morning, when I scooped the towel up and shook it out of the window. The bathroom still flooded whenever we released the plug, the ensuing dampness must have attracted our unwelcome guest.

When we had fixed our hotel at the airport we had been issued with a voucher for our taxi ride back for our departure, and all we had to do was to hand it to the traffic captain who stood at his desk outside the hotel entrance. At the appointed time a taxi arrived, but unfortunately it broke down almost immediately. Another cab was summoned without much delay and soon we were on our way. The early Sunday morning traffic was light and we reached the airport in half the time it had taken when we arrived. As anticipated, the place was packed with people milling around but to our surprise it did not take long to get through all the formalities; our luggage had to be X-rayed before it was checked through, otherwise the procedure followed the usual routine. Time passed quickly in the departure lounge, where we browsed through its arcades of shops.

The hostesses of Thai Airways greeted us with buttonholes of mauve orchids, then having settled comfortably for our short flight to Vientiane, we were served a light snack followed by flannels impregnated with toilet water to wipe our face and hands. Haze shrouded Thailand, we could barely see the muddy river and only glimpsed the faint outline of the rice paddies in the lowlands, followed by mountains. After we landed we had to line up in queues and wait for a considerable time to pass through immigration. Having completed the formalities, we were lucky to see a young man holding up a placard with seven names on it – ours amongst them. As soon as we had collected our luggage we joined the rest of our party consisting of two couples from Canada and one lady from Australia. Henry from Canada was born in Berlin and Bill came from Aberdeen. Jean, the single lady, hailed from Sydney.

Our drive took us through dusty streets to 'the best hotel in town', which was a large building with three floors but no lift. The dining room was a big hall with a high ceiling, thick wooden pillars and wood-clad walls. Food was plentiful and beautifully presented; a four-course meal was served with coffee or tea to follow. The tub in the bathroom, which was en suite, was most extraordinary since it was almost square, with wall tiles on all sides and a multicoloured tessellated floor.

After lunch we set off to see some of the sights accompanied by a twenty-two-year-old guide who spoke scant English. Unfortunately his accent was so pronounced that it was difficult to understand him at all. He informed us that he had trained as a pharmacist in a small town in the Caucasus for seven years and had worked in a brewery on his return but had left this job one month ago to become a guide because it was better paid. Vientiane struck us as a strange town when we first drove along wide dusty roads and it seemed difficult to realise that it is the capital of a country the size of France, but with a population of only a four million. Some of the houses standing in their own grounds looked quite imposing and we were told that they were foreign embassies, whilst the former Royal Palace now housed Government offices. Our first stop was the Pha That Luang – the Sacred Stupa – now used as a museum, where only foreign tourists pay an entrance fee. It was entirely surrounded by a high-walled cloister with tiny windows. The great stupa rose, beautifully proportioned, in a simple curved line from the square hemispherical base, which resembled a lotus bud. We ascended the staircase to walk around the three levels. The first walkway was a square, 74 by 74 yards, supporting 323 ordination stones or *sima*. There were also four arched prayer gates, or *haw wai*, one on each side, leading up to the two remaining levels. The second walkway was 52 by 52 yards square and was surrounded by 120 lotus petals. Here were 288 *sima* as well as 30 small stupas symbolising the 30 Buddhist perfections. Arched gates led up to the third level, which was 30 yards long on each side. The tall central stupa consisted of a brick core which had been stuccoed over and was surrounded by lotus petals at its base. The numbers and the various architectural features are of great significance to the devout Buddhist.

The second temple we visited was the Wat Si Saket, which, like Wat Pha Kuang, also served as a museum. The cloisters which again surrounded the entire courtyard were honeycombed with niches which contained miniature Buddha figures, usually two to each niche. Some were made of silver, others were ceramic figures; they totalled 2,000, whilst another 300 were displayed on long shelves below. These were either seated or standing and were made of wood, stone or bronze. A Khmer-style Buddha sat on a coiled snake which kept him dry in floods and protected his head from the rain with its multiheaded hood. A pile of broken and half-melted Buddhas from the 1828 Siamese war lay in one corner.

The walls inside the *sim* (shrine) contained hundreds of Buddhas in niches as well as badly damaged Jakata (Buddha's life story) murals. The high ceiling bore golden flowers on a red background. A young painter was busily copying the faded murals for his thesis.

The nearby Wat Pha Keo, formerly the Royal Temple, had also been converted into a museum and was no longer used for worship. Royal temples carry the symbol of kingship in the form of numerous ceremonial umbrellas, made of silver, on top of the highest roof. Roofs were high-peaked, with a steep pitch, and layered in uneven numbers. Their edges nearly always featured a flame motive, terminating with claw-like hooks said to catch the evil spirit, thus protecting both the shrine and the people who came to worship. A heavily ornate roof usually projected over the front porch. Like most temples in Laos this too had been destroyed and rebuilt, with little remaining from the original building; only one heavily carved wooden door had survived, which was badly damaged but still showed traces of colour and had beautifully turned spindles barring the windows. Inside the *sim* stood the royal requisites, such as the gilded throne. This temple had been built to house the Emerald Buddha and to serve as private chapel to the King. It now contained a copy of the Emerald Buddha, which was known as Pra Keo, and also gave a home to many Buddha images and Buddha heads, including two very ancient terracotta ones. Dusty stelae and wood carvings stood around. A long wooden trough, known as *hang song ham phra* or image watering rail, carved to resemble Naga the Snake God, was still being used to wash all Buddha images for the Lao New Year. A large wooden bird, also a symbol for the New Year, stood in a corner. On the back terrace (all temples were raised above the ground) we saw a collection of stelae inscribed in both Mon and Lao script. From here we looked down on the garden, where a bodhi tree sheltered an enormous jar which came from the Plane of Jars, a high plateau strewn with gigantic jars whose origins remain a mystery. Along the banister of the stairs leading down from the temple curled Naga, whose multiheaded hood was raised to protect the temple.

Numerous Buddha figures had been assembled in the surrounding cloister, some of which were made of stone, others of wood or bronze. Several sitting or standing Buddhas in bronze were also displayed which were in typical Lao style with simple elegant lines and often in certain attitudes, such as a standing Buddha with arms by his side calling for rain or with both arms stretched out with palms upturned, protecting, or with hands loosely crossed at the wrist and eyes closed, contemplating the tree of enlightenment.

Our last visit took us to a weavers' village where the houses stood on stilts and the walls consisted of bamboo matting. Little girls of fourteen or less sat at their looms beneath the wooden floors, working away, using silk and cotton and sometimes golden thread following traditional patterns for the borders of sarong lengths. Somebody asked the price of a length of silk and out of the blue came the answer: 100 dollars, which seemed far too much.

On our journey back to the hotel we stopped briefly at the Pratuxai, which, seen from the distance, resembled the Arc de Triomphe and had been built to commemorate the men who died in the pre-Revolutionary wars.

259

After a short rest we walked to the back of the hotel across a car park which had been marked out for basketball and came upon cages containing monkeys, bears and one evil-looking crocodile in very confined spaces; no wonder they all looked miserable. To our great surprise we also found a swimming pool with sunbeds, changing rooms and a bar looking exactly like the picture we had seen on the brochure of the hotel. The back gate of the hotel led to a square with a fountain, around which a travel office, a French restaurant and a few shops clustered. Everything, however, was firmly closed since it was Sunday – except a booth selling soft drinks and snacks in which a radio blasted away. Youngsters sat at tables enjoying their drinks whilst children played near the water's edge. Wandering on, we came upon a stupa which looked old and romantic with plants and grass growing up from its base. This was known as That Dam or Black Stupa.

By this time it was getting dark and broken pavements as well as open gutters presented hazards in the fading light. When we returned to our hotel we met up with a Norwegian pilot-surveyor who told us that he had been in the country for the month with two of his countrymen, a pilot and a navigator, working for a Finnish firm surveying the Mekong River. They were waiting for instructions from their firm, whether they were to extend their survey to the entire water system of Laos. Apart from work there was nothing for them to do in Vientiane, which he found very tedious. We asked him who provided the money for all the goods we had seen in the shops, such as Japanese motorbicycles, bicycles, tinned milk and other food from Malaysia and goods from Thailand, etc. He told us that most goods were paid for by foreign powers. Merchandise seemed to be plentiful in the numerous small shops. Apart from shops, we had passed many bars and had remarked on the many stalls along the streets which prepared fresh fruit and salads almost non-stop. Back in our room we were delighted to find that our sinister-looking boiler produced plenty of hot water for us.

After a dinner as elaborate as lunch had been (although we skipped the main course and side salad) we went out once more and found that young people were still about, congregating around the fountain or drinking in small pavement bars and chatting in groups at street corners or just strolling along. Some shops were still open and we also passed a number of hotels of varying kinds, some looking slightly seedy, others quite nice. There were also offices, one was a computer office advertising a fax service; next to it was a big depository and close by a money exchange and a bank. Families lived at the back of their little shops, where they all seemed to be glued to their televisions. It appeared strange to us to have television, gleaming motorbikes and big cars in a town which was full of broken houses and unmade roads and an uncertain electricity supply. Families slept either on mattresses or on the bare floor in the shop, with their prize possession – either a bicycle or motorbike – sharing the confined space. Big baskets looking like lobster pots stood along the street; next morning we saw two turkey cocks strutting around in one and learned that cockfights were the national sport. Dogs barked late into the night and cocks crowed in the early morning, taking over where the canines had left off.

Next morning we had time to stroll along the way we had walked the night before, and stepped into a temple complex which served as school. Little tots played happily in the sandy courtyard, older children sat earnestly behind desks in classrooms which were housed in the monks' quarters. From here we found our way down to the Mekong River, whose waters had receded, leaving a sandy beach behind. Ships and barges plied the muddy waters of the mighty river, which in Laos is fully navigable through its entire course. Near the river stood a temple which was being restored, with one man on bamboo scaffolding carefully cementing precast stylised decorations around window frames, whilst an old man was in the process of dismantling scaffolding to reveal a new painting at the entrance to the shrine. Mats had been placed on the floor of the porch for the workmen to sleep on and also to sit to have their simple meals of rice. Straw baskets served a double purpose: turned one way they acted as tables, whilst the other way they made a tray.

Returning finally to our hotel and approaching it from a different direction, we were amazed to see how big it was and also became aware of the fact that a nightclub was attached to the main building. Apart from the Norwegian pilot we had not seen any other guest during our stay.

Then we collected our luggage and proceeded to the airport, where we sat for the next few hours on hard plastic chairs in a big hall, waiting to be called to board. Local travellers joined us, weighed down with enormous piles of cabin luggage. Many of them carried large quantities of the delicious French bread which we had enjoyed so much with our meals. Loaves of this appetising-looking

261

bread, as well as cakes, were laid out on a table for sale in the departure hall. Most of these travellers (obviously used to the delay) arrived a mere half an hour before the scheduled take-off time and presented their tickets to four officials sitting at a table in the hall, who cast a cursory glance at them. Finally we took off in an old Russian plane and, although we had received numbered boarding cards, we could sit where we liked. Almost immediately we had sat down we were served with a cup of Pepsi and offered an ice-cold face flannel impregnated with toilet water to wipe our hands and face. Just before we landed bumpily in Luang Phabang after our short flight, we could see the wide Mekong River, paddy fields and wooded mountains. The airport consisted only of a landing strip and a shed, half of which served as departure and arrival lounge, the other as a simple bar. A charming local guide dealt with our luggage and soon we were on our way to the hotel on the slope of Kite Hill, which was extremely pleasant, with friendly staff who were eager to please. Our room was very basic but had a bathroom attached and a superb view from the balcony, sweeping over a valley where little homesteads stood beneath palms, across the Mekong River and up to the green hills on its other bank.

After lunch we set off to see some temples down town. The first one was Wat Wisunarat or Wat Visoun, the oldest operating temple in this former capital. Once upon a time it had been a royal temple and therefore carried the royal emblem on top of the highest roof. (All temples are crowned by a number of tiered roofs sweeping low down to the ground.) The original temple, built in wood in 1513, burnt down in 1896 but was restored two years later in brick and stucco. An attempt had been made to make the balustraded windows simulate turned wooden spindles. This feature is alien to Lao style but typical of Khmer work. The *sim* contained the largest Buddha in the country and was full of Buddha images in various typical Lao attitudes. Our guide pointed out the wooden bird which is one of the seven ceremonial animals appertaining to the New Year and the *simas*, ordination stones, dating from the 15th to the 16th century. The main stupa facing the *sim* rose gracefully into the air, resembling a watermelon. As we walked past the monks' quarters we noticed the sticky rice laid out to dry, to be used later to feed the pigs.

The second temple we visited, the Wat Xieng Thong, stood at

the confluence of the muddy Mekong River with the green waters of the Mankhan. The Wat Xieng Thong was a most magnificent complex, living up to its name, which means Golden City Temple, and was richly decorated with gold. Wooden columns covered in golden design supported the ceiling, which in turn was adorned with the Dharma Wheels. The rear wall of the temple featured an impressive Tree of Life mosaic on a red background. To one side of the *sim* stood several chapels, one of them on stilts contained the big drum, whilst another one housed a Reclining Buddha, rare in Laos. Near the East Gate rose the elaborate Royal Funeral Chapel, with the 36-foot high funeral chariot and a number of funeral urns containing the ashes of members of the royal family within, whilst sumptuous gilt panels covered the walls outside, depicting episodes from the *Ramayana*. Huge banners hung suspended from long poles crowned by a bird symbolising the ladder on which the spirit of the dead can climb up to heaven. We had already seen a collection in the museum in Vientiane.

Our visit continued to Wat Aham, which lay on a hill and looked peaceful in the last rays of the day's sun. A few young novices with saffron-coloured woollen hats stood shyly beneath a Bodhi tree, looking at us with big eyes. Two rows of wooden cabins resembling our beach huts stood on stilts and served as retreats for meditation.

As the day drew to a close we drove to a temple standing above the Mekong River to rest and wait for the sun to set. The temple itself was being repainted by novices in brilliant colours of yellow, green and red. This temple had been built to protect a cave in the cliff below it which harboured an enormous imprint of Buddha's foot and was sacred to the many pilgrims who came to honour and venerate it. Here we sat next to the cave, enjoying the peaceful view. A small boat drew alongside a sandbank and a young woman standing in the bow helped an old lady ashore. The old lady performed a ritual in front of a small mound, producing a net which she swung in large circles around her. This ritual is performed when a child is ill, and it is always the grandmother who goes out to catch the spirit of health to bring back to cure the sick child. Our guide explained that he had lived with his grandmother at a temple for seven years, having lost his parents when he was very young, and remembered well that this was what she always used to do whenever he ailed and it inevitably restored him to rude health again.

When the sun had set over the river we returned to our hotel

263

where we later talked to a Dutchman who worked here in an advisory capacity for the EEC and had a team working on a project to improve roads and to help in setting up education and health projects. It was his third assignment in Laos, and although funding was a great problem, he felt very optimistic that the country would win through since in his experience as long as one was prepared to listen to the people and was willing to give them the opportunity to ask questions, progress was made. It was extremely interesting to talk to this man.

Once the sun had disappeared it grew cold and made us shiver as we walked through the little garden of the hotel, where a couple of monkeys were kept in small cages beneath palm trees. On reaching our room we saw that there was no blanket on my bed. A sweet young maid, upon being asked, immediately came running along with two warm blankets, which meant we could settle for the night in great comfort.

It was misty when we woke, and chilly, but we had come prepared, having been forewarned about cold mornings and evenings up in Luang Phabang. Sharp at 8 a.m. the electricity went off and remained off until 6 p.m.

Soon after breakfast we set off to visit the market, which sold mostly food and some other commodities (mainly imported from Thailand). The vendors, who were all women, sat on low basket-weave stools which they carried around with them. Layers of sugar-cane lay placed between palm leaves before being boiled to extract the syrup, which was spread on flat tins and left to dry and when set was cut into small pieces of sugar! All the vegetables, salads and herbs looked beautifully fresh; baby cauliflower were sold on stalks, resembling our sprouts. Buffalo hide was cut into strips and mixed with chilli, constituting a special relish. There were many types of rice for sale: black rice was used for special ceremonies or fermented with yeast to produce a sherry-like drink. (Since we bought some for our evening meal we knew the taste!) Thin noodles were cut by hand. Pancakes were yet another speciality, which we sampled at a later date; thicker than we are accustomed to make they tasted delicious and provided a very substantial breakfast. The whole of the market presented a lively scene with many smiling faces.

To reach Wat That Luang we crossed the street and walked along the stadium to climb up steps between stone walls crowned by *nagas*. Wat That Luang was yet another royal temple with the usual silver emblem on the highest roof and was built in classic Laotian style, with multiple roofs sweeping down to the ground, carvings on doors and windows, and pillars supporting the overhanging porch. The ashes of King Sisavang Vonga were interned in the central stupa. In one corner stood a delightful double-gabled building which had dainty stucco designs adorning the windows and the central door. This used to be the chief abbot's home. The temple still housed the largest contingents of monks in the country.

We set off on a day's outing into the countryside along unsealed roads which were in a reasonable state of repair though the Dutchmen had warned us the night before that this was a 'terrible' road according to his recollection of two years ago. Two bridges had collapsed but these could be bypassed. Obviously work had been carried out in the intervening years. The scenery was lovely and we felt happy to be on our way to see more of this land. At the unspoilt village of Watlakham we stopped and found ourselves almost immediately surrounded by excited children who with laughing happy faces, just looked at us. A black sow was suckling five piglets, a herd of buffaloes with pink calves was being driven home, small dogs abounded (later we learned that dogs are eaten by the villagers.) The blacksmith was working with his assistant, who kept the charcoal fire smouldering by pumping air through a hollow trunk whilst the smith plunged the hot iron into a shallow trough of water. Girls were husking rice. Houses with walls consisting of bamboo matting, or occasionally made of wood which had been beautifully assembled resembling parquet flooring, stood on stilts. The roofs were thatched; they contained one large room, with an open terrace in front on which an urn filled with water with a ladle nearby, stood at the head of the stairs to provide a place to rest and a drink for any stranger. The village lay near the river and since boats did not sail at night, any traveller would alight and stop for the night.

When a new house was being built, all the villagers lent a hand; they received no pay but were fed. The foundation of a house was being laid whilst we were there and we watched one man busily making a mould of rough wood for cement blocks whilst another with plumb line in hand marked out the position where they were to go. Cots and hammocks hung suspended below the houses. Babies often cried when they saw our unfamiliar faces. Big Ali

Baba-like jars made of canes strengthened with a mixture of dung and powdered lime also stood beneath the dwellings; these were used to store rice. A separate small hut served as a kitchen. Old women with teeth stained brown from betel-nut looked after the small children. Everybody, men, women and children alike greeted us with smiles; children waved to us wherever we went, no one begged. Accompanied by a horde of happy children, we walked past the temple, where a big wooden bell stood close by, and back to our bus to continue our journey further up the valley.

The main village of the district through which we drove boasted a secondary school. Schooling was not compulsory but was free. Great efforts were being made to train teachers and to improve education. In a second village where we stopped, everybody was involved in processing cotton. Little girls sat on low stools, turning the handles of miniature mangles to remove the seeds, whilst women deftly beat the cotton with a stick which looked like a violin bow with a single string attached to either end. The seedless cotton was placed inside a hollow trunk, which was turned with one hand whilst the other wielded the stick. This cotton was not used for spinning but to stuff pillows and overlays. It felt lovely and soft lying in snowy white heaps in the sun to dry, resembling fluffy clouds. As we walked through the village we saw the simple way a fire was constructed: a deep notch was cut into a thick branch, almost dividing it into two halves. Each cut end was lit and both ends were gently pushed inwards to feed the flame. Little children huddled over the fires to keep warm and even stirred food in black pots.

Driving on, we reached the Khouansy Waterfalls at the end of the valley, a romantic, peaceful place and a favourite spot for the townspeople to come for a picnic. One of the sweet-faced waitresses from our hotel had come along with us to set out our lunch, which had been carried in huge baskets in the bus. She had sat busily crocheting whilst we drove along. Like all Laotian girls and women, she wore a short sarong with the traditional border with a silver belt encircling her slender waist.

On our way back we stopped once more to visit a third village, where girls sat spinning and weaving below the houses, sheltered from sun and rain. Children pulled crudely fashioned toys along the sand; one small cart was made of wood, whilst a boat had been formed from a palm leaf. A little toddler played with two live mice which were tied together with string. A woman sat stirring her pot over the fire containing fresh vegetables and rat meat. Rats were shot with long barrelled guns in the rice fields. A little boy was gnawing a roasted leg of rat.

To watch two water mills grinding away, we walked to the stream where kapok trees grew. I continued upstream where it widened out into a pond. A pretty young girl, her hair wet, her sarong tightly wrapped around her supple body, two small children by her side, stood motionless like a painting at the edge of the water. Feeling an intruder I hastily withdrew.

Returning to Luang Phabang, we visited more temples. The Wat Mas, known as the New Temple, was interesting: built in the classic five-tiered style and sumptuously decorated in shimmering gold on a red background. Redecorating was in progress whilst we were there. The painter used stencil to apply the golden pattern on the newly-painted red background. The *sim* was quite remarkable for its decorated columns and for the elaborate golden relief door panels which recounted scenes from Buddha's life before he obtained enlightenment. A shelter housed two long racing boats which were used for the New Year celebrations and again in October during the Water Festival. The second temple, the Wat Po Huak, stood on a ridge above the river at the back of the former Royal Palace. It had a large courtyard, a classic *sim* and old stupas standing behind the shrine. Stone stairs with *naga* balustrades led down to the road, linking with further flights of stairs which led down to the landing stage on the Mekong River.

When we reached down town Luang Phabang we left our party to walk around on our own and strolled through the covered market, which sold mostly imported merchandise, and further along past the Phousy Hotel, where a monkey fastened by a long rope swung from a tree. First we looked for the post office but found it firmly closed; next we located the tourist office, where we found two young Australians sitting dejectedly on the stone steps. They had wanted to go upriver to visit the famous Buddhist Caves but had been asked to pay sixty American dollars each, which they could not afford. Pong, our charming local guide, appeared on the scene at the right time and we asked him whether we could accommodate the youngsters on our boat next day. Since he agreed we arranged to meet them at 9 a.m. at the National Museum next morning. Nothing of interest was available at the tourist office. A

267

new hotel was being built in the complex. The Parliament of the Province of Luang stood opposite but photography was strictly forbidden. Strolling on, we discovered a whole string of old temples along the ridge on which Wat Po Huak stood which were interconnected with flights of stone steps. Walking along the dusty roads we watched women sitting at their looms and men mending their fishing nets. It did not take us long to reach our hotel, where we were again impressed by the service which we received. The man in charge of the dining room could not have done more to please everyone; some of our party wanted local food whilst others refused and asked for western fare. Next to us sat a party of Japanese who worked in Laos.

As night descended a full moon rose, spreading magic over the Mekong Valley.

The morning mist lifted earlier than on the previous day and it was less cold when we started with a visit to the National Museum, where opening hours were a moveable feast and visits had to be arranged in advance. The museum was housed in the former Royal Palace, which had served as a venue for State occasions. Two charming girls greeted us at the bottom of the stairs and led us along the tiled terrace. We looked through grilles into the royal chapel, which contained the most highly prized of all the treasures in the museum, including the Gold Standing Buddha, known as the Prah Beng, a present from the Khmers in the 14th century to commemorate the legalisation of Buddhism by royal decree by King Fa Ngum. Here we also saw three beautifully embroidered silk screens and one which was inlaid with mother-of-pearl. Large elephant tusks engraved with Buddhas stood in the centre. Khmer-style sitting Buddhas were displayed side by side with Luang Phabang standing ones. A splendid temple frieze with elephants adorned one wall.

Entering the palace, we stepped into the lofty hall where the Throne for King of Monks – the Supreme Patriarch of Lao Buddhism – stood raised above the hereditary King's place, which was on the floor below to indicate 'humility'. We admired a head of Buddha, a present from India, and also a reclining Buddha next to a classic figure with his eyes closed, hands lightly resting in each other, palms turned upwards in the attitude of contemplating the bodhi tree – all sculptured in white marble. This position of Buddha contemplating, as well as the other typical Lao attitudes such as

Buddha praying for rain or calming the ocean, were particularly lovely in their elegant simple line, always with a smile hovering round Buddha's lips.

A room to the left of the hall was filled with presents from many other countries, with paintings specific to each country, such as the wintry scene from Russia, hanging on the wall above each gift. The next room on the left served as the Queen's reception room and was dominated by large paintings of King Savang Vatta, his Queen and the Crown Prince painted by the Russian painter Illya Glazunov. Friendship flags from China and Vietnam were prominently displayed, whilst bronze drums decorated with frogs, the symbol for rain, stood in the corner. Some of these had three single frogs sitting on the circumference, whilst others had two or even three placed on the three basic ones, denoting the owner's rank.

The King's reception hall was to the right of the entrance lobby and contained busts of the Lao monarchs and murals depicting traditional scenes from Laotian life. Behind the entrance hall lay the former throne room, which was a lofty place where the walls were covered with eye-catching scenes laid out in coloured glass and where the magnificent royal throne in gold stood flanked at either side by the golden crown boxes (though the ceremonial crown was actually kept in the bank). A golden chest contained the original constitution, and a glass case displayed the five royal insignia: the crown, denoting royalty and responsibility to govern with wisdom; the sabre, standing for strength; the whisk to sweep all evil away and the two-sided sword for justice; a staff symbolised long life since only the very old require sticks. A collection of crystal and golden Buddhas which had been found in the Thai Mak Mo – the Watermelon – stupa were shown in one glass cabinet, whilst the royal robes were displayed in another. Long gold framed benches with silken cushions stood in neat rows.

Next came the King's private apartments, containing the library with the Triptikatas of successive monarchs in a glass case, followed by the King's bedroom, with a large bed in the centre of the huge room adjacent to the Queen's chamber. Another room housed a collection of weapons, whilst the most interesting objects on display were Laotian classical musical instruments and masks used for the performance of the *Ramayana* dance-drama. Photographs of the royal family hung on the wall, with a stunning picture of the late King's mother and a photograph of his five children leaving a poignant impression. The King and Queen and two of their sons are now dead, whilst two of their sons live in France and only one daughter remained in Luang Phabang.

Opposite the Royal Palace, steps led down to the former royal landing stage, where guests used to alight to be greeted by their royal hosts. Here we boarded a longboat for a trip up river to visit the Pak Ou Caves. The Mekong River is wide and lined by many fresh vegetable plots on its shores. These thrive because of the silt the river leaves behind after the floods of the rainy season have subsided. Many junks and long-boats carrying passengers and goods passed us on our journey, fishermen skilfully threw their nets, banana groves grew neatly between lush vegetation, houses raised on stilts stood at the water's edge and roofs shimmered through the trees. The river was low. Awesome cliffs towered above where the Mekong joined the Nam Ou River; here we anchored and disembarked and climbed up numerous uneven steps to reach the upper cave, outside which stood a remarkably big-bellied figure with an ugly face. He was said to be one of Buddha's disciples who made himself ugly so as not to tempt the many beautiful maidens he met on his way and was therefore known as the Big-Bellied Disciple. The cave was full of Buddhas of all sizes in various attitudes, many standing erect in the lovely classic Laotian style. Bundles of sticks were inside a tube-like container, waiting to be shaken out onto the floor. The number of sticks which tumbled forth corresponded to numbers on an inscription on the wall which forecast the future. It always promised good fortune!

Our picnic lunch lay spread out on a rough table covered by a snowy-white cloth, waiting for us down some stairs where tables and benches stood beneath a roof. After lunch we climbed further down to reach the lower cave, smaller and less deep, containing more Buddha images. A New Year flag stood in the centre, consisting of a banner depicting the eight animals representing the years. Each person starts to count up to their present age to reach the sign of the New Year. On New Year's Day these banners are placed on top of a stupa made from sand.

On our journey back to Luang Phabang we stopped at the pottery village where whisky was being distilled on the banks of the river, utilising oil drums as crude stills and charcoal as fuel and feeding the waste to the pigs. The distilled liquor was left to ferment in the sun, stored in large pottery jars. The smell of the fermenting brew was so strong it almost knocked us over as we climbed up the steep bank. Sadly this village was dirty and the inhabitants proved less friendly than anywhere else we had been; they had seen more tourists and were used to strangers. Men were building a brick wall and gate for the village and asked us to contribute, assuring us that this would 'earn us merit'. Continuing our journey down river, we returned to the landing stage and drove east of the town to Ban Phanon Village, which was well known for its weaving. However, since the looms beneath the houses stood idle we were somewhat disappointed. The ladies sat on the floor around a big hall, selling shawls, bags etc.

At dinner we watched a large party of Japanese celebrating. The table was beautifully decorated, food attractively presented and by the time they had consumed three bottles of best French brandy they became noisy and very lively.

After our meal we strolled out into the balmy air and met an Indian couple: he was a distinguished-looking white-haired man, she an elegant younger lady wearing a silk sari and speaking in a gently pleasing voice. He was a diplomat who had been ambassador to Laos thirty-six years ago and this was their first visit after all these years; they were staying with friends in Vientiane. It was quite apparent that they loved the local population and felt happy to have returned and they, like the Dutchman on the previous day, were convinced that the country would steadily advance. They were interesting people to meet and we learnt that they lived apart, since he had returned to his native Delhi after he had retired whilst she lived in London and was involved in helping black women in South Africa. Briefly we also talked to two German women who had flown into Laos with us. We had presumed they were friends but learnt to our amazement that they were mother and daughter. The daughter, who was a pretty young girl, lived in Beijing studying Chinese and hoped to marry her Chinese fiancé the following August, intending to return with him to Germany after the wedding.

Thick mist covered the landscape which was slow to lift when we rose next morning. For the last time we sampled the delicious local pancake for breakfast before we met up with Pong, who told us that the exact time of our departure from Luang Phabang was uncertain since it depended entirely on the weather conditions; planes could not take off in fog. The mist remained thick, delaying the arrival of the plane from Vientiane until it had cleared enough

271

for a safe landing. Our luggage was loaded on our minibus, which dropped us off at the foot of Phu Hill and proceeded to the airport, whilst we climbed up 364 steps, stopping to admire the large bo tree – a gift from India – which had been planted as a sapling (a twig of the original bo tree) by the former ambassador we had met the night before. On top of the hill stood Wat Cho Sia, a modest temple which served as starting point for the colourful Laotian New Year Procession. A natural cleavage in the rock behind Wat Cho Si was worshipped as a shrine by the local population. On the spur of the rock sat an old Russian anti-aircraft cannon, a sinister memento of the recent past.

The fog still had not disappeared when we climbed down, therefore we had ample time to stroll leisurely through the streets and observe the people around us. Monks wore yellow woolly knitted hats to keep their shorn heads warm; State Lottery tickets were being sold at the kerbside; children skipped happily and played the same games as children of their ages will do all over the world, with one little girl balancing precariously in her mother's shoes. A barber was busily following his trade, shaving a customer reclining in an ancient dentist's chair. From the lively pavement we slipped into the peaceful courtyard of a *wat* which lay almost hidden behind the densely populated area and found young novices trying to keep warm over a small fire. Out in the street, children huddled over a burning stick encased in a big tube lying on its side. Here we saw Mons people in their national dress, with women wearing long black skirts, aprons in stripes of black and blue, and black cloth twisted like a turban on their heads. Men were in black jackets and long trousers, sprouting tall hats resembling the old Welsh ones. Some of the features around us, such as an old lady with grey hair and a round face, looked very French.

Our next visit was to a famous silversmith, where four men sat on low stools in a yard busily working away, cutting silver sheeting, shaping, filing, hammering and etching delicate designs, using wooden blocks to support the metal. Some members of our party bought trinkets in the little 'shop', which was simply one showcase in the family room, which housed the prized possession: a Honda motorbike.

Finally we called on a master woodcutter but unfortunately he was old and ill and unable to work any more. Instead, a young man brought out the exquisite carvings cut from teak, rosewood and honey-coloured wood from a special tree. The Buddhas were expertly carved, wall plaques were of intricate detailed design but all the articles were very expensive and also too delicate for the long journey which lay in front of us. There still was no news of the flight when we returned to our hotel for lunch at the poolside, with its peaceful view across to the mountains and down to the lush valley where the Mekong flows. Whilst having our snack lunch we were informed that our plane had just left Vientiane. It was sad to say goodbye since we had felt happy in Luang Phabang, where the simple hotel was so expertly run and where everybody had been friendly and kind.

At the airport we again met the Australian couple – brother and sister – who had come on our river trip. They had been told to report at the airport at 6 a.m. and had used the long hours of waiting to wander around visiting nearby villages to see how people lived. Maureen was a teacher in Melbourne and many of her pupils were immigrants from Vietnam, where she had already been to collect information for a project about this country as well as about Laos and Cambodia. She was trying to understand her pupils by coming to their country of origin and hoped to be able to teach them about their own culture.

The plane had landed when we arrived at the airport and our luggage was being loaded as soon as the hold was clear. There was no hustle at all and after a very short wait we boarded the Bulgarian plane, now belonging to Lao Air, which was a big plane but not full. For the last time we glanced down on Luang Phabang set on the shores of the mighty Mekong River, and flew over many shallow rice paddies well irrigated by numerous canals before clouds swallowed the scene below us. Soon we landed once more at Vientiane. Once installed, we wandered out in search of the Morning Market, which actually functioned from 6 a.m. to 6 p.m. Stalls selling delicious fruit clustered around a big new hall, covering two floors, which housed a vast number of stalls selling all kinds of goods. The amount and diversity were bewildering: there were jewellery stalls selling mainly silverware, and stalls of textiles, glass, pottery etc. Some shopkeepers were far too involved watching television to be prised away to serve, but we managed to buy a silver belt. Every woman in Laos wore a silver belt as part of their daily dress, some of them being more elaborate than others, some heavier and therefore more expensive since the price of silverware depended

273

upon its weight. A pretty young girl peeling a root handed one to us to try. It was a mild juicy radish and most of the local population seemed to be chewing them. After purchasing some textiles we briefly looked into a small supermarket before walking out of the hall where many small shops sold imported manufactured goods.

Crossing the main road we reached the Khun Kham Market, also known as the Evening Market, which sold fresh products. Motorbikes and motorised trickshaws stood waiting to serve as taxis to take the shoppers home with their heavy loads. (In Bangkok we had seen motorbikes used as taxis in the dense traffic.) Fruit, vegetables and salads looked very appetising and fresh but we took flight when we reached the section selling meat, since flies, stench and dirt chased us away. Later I walked out by myself to buy some postcards. By then it was dark but the streets were still full of life, motorbikes and bicycles still plied the roads. I saw a bridal pair in European dress in a restaurant having their photograph taken. At dinner we marvelled again at the impeccable manner in which waiters and waitresses served and the way tables were laid and food presented.

Cambodia

A cheery smile greeted us at 5.30 a.m. when we arrived for breakfast and again the service and the food were as perfect as they had been the night before. Soon we were speeding through the dark, silent city sorry to leave Laos behind us. The flight was short, just one and a half hours, and we first looked down on the rice paddies again before we rose above the clouds where the view of the countryside was blocked. Pleasant girls served us with a pre-packed lunch, but since we could not eat at this early hour we asked whether we could take it with us. Almost every passenger did this except our Australian couple who had not had any breakfast before they boarded, doing the whole extensive trip on a shoestring budget. Again and again we met the same people since every tourist seemed to be following the same route. One of them was a bluff jolly Irishman who had booked his tour in Bangkok and had spent one week in the Philippines before arriving in Lao. He bought a silver belt for his American wife amidst a great deal of laughter and bargaining, teasing the pretty airhostess during the transaction.

274

Nearing Phnom Penh, we caught sight of two rivers: the broad Mekong and the Tonle Sap, followed by a network of waterways and a large lake in the distance. Water seemed to glitter everywhere. The Tonle Sap drains the big lake during the dry season but reverses its flow during the rainy season, refilling the lake. The Mekong River, which rises in Tibet, is a mighty waterway, reaching a width of 5 kilometres at one point. At Phnom Penh it divides into two arms and finally forms a big delta in Vietnam to pour into the South China Sea. Clouds obscured our view once more until just before we landed, when we saw a row of little new houses standing at the side of a straight tree-lined road.

Once we landed, confusion reigned in the densely crowded reception hall since some travellers had been issued with forms whilst others had none. Two duplicated forms were given to us to fill in, one for customs the other for the police. We also had to identify our cases on the tarmac before we were allowed to proceed through passport control and customs. Everything then went surprisingly smoothly, contrary to what we had been told, and all the pleasant customs officer asked was the amount of money we carried and the contents of our luggage. Again we were met by a local guide, our baggage was stowed away in the boot of a small air-conditioned bus and we were away into town to our hotel, driving along wide, tree-lined well-surfaced avenues with houses shot to ruins standing to either side. The town bore witness to its former elegance, the scarred buildings spoke of a gracious past.

Soon we reached Hotel Cambodia, a brand new hotel built by a Cambodian who had made his money in Hong Kong, in conjunction with an Indonesian company. The gate, the approach to the building and the entrance hall were all very grand but the bedrooms although well furnished, were not finished and there was a marked shortage of well-trained staff. The hotel stood on the river, where many vessels, big and small, plied up and down. A big wet area next to the Cambodia was being filled in with mud dredged up from the river-bed to form the foundation for another hotel, whilst a motel was being built on the other side. Many business people and aid personnel had their offices in the Cambodia Hotel and many chauffeur-driven Mercedes, often with flags unfurled, frequently drew up outside the entrance hall.

We walked out of the cool building into the scorching heat. Outside the gate we were besieged by the 'cyclo' brigade (cyclos are the man-driven three-wheelers used as taxis in Cambodia and Vietnam) but we waved them aside and crossed the wide Lenin Boulevard. The street plan was quite simple, based on the grid system with named boulevards constituting the main arteries and the side streets being clearly marked with numbers. Slowly we walked along the high wall of the Royal Palace; its many roofs shimmered in the bright sunlight above the enclosure. It was horrendous to see the war-damaged city with house after house a mere shell, whilst the population lived like cave dwellers in terrible conditions of filth amongst the rubble, without water, sanitation or electricity. Realising that the hotel stood a long way away from the centre of the city, we returned to cool off in the swimming pool and wait for our city tour scheduled for the afternoon.

Once again we met our Australian couple, who were on their way to book a tour to Siem Reap to visit Angkor Wat, since at that time you could not get to this important site independently. Inviting them into our hotel, we took them up to the fifth floor to enjoy the splendid view over the river and to relax, fanned by the gentle breeze.

When we finally met up with our group we found that we could barely understand our young local guide and he certainly failed to understand us. He did, however, change our dollars on the black market, which was quite official and gave us a better rate of exchange than the hotel would have done, but less than a bank, but saved us the hassle of having to fill in endless forms if we had managed to find a bank.

Our tour started with the Silver Pagoda, where we had to pay to be allowed to take photographs. Since the return of Prince Sihanouk the Silver Pagoda was the only building in the complex open to the public. His photograph as a young man was everywhere prominently displayed. The Silver Pagoda stood entirely surrounded by a wall which was decorated with painted scenes from the *Ramayana*, but although only created in 1900 the paintings were in a poor state. The Pagoda itself had been originally built in wood in 1892 by King Norodom, the grandfather of Price Sihanouk; it was rebuilt in 1962 and fortunately the pagoda and its contents had been preserved by Khmer Rouge as a museum. Various structures stood outside the enclosure as well as inside, such as the *mondap* or library, which used to house illuminated sacred texts written on palm leaves, and the grey sandstone stupa of King

Norodom (1859–1904) decorated in traditional Khmer style, which has a distinctive element of Hindu mythology included in its ornamentations. Near this monument rose the splendid equestrian statue of the King on his white horse. We admired the stupa of King An Duong (1845–1859) and glanced at a pavilion containing Buddha's footprints in bronze, which lay hidden amongst foliage on an artificial hill; the footprints had come from Sri Lanka. Passing the Phnom Mondap brought us to the stupa of Sihanouk's daughter, who had been a famous dancer and died when she was fifteen years old. Next to this stood the pavilion used for royal celebrations, followed by the stupa of King Norodom Suramarit (father of Prince Sihanouk) and lastly the bell tower, which used to issue the call to open and close the gates.

Our guide told us that we were not allowed to enter the Silver Pagoda, which dominated the centre of the courtyard, but fortunately a French group appeared on the scene and their guide managed to gain entrance and we were able to follow them up the smooth marble steps. Dutifully we took off our shoes to enter this temple with its floor entirely covered by the solid silver tiles from which it derived its name. It is also knows as Wat Phra Keo, Temple of the Emerald Buddha, who – made of Baccarat crystal – sat supreme high up on a gilded altar below a magnificent French chandelier. Below the Phra Keo stood a life-sized statue of the Buddha which our guide claimed was the image of the King and was adorned with priceless diamonds. Directly in front of this statue, protected in a glass case, a miniature gold and silver stupa contained a relic of the Buddha brought from Sri Lanka and to either side sat bronze Buddhas as well as one delightful silver statue; all of them with the same blissful smile playing round their lips. A small glass cabinet contained scenes from Buddha's life cast in golden miniatures; amongst other events was his entering Nirvana with his mourning disciples by his side. The delicate Tree of Life, which is always present in every shrine, was also faithfully represented in the Silver Pagoda. A wonderful tall marble Buddha from Burma stood guard behind the altar, and next to it the King's litter, used at his coronation, had its place. This was partly made of pure gold and had to be carried by twelve men. A glass case at the back of the hall housed two golden Buddhas heavily adorned with diamonds, whilst all along the walls glass cases exhibited a variety of articles of Khmer craftsmanship, including bejewelled masks in

277

solid or hollow gold used in classical dance. Poignantly one show-case protected the golden regalia worn by Sihanouks' daughter when she danced.

Our next visit took us to the National Museum of Khmer Art and Archaeology, housed in a red building of classic design which had been a palace in the past. The beautiful sculptures were well displayed, set out in chronological order in galleries around a courtyard which itself had been laid out into a pretty garden around a central dais on which the Leper King from the Leper Terrace of Angkor Wat sat. Excavations dating back to prehistoric times were neatly displayed in showcases, superb sculptures from the prehis-toric Funa and Chelna period (1st to 9th century), followed by the Indravarman period (9th to 19th century) and the classic Angkor period – the Golden Age of Khmer Art – (10th to 14th century) up to the post-Angkor time (after the 14th century) were on display. Hinduism flourished alongside Buddhism from the lst to the 14th century. From the 1st to the 6th century BC the south of the country was part of the Indianised Kingdom of Funa. The Indian influece is easliy seen in Harihara, the figure which combines the Hindu gods Siva and Vishnu. Funa was attacked by the pre-Angkorian kingdom of Chelna, which gradually absorbed the country. Buddhism itself went through various stages. Before the 9th century the Hinayana school of Buddhism prevailed but after the 9th century it was replaced by Mahayana Buddhism which was mainly adhered to until the 13th century, when a form of Hinayana Buddhism arrived from Sri Lanka via Thailand with the Pali script which replaced Sanskrit. I found it (and still do) extremely difficult to understand Buddhism and particularly the difference between the Hinayana or Theravada (the Lesser Vehicle) and Mahayana Buddhism (the Greater Vehicle). The Theravada school of Bud-dhism is an earlier form of Buddhism and its followers strive to become perfect to reach Nirvana, whilst the adherers of Mahayana Buddhism try to imitate the Bodhisattva (Buddha to Come), per-fecting themselves in the necessary virtues (such as generosity, morality, patience, vigour, concentration and wisdom) but even after attaining perfection choose to remain in the world to help others. They consider Gautama Buddha to be only one of the many manifestations of the one ultimate Buddha. The Theravada school stresses three principal aspects of existence:
1) suffering, unsatisfactoriness, disease 2) impermanence, the tran-

gave him one US dollar; but he did not forsake her and kept steadfastly to her side until the bitter end.

The next three hours we spent walking happily around the central temple, which consisted of three storeys, each enclosing a courtyard surrounded by interlinking galleries. Wherever we looked, the walls, door jambs, lintels and window frames were covered with the most skilful carvings. Corbelled ceilings met our upturned gaze, columns had been expertly turned to simulate wooden spindles. Well-worn steps led up to different levels and down again. Sunken pools now empty must have provided blessed coolness when the sun beat down. A most superb bas-relief covered every inch of an 800-yard-long esplanade which ran around the central temple. These used to be protected by wooden roofs but one single beam was all that remained. *Apsaras*, the graceful wood nymphs, adorned the walls everywhere.

The southern wall of the western gallery depicted battle scenes from the Mahabarata, whilst the western section of it showed scenes from Khmer history with Suryavarma the Second (1112–1152), mounted on an elephant, wearing the royal tiara, armed with a battle axe, shaded by fifteen umbrellas and fanned by legions of servants. Proud warrior chiefs were depicted, seated on elephants, fighting the Chams (Muslims), helped by Thais. Thai mercenaries wore headdresses and skirts and carried tridents, whilst Khmer soldiers had square breastplates to protect them and were armed with spears. The Chams were easily spotted by the topknots on their heads. Rectangular holes in the carvings were due to the belief that these stones contained magic power, and many people therefore removed small portions.

The carvings on the eastern side of the south gallery corresponded with the Christian concept of the Last Judgement, depicting reward and punishment in the thirty-seven heavens and thirty-two hells: On the left upper and middle register fine gentlemen proceeded towards the eighteen-armed Yama – the Judge of the Dead – who was seated on a bull. Below him were his assistants; Dharma and Sitragupta, whilst the lower register symbolised the way to hell along which the dammed were dragged to their doom. On Yama's right side in the upper register the good people reaped their deserts by being shown as living in beautiful mansions being served by women, children and attendants, whilst down below the

283

wicked people were being punished suffering terrible torture being strangled by snakes and attacked by fierce lions.

The south section of the east gallery bore the most famous relief of all at Angkor Wat, known as 'the Churning of the Ocean of Milk', where eighty-eight *suras* (devils) to the left and ninety-two *devas* (gods) with crested helmets to the right were seen churning the ocean to extract the Elixir of Immortality, which both factions desired. This process was being accomplished thanks to the huge serpent Vasuki – who was entwined around Mount Mandara and rested on a turtle in the centre – rotating. Vishnu was assisting on the side of the mountain, whilst Indra calmly surveyed the whole scene from up above. Other figures watching the churning were Siva, Brahma and Hanuman the Monkey God, all mounted on their respective steeds. The sea teemed with lively fish and sea monsters, whilst *apsaras* (nymph-like dancing girls) danced up above.

The unfinished northern section of the east gallery showed a furious Vishnu seated on the Garuda engaged in battle with a group of devils, whilst the incomplete eastern portion of the north gallery portrayed Krishna arriving in front of Soitaput – the residence of Bana, who had raped Aniruda – where a wall of fire blocked his way. This was quelled by Garuda, thus enabling Krishna to defeat Bana and take him captive. However, Siva, shown with a halo and with his trident, intervened to spare Bana's life.

The western side of the northern gallery depicted the battle between *devas* and *suves*, ending in the duel between Vishnu and Kalameni.

In the northern half of the west gallery we admired scenes from the *Ramayana* showing Rama on the shoulders of Hanuman, with his army of monkeys fighting the ten-headed Ravana.

At this point we had reached full circle and commenced our tour of the interior, wandering through corridors and admiring shrines in which Vishnu had been replaced by Buddha. Climbing up to the third level, we stopped again and again to look at the exquisite carvings present everywhere. In the central tower which rose from the top floor were four shrines dedicated to Buddha.

In one section we met an Indian craftsman from Madras who worked with a team restoring Angkor. They were only able to work during the dry season, returning home for six months during the rains. As far as we understood, this project was scheduled to continue for the next fifteen years.

284

Slowly we retraced our steps and returned to the Grand Hotel. After a short rest we strolled into town on our own, following along a main road which led through a small park with stone benches and statues of lions around a fountain where – it being Sunday – the young people of Siem Reap had congregated. Streams of cyclists passed us merrily, many of the women, wearing trilby hats, cycling with children hoisted back and front. I even saw a baby slung in a mini-hammock between the handlebars. There were very few cars but a large number of motorbikes, which were often ridden by women. Women when riding pillion occasionally sat sideways.

Crossing a river, we found ourselves amidst a lively scene where most houses – which were built of wood with thatched roofs – served as shops as well as homes. There was no street lighting and the houses had no electric light but some light was provided by fires which people had lit in front of their homes. A hairdresser proclaimed his trade with a graphic sign of a pretty young woman, whilst the dentist was easily found by his vivid painting of a giant molar. A gaily striped awning and twinkling lights adorned a fish restaurant.

By this time it had grown dark, hence we returned to our hotel. At dinner, having drunk excellent wine in Luang Phabang in the pleasant hotel on Kite Hill – we asked for some wine in the Grand Hotel. A boy was sent out to purchase a bottle from a stall. It tasted like rough brandy but was quite palatable when mixed with 7-Up and later, when we triumphantly found it in the bar, with Schweppes soda. Through our entire stay in this hotel we were impressed by the service and attention we received. I enjoyed the Cambodian food, which I found light and very agreeable indeed.

Finally we went to bed, tucking the mosquito nets carefully around us, and slept remarkably well.

Next morning we had time to walk along the river, watching people taking their morning bath and doing their laundering. Bulls and calves grazed in the dusty grass and cyclists were on their way to work. Women passed us, carrying wooden poles across their shoulders with heavy baskets full of goods or buckets filled with water suspended at each end. There was barely any begging, except now and again at temple sites a child would stretch out a hand. Children were bright-eyed and clear-skinned, clad in rags, but seemed extremely quick-witted and picked up English phrases easily. No schooling had been available up to a year ago but since then the Government had been trying hard to establish education.

At 8 a.m. we set off for Angkor Tom, which means Celestial City. It was a fortified town whilst Angkor Wat was a temple complex. Angkor Tom had been built in the 12th century and stood surrounded by a wall and encircled by a moat, with four monumental gates. When we arrived at the south gate we stood rooted to the spot at the sight of four gigantic faces of the Bodhisattva Avalokitesvara smiling down on us in every direction from above the gate. Leading up to the gate sat fifty-four gigantic gods to the left of the causeway, with a pleasant smile playing around their lips, whilst to the right fifty-four huge devils sat with the corners of their mouths turned down. Each of these massive figures had its hands clasped firmly around the body of the *naga*, which reared its many-headed hood in front. Whilst we stood in amazement, one of the men in our group shrieked in utter fright as a terrified little frog came hopping in his direction. Quick as a flash of lightning an old woman caught the creature and bagged it in a sack which wriggled ominously with many more amphibians. Frogs are a delicacy in Cambodia, as in France.

As we wandered from level to level we saw the smiling giant's face from every angle: full face, profile, almost at eye level looking down upon us from high above, bathed in brilliant sunshine or deep in shade. Having entered the complex, we followed the usual approach up to the gate between the *naga* balustrades and the fierce lions which stood guard. Inside lay pools to either side. Our tour started with the most important temple, the Bayon, which stood at the exact centre of the Celestial City.

Like all temples in Angkor Tom, Bayon too had originally been a Siva temple (in the late 11th century) but was changed into a Mahayana Buddhist shrine. Some of the Buddhas were later re-carved into bunches of flowers when Hinduism once again was in ascendance. There were three levels in this temple. Superb bas-reliefs depicting scenes from daily life in Cambodia covered the outer surface of the wall around the first level. These excellent carvings were a more vivid portrayal than any pages of history books or any sociological report. On the first panel meals were being prepared; a pig was being lowered into a cauldron whilst birds sang and monkeys played in the trees above. Chams with their topknots faced Khmer soldiers in the next picture whilst further along we saw a cockfight. Near a doorway a woman was giving birth. People picked lice out of each other's hair – a sight we had become familiar with along the roadside. Next came a battle between Chams and Khmers on the high sea, with crocodiles and pelicans catching fish to eat. In one corner Hindus worshipped the lingam.

A three-tiered panorama was carved to the south of the east gate, showing Khmer soldiers marching into battle accompanied by elephants and oxcarts in the first register; in the middle register coffins of the dead were being carried off the battlefield, whilst in the centre of the third tier Jayavarma the Second (the builder of Bayon) sat astride his horse shaded by parasols, followed by legions of concubines. The horse was beautifully carved with its feet raised, caught in swift motion. The battle continued and the next three panels showed the Khmers facing the Chams, with the two armies being engaged in fierce battle in the middle register. A Cham soldier was seen cutting off a Khmer's foot and a severed head lay on the ground. Dead soldiers lay at their marching comrades' feet. Another confrontation of the two armies followed. Up to this panel Chams had been defeated (in 1181), though in an earlier battle (in 1177) it was the Khmers who had been vanquished by the Chams: an event which had been immortalised in the next two sculptures, to be followed by a scene in which the Chams advanced again until finally (as shown in an unfinished three tiered carving) the Chams were defeated and expelled from the Khmer Kingdom.

Since it would have taken weeks to study all the panels, we left the remaining ones and climbed up to the second level to continue through courtyards and truncated galleries to the third floor, which was surrounded by forty-nine towers, each with a smiling face of Avalokitesvara on its four sides.

With heads still spinning with all we had seen, we moved on to the pyramidal structure representing Mount Meru (the sacred mountain) of Baphuon. I climbed the central structure up a narrow flight of stone steps. The view across the jungle was breathtaking, the sculptures around the door frames, lintels and on the octagonal columns were particularly fine and often quite intricate and delicate. I descended on the west side. As all temples, Baphuon consisted of three levels. In the 17th century the retaining wall of the second level on the west side had been fashioned into a 40-yard-long reclining Buddha. Alas, I was unable to see this figure since vines and shrubs had grown over it, obscuring it all.

From here we drove to the Royal Enclosure, where once upon a time many wooden houses had stood but had long since perished. Two sandstone pools for the use of the King were barely visible. The Phieanakas, the Celestial Palace, built in the 10th century, rose as a pyramid in the centre, representing Mount Meru. It was sadly dilapidated and I climbed the west side, which was in a better condition, to look down on the Royal Enclosure, which had in the past been surrounded by a double wall pierced by five gates for access. A deep moat used to lie between the walls. I looked eastwards to the Elephant Terrace, south to Baphuon and north to the Terrace of the Leper King. To climb up to the Terrace of the Leper King we passed through the eastern gate. This terrace used to serve as a gigantic reviewing stand for public ceremonies and formed the base of the King's audience hall. It was supported by walls which had been superbly carved with human-sized Garudas and lions, with the famous parade of elephants which gave the terrace to either side its name. It was an impressive sight. Making our way to the north of the Elephant Terrace, we climbed down to admire the retaining wall of the Terrace of the Leper King, which showed five tiers of exquisitely carved seated *apsaras*, and kings wearing pointed diadems and carrying short double-edged swords, followed by courtiers and princesses whose slender necks were adorned with rows of pearls. On the terrace stood the replica of the Leper King, a sexless, headless, nude figure, possibly of Siva, though the local population believed the seated figure to be King Yasovar-man, the founder of Angkor, who according to legend died of leprosy.

Driving on through the jungle we admired the old trees, some of which were four hundred years old. Many bore deep gashes which had been cut into their trunks to collect the resin. A deep cut was made first, then a fire was lit to soften the resin so that it would pool at the bottom of the hollow, to be collected after a few days. The trees showed the scorched scars. Presently we halted between two temples: Chau Say Tevoda to the south, Thommanon to the north, both built in the 12th century and dedicated respectively to Siva and Vishnu. Sadly both temples were in a very poor state. Smiling gods hugging Naga sat to the right of the causeway, whilst devils with dropping mouths sat to the left, also clutching Naga, who raised his many-headed hood up into the air at the end of the balustrade. Many of these figures, gods and devils alike, were headless, and the Army was now employed guarding this monument since some of the heads had been stolen. The soldiers with rifles in hand looked mere children.

First we visited Chau Say Tevoda, which, like all the temples, stood surrounded by a wall which was badly broken. Stepping through the gate, we walked through gallery after gallery with broken masonry blocking some of the side wings, but even in this dilapidated state the remaining carvings were quite exquisite. Siva's lingam stood in the centre of the temple; the library, as always a separate building, was easy to define. Once again I was enchanted by the carvings on frames and lintels and on numerous blind doors, and I was intrigued by the graceful spindles screening the windows, which simulated turned wood.

Thommanon had a tall tower, which I climbed to look down on what must have been a splendid compact temple but had been encroached by dense jungle. Again carvings when visible were beautiful, such as the splendid sculpture of Rama and Sita above one door. At both these temples we were the only people (apart from the soldiers guarding Chau Say Tevoda) and even the swarm of children with their ice buckets of canned drinks, their home-made clappers and pipes which they offered for sale were missing. Near these temples stood Ta Leo, built in the reign of Jayavarman the Fifth (968–1001) which was dedicated to Siva and was entirely constructed of very hard sandstone. Because of this hardness the decorations had never been completed. I found a beautiful Nandi (Siva's bull) sitting in a courtyard amongst broken masonry.

Continuing through the jungle, we reached Ta Prohm, which had been built as a Buddhist temple in the 12th century. The French archaeologists who had found this Khmer edifice from the Angkor period over a century ago left it in the exact state as it was when they first discovered it. It had never been restored and nature had taken over; trees with enormous roots like snakes threatened to strangle the structures and mighty trunks had fallen on walls, reducing them to heaps of rubble. It was an eerie place, with its broken walls, delicate carvings and jumble of fallen masonry. Everywhere were children from the nearby village enjoying the heaven-sent adventure playground. They seemed to own the place, playing happily amongst the broken buildings, climbing trees, sitting on remnants of roaring lions – barefooted and in rags but bright-eyed and clear-skinned. Wonderful butterflies in shades of yellow, russet and blue skimmed through the thick foliage, whilst birds chirruped away, hidden amongst dense leaves. I heard a copper bird beating its rhythmic tune. Picking our way carefully through the whole complex, overawed by the wholesale destruction nature had wrought, we arrived at a terrace at the back of the temple where we rested, under the frank stares of the children. Retracing our steps, we came upon an Australian television producer who was taking photographs for a programme he intended to make. Jean, our Australian, talked to him, only to discover that his late boss had been a close friend of hers; strange to meet in the depth of the jungle.

The sun was gently sinking, bats were beginning to stir and a tiny bird high up in a tree added its crescendo to the orchestra of the jungle. Stopping briefly, once again we admired a gigantic water-wheel which was still being used for irrigation and halted a second time outside Victory Gate to take photographs which would show its great height of 60 feet, with the four smiling faces of Avalokites-vara towering high above and with stone elephants' trunks decorating either side of the passageway.

Outside the thick wall of Angkor Wat we skirted the wide moat and sat on the grass in one of the outer courtyards to wait for the sun to set. In vain we waited since the trees obscured our view, but we were content, enjoying the vista of this great complex in the fading light and to listen to the chorus of frogs. Five old ladies with shorn heads and smiling faces showing their teeth stained brown with betel-nut juice came walking along. They wore the ancient Khmer dress of short sarongs tucked between their legs and anchored in their belts at the back. These were black, like the long-sleeved high-necked blouses which they wore fitting tightly to their bodies. They carried various baskets. When they spotted us they changed direction and came over to see us, laughing good-naturedly and appearing to be highly amused. I would have liked to take a photograph but they firmly refused. They cooked for the four monks who looked after Angkor Wat and lived in simple quarters which stood well hidden in its shade, obscured by trees.

It had been a full and satisfying day. On our way back from our morning visit we had stopped briefly at the local market which was a jolly affair. Amongst the various goodies I spotted gulls' eggs and clams for sale.

In the evening we talked to the Swiss gentleman who was a director of a hotel company which had bought the Grand Hotel at Siem Reap and planned to convert it into a luxury hotel with a swimming pool, tennis court, riding stables etc. His company intended to extend it, lay out gardens, refurbish the whole place and import a French cook. He had done the same job all over the world, in Africa, Pakistan and Iran, to name just a few places, but a French company had pipped him at the post in Rangoon and had bought the Strand Hotel. Being full of enthusiasm, he seemed certain of his abilities to achieve his goal and was convinced that the Grand Hotel of his dreams would live up to its name and would benefit the local population. This transformation, so he assured us, would be completed in twelve months. In the meantime we watched him reorganising the shabby furniture from time to time and getting the pleasant staff to dust and polish very half-heartedly. On balance we were glad that we had come now before changes had been made, even if this meant slight inconveniences from time to time when the lights failed in the dining room or when we were without water for twenty-four hours because the pumps had failed. A bucket of cold water and a huge thermos of hot water tided us over this problem. Once again the electricity and with it the air-conditioning stopped at 1 a.m. but returned at 5 a.m. But in spite of these obvious difficulties we had clean sheets and towels each day during our stay.

The United Nations were very much in evidence and we talked to a tall black soldier from Senegal whilst our Australian friend chatted with one of her countrymen. Four Australians were stationed in Siem Reap, engaged to establish a communication system. They got very bored with too much free time on their hands and therefore frequented the dingy bar in the hotel, chatting up the pretty local girls, who coyly hid their faces and giggled behind their hands. One of these youngsters had a pale skin. I heard her explain to one of the surprised Australians that her grandfather had been European and that an uncle of hers lived in Sydney.

On our second night we dispensed with our mosquito nets, feeling perfectly safe. No insect disturbed our night, only the heat made us restless until the early hours of the morning when it became cold.

The day started brilliantly, like a clear English summer's morning. It was pleasant to drive the now familiar way past Angkor Wat with its wide moat almost obliterated by lotus flowers. Hordes of bicycles, with a sprinkling of motorbikes, streamed into town. We seldom saw people riding bikes on their own. If they rode singly they sat bolt upright, carrying a full load behind consisting either of baskets full with wood, sacks of rice or some other merchandise. More commonly, two adults and one or two children rode on a single bicycle. Women nearly always wore hats, either a trilby or a broad-brimmed straw coolie hat. Small novices as well as very old monks were tenderly conveyed on the trusty steed.

Once again we made our way into the jungle, this time visiting Preah Khan – the Sacred Sword – taking its name from the fact that when seen from the air it looked like a sword. It had been built in the late 12th century and most of its carvings depicted Hindu epics, which were later defaced when Buddhism asserted its supremacy. I saw a wonderful Garuda riding on a *naga* and also a scene of the Churning of the Ocean of Milk.

The next temple we visited was the Temple of the Entwined Naga, lying peacefully in a sunny clearing and dreaming sleepily of the past. This was a late 12th-century Buddhist temple consisting of three large basins where the temple stood in the middle basin surrounded by two entwining *nagas*. Buddha's horse, with forelegs raised and with his disciples crowding beneath, rose to the right of steps leading up to the shrine in which sat the Buddha image. A three-headed elephant, Indra's emblem, adorned each corner on the outside, whilst carved lotus blossoms formed the base. Four pavilions, one to the north, one to the south, one to the west and one to the east, rose at the periphery of the large basin. One gave access to the temple, two connected to the lateral basins, the fourth was purely ornamental. A stone elephant appeared to grow out of the rear wall of each pavilion. The trunks of the elephants in the lateral basins served as spouts to allow water from the central pool to spill over to either side. When we were there the basins lay empty and overgrown; until a fisherman came along, carrying two elongated baskets which looked like our crayfish pots and hung suspended from the ends of his shoulder pole. We had been the only visitors to disturb the peace. In the past this temple had been used for ritual purification.

To the east of Preah Neak Pean lay Tom Som, another 12th-century temple, where again we were the only visitors to admire the exquisite carvings in this ruined building.

From here we drove to the Eastern Baray and Eastern Mebon. The Eastern Baray used to be an enormous reservoir fed by the Siem Reap River and was the most important public work constructed in the 9th century. A stele used to mark each of its four corners. Nothing had remained of the big reservoir, only five elaborate brick shrines, known as the Eastern Mebon, raised on what used to be the central island, were still standing. Once again I climbed up to admire the traces of carvings and to enjoy the view.

Continuing our temple tour, we reached Pre Rup: The Return of the Corpse Shrine, where we walked along long corridors to arrive at a courtyard with the square cremation shrine where the bodies had been burnt in its centre. Behind the shrine stood a lingam demarcated into three zones: one dedicated to Siva, the second to Vishnu and the third to Brahma. Climbing right to the top, we could see Angkor Wat silhouetted against the sky in the far distance and also the five towers of the Eastern Mebon. Looking down on the rural scene around the temple, we saw buffaloes grazing between rice fields, honey-coloured cattle (calves and oxen but no cows) chewed the cud and oxen carts – exactly resembling the carvings we had seen sculptured on the ancient walls – trundling along the dusty road. Farmsteads stood amongst the fields. Since the rice had been harvested, the buffaloes who had worked in the fields grazed freely, enjoying their well-earned holiday.

The last temple we visited on this hot morning was the Prasat Kravan, a Hindu shrine built before the Angkor Wat period and partially restored by the French in 1968. The original building had been constructed of brick, and holes were still visible which had been used to insert rods to hold the bricks securely in place. New bricks used for restoration carried a stamp to distinguish them from the original building material. Climbing down from the high terrace on which the five towers stood, we found a small group of children gathered at the base of the temple and staring at us. Little girls carried their sleeping younger siblings tenderly in their arms. They were friendly – looking at us with their large innocent eyes in utter amazement.

After a welcome siesta we set off once more, travelling this time in a different direction, crossing the Siem Reap River and driving past the market along Highway Number Six, which was a bumpy, dusty road. Our driver skilfully circumvented potholes and negotiated a very precarious bridge which consisted merely of logs slung together, leaving a gaping void between them. Further along we passed a bus without any glass in its windows, piled high with not only passengers but with sacks of rice and baskets filled with other merchandise. A lorry with a gigantic load of rice stopped to let people climb up for a ride into town. Children played in muddy pools, buffaloes took refuge in small puddles, trying to keep cool, and we actually saw a pink buffalo calf. Hens with tiny chicks clustering around them scratched at the dry earth. Farmsteads stood amongst rice fields, coconuts and bananas grew in abundance. Women cut rushes, which they laid out to dry before weaving into matting to serve as walls for their houses. After 13 kilometres we passed an Army camp before reaching Lolei, whose four brick towers dated back to pre-Angkor times and had originally stood in the centre of a reservoir, but now rose from a platform above rice fields. Two of them were 'male' and two 'female' towers, guarded respectively by male and female figures carved into the wall. One of these shrines contained, apart from indifferent seated Buddha figures, two gilded elongated Hindu images carved of wood. A superbly preserved Sanskrit inscription inside a doorway stated that King Yasovarman dedicated these shrines to his father, mother and to his grandparents on 12th July 893. A group of later stupas stood to one side near a plain open-fronted building with a tiered roof which was probably being used as a meeting hall.

From here we proceeded to Preah Ko, another Hindu temple, also known as the 'Sacred Oxen Temple', named after the three Nandis standing at the base of six brick towers. Silos with perforated brick windows for circulation stood in one corner of the courtyard. At the base of four flights of steps which led up to the raised platform lay double half-circular stones, beautifully shaped and delicately carved at the edges, reminding me of the moonstones in Sri Lanka. Climbing up them we were able to peer into the shrines, in one of which sat a statue of Siva in the lotus position with folded hands raised in mediation, sprouting a long beard. The brick-built towers were decorated with carved stucco and carved sandstone. Elephants graced the corners of the platform. There was a particularly fine blind door with most intricate carvings; blind doors had been a feature in all the temples we had seen. From the upper terrace I looked across into the courtyard of the attached monastery, where stupas made of sand stood in a row. At the bottom of one flight of steps an old man with shaven head prayed as he offered his modest gifts. In one corner of the courtyard belonging to the temple lay the broken remains of the former splendid library and outside the complex stood an open-sided schoolroom with crude tables and chairs. Close to this an old monk was supervising the planting of young coconut palms. As we descended to climb back on our bus to drive to our last temple, we heard chanting, which seemed a fitting send-off to our visit to this tranquil place.

Bankong Temple was also dedicated to Siva and built to resemble Mount Meru. It consisted of a five-tiered pyramid of sandstone flanked by eight towers which were built of brick and sandstone, some of them still covered by their original stucco work. Elephants stood at each corner of the first three levels of the central shrine, whilst twelve stupas, three on each side, rose from the third level. A modern Buddhist monastery had been built in the north-east corner of the sandy courtyard which lay in front, with charming paintings adorning its shutters.

To return to Siem Reap we had to regain Highway Number Six again. Further on we stopped at a village which lay to either side of the road. A large roofed veranda built on stilts loomed near the highway, where a big earthenware pitcher with a ladle placed on its wooden lid stood in one corner ready to refresh the weary traveller. It was the rest house of the village, meant to be used by any passer-by who wished to stop to rest for a while. I wandered off on my own and came upon a farmhouse where brand new woven baskets bulged out from beneath it, whilst a stall selling drinks stood near a murky pond on which ducks glided by. A small boy came riding along on the back of a buffalo. Women were busy winnowing rice. Egrets sat on the backs of cattle, looking for insects. Hens with their chicks and dogs were around in large numbers and cats lay sleeping in the sun. A young beauty was stirring the fire and eating her meal whilst another young girl rested in a hammock in the shade of a tree. When I greeted them the young lady dropped her metal dish to be able to raise both hands in the customary greeting. I indicated that I would like to take her photograph and smilingly she posed for me. Crossing the road in search of my friend, I found her surrounded by children distributing sweets which she had just bought. None of the little mites were greedy, in fact some were too shy to accept the offered gift and the bigger ones pushed the smaller ones forward. None took more than one for themselves, frequently passing a second sweet to a child who was too timid to stretch out a hand. Watched by the entire village we bought a bottle of fierce spirit off the stall by the pond before we returned to our bus.

On our way back to our hotel we had a 'city tour' when we realised the true size of the town, which was bigger than we thought. Driving along the river, we saw people having their evening wash and even cleaning their teeth in its water. The houses along the river were quite large and stood in their own grounds. Crossing the river, we passed the wooden houses of the old market, now closed, and saw the hospital and the headquarters of Médecins sans Frontières before reaching the centre, where a new market was in full swing. Our drive took us past apartment blocks which looked rather run-down, with crude boards nailed over the former shops which had been converted into living quarters for whole families.

Back at our hotel we found that the water had been restored. Finally we enjoyed our last dinner. I ate Cambodian food, as I had done throughout our stay. The big dining hall was extremely well-run by an elderly man with a kind face. The service was superb.

We had asked our charming guide whether it would be possible to watch the sun rise over Angkor Wat and she arranged to meet us at half past five next morning. We had spent a peaceful night during which we only heard the steady steps of the night watchman doing his rounds echoing on the stone floor.

The electricity went off just before 2 a.m. and had not returned when we got up to dress, which meant we had neither light nor air-conditioning, but we had candles and it was not too hot at that hour so all was well – except we had no water either, since electricity was needed to pump it around.

Three of us met in the hall clutching our torches. An Englishman travelling on his own had joined us at our invitation since we felt sorry for him. He was a strange man who always journeyed on his own in the Far East. He was a book dealer living in Islington. Later we were told by the young Japanese couple that he had converted to Buddhism. It was his first visit to Laos and Cambodia but unfortunately 'nothing had gone right for him'; he was full of complaints.

Our charming guide appeared, looking as fresh as a daisy and collected the driver to set off through the dark countryside on our last journey to Angkor Wat, where we waited and watched the sky grow lighter, saw the subtle colour change but searched in vain for the sun. Another party of tourists joined us and some members of this mixed group whiled away the time performing the most remarkable exercises which helped to amuse and entertain us. When we felt tempted to call it a day our guide would not budge and suddenly the sun burst forth as a large fiery ball. At least we had not waited in vain and felt satisfied. As we were leaving, a stream of women poured into the temple; these were the Mrs Mops of Angkor Wat, who cleaned, brushed and swept so that skilled craftsmen could set to work restoring the ancient building.

When we returned for our breakfast, electricity and water had been restored. Leaving the hotel for the last time with all our belongings safely stored in the coach, we deviated from the road leading to the airport and drove through open countryside to see an enormous lake which had been dammed many centuries ago to serve as a reservoir for irrigation during the dry season. It was eight kilometres long and four wide and had been restored by the French. It was a peaceful place, with the sun shimmering on the cool water.

The airport lay close to the reservoir, hence we reached it in plenty of time, passing a country market already in full swing, but our plane had not arrived. This gave us ample time to chat again to the young Japanese couple and hear where they had been since they left home in October and to learn about the route they intended to take, which included England, where they hoped to arrive in August. When we gave them our address to contact us in due course, they insisted on taking our photographs lest they forgot what we looked like! Finally our plane arrived and a group of very old Chinese passengers disembarked, shuffling along. After a three-hour wait we boarded to fly back to Phnom Penh. The last to come aboard were the bevy of air hostesses, laden with shopping, including fish.

A herd of buffaloes took fright when the engine started up, and the plane rose noisily into the air to fly over dried-out rice paddies with isolated palm trees standing forlorn in the landscape. Bright green fields greeted us around Phnom Penh before we saw a broad river which fanned out into a network of waterways shimmering through haze. Water and land covered by mist lay below us as the plane descended rapidly over the wide Mekong River and landed way out at the edge of the airfield, where fire engines were waiting to hose down the hot tyres. Later we learnt that the crowd we had seen from the air was waiting for Prince Sihanouk to arrive fifteen minutes after our plane had landed.

Our guide was waiting to take us back to the luxurious Cambodia Hotel. This time we had a room on the top floor but although it was comfortable it had not been finished, the ceiling light in the hall had not been fitted, a picture stood leaning against the wall waiting to be hung and the refrigerator was missing, although the housing had been installed, but work was progressing in the long corridor outside our room.

For lunch we were taken to a local restaurant on Boek Kak, a lake with an amusement park, a small zoo, paddleboats for hire and two restaurants, one of which looked quite smart and proclaimed nightly performances of local dance, but it was closed at lunchtime. The second restaurant, where we ate, looked most dilapidated and to reach it we had to walk across a big terrace built over the lake, which was littered with debris of all kinds and where a mangy dog lay on a heap of garbage fast asleep. It was a very busy eating place, also built above the water, where I sat by the window looking down on the graceful lotus flowers festooned with cans and plastic bottles. On the banks stood wooden shacks huddled together and crammed with families, but in spite of the somewhat dubious ambience the meal was quite excellent.

After lunch we drove to Wat Phnom – *phnom* means hill – which stood on top of a tree-covered hill visible from all over town. According to legend the first pagoda had been erected here in 1373 to house four statues of Buddha which had been washed ashore by the Mekong River and had been found by a woman called Penh, hence the name of the *wat* and of the city. A grand staircase led up to the shrine, which had been rebuilt at various times. Flashing lights seemed to be working overtime inside the temple but the objects were difficult to discern, except for a stele with many Buddha images which was well lit and looked rather splendid, whilst the remaining golden Buddha figures were just shining objects in the dim light.

West of the sanctuary rose an enormous stupa containing the ashes of King Panhea Yat (1405–1467). A cave dedicated to the genie Preah Chau sheltered below the terrace on which the shrine stood. A guardian sat to either side of the entrance to the cave, where the statue of Preah Chau presided over an array of offerings inside with the eight-armed figure of Vishnu standing to his left. In front of the guardians, who were armed with iron bats, we saw a tiled table with drawings of Confucius and two Chinese sages. Stone effigies of lions to one side of the offering table were covered with food. Pieces of fat pork lay across their noses, melting in the fierce sun, which was neither a pleasant sight nor a fragrant smell.

Slowly we walked down hill and spent some time in the nearby Central Market, which was housed in the most extraordinary ochre and white building constructed in Art Deco style by the French. Stall hustled for space with stall, spilling over with merchandise. Outside the hall attractive flower stalls sold pot plants and shrubs (which had been grown over wire frames in the shapes of animals). Ceramic flowerpots were particularly pleasing and widely used in public places; we had noticed them throughout our hotel and also in the hotel garden. Second-hand clothes lay in heaps on the ground. An abundance of fresh fruit, vegetables and salads were on sale, as well as cooked food which could be eaten sitting at rough low tables. Another part of the market sold jewellery, mostly gold and precious stones, and copies of well-known makes of watches. There were also very realistic-looking replicas of pistols, revolvers and guns of known makes. Special parking places were marked out near the Central Market where weary shoppers laden with their spoils could hire cyclos or could choose to ride home on the back of a motorbike.

Finally we returned to our hotel, where we had a splendid view from our room on the fifth floor over the city, with the Victory Memorial in the shape of a stupa soaring into the cloudless sky. The last beams of the sun reflected off the many-tiered roofs of the Palace and caught the graceful spire of the Silver Pagoda. Cool water spilled over a wall into a pool to either side of the hotel entrance. But a muddy place where children played and pigs shared the mud with them, wallowing in the dirt, stretched just beyond the well-kept hotel garden. And behind the hotel, facing the river, stood completely derelict houses serving large families as their homes, without any water, without electricity or sanitation of any kind; but private enterprise had already opened a shop.

Phnom Penh was a remarkable city, still bearing the deep scars of the time when Pol Pot reigned, wiping out whole generations of learned people, of skilled women and men, destroying an ancient culture, smashing monuments and shrines, hurling statues into the river, burning books – and yet its people seemed incredibly resilient, managing to survive and build again for the future. There were relatively few beggars, only the maimed had to rely entirely on alms for their sole support. At all times we felt perfectly safe and secure walking on our own through the streets. People smiled and children waved to us wherever we went. The hotel was still being extended but had already three restaurants and one coffee bar and was well run and spotlessly clean, with adequate staff, who were without exception friendly and helpful at all times. Food was attractive and well served in restaurants and in the coffee bar – the only strange thing was the absence of coffee spoons, which according to the French manager, 'just disappeared'.

Our guide suggested a visit to Pot Pol's Killing Fields and Interrogation Centre but we declined this horrendous outing, walking instead along the river and enjoying the lovely scene. Our walk took us past the Palace Square, where the Royal Palace stood at the edge of the river from where His Royal Highness watched special water festivities. The Water Festival, or 'Festival of Reversing Current', takes place in late October, early November. It corresponds to the moment when the Tonle Sap River, whch since July has been filling the Tonle Sap Lake with water from the Mekong, reverses its flow and begins to empty the water from Tonle Sap Lake back into the Mekong. Soon we reached the tourist office and Wat Ounalom again and found the whole temple complex spotlessly clean, not even one single grain of rice soiled the ground. Behind the famous stupa we entered a warren of houses which constituted the Centre of Buddhism, where private tuition could be obtained. 'English book one and two' were proudly advertised on the fence along the road.

Starting to walk back to our hotel, we heard music and saw blue striped awning over one of the sidewalks. Thinking fondly that this was a coffee bar (we were getting thirsty by this time) we crossed the road, only to find that a traditional Cambodian wedding was about to begin. A shrine with glittering lights had been erected in a ground floor room which normally served as a shop, and round tables with chairs had been placed on the pavement, whilst a kitchen had been set up on the opposite side where soup bubbled away in gigantic cauldrons. Large metal wash bowls were filled with the steaming broth and carried across to be placed on each table. Everybody laughed joyfully and chatted away, children clutching biscuits and fruit in their hands rushed about happily. Some of the little girls were dressed in glittering party dresses and were heavily made up. We were invited to sit down near a table in front of the shrine on which various silver bowls and silver salvers stood. Flowers and trays of fruit had been artistically arranged and incense permeated the air. A photographer with a video camera poised on his shoulder stood waiting in the wings and a local band sat inside on the floor of the shrine. The bridegroom was the first to appear, accompanied by two attendants who were dressed in grey city suits; but the bridegroom himself wore traditional dress, consisting of an orange sarong tucked between his legs and secured in his belt at the back, a tight-fitting long-sleeved jacket covering his top and a shimmering turban crowning his head. His bride advanced from the other side with two female attendants. She wore a similar orange sarong; her golden top was sleeveless with modest décolletage. A golden necklace with glittering stones adorned her slender neck and her face was heavily made up beneath the small golden crown which sat on her smooth black hair. They settled on two chairs which had been covered with a big shawl, with their respective attendants standing at either side. The girls were beautifully turned out in pink close-fitting shifts with their faces also heavily made up, their hair elegantly coiffured. The bride's mother fussed over her daughter, as all mothers are wont to do. An elderly gentleman in a long white jacket over grey trousers took his place by the offering table and began to chant. His attendant lit the incense sticks and handed him a silver salver which displayed a silver mirror, silver comb and brush, toilet water and a pair of scissors. This salver he raised towards the bridal pair, blessing it and them. The ceremony, completed, a 'funny man' appeared, made up like a clown and wearing a coat of many colours. He began to dance, to sing, and to tell funny stories which made everybody laugh. A girl in a tight pink dress of shining silk joined him and danced and sang, coyly rebuffing his bold advances. Street urchins had gathered to watch with big eyes as he danced and pirouetted, then knelt down before some of the old ladies, making them laugh with his unashamed flattery. He also made good-natured fun of us, the only strangers amidst this large gathering, and jokingly frightened children but only made them squeal with delight.

Leaving this jolly party, we continued to walk back to our hotel, stopping to buy an enormous pamplemousse off a barrow, much to the delight of all the bystanders who watched the vendor's effort to find a plastic bag big enough to contain this large fruit to make it easier for us to carry it safely back. Cyclos stood waiting outside the gate of our hotel, which was guarded by day and closed at night. Boys had caught a wild cat, which was securely confined in a bamboo cage, and offered the creature to us for sale but we politely declined.

Siesta time passed quickly, when we sat at the poolside observing the international clientele around us. Small children jumped fearlessly into the water, swam and disappeared below the surface. Two little girls, having enjoyed their swim, then dressed and chose coffee and cake, for which they signed, before trotting off happily hand in hand, with some of the goodies. Outside the gate they calmly and with great self-possession climbed into a cyclo each and off they went to their respective homes.

At 4 p.m. we met up with the rest of our party for a boat ride, boarding at the landing stage of the adjacent Cambodia Inn, which was a modern motel complex being entirely rebuilt and refurbished. Four rivers meet at Phnom Penh: the Mekong River divides into the Upper and Lower Mekong and is joined by the Bassac and Tonle Sap. The waters were teeming with fish. The next hour we spent enjoying gliding gently downstream and across to an island where fishermen and their families lived on boats. They built reservoirs out of bamboo to store their live catch, for which they cast their nets from their long narrow fishing boats. Up on the bank stood little huts on stilts. The island was extremely fertile, thanks to the rich silt of the river, and was well-cultivated. White cattle with humps grazed peacefully, dogs frolicked with children, hens with their chicks pecked around the houses. It seemed hard to believe that three months ago the whole community had been entirely flooded. Laughing children waved to us, adults stopped work to greet us as we passed by. Men sat mending their nets, whilst women laundered their clothes and men and women alike performed their ablutions. It was a lively scene. Enormous rusty barges carrying large containers chugged by, pulled by tugs, and a big container boat from Singapore, laden with second-hand cars which had been neatly lined up on deck, sailed past us. Our boat changed direction and turned upstream, where a rusty ferry laden to the brim had docked, discharging a large crowd of passengers. The broken skeleton of Chrouy Bridge, built by the Japanese and blown up by Pol Pot in 1975, and waiting to be reconstructed, loomed up in front of us. Here we finally turned and, passing Ounalom Pagoda as well as the Palace complex, we returned from a pleasant hour spent cruising on the Mekong River.

That night Phnom Penh was plunged into darkness; even the Palace was blacked out. The only light piercing the dark night came from the front of our hotel and from the big ship the *Ocean Princess* anchored upstream, which served the members of the United Nations and their families as a holiday resort.

Our last day in Cambodia dawned and we set off to visit the workshop of the Academie de Beaux Arts behind the National Museum. The students were engaged in woodcarving, stone sculpture and carving in marble and ivory. Carpenters were at work, attractive traditional masks were being created, silk painting was being carried on, embroidery and weaving were being produced inside bare huts where conditions were very primitive. Oil paintings, without having recourse to models of any kind, looked sadly stereotyped and many of the paintings of Angkor Wat appeared stilted and flat since none of the artists had ever been there. A whole generation of artists, artisans and teachers had been entirely wiped out, books destroyed, paintings burnt, sculptures smashed, therefore the poor Cambodians had to start afresh without any role model to teach them.

Returning once more to the Central Market, we bought a handmade hammock.

Reluctantly we left to drive to the airport. The road was almost deserted since it was midday, siesta hour, and extremely hot. Our drive took us for the last time through the town, skirting Wat Phnom on its hill and passing the handsome railway station and some temples and villas of former elegance, the hospital and university buildings, which looked somewhat the worse for wear, with the ultra-modern complex of the Institute for Sociology providing a stark contrast. A mother perched with her little girl on top of a lorry which was piled high with mighty tree trunks. Two young girls rode on a motorbike pulling a carrier containing an enormous drum. One car was almost entirely obscured by its load of unplucked dead chickens. At the outskirts of Phnom Penh little houses stood on stilts between fields, ponds were covered by water lilies and cattle grazed peacefully by the roadside.

Vietnam

Utter confusion reigned at the airport when we arrived and we had to fill in form after form in duplicate. Again we flew Cambodia Air in a Russian plane which was ill-maintained and had no adequate ventilation, and since it was very hot indeed steam billowed into the cabin as soon as the pressure dropped. Cambodia lay below us, with brown fields where rice had already been harvested and with the gleam of its big rivers and network of waterways shimmering in the sun, but then haze covered the landscape. The flight was short and soon Vietnam greeted us with green fields, since here the rice had not as yet been gathered as they were able to grow two or three or, in some areas, even four crops a year. The landing was rough and again pandemonium reigned in the arrival hall, where more forms had to be completed. I passed through passport control but had to go back to collect yet another stamp when I tried to have my luggage checked. Neither staff nor passengers had the faintest idea how to proceed. One couple had to open their suitcase since a metal mask had shown up on the X-ray and they had a hard time trying to convince the customs officer that this was not an antique but that they had only paid three US dollars for it. Jean, our Australian lady, had problems with her cine-camera, which they wanted to X-ray. She refused since we had been warned that the antiquated X-ray machines would cause damage to exposed and unexposed films alike as well as to cameras. Everybody in our little group took films and cameras through in person. Ruth had to open her case, only to close it again. In spite of the chaos everybody was friendly and smiled, making up for the lack of communication since their English was very limited and our Vietnamese non-existent. Finally we were able to pile our luggage on a trolley which was broken and had to be nursed along through the dense crowd waiting outside. It took a little while to find a banner saying 'Orbi Tours' and our names. A young man and a young woman introduced themselves as our guides. The young man was married, with a daughter of twenty-five months, the young lady was thirty years old, born in Hanoi, married with a little boy of four, and her husband was also a guide. She had graduated from Hanoi College in Russian and English, had taught for three years and had only started this job ten days ago and we were her first English tour; she had never met English-speaking people before. Both these young people were quite obviously 'good party members', since she told us how poor the country was, how friendly her people were towards foreign tourists from anywhere in the world and that they hoped foreigners would invest in Vietnam, whilst the young man stated that 'a happy family was a family with one or two children, no more'.

As we sped along the wide road teeming with bicycles and motorbikes, we were regaled with facts and figures relating to Saigon. Our hotel was the very luxurious Saigon Floating Hotel, which was an Australian-built ship originally anchored outside Cairns to be used as a hotel. When this ventured failed, it was towed all the way across the sea to Saigon, where it had found its place on the Mekong River. Actually, apart from the very ornate entrance hall, our room, called a 'cabin', was compact and very comfortable, with slippers and robes provided and every detail taken care of. It was pleasant to be able to drink tap water once again rather than having to rely on bottled water or boil every drop.

As soon as we had settled we walked out into the warm air and followed the riverside, where young men touted for business for dinner cruises on boats. The number of people crowding the pavements, sitting at the kerbside on little stools or on the ground, crossing the busy road, riding bicycles or motorbikes or driving the occasional car, hanging on for dear life to dilapidated windowless buses or lounging about propped up against houses, was simply overwhelming. Along a broad avenue, shops were still open, selling all kinds of merchandise: jewellery, furniture inlaid with mother-of-pearl, antiques, silks, dresses, ivories and many more. The money exchange, however, was closed. Small spirit lamps glowed at the kerbside, placed next to simple hand pumps to inflate tyres which had lost their air. To cross the streets we had to take our chance since nobody on wheels would stop and traffic lights were extremely rare. Walking past a few hotels and coffee bars, we reached a square with the main hotels and the theatre, then cutting across a wide avenue we saw the very French-looking town hall, which was well lit up and had a nicely kept park gracing its front. The avenue was partly closed for traffic to provide space to display plants. Next

305

day we returned to the park and walked amongst the profusion of colours where we admired the vast numbers of ornamental orange trees all trained in the same cone shape and heavy with fruit. This was a special display for the forthcoming Chinese New Year on 4th February. The coming year stood under the sign of the Monkey. Red, the festive colour in the East, was very much in evidence but it was very strange to see 'Merry Christmas' everywhere and to find small replicas of the Eiffel Tower decorating many places. Tired by the end of the day, we returned to our hotel.

First thing in the morning we had time to wander out on our own after breakfast. Changing money proved an extremely simple trans-action. A young lady standing outside the money exchange approached us, offering a rate which was slightly higher than we would have got at the hotel or in a bank.

Leaving by coach, we drove through the city, past parks, hotels, the big Notre Dame Cathedral and the imposing former Presiden-tial Palace. Saigon is a far-flung, large town. Our journey continued along Highway 22 through the green belt which surrounded the town. Field after field of young fresh rice lay to either side of the road, as well as diligently cultivated vegetable plots. Bananas grew in large quantities. Vendors sat beside mountains of pineapples and watermelons, and French bread lay neatly stacked, gathering dust, whilst rice paper had been placed on special frames to dry in the sun. Skilfully constructed brick towers protected young palm trees. Oil and petrol for motorbikes were on sale in big plastic bottles with funnels balanced on their tops. An enormous pink pig grunted in a sty and we saw another one being transported in an elongated basket on a truck behind a motorbike. White Brahmin cattle with their humps grazed along the wayside, buffaloes searched for water to keep cool. Houses were small, with thatched roofs and walls made of matting or mud, and each harboured either a small shop or a workshop producing wooden furniture or bamboo beds, or repairing motorbikes – making or mending all kinds of articles. Family graves lay scattered between fields beneath shady trees. Our way led passed the US Airforce Base, lying idle and waiting to become an international airport. Driving along the river we watched a farmer irrigating his field by hand, using a leather pitcher.

Finally we arrived at the amazing underground complex of Cu Chi, seventy kilometres out of town. This warren of tunnels built on three levels constituted a complete town and stretched from

Saigon almost to the Cambodian border. It had been constructed by the guerrilla forces during the war. First we were shown a video of very poor quality portraying the construction of Cu Chi, when these tunnels had been dug by hand into red soil to produce bedrooms, living rooms, meeting places, conference rooms and hospitals, apart from the miles and miles of corridors. Well-camouflaged trapdoors led down into the tunnels where evil-looking spikes were intended to delay the enemy, whilst ventilation shafts strategically placed provided fresh air. Pepper or American soap had been put near grilles to confuse sniffer dogs. Many children had been born underground. We climbed down into the demonstration dugout which had been specially widened for tourists and also visited the General's Quarters. It was with great relief that we surfaced again and returned to the city for lunch in a local restaurant. As in China, tourists ate upstairs whilst local patrons took their simple meals downstairs. Here we met the couple from California we first came across in Vientiane and later again in Siem Reap. This eating place was obviously on the 'tourist route'.

Our next visit was to Cholon, the Chinese quarter, where we walked through the market. To be correct: we struggled through the dense excited crowd, fighting our way through mountains of merchandise. I have never seen such a profusion of goods nor such crowds in a confined space. The festivities for the Chinese New Year were only just beginning, with banners and decorations in red everywhere and with Chinese firecrackers adding to the noise and confusion. The sense of excitement hung almost palpably in the air.

Two temples – the only ones we had seen so far, although we had noticed a number of churches and one mosque – were on our agenda. First we were taken to the Vinh Nigheim Pagoda, known for its eight-storey tower, which, however, was closed. Each of its levels contained a statue of Buddha. It was built in 1971 with the help of the Japanese–Vietnam Friendship Association and showed Japanese influence in its architecture. The tower, visible from afar, stood separately from the shrine. Finally we visited the Thien Hau Pagoda, dedicated to the Lady of the Sea and protecting fishermen, sailors, merchants and anyone travelling by sea. This pagoda was decorated with the most elaborate friezes both on the outside and in the interior, whilst wooden carvings adorned the walls. Cleverly fashioned large cones of incense hung suspended from the high ceiling and beautiful bells stood waiting to be rung, together with a mighty drum to be struck. Two elaborate ships were prominently displayed and three figures of the goddess graced the altar, one standing behind the other, each flanked by a guardian on either side. The smallest of these images was taken out in a special litter on a festive day to be paraded around the city. On a side altar stood another goddess: Long Mau, the protectress of all mothers and their new-born children. A 200-year-old turtle, venerated as the true protectress of the sea, lived in a tank, whilst young turtles were kept in a large tank behind a grille. This visit concluded our official programme for the day. Before we parted the young lady guide presented each of us with a bag of boiled sweets.

Later we went out in search of a bottle of brandy to go with the tins of Schweppes we had bought, and we strolled along amidst the excited crowds getting ready to celebrate the New Year. Having completed our mission, we returned to our hotel, where we discovered some paintings on show upstairs; some of which were by children and others by the painters who had taught them.

Once again we dined in the coffee shop where both food and service were excellent and whilst we were eating a cook in uniform joined another man sitting at a table. Ruth went to compliment the chef on the fare and was told that the man in mufti was the chef, the other his assistant. The former was Swiss, the latter Austrian. They had worked together in New Zealand and in Australia and had been in this hotel for the past two years. They loved it in Saigon.

Next morning we drove to the former Presidential Palace, now known as the Unification Palace or Independence Hall, which was a handsome building set in a well-kept park. Because of the forthcoming Vietnamese New Year, known as Tet, flowering shrubs in ornate china pots had been grouped throughout the grounds, providing splashes of brilliant colour. The French built a Residence on this site in 1868 for the use of the Governor of Cochin-China which was destroyed. It was rebuilt between 1966 and 1988 by a Vietnamese architect who had been trained in France. The official rooms were spacious and tastefully furnished. When we walked in cleaners were waxing the floors in the grand hall by hand. We saw the conference room with its large boat-shaped table, and the presidential reception room, where the chairs were covered with red silk and fine red and gold lacquered cabinets stood against the wall. An elegant meeting room followed. In the Vice President's

Office the chairs were covered in gold silk. Beautiful hand-woven carpets lay on all floors. A 'Retiring Room' occupied a large area on the third floor, furnished with a bar, a card table and a movie screen. This floor gave access to an open terrace which served as a heliport and also offered a splendid view over the city.

A special guide clad in traditional dress gave the commentary, which our guide translated into English for us. Halfway through the tour we had to watch a very poor quality video with an equally poor soundtrack relating to the horrific history of the American-Vietnamese war.

To complete our visit, we were taken into the basement and led through a warren of passages serving as a shelter, which consisted of offices, command headquarters with maps pinned to the walls, sleeping quarters and large kitchens. Gratefully we emerged into the sunshine and fresh air from this sinister dungeon.

Our next stop was the Military Museum but we declined politely and strolled happily on our own. Finally we sat in a shady garden sipping cold drinks. To conclude our tour we were taken to a lacquer factory, where we were first shown the salesroom, which was crammed with the most exquisite ware: from tiny boxes to large pieces of furniture. Many of the articles were skilfully inlaid with mother-of-pearl. Some of the goods were made of tortoiseshell and a small candlestick was made of sweet-scented cinnamon wood. A collection of authentic musical instruments in miniature was particularly attractive. Next we were shown the incredibly primitive workroom where men polished tables and trays with their bare hands, using a black powder, whilst women stood ankle-deep in water to wash articles under the running tap. Pictures were first scrubbed then submerged into large tanks. When we purchased a few minor articles costing only a small sum, one man wrote the bill in triplicate, another accepted it and coped with our credit card and he too made out the receipt in triplicate. Finally we were able to collect our modest purchase from a third man, who had carefully packed each article and put it in its individual box. Incidentally, lacquerware in Vietnam was carved from the hard wood of the lacquer tree, unlike in Burma, where resin was applied to layer upon layer of cloth. Inlay of mother-of-pearl was used in both countries and all ware was finally highly polished, wherever it had been made.

When we returned to our hotel we went once more upstairs to

study the paintings and bought two which the children had painted. They were not priced but purchasers were asked to give a donation which went entirely to the children's foundation.

The afternoon was free and Jean our Australian friend joined us to stroll leisurely through the dense crowd, skilfully avoiding bicycles, motorbikes and cyclos when attempting to cross the busy roads.

We enjoyed the Flower Market, set between shrub-lined boulevards, where plants were massed together in baskets and pots. Women in their attractive traditional dress, little girls in frilly pink or white party dresses, teenagers dressed up to the hilt all wandered around admiring the flowers and choosing with utmost care those they wanted to take as gifts for the New Year. Photographs of young beauties posing against a bank of flowers were duly taken.

Intending to visit the Pagoda of the Emperor of Jade, we made our way to the city centre near the town hall and asked various people for directions; some did not understand us, others understood but either did not know or could not explain in English how to get there. Finally we asked at a stall where the stallholder, aided by his wife and a bystander, drew a map for me with street names clearly marked and pointed out that it was four kilometres distant and too far to walk. Thanking him and clutching the precious piece of paper, we hired dilapidated-looking cyclos and off we went on an incredible journey, competing with all other cyclos, bicycles, motorbikes and the few cars along the way, weaving in and out of dense traffic, narrowly missing pedestrians and other vehicles. The cyclo-men kept close together and managed without any problem to take us to our goal, where they settled beneath a tree to wait for us patiently.

This pagoda was built in 1909 in pure Chinese style and the graceful roof was covered with elaborate tile work. It was dark inside; incense and smoke filled the air and our eyes had to become accustomed to the darkness after the brilliant sunshine outside. Only with much effort were we able to make out dimly the fearsome guardians standing in elaborately carved wooden cases: the God of the Gate to one side and the God of the Land to the other. The altar stood in the centre, with the figure of the Mother of the Five Buddhas and the Buddha to come as well as a charming small edifice of the Goddess of Mercy all standing between offerings and incense burners. These statues were made of reinforced papier-

310

mâché. A bas relief portraying Sakyamuni decorated the front of the altar and a Buddha carved from sandalwood sat immediately behind it. Two awe-inspiring figures protected the altar on either side, one being the General who defeated the dragon and was shown stepping on the monster, whilst the General who defeated the white tiger had his feet firmly placed on the snarling beast. The main altar at the back of the hall was dominated by the Emperor of Jade dressed in luxurious golden robes, flanked to either side by his two guardians, the Diamonds. In front stood a group of six figures: three to the right, three to the left, representing the God of the North Pole, the God of Longevity, the God of the South Pole and the God of Happiness between their two gigantic guards. To the right of the Emperor posed the Mother of the Five Buddhas who had eighteen arms. The Five Buddhas represented the North, South, West, East and the centre of the Universe. A face was attached to either side of the Goddess's head behind her ears to enable her to see everything. Above her rode Sakyamuni on a phoenix and below her grouped the good people whom she protected. On the left of the Emperor sat his Incarnation holding a sword, with one of his feet said to rest on a turtle and the other on a snake, but we were unable to see his feet. On the wall was the God of Lightning, who slayed bad people. These three alcoves described above were separated from each other by pillars which bore the Goddess of the Moon and the Goddess of the Sun up above. Behind the altar stood yet another altar, which was tiered, poised high above the floor and also presided over by the Emperor of Jade surrounded by his four Diamonds with his Incarnation to one side, the Mother of the Five Buddhas to the other. The God of the Sun with the God of Happiness stood to one side, the God of the Moon with the God of Longevity to the other. On the step below, the God of Lightning had his place, whilst the Military Commander occupied the lower tier. The Emperor himself rose between these two groups, shimmering in gold. It all dazzled our eyes.

Proceeding through a narrow corridor led us to another chapel, which was divided into two parts: in the dark back room stood Than Hoang, the Chief of Hell. Six figures lined the wall, which were God of Yang to his right, God of Yin to his left and the other four Gods, dispensers of punishment for evil deeds and rewards for good ones. To his left towered a life-sized statue of his horse. The second part of the chapel represented the Ten Hells. Carved panels on the wall depicted various torments which awaited sinners in the ten regions of hell most realistically. Above each panel presided a judge examining a book in which the deeds of the deceased had been listed.

On the wall opposite Than Hoang a charming relief depicted Quan Am Ti Kinth, the guardian spirit of mother and child, standing on a lotus flower. To her right was her guardian spirit and to her left a very young Buddha, known as Long Nv, who was her protector. From the hall we stepped into a small room in which twelve ceramic figures of women overrun by children sat in two rows of six. They represented good or evil traits in human nature, such as the woman drinking alcohol out of a jug. Each figure also stood for one year in the twelve-year Chinese calendar. Walking back into the main body of the temple, we stopped briefly in a side room dedicated to the dead. Photographs with red banners gave their personal details, biographies listed their deeds. Finally we climbed up to the floor above the sanctuary and stepped out on a balcony from which we looked down on a tranquil pond set in a shady garden surrounded by the monks' quarters. Looking upwards, we were able to admire the elaborate tile work covering the roofs.

Delighted with our visit to the splendid shrine in spite of the long journey to reach it, we decided to see another pagoda, the Giac Lam, dating from 1744, the oldest in Saigon. When we asked our patient men to take us there, they scratched their heads since none of them knew where it was. Just then a tourist bus drew up before the gate and the driver, who spoke English well, was able to give our men precise instructions.

Off we went in our carriages for miles and miles of a long ride, fearing that we would never reach our goal, but since we literally traversed this amazing town from one side to the other we saw a great part of it and were amazed by the conglomeration of buildings and the profusion of cycles, cyclos and motorbikes. Whole families rode on one machine and everything from furniture, livestock and other vehicles was transported by cyclos. There was never just one adult riding a bike on their own without any ballast, there were always at least two riders on one machine, frequently with a child between them or even two, the second on a small seat at the back. The same applied to motorbikes, with babies (in both cases) clutched tightly to their mother's breast or cradled by their siblings, feeling secure enough to sleep peacefully unaware of all the tumult surrounding them. From four years onwards they sat fearlessly bolt upright on their special little seat behind the adults.

The town was seething with excitement with everyone preparing for Tet, flowers and plants and festive red banners were everywhere, colourful stalls selling trinkets and ornaments of every kind lined the streets. The terrible noise and smoke from Chinese firecrackers being set off added to the confusion. Leaving the asphalted roads behind, we bumped along a busy dusty lane with various workshops to either side, eventually reaching a sandy track which brought us to an oasis of perfect peace. Big old trees provided shade for the tombs of venerated monks.

A small slender monk invited us graciously to step inside, greeting us solemnly. He led us into the main sanctuary, making us take off our shoes before we passed from rough red floor tiles to smooth grey ones. A whole plethora of gilded statues displayed on a high platform met our eyes, with Amitabha – the Buddha of the Past – standing on his own in the centre at the back presiding over the rest of the tableau. In front of him rose Sakyamuni between the two disciples Anand and Kasyan. They were flanked by Nhila Daig Buddha and Tini Buddha. In front of Sakyamuni stood a delightful figure of Buddha as a child, dressed as always in yellow robes. A fat laughing fellow with five children climbing all over him took up the space in front of the tiny figure who was Ameda, a disciple. To his left rose the Emperor of Jade. The front row was occupied by a statue of Sakyamuni with two Bodhisattvas at either side. Altars along the side walls bore various Bodhisattvas and a row of earnest-looking judges who each held a scroll resembling the handle of a fork in their hand. In one corner stood a red and gold tree whose every branch carried a lamp and a miniature statue of a Bodhisattva where people prayed for sick relatives and for happiness and in return contributed kerosene for lamps. They wrote the names of the sick relatives on slips of paper, which they attached to the tree. A large bronze bell adorned the other corner, with slips of paper bearing the names of the sick and the dead and those seeking happiness fastened to its frame. Worshippers believed that when the bell was rung the sound would vibrate right up to heaven, carrying their wishes with it.

Returning to the reception hall, we saw funeral tablets and photographs of the deceased lining the wall. Beautifully carved

313

hardwood columns bore gilded Vietnamese inscriptions written in the ancient Nom characters: this script was used before the Latin-based writing had been introduced into the country. The wall to the left was covered by portraits of great monks of the past with their particulars and biographies recorded on vertical red tablets in Nom script. In the centre of the hall stood one of the forms of the eighteen-armed Goddess of Mercy, whilst at the back of the big room, separated by a row of columns, were long benches and tables constituting the schoolroom where the young novices were not only taught but also ate and slept. Being Tet, they were on holiday and tables and benches stood empty.

Our guide led us out into a secluded courtyard to show us a stone tank where, leaning over it, he rippled the surface to make an enormous fish appear. Looking, up we saw a row of charming blue and white porcelain tiles decorating the roof line both inside and outside. When I asked the young monk to show us the bo tree, which had been a gift from Sri Lanka, he took us to the peaceful garden where a white statue of the Goddess of Mercy rose from a lotus blossom beneath the tree. A small band of children materialised from nowhere and clustered around us gazing at us with wide open eyes. With a little coaxing we managed to get all these urchins except one to stand still long enough for us to be able to take a photograph. When we thanked our charming guide he countered with the phrase: 'Not at all, not at all' which he seemed to enjoy, repeating over and over again.

Our steadfast three had settled around a table to chat with some monks, content to wait for us. They peddled cheerfully back through dense traffic, past an enormous modern church from where an angel seemed to be in the process of descending at a somewhat precarious angle. We also caught a glimpse of a Hindu temple and of a mosque but actually saw more churches than temples on our way back to the centre of town. Having paid our drivers handsomely for the work they had done in driving us for many miles so cheerfully in the heat, we walked back to our hotel, just in time for a wash and change to go upstairs to attend the opening of the exhibition of the paintings of the Christina Noble Rigg Foundation. Here we had an opportunity to talk to the teacher who taught the two children whose paintings we had bought. One of them was a little girl aged ten who had lost all her family and, as he put it: her

314

idea of a happy family was 'painted from her heart' with mother and father sitting to either side of a round table covered by a tablecloth and bearing a vase of flowers in the centre. A small dog sat at the feet of father, lace curtains framed the window. The second picture was painted by a gifted boy of fourteen and portrayed a row of houses in a street with cars driving along it and birds above in the blue sky. A big sun smiled down on green trees.

Later we dined from a buffet set out around the pool and watched a splendid performance to celebrate the New Year. Loud music heralded the appearance of two dragons who engaged a masked man in fierce battle but after some struggle he managed to vanquish them both. A group of acrobats, including two little boys, performed some feats. They were followed by music played on authentic Vietnamese instruments. Both the orchestra and the soloists performed most splendidly, especially one girl who played with impressive skill on a bamboo instrument which resembled a large xylophone. A man with a very pleasant voice sang a playful duet with a girl, whilst handsome girls danced a graceful ballet followed by a dance in which they tempted and cajoled a male dancer, who in turn teased the bevy of pretty females. Another couple performed a beautifully measured classical dance whilst two small children in the wings copied each movement as it took place on the stage. Once this performance had ended no time was lost to dismantle the stage to make room for a group of Philippino musicians, three boys and one girl singer, to take over the entertainment. Finally we left to collect our paintings and to pack.

We were up early next morning to settle our bill and to leave for our flight to Hanoi, clutching one picture and two coolie hats, a thoughtful present from our guide, which we had been unable to stow away in our cases. Our guide appeared dressed in his traditional dress as promised and we set off on empty roads for the short journey to the airport. Formalities were quickly completed in spite of the fact that even for an internal flight each piece of luggage had to be X-rayed. The plane, built in eastern Germany, was fairly full with predominately Vietnamese bringing large amounts of hand luggage on board. Our plane left on time and we looked down on the sprawling city with its broad waterways before mist obscured our view. At one point high mountains eerily pierced the grey clouds, resembling a Chinese painting. A box of food was handed to each passenger but we found little to please our palate. The flight took roughly two hours and just before we landed in Hanoi we saw many neat fields, houses and trees.

Without any delay we collected our luggage and met up with our guide, who welcomed us to 'this old city'. Leaving the airport, we drove through open country where many people were planting young rice and crossed two bridges: the first spanned the Dong River, the second took us along the Bien Bridge over the Red River, which is the longest river in Vietnam. This long bridge, carrying the railway as well as the road, had been bombed and bombed again during the war but the Vietnamese always managed to repair it and keep it open for traffic running into Hanoi. Rusty trains stood in a siding, waiting to be transferred to a Transport Museum. The road surface was exceedingly rough but soon we reached the city, which was teeming with life; the profusion of people as well as merchandise is difficult to describe. At a railway crossing we had to stop; but although the barrier was down, it took the lady traffic warden a considerable time to stop pedestrians calmly wandering across the track before a dilapidated steam train came rumbling along. Some very rusty buses full to the brim had passed us, or we them, on our way. Fruit and vegetable stalls lined either side of the road, in fact the whole town resembled a never-ending open-air market. Soon we left the busy city to drive to our hotel through open country, ending up between two lakes: the smaller called Truc Bach, or White Silk Lake, the larger Ho Tay, or West lake. Our hotel, called Thang Loi Hotel, had been built on pylons above West Lake. It was a large complex with some attractive bungalows set into a landscaped background but had extraordinarily long corridors and a very grand entrance hall with ponds and fountains, pebbles on the ground and trees. It had been built in the seventies by Cuba but by 1992 it had fallen into a sad state of disrepair in contrast to its grandiose layout. It reminded us very strongly of the Inya Hotel outside Rangoon, which was Russian-built in a similar style. When we took our lunch in the enormous dining hall four young English-speaking people appeared who were travelling on a tight budget and lived cheaply in town but had to come to our hotel to be able to change traveller's cheques. A group of solemn-looking gentlemen in dark city suits were also dining; they were staying in the hotel and were either Russians or came from one of the East European countries. One Swedish lady had come to see her husband, who worked in Hanoi.

After lunch we set off on our city tour, driving first through intensely cultivated rural areas. The central square, called Ba Dinh, was most impressive, surrounded by large handsome buildings with Ho Chin Minh's Mausoleum – a stark grey edifice – dominating one side, flanked by the attractive yellow Presidential Palace and with the National Assembly opposite, next to the rambling Ministry of Foreign Affairs. Driving along extraordinarily wide streets with large trees to either side we passed the remains of the Cocoa Citadel, dating back to the 3rd century BC. Embassies were housed in grand impressive villas and the Workers' Cultural Palace rose as a massive solid building. Finally we arrived at an open space with a gigantic statue of Lenin in its centre, from where we made our way to the enchanting Hoan Liam Lake in the middle of Hanoi, where we parked our minibus and braved the dense traffic to cross the busy square and reach a bridge leading to a small island which bore the tiny Tortoise Pagoda on its shore. Its two shrines were blackened by the eternally burning incense sticks. Buddha sat surrounded by offerings which were artistically arranged on plates, consisting of apples, bananas and sweetmeats – even cigarettes had been neatly displayed. Our guide bought a bundle of incense sticks which he clasped firmly in both hands and shook in all directions before he lit one for each of us and placed them into the sand in a pot which stood in front of the Buddha, thus ensuring our happiness during the New Year. He told us that later in the evening most families would promenade around the lake. Before leaving the island we admired some paintings in the adjacent souvenir shop but were content to purchase some greeting cards painted on silk.

Continuing our city tour, we drove to a quiet corner of the town to visit the very old Stone Figure Pagoda, which had originally been built in the 8th century. The story related that when the foundation was being dug a stone figure of a goddess was unearthed, which gave the pagoda its name. The main shrine contained exquisite figures of Buddha, his disciples and his guardians made of papier mâché. At the back of the temple stood the schoolroom, deserted because of Tet, whilst the monks' quarters basked sleepily in the sun. The whole complex, although not very far from the bustling town, provided a peaceful oasis. Emerging into the sunlit street we crossed over to walk to an adjacent square in front of St Joseph's Cathedral, which had been inaugurated in 1886 and was built in the neoclassical style. Actually it looked far older, since its grey stone had weathered so much. Leaving this quiet corner, we spent the next hour engulfed by happy crowds and colourful merchandise in the Old City, where the streets – although in parts quite wide – were absolutely choked by crowds and where stall stood next to stall, with living quarters or workshops up above. Families always embraced at least three generations, with far-flung relatives included in the close circle. Most of the houses seemed to be under the threat of collapse, with shrubs and trees growing on balconies and roofs and some kind of vegetation poking through the fabric of most buildings. One store we passed was Government-owned, whilst the rest was private property. We did not visit the Covered Market but fought our way through the profusion of flowers of all kinds, all sizes, all colours and all lengths. It was not just a question of struggling through the crowds but we also had to find our way past heaps of garbage through which poor people raked.

Back at the hotel, we watched the sun sink slowly down over the water. Two girls suddenly appeared on the terrace below. When we called 'Happy New Year', one of them replied that it was not her New Year since she was Cambodian. They asked whether they could join us and came up to Jean's room introduced themselves: one was thirty years old and came from Phnom Penh and had arrived in Hanoi three months ago, having travelled by train from Cambodia. She intended to stay for nine months to perfect her Vietnamese. Her English was remarkably good. In the past she had spent three years in a small town in Georgia to learn electrical engineering. Her parents had retired and lived in Cambodia, whilst her sister had fled from a camp to Newcastle in Canada and kept on urging her to join her. She had never seen a map and had no idea where Canada was but nevertheless thought one day she might follow her sister. Both girls were living in hall at Hanoi's university. The second girl was a quietly-spoken Japanese who taught in Hanoi, where she had arrived four months ago, having taught in Saigon for one year. She planned to return home in nine months time. According to her, Hanoi was the better of the two towns to live in since it was cleaner and with fewer problems than Saigon. It was interesting to chat to them.

Our balcony faced a small community on the water's edge where each little house had a small well-tended garden, in one of which grew delphiniums. All houses had access to the lake and each property included a stretch of water, thickly covered by water lilies, which was contained between poles and wooden planks. The leaves of the water lilies served two purposes: they were fed to the pigs and also used as fertiliser. Many of these water plots lay scattered across the lake and I watched the owners row out to them in their small boats, working the oars with their legs. They started their day early in the morning, when they washed everything in sight: themselves, brushing their teeth, laundering their clothes, scrubbing the flip-flops they wore on their feet, bringing out mats to clean, pots and pans, buckets and other domestic utensils. Buckets were filled with the murky water from the lake. When I waved they all waved cheerily back. These families provided a never-ending interest for us to watch their daily lives unfold before our eyes.

After breakfast we set off to drive through town, where everybody seemed to be on the move on bicycles, all streaming into the city. Most people carried either delicate pink peach blossoms or kumquat trees laden with golden fruit as they cycled along, whilst country folk sat along the dusty roadside offering their home-produced goods for sale: fresh fruit and a large variety of superb vegetables such as cabbages, cauliflowers, kohlrabi, salads etc. A rusty bus was fully laden with the baskets which were usually carried at either end of a pole across the shoulders. Many bicycles had cylindrical bamboo panniers hanging to either side of their rear wheels. Ugly large blocks of flats loomed up at the outskirts on the other side of town and were used to house foreigners from the West; beyond these we passed the Lake of the Zoo, with the attractive zoo complex on its distant shore. Much building appeared to be in progress in various districts which we travelled through. Suddenly we saw a big dilapidated building loom up in front of us: this was the Dancing School of Hanoi.

Having left the town behind, we drove through flat countryside, where every inch had been cultivated and where rice paddies occupied different levels. Round reservoirs surrounded by low walls were fed by pumps with water from the river, whilst fields were irrigated by hand, using either a wooden trough on a long handle or by a bucket made from bamboo which hung suspended from ropes to either side. Each rope was firmly grasped by one man

319

before both swung the bucket skilfully into the river to fill it, and then transferred it deftly to the field, where they tipped the contents onto the soil. Vegetables grew between rice paddies, whilst flowers blossomed in nurseries. Here and there maize fields appeared, where buffaloes and zebus pulled wooden ploughs through muddy grounds whilst farmers, with their faces well shaded by coolie hats, trotted behind them. Every village we passed had a crowded market in full swing and everywhere were bicycles. Many men wore khaki tops and frequently khaki jackets or trousers. Temple complexes graced each village, whilst military cemeteries stood on their outskirts, with a tall column in the centre which bore the names of those who had perished in the war. Family graves stood in the midst of rice paddies and were frequently surrounded by water. Passing a big lake with a dam, we came to a village with a church and a graveyard nearby with crosses rising above the rice. Bricks lay in a heap waiting to be fired in a big kiln and we also saw some lime kilns standing in the countryside. Houses were constructed from matting, wattle and daub or brick. All we saw made our journey to Buffalo Mountain most interesting. This mountain rose quite suddenly before us and we could see why it had acquired its name.

As soon as our bus stopped, we were surrounded by children offering colourful flat woven fans for sale which bore the words: 'Good Luck for 1992'. The hordes of little urchins followed us up the 210 steps to reach Tay Phuong Pagoda on top of the mountain. A sweet-faced old nun with shaven head and teeth stained brown from betel-nut juice greeted us with a gentle smile, inviting us into a small open-sided hall, part of a simple building where we sat at rough tables to drink green tea out of tiny handleless china cups. The teapot was kept hot in a lined bamboo basket with a padded lid.

The old nun took care of the pagoda, which consisted of three single-storey buildings, one of which contained the most treasured possession: seventy-six figures skilfully carved from jackwood, most of which had been produced in the 18th century. The building itself dated back to the 8th century. The carvings on the wooden beams were particularly intricate and beautiful, whilst each of the figures deserved careful attention. Every single one had its own individual facial features and expressions, and each one was portrayed in a different posture and clothed in different styles, each of them representing a specific human attribute. Buddhism had been introduced to Vietnam from India and therefore Vietnam looks towards the West not to the East, which was apparent in the Indian features of these *arhats* (monks who have attained Nirvana), as well as the slender bone structure obvious in their long hands. I wished I could describe each *arhat* or at least had been able to take photographs, but it was far too dark. A statue of a lady cradling a baby fronted by a tiny figure of a man and a woman stood in one corner. Our guide told us a very complicated story connected with this group. As far as I could follow, legend had it that a young girl disguised as a boy fell in love with a monk and had a child. This group somehow resembled the Virgin and Child and had been most tenderly executed.

As in the other pagoda our guide bought again a bundle of incense sticks, shook them, lit them and did homage to Buddha before handing each of us one to place into the pot filled with sand which stood at the foot of the Buddha image. Enormous guardians filled one section of the dark interior almost entirely; during the war these had been hidden in caves to keep them safe. Before we left we bought a fan from a deaf and dumb girl and were told that deaf and dumb children presented a great problem in Saigon. One member of our party signed the visitors' book on behalf of us all and we each took a photograph of the old nun before climbing down the 210 steps, still accompanied by the children.

From the Buffalo Mountain we drove to the 11th-century Thay Pagoda, passing paddy fields with ducks swimming on the water of the reservoirs and overtaking handsome village girls balancing their heavy baskets suspended from shoulder poles with apparent ease and walking along the dusty road with a natural grace. Suddenly jagged rocks in weird shapes rose out of the flat countryside, with Thay Pagoda nestling in the shade of one of them. Leaving the busy road to reach our goal, we travelled through a tiny village asleep in the hot sun where a small lorry minus its driver obstructed our path. Our driver removed the awning outside a little stall opposite the parked vehicle without much ado and with barely an inch to spare, he skilfully manoeuvred our bus past the obstacle. Finally we reached a lake with a pavilion on an island in its centre from which three naked boys jumped off for a swim.

Thay Pagoda is specially used for water festivals, when the monks stage water puppet shows. A small bridge gave access to a little fishing village on the distant shore. A group of young girls were washing their linen in the lake, whilst cattle lay resting in the shade and small boys tucked incense sticks into our hands before we entered the pagoda. Nhan Tong was a monk here before he became King, and his statue, dressed in plain robes, stood on a big stone pedestal supported at each corner by Garuda with lotus petals adorning the rim. A lacquered table bearing a teapot and cup had been placed in front of the King, whilst two Buddha images, one carved from jackwood, the other sculptured in copper, rose in front of the table. An elaborately carved altar supported Buddha as a baby, surrounded by nine dragons, whilst to the left of the main altar stood the figure of the King again, but this time he rose from a dais elegantly gowned and wearing his crown, with two jolly-looking guardians kneeling below him. Golden robes were displayed on the other side of the altar, behind which a closed chariot protected the articulated skeleton of Nhan Tong, which on a special day was carried around in procession, dressed in its golden robes and raising his arms.

In a second shrine stood the Buddha of the Present, flanked by the Buddha of the Past and of the Future, carved in wood with three Buddhas standing in a line behind this group, representing first the thin one who knew all about hardship, carved in wood, followed by the fat happy one cast in copper and finally the wooden one of compassion with his many arms. On a lower level stood Buddha as a child again, protected by nine dragons. A large ceremonial horse rose at the side of this altar.

Again we were invited to take tea in an open-fronted hall and again we were asked to sign the visitors' book. The veranda where we drank our tiny cups of fragrant tea housed a shrine dedicated to the memory of the founder abbot of the temple. A stele gave details about him and the life he had led, whilst photographs of monks and nuns with their particulars lined the walls; one picture of a nun with a strikingly beautiful face stood out amongst them all.

Following the Dyke Road high above the fields, we set off on our return journey. Around Thay Pagoda graves were shaped like enormous armchairs (as we had met in Korea). People were streaming back from town with empty baskets dangling from their poles. Markets in the villages were still carrying on a brisk trade but back in town business had finished and streets were being cleaned and all rubbish which had been simply tipped into the street was swept up, raked together and shovelled into handcarts. All this work was

322

carried out by women. Water carts followed to wash down the streets.

When we returned to the vast dining hall for a late lunch, we were able to choose from a menu which eliminated the confusion of the previous day, when we really did not know what we were being served. Back on our balcony we were almost deafened by the continued noise of Chinese firecrackers. Looking across to the tiny gardens, we found them bare – all the delphiniums had been cut since they had been specially grown for Tet. A poor chicken ended its day by having its neck first wrung then slit for the blood to drain. It was plunged into the lake prior to being doused with boiling water to be plucked ready for the pot.

As it was New Year's Eve we were taken down town in the evening, where we found Hanoi lit up with fairy lights making it into a very festive scene. Walking round Hoan Kiem Lake, where we had visited Tortoise Pagoda, we found both the bridge and the pagoda illuminated. Suddenly half of the lights failed, since photographers who had set up shop along the lake had run their lights from flats across the street, overloading the power and causing partial blackout all round. After having mingled with the crowd to stroll along the lake, stopping to look at the various stalls, we were taken to a banquet and floorshow in honour of Tet. Like all the other groups of tourists, we were taken to a special hall upstairs in an official building where we were treated to splendid singing, dancing, juggling, magic and quite excellent miming. The men's voices were dark and warm, whilst the girls sang in shrill tone. We again admired the virtuosity with which one girl played the bamboo instrument resembling a xylophone and were also impressed by a man who produced birdlike tunes on a string instrument, whilst another musician brought forth full bass notes on his xylophone. Here we had an opportunity to talk to our guide and learnt to our astonishment that he had lived in Britain for two years. He was forty-two years old but looked much younger than his years. His father had been killed in a massacre during the war with France when he was one year old. His mother died seven years ago aged eighty-four. He taught English and was sent in a group of fourteen to Britain in 1978/79, where he had first lived in Edinburgh near the Castle for one year. He spent the second year in London, living in Wimbledon and attending Ealing College for Adult Education. His wife taught Russian and his oldest daughter Ma had been learning English these past two years. Unfortunately we could not continue our conversation since he was wanted to interpret the programme to the audience.

The whole town was teeming with life when we left to return to our hotel. With the crowds and the traffic, the noise was quite indescribable. Fireworks went off over the lake and these, as well as Chinese firecrackers, continued throughout the night. A big party in the hotel added their share of noise.

All traces of the party from the night before had been cleared away by the time we appeared for breakfast but smoke still hung about and soon Chinese firecrackers were being let off again.

When we drove into town there were no stalls anywhere to be seen on this festive day. People dressed in their Sunday best were on bicycles and motorbikes on their way to visit relatives and friends or to pay homage at the temples.

Having driven round the main square we parked and walked solemnly two abreast from one guard to the next to visit Ho Chi Minh's Mausoleum, which is a great big grey edifice said to look like a lotus flower when seen from the air. Moving sedately up the grey steps into the cold marble hall, past guards stationed at regular intervals, brought us into the sanctum which housed the glass sarcophagus in which the great man lay as if asleep. We were quite relieved to step out again into the fresh air and to walk along an avenue planted with different shrubs from various parts of Vietnam. Our way led past the Presidential Palace, built in 1906 by a German architect for the French, but which was only used for State occasions since Ho Chi Minh refused to live in grandeur, preferring his modest home in the adjacent park. However, he did proclaim Vietnam's freedom from its majestic steps. The Presidential Palace was a handsome, well-proportioned building.

To reach the little ochre building standing on the shore of the lake where he used to live until a simple wooden house on stilts was ready for him on the opposite side, we walked through well-kept gardens. He stocked the lake with carp and used to come down the steps and clap his hands, when they swam along to be fed. Food was still being kept to be thrown on the still waters, when big fish appeared to claim the bait. At his death the house was left in exactly the same state as it had been during his life, with table and chairs beneath the house where he used to work during the hot summers. A helmet lay next to the telephone in case of air raids and bench seats surrounded this cool spot, inviting children to come and sit here and talk to him. In winter he transferred to the small simple study on the first floor. His bedroom was equally modest, graced by a vase of flowers since he loved flowers and children. A small radio which had been a cherished present was the only luxury he indulged in. A veranda ran around the entire building to keep the air circulation and keep the two rooms cool. A simple hand bell attached to the gate allowed visitors to announce themselves. A small room containing desk, chair and bed led to a shelter: His previous home, the little ochre house on the opposite shore, had been turned into a kitchen and dining room where he took his meals, refusing to be waited on, whilst his Prime Minister occupied the bigger house next to the ochre building since he was a married man with a family. Ho Chi Minh was on his own.

From this rather poignant visit we drove to the One Pillar Pagoda, a tiny shrine emerging out of a lake like a lotus flower. Except for the steps and one stone pillar, everything else was wood. Here the statue of Buddha was illuminated by flashing lights. Nearby lay the equally small Dien Huu Pagoda, surrounded by a charming courtyard which had been laid out as a delightful garden. An elderly monk oblivious of all around him was chanting away and gently tapping the bell to one side and a wooden shell to the other with a stick.

Continuing our sightseeing, we drove past the 'Hilton Hotel', the former prison where American captives were held (which we politely declined to photograph,) to visit a delightful temple (whose name I unfortunately do not know) dedicated to a hero who freed the terrified neighbourhood from a nine-tailed fox. The temple also honoured the ancestors of all copper workers. Here we joined the dense crowd and admired the intricate bas-relief cast in copper which hung suspended from the ceiling in the porch. Every worshipper bore a lighted incense stick, which produced so much thick, acrid smoke that it proved quite difficult to find the way round to the square shrine, but once my eyes had become accustomed to the darkness and smoke I could see the beautiful vessel cast in copper displayed on a pedestal in front of the main altar and the beautiful pure copper figure of the hero occupying the shrine. In alcoves to either side of the altar stood superb phoenixes poised on the backs of tortoises, with one guardian and one mandarin standing beside the graceful birds.

Driving back to our hotel, we marvelled at the festive crowd. Little girls were dressed up in their best party frocks and old ladies wore black or brown shifts over their silk bell-bottom trousers and velvet bands round their heads, whilst some ladies were clad in elegant velvet shifts or plain cotton ones.

After lunch we went back to town to visit the Temple of Literature, which was founded in 1070/4 and dedicated to Confucius. In 1076 Vietnam's first university was established here, initially to educate princes and princesses and later children of noblemen too. Once they had passed their examinations they became mandarins (Civil Servants). The Temple of Literature consisted of five courtyards divided by walls and pierced by gates. The straight central pathway was reserved for the King, whilst curved paths to either side served the mandarins. The complex stood at the shore of the Lake of Literature. Outside the gate an inscription on a pillar invited the visitor to alight from his horse and step through a splendid gateway into the first courtyard, where two pools were provided for the use of the students. The Khue Van Pavilion, built in 1802, stood in the second courtyard and represented a fine example of Vietnamese architecture. The next gate, the Gate of Literature, was decorated with two fishes to either side of an urn, whilst the third courtyard contained 82 stelae, 41 to either side, which were all carried on the back of a tortoise, with each being decorated in a different style and inscribed with Chinese characters listing the names and achievements of students who had passed the examinations. The fourth courtyard contained a chapel with an elaborate shrine, whilst the last one, known as the National College, constituted the students' quarters and contained the Khai Than Temple, dedicated to Confucius. His statue stood in the centre of the shrine flanked by slender cranes. Tucked in one corner were desks, chairs and a blackboard, where Chinese children came for their lessons.

The plan was to visit the History Museum, which stood near the handsome Opera House but – because of Tet – it was firmly closed for four days, which was very disappointing since we had come up against the same situation in Saigon. Instead we were taken to the largest park in Hanoi, where all families with children seemed to have foregathered. Little ones in their fineries posed on yellow tricycles to be photographed, whilst older girls vied with each other in their smart dresses, heavily made up and with ribbons in their